THE HISTORY OF AL-ṬABARĪ

AN ANNOTATED TRANSLATION

VOLUME XXXIII

Storm and Stress along the Northern Frontiers of the ʿAbbāsid Caliphate

THE CALIPHATE OF AL-MUʿTAṢIM

A.D. 833–842/A.H. 218–227

SUNY

SERIES IN NEAR EASTERN STUDIES

Said Amir Arjomand, Editor

The preparation of this volume was made possible in part by a grant from the National Endowment for the Humanities, an independent federal agency.

Bibliotheca Persica
Edited by Ehsan Yar-Shater

The History of al-Ṭabarī

(Ta'rīkh al-rusul wa'l mulūk)

VOLUME XXXIII

Storm and Stress along the Northern Frontiers of the ʿAbbāsid Caliphate

translated and annotated
by

C. E. Bosworth

University of Manchester

State University of New York Press

Published by
State University of New York Press, Albany

Printed in the United States of America

For information, address State University of New York
Press, State University Plaza, Albany, N.Y. 12246

Library of Congress Cataloging in Publication Data

Ṭabarī, 838?–923.

[Ta'rīkh al-rusul wa-al-mulūk. English. Selections]

Storm and stress along the northern frontiers of the ʿAbbāsid caliphate/translated and annotated by C. E. Bosworth.

p. cm.—(SUNY series in Near Eastern studies) (Bibliotheca Persica) (The history of al-Ṭabarī-Ta'rīkh al-rusul wa 'l mulūk; v. 33)

Translation of extracts from: Ta'rīkh al-rusul wa-al-mulūk.

Includes bibliographical references.

ISBN 0-7914-0493-5 (alk. paper).—ISBN 0-7914-0494-3 (pbk.: alk. paper)

1. Islamic Empire—History—750–1258. I. Bosworth, Clifford Edmund. II. Title. III. Series. IV. Series: Bibliotheca Persica (Albany, N.Y.) V. Series: Ṭabarī, 838?–923. Ta'rīkh al-rusul wa-al-mulūk. English; v. 33.

DS38.2.T313 vol. 33
[DS38.6]
909'.1 s—dc20
[909'.097671] 90-33516
CIP

10 9 8 7 6 5 4 3 2 1

Preface

The History of Prophets and Kings (*Ta'rīkh al-rusul wa'l-mulūk*) by Abū Ja'far Muḥammad b. Jarīr al-Ṭabarī (839–923), here rendered as the *History of al-Ṭabarī*, is by common consent the most important universal history produced in the world of Islam. It has been translated here in its entirety for the first time for the benefit of non-Arabists, with historical and philological notes for those interested in the particulars of the text.

Al-Ṭabarī's monumental work explores the history of the ancient nations, with special emphasis on biblical peoples and prophets, the legendary and factual history of ancient Iran, and, in great detail, the rise of Islam, the life of the Prophet Muḥammad, and the history of the Islamic world down to the year 915. The first volume of this translation contains a biography of al-Ṭabarī and a discussion of the method, scope, and value of his work. It also provides information on some of the technical considerations that have guided the work of the translators.

The *History* has been divided here into 39 volumes, each of which covers about two hundred pages of the original Arabic text in the Leiden edition. An attempt has been made to draw the dividing lines between the individual volumes in such a way that each is to some degree independent and can be read as such. The page numbers of the Leiden edition appear on the margins of the translated volumes.

Al-Ṭabarī very often quotes his sources verbatim and traces the chain of transmission (*isnād*) to an original source. The chains of transmitters are, for the sake of brevity, rendered by only a dash (—) between the individual links in the chain. Thus, "According to Ibn Ḥumayd—Salamah—Ibn Isḥāq" means that al-Ṭabarī received the report from Ibn Ḥumayd, who said that he was told by Salamah, who said that he was told by Ibn Isḥāq, and so on. The numerous subtle and important differences in the original Arabic wording have been disregarded.

The table of contents at the beginning of each volume gives a brief survey of the topics dealt with in that particular volume. It also includes the headings and subheadings as they appear in al-Ṭabarī's text, as well as those occasionally introduced by the translator.

Well-known place names, such as, for instance, Mecca, Baghdad, Jerusalem, Damascus, and the Yemen, are given in their English spellings. Less common place names, which are the vast majority, are transliterated. Biblical figures appear in the accepted English spelling. Iranian names are usually transcribed according to their Arabic forms, and the presumed Iranian forms are often discussed in the footnotes.

Technical terms have been translated wherever possible, but some, such as dirham and imām, have been retained in Arabic forms. Others that cannot be translated with sufficient precision have been retained and italicized, as well as footnoted.

The annotation aims chiefly at clarifying difficult passages, identifying individuals and place names, and discussing textual difficulties. Much leeway has been left to the translators to include in the footnotes whatever they consider necessary and helpful.

The bibliographies list all the sources mentioned in the annotation.

The index in each volume contains all the names of persons and places referred to in the text, as well as those mentioned in the notes as far as they refer to the medieval period. It does not include the names of modern scholars. A general index, it is hoped, will appear after all the volumes have been published.

For further details concerning the series and acknowledgments, see Preface to Volume I.

Ehsan Yar-Shater

Contents

Abbreviations

BGA: Bibliotheca geographorum arabicorum
BiOr: *Bibliotheca Orientalis*
BSOAS: *Bulletin of the School of Oriental and African Studies*
CT: *Cahiers de Tunisie*
EI[1]: *Encyclopaedia of Islām*, first edition
EI[2]: *Encyclopaedia of Islam*, second edition
EIr: *Encyclopaedia Iranica*
GAL: C. Brockelmann, *Geschichte des arabischen Literatur*
GAS: F. Sezgin, *Geschichte des arabischen Schrifttums*
GCAL: G. Graf, *Geschichte der christlichen arabischen Literatur*
GMS: Gibb Memorial Series
HJAS: *Harvard Journal of Asiatic Studies*
IC: *Islamic Culture*
Iran, JBIPS: *Iran, Journal of the British Institute of Persian Studies*
Isl.: *Der Islam*
JA: *Journal Asiatique*
JAL: *Journal of Arabic Literature*
JAOS: *Journal of the American Oriental Society*
JESHO: *Journal of the Economic and Social History of the Orient*
JHS: *Journal of Hellenic Studies*
JIH: *Journal of Indian History*
JRAS: *Journal of the Royal Asiatic Society*
JSAI: *Jerusalem Studies in Arabic and Islam*
JSS: *Journal of Semitic Studies*
JTS: *Journal of Theological Studies*
MW: *The Muslim World*
REI: *Revue des Etudes Islamiques*

RSO: *Rivista degli Studi Orientali*
SI: *Studia Islamica*
St. Ir.: *Studia Iranica*
WbKAS: *Wörterbuch der klassischen arabischen Sprache*
ZDMG: *Zeitschrift der Deutschen Morgenländischen Gesellschaft*

Translator's Foreword

Al-Muʿtaṣim's reign of almost nine years saw a recrudescence of conflict and disturbance such as had characterized the early years of the previous caliphate, that of his brother al-Maʾmūn, but with the difference that the focuses of discontent were now no longer Baghdad and Iraq but rather the northern fringes of the Persian lands and, to a lesser extent, Syria and Palestine.

It is not therefore surprising that in this section of his *History* Ṭabarī should devote a great amount of space to, and provide the most detailed and graphic historical accounts that we possess of, the last years and final overthrow of Bābak and his Khurramī movement in Ādharbayjān and Arrān, as well as the eventually unsuccessful rebellion of the Qārinid prince Māzyār b. Qārin in Ṭabaristān and the Caspian provinces. The ideology and beliefs of the Khurramiyyah are unfortunately insufficiently known for us to decide whether the primary impulse behind the movement, of which Bābak was only the latest leader, was religious, perhaps a recrudescence of neo-Mazdakism, or whether the movement was one of social protest or of incipient Persian national feeling directed against the Arab political domination of Persia.[1] It is,

1. Cf. A. H. M. Jones, "Were Ancient Heresies National or Social Movements in Disguise?" *JTS*, N.S. 10 (1959): 280–98. Jones is very skeptical that ethnic or "nationalist" motivations were at work among the heterodox Christian sects of the later Roman and early Byzantine empires; for example, North African Donatism or Egyptian Monophysitism. We should probably be equally wary of imputing similar motivations to early Islamic religious dissidence in the Iranian world.

however, certain that the aim of Māzyār, himself a convert to Islam in the previous reign, was eventually to extend his own political authority over neighboring petty dynasties and to achieve a position within the Caspian provinces comparable to that of his rival ʿAbdallāh b. Ṭāhir in Khurāsān, rather than to subvert the position of Islam in Persia by engaging in a grand conspiracy against it in alliance with al-Afshīn, the prince of the Transoxanian principality of Ushrūsanah.

Ṭabarī likewise devotes considerable space and detail to the external campaign that established al-Muʿtaṣim's reputation as a great *ghāzī*-prince and hammer of infidels, the attack in 223 (838) on the Byzantine city of Anqirah (Ankara) and the sack of another great fortress of central Anatolia, ʿAmmūriyyah (Amorion), the original home of the ruling Amorian dynasty, in retaliation for a preceding Greek attack on the Muslim population of Zibaṭrah in the Byzantine-Arab marches.

Ṭabarī's interest as a chronicler of the ʿAbbāsids was in the heartlands of Islam, so that we lack from him any information at all about the eastern and western wings of the caliphal dominions—a general characteristic of his treatment of other ʿAbbāsid caliphates. Thus we learn nothing about what was happening in Sind under its Arab governors; about events in Sīstān and eastern Khurāsān, where serious Khārijite uprisings continued to disturb the countryside; or about the political processes in Transoxania, where the Sāmānid family was consolidating its power under the aegis of the Ṭāhirid governors in Nayshābūr. Regarding the Muslim west, Ṭabarī tells us nothing about Egypt, the Maghrib, and Spain, though these years were areas in which, for example, the Aghlabid conquest of Sicily from the Byzantines was proceeding apace.

Even information on what was happening in Iraq and the traditional capital of the ʿAbbāsids, Baghdad, is sparse compared with Ṭabarī's concentration on events there during al-Amīn's brief caliphate and al-Maʾmūn's early years, when he was still based in Marw in Khurāsān and Baghdad itself was for the most part in hands hostile to him. The major happening in Iraq during al-Muʿtaṣim's reign was, of course, the Caliph's decision to transfer the military and administrative capital of the ʿAbbāsid empire from Baghdad to Sāmarrā in 220 (835) and to buttress his personal power there with a professional army, in which Turkish slave soldiers were prominent. Although the sources are not explicit, the research of scholars like David Ayalon have made it abundantly clear that al-Ma'mūn came to feel, in view of the support that the *ahl Baghdād*, the Abnā' (the Arabs from Khurāsān who had migrated westward to Baghdad and become the mainstays of the first ʿAbbāsid caliphs), had given to his rival al-Amīn in the civil warfare of 195–98 (811–13) and their subsequent chronic disaffection, that he could never thenceforth rely on them and must accordingly seek his personal military support elsewhere. Al-Muʿtaṣim carried the process farther and came to realize—as the sources frankly state—that his new Turkish slave soldiery would never be welcomed in Baghdad by the Abnā', who were dominant there. He thus planned his new capital a safe seventy miles away at Sāmarrā.[2] The wisdom of his policies must have been further apparent to al-Muʿtaṣim when he was nearly toppled from his throne on his way home from the ʿAmmūriyyah campaign by a conspiracy largely mounted by the Arab and Khurāsānian commanders to raise his nephew al-ʿAbbās b. al-Ma'mūn to the caliphate. In this abortive putsch, Turkish commanders of the army like Ashnās and Bughā remained conspicuously loyal, and their influence in the state grew proportionately. The condemnation in 225 (840) of al-Afshīn, who had been the victor over Bābak only three years previously, may be viewed as a further diminution of the influence of the ʿAbbāsids' traditional support from the peoples of the eastern Iranian world, whether the Arabs originally settled in Khurāsān or, in the case of al-Afshīn, Iranians from the pre-Islamic local aristocracy. Only in Khurāsān itself was al-Muʿtaṣim wise enough to retain ʿAbdallāh b. Ṭāhir in Nayshābūr as the supremely capable and knowledgeable controller of events in the east, and ʿAbdallāh's first cousin Isḥāq b. Ibrāhīm b. Ḥusayn b. Muṣʿab, governor of Baghdad for the Caliphs, always remained one of the closest confidants of both al-Ma'mūn and al-Muʿtaṣim.

If we depended solely on Ṭabarī for information on al-Muʿtaṣim and the events of his reign, we would be unaware of the major

2. See Ayalon, *The Military Reforms of Caliph al-Muʿtaṣim*, pp. 4–12, 31–33.

event of intellectual and theological significance during these years; that is, the continuation by al-Muʿtaṣim of the *Miḥnah*, or inquisition, involving the requirement of assent to Muʿtazilī doctrine on such questions as the createdness of the Qur'ān as a condition for holding official legal and theological posts. Al-Ma'mūn had put these measures into effect in Iraq during the last year of his life, and al-Muʿtaṣim had been his close lieutenant in this.[3] Thus it was al-Muʿtaṣim who in Jumādā I 218 (June 833), two months before his brother's death, had written to the governor of Egypt, Naṣr b. ʿAbdallāh Kaydar,[4] and to the governor of Syria, Isḥāq b. Yaḥyā b. Muʿādh al-Khuttalī,[5] obliging them to enforce the stipulations of the *Miḥnah* in their provinces. These Muʿtazilī measures were enthusiastically promoted, and the caliph's resolution was stiffened by one of al-Muʿtaṣim's closest intimates and the most decisive single influence on him, his chief judge, Aḥmad b. Abī Duwād.[6] In Ramaḍān 219 (September–October 835) the spearhead of the conservative, orthodox opposition to the new official policies, the Imām Aḥmad b. Ḥanbal, was summoned before the caliph and, after refusing his assent to Muʿtazilī measures, was severely beaten and jailed for two years.[7] There seems also to have been an intensification of inquisitorial activities in the year or so before al-Muʿtaṣim's death, both in Egypt under the Muʿtazilī *faqīh* Muḥammad b. Abī al-Layth al-Aṣamm and in Baghdad under the judge Shuʿayb b. Sahl.[8]

The picture of al-Muʿtaṣim's character and aptitudes that emerges from Ṭabarī's pages is not very clear, except that his strategic skill and generalship are demonstrated by his careful planning of the Anatolian campaign, involving a meticulously timed pincer movement on the Anatolian cities executed by the

---

3. For Ṭabarī's account of these developments, see vol. III, 1112–33; trans. Bosworth, *The Reunification of the ʿAbbāsid Caliphate*, pp. 199–222.

4. Kindī, *Kitāb al-wulāt wa-kitāb al-quḍāt*, pp. 193, 445–49.

5. Ibn ʿAsākir, *Tahdhīb ta'rīkh Dimashq*, vol. II, p. 458.

6. On him, see p. 33 n. 127 below.

7. W. M. Patton, *Aḥmed ibn Ḥanbal and the Miḥna*, pp. 90–113; W. M. Watt, *The Formative Period of Islamic Thought*, pp. 178, 292.

8. See *EI*[2], s.v. "Miḥna" (M. Hinds).

two wings of the Muslim army led by himself and al-Afshīn respectively. His personal bravery also seems established. Ibn Shākir al-Kutubī's biography of him illustrates, with several episodes recounted on the authority of Ibn Abī Duwād, al-Muʿtaṣim's great physical strength,[9] and it emerges from Ṭabarī's own pages that he was a lover of the game of polo.[10] Also, his kingly presence and dignity were regarded as particularly awe-inspiring.[11] It does, however, appear that these features and traits of character were combined with what was at times a violent temper and lack of self-control.[12]

Intellectually, he appears insignificant beside his brother al-Ma'mūn, with his wide-ranging scientific and philosophical interests, and is described in some sources as totally lacking in learning (though some Arabic verses are nevertheless attributed to him).[13] Subkī was doubtless right when he asserted that al-Muʿtaṣim had not the intellectual formation to make an informed decision on the correctness of the Muʿtazilī measures being enforced under the *Miḥnah* but was largely impelled to continue them by al-Ma'mūn's dying charge to him[14] and the influence over him of Ibn Abī Duwād and others.[15]

The sketchiness of Ṭabarī's portrayal of the caliph is emphasized by the paucity of anecdotes about his conduct and character that he retails, compared with the number of similar stories given for Hārūn al-Rashīd and al-Ma'mūn, for example. For amplification of such material on al-Muʿtaṣim, one has to go to such works as the *Kitāb al-aghānī* and the *adab* collections.[16] One facet of culture, in the widest sense, does seem to have interested the caliph, however: He appreciated food and was interested in the *haute cuisine* of the time, as were other members of his

9. *Fawāt al-wafayāt*, vol. IV, p. 49 no. 500.
10. Ṭabarī, vol. III, pp. 1326–27 (p. 213 below).
11. Kutubī, *Fawāt al-wafayāt*, vol. IV, p. 49 no. 500: *min ahyab al-khulafā'*.
12. Cf. Ṭabarī, vol. III, p. 1326 (p. 212 below).
13. Kutubī, vol. IV, pp. 49–50.
14. Ṭabarī, vol. III, pp. 1136, 1137–38; trans. Bosworth, pp. 225, 227–28.
15. Cited in Patton, p. 114.
16. Some material additional to that of Ṭabarī was adduced by E. Herzfeld, *Geschichte der Stadt Samarra*, pp. 153 ff.

family.[17] This emerges from a passage in Masʿūdī describing how, at his Jawsaq palace in Sāmarrā, al-Muʿtaṣim brought in Ibn Abī Duwād to adjudicate various dishes of food prepared by his boon companions.[18] In addition, a *nuskhah* (list, collection of recipes?) on practical cookery by al-Muʿtaṣim is mentioned—together with similar *nusakh* and *kutub* by Yaḥyā b. Khālid al-Barmakī, al-Maʾmūn, al-Wāthiq, and the like—in a later fourth-century (tenth-century) cookbook, Ibn Sayyār al-Warrāq's *Kitāb al-Ṭabīkh*.[19]

The editor of this section of Ṭabarī's *History*, the general editor, M. J. de Goeje, had at his disposal as the basis for his text two manuscripts, one in Istanbul, Köprülü 1040-2 (C), and one in Oxford, Bodleian Uri 650 (O).[20] Muḥammad Abū al-Faḍl Ibrāhīm used the Leiden text as the basis for his Cairo edition of 1960–69 but in this section of the text he added a few readings from another Istanbul manuscript, Ahmet III 2959;[21] the extra information is, however, negligible.

This section of Ṭabarī on the caliphate of al-Muʿtaṣim is the only substantial portion of the Islamic part of the *History* treating an entire caliphal reign that has previously been translated into a Western language, in Elma Marin's *The Reign of al-Muʿtaṣim (833–842)* (American Oriental Series 35, New Haven, 1951), prepared under the guidance of the late G. E. von Grunebaum.[22] It has been discussed at some length by F.-C. Muth, who noted the views and comments of various reviewers soon after the book's appearance.[23]

In general, these reviewers welcomed Marin's rendering as the first sizable portion of Ṭabarī's text to be translated since Theodor Nöldeke's exemplary *Geschichte der Perser und Araber* some

---

17. E.g., Ibrāhīm b. al-Mahdī, whom David Waines describes as the author of the first, practical, comprehensive cookbook; "A Prince of Epicures: The Arabs' First Cookbook," *Ur*, 3 (1984), pp. 26–29.

18. *Murūj al-dhahab*, vol. VII, 214–20 = pars. 2898–2904.

19. At p. 265, specifically for the confecting of the sweetmeat *lawzīnaj*.

20. See *Introductio*, pp. XLVII–XLVIII, LV–LVI, LXV.

21. See the *muqaddimah* of his edition, vol. I, pp. 30–31.

22. Cf. F. Rosenthal's brief words on translations of Ṭabarī, in *The History of al-Ṭabarī, vol. I*, 144–45.

23. *Die Annalen von aṭ-Ṭabarī im Spiegel der europäischen Bearbeitungen*, 61–63.

seventy years before, while disagreeing with her opinion that Ṭabarī's style is flat and uninteresting and his narrative consequently dry and jejune. Their main criticism of her work, however, was that it is in general too free, often without regard for the subtleties of Arabic syntax, as for example, in the use of dependent circumstantial clauses, relative clauses, and the like.[24] Their criticism is, indeed, quite justified; one might add that the connections, distinctions, and changes brought into the flow of the narrative by Ṭabarī's choice of *wa-*, *fa-*, and *thumma*—the usage of which in Arabic is never haphazard—were not always recognized by Marin and taken into account in her rendering. Also, some of the technicalities of early ʿAbbāsid history eluded her, for example, the identification of the troops of the Ḥarbiyyah quarter of Baghdad (Ṭabarī, vol. III, p. 1179 l. 14 = trans. Marin, p. 15 and n. 105a) and of the Abnāʾ (vol. III, p. 1181 l. 3 = trans. Marin, p. 16; cf. p. 7 n. 57). It is only fair to observe that much less was known about these groups forty years ago, before the work of Ayalon and others on the military foundations of the early ʿAbbāsid caliphate, though research centered on Sāmarrā by Ernst Herzfeld (not used at all by Marin) might have put her on the right track.

There remains the pleasant task of thanking those scholars who have given advice and help on certain difficult passages and on certain doubtful points, the sorts of problem from which no substantial passage of Ṭabarī's *History* is free; as Helmut Ritter stated, there is an ever-present danger of becoming lost in the Arabic/Arabian desert ("in der arabischen wüste").[25] In particular, I am grateful to my colleague Dr. Norman Calder and to Professor Josef van Ess (Tübingen), Professor Wilferd Madelung (Oxford), and Dr. David Waines (Lancaster), while Dr. P. O. Skjærvø and Dr. Estelle Whelan (New York) have provided valuable corrections to my text in the fields of Iranian philology and Islamic art respectively. Nevertheless, I must add the usual disclaimer that any errors and imperfections are my responsibility alone.

C. E. Bosworth

---

24. Cf. H. Horst, *ZDMG*, 105 (1955): 219.
25. *Oriens* 6 (1953): 157.

Table I.
Genealogy of the ʿAbbāsids, with Special Reference to Members of the Family Mentioned in This Section of al-Ṭabarī's *History*

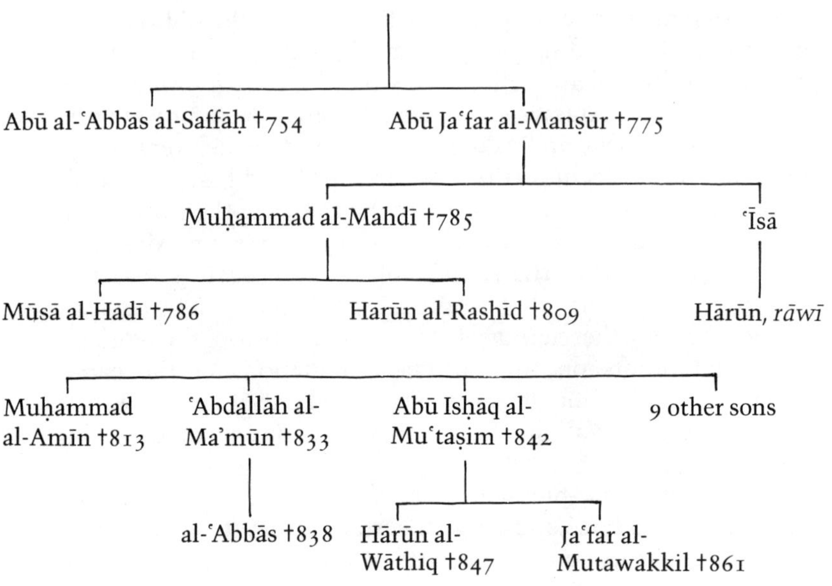

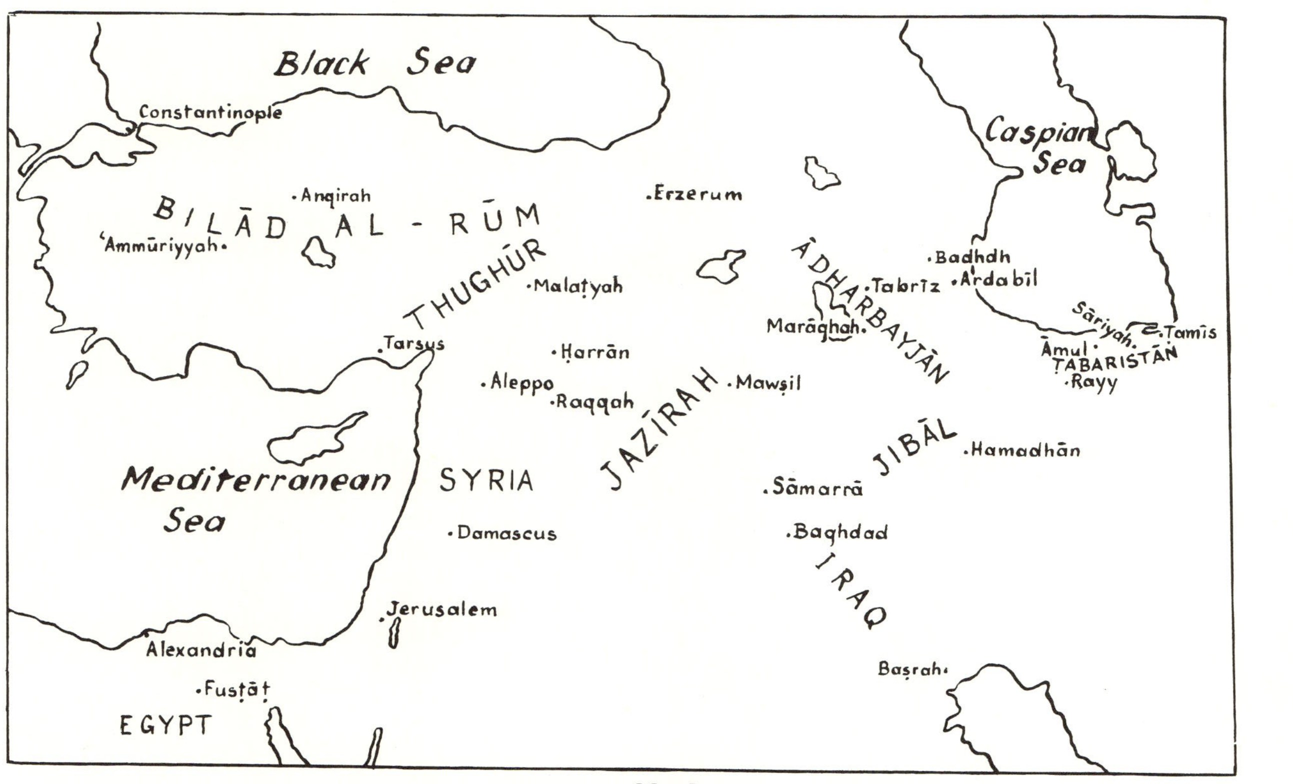

Map I.
The Central Lands of the Caliphate during the Reign of al-Muʿtaṣim

The Events of the Year [1164]

218 (cont'd)

(JANUARY 27, 833–JANUARY 15, 834)

The Succession of Abū Isḥāq al-Muʿtaṣim on His Brother al-Maʾmūn's Death

In this year, on Thursday, the eighteenth of Rajab 218 (August 9, 833),[1] allegiance was given to Abū Isḥāq Muḥammad b. Hārūn al-Rashīd b. Muḥammad al-Mahdī b. ʿAbdallāh al-Manṣūr as caliph. It has been mentioned that the populace (*al-nās*) had been perturbed lest al-ʿAbbās b. al-Maʾmūn dispute with al-Muʿtaṣim over the caliphate, but they had been spared that. It has been mentioned that the army (*al-jund*) rioted when allegiance was given to Abū Isḥāq as caliph; they sought out al-ʿAbbās and hailed him with the name of caliph. Hence Abū Isḥāq sent for al-ʿAbbās and summoned him to his presence, and the latter gave allegiance to him. Then al-ʿAbbās went forth to the army and said, "What is the use of this pointless devotion? I have already given allegiance to my paternal uncle and have handed over the caliphate to him." The army thereupon became calm again.[2]

1. Actually a Saturday, though stated by Yaʿqūbī, *Taʾrīkh*, II, 575, to be a Friday.
2. Yaʿqūbī, *Taʾrīkh*, II, 575, says that the army regarded al-ʿAbbās's backing down as feeble and inadequate; hence they reviled him for his weakness before

In this year al-Muʿtaṣim ordered the destruction of all the construction work that al-Maʾmūn had commanded to be done at Ṭuwānah.[3] He carried away all that was transportable there of arms, equipment, and so on, and what he was unable to transport he burned. He also ordered the removal back to their original home territories of all those whom al-Maʾmūn had settled at Ṭuwānah.[4]

In this year, al-Muʿtaṣim, accompanied by al-ʿAbbās b. al-Maʾmūn, returned to Baghdad, entering it, according to what has been mentioned, on Saturday, the first of Ramaḍān (September 20, 833).[5]

[1165] *An Expedition Sent against the Khurramiyyah*

In this year, according to what has been mentioned, a great number of the people of al-Jibāl, from Hamadhān, Iṣfahān, Māsabadhān and Mihrajānqadhaq,[6] embraced the Khurramī faith (*dīn al-Khurramiyyah*).[7] They banded together and then en-

---

finally acquiescing in al-Muʿtaṣim's succession. See Dīnawarī, *Kitāb al-akhbār al-ṭiwāl*, 401; Masʿūdī, *Murūj al-dhahab*, VII, 102–3 = par. 2786; *Kitāb al-ʿuyūn*, 380; Ibn al-Athīr, *al-Kāmil*, VI, 439; Ibn al-ʿAdīm, *Bughyat al-ṭalab*, I, 68. Although, while dying, al-Maʾmūn had nominated his brother as his heir (Ṭabarī, III, 1133), in a later tradition it was alleged that al-Maʿmūn had, at least at some point in his caliphate, expected his son al-ʿAbbās to succeed him (Ṭabarī, III, 1469). Certainly al-ʿAbbās had experience of fighting on the Byzantine marches and had been governor of Syria and al-Jazīrah for his father, an office in which al-Muʿtaṣim confirmed him (Ibn al-ʿAdīm, *op. cit.*, I, 68); and in 223 (838) he was to be the focus of an abortive plot against al-Muʿtaṣim by discontented commanders during the march against Anqirah and ʿAmmūriyyah, being subsequently arrested and killed at Manbij after that campaign had been successfully concluded (Ṭabarī, III, 1249–50, 1256–67; pp. 112–13, 121–33, below). See also M. A. Shaban, *Islamic History*, 61.

3. The classical Tyana in Cilicia. See Yāqūt, *Muʿjam al-buldān*, IV, 45–46; G. Le Strange, *Palestine*, 547; idem, *Lands*, 139. Al-ʿAbbās had fortified it on al-Maʾmūn's orders earlier in the same year; see Ṭabarī, III, 1111–12.

4. Azdī, *Taʾrīkh al-Mawṣil*, 415; see also Shaban, *op. cit.*, 61–62.

5. This date is confirmed by Yaʿqūbī, *Taʾrīkh*, II, 575, with more details of the new Caliph's journey than Ṭabarī in fact gives: that he traveled via al-Raqqah and while there appointed Ghassān b. ʿAbbād, the former governor of Khurāsān, governor of al-Jazīrah and the frontier fortresses (*al-ʿawāṣim*) there. See also Ṭabarī, trans. Balʿamī, IV, 523.

6. These two last being districts of the province of al-Jibāl, in modern Luristān, to the northeast of the Pusht-i Kūh. See Yāqūt, *Muʿjam*, V, 41, 233; Le Strange, *Lands*, 202; P. Schwarz, *Iran im Mittelalter*, 464–73.

7. Khurramī unrest in the mountainous regions of northern Persia, in the three distinct regions of Khurāsān, al-Jibāl, and Ādharbayjān, is mentioned from the

camped in the province of Hamadhān. Al-Muʿtaṣim accordingly sent troops against them, the last army sent against them being that which he dispatched under the command of Isḥāq b. Ibrāhīm b. Muṣʿab,[8] whom he appointed governor of al-Jibāl in Shawwāl of this year (October–November 833). Isḥāq set out against them in Dhū al-Qaʿdah (November–December 833), and his dispatch announcing victory was read out (in the capital) on the "Day of Refreshment" (*Yawm al-Tarwiyah*, the eighth of Dhū al-Ḥijjah [December 25, 833]).[9] He killed 60,000 of them in province of Hamadhān, and the rest fled to Byzantine territory.[10]

---

middle years of the second (eighth) century onward, but the major outbreak, which convulsed northwestern Persia for more than twenty years under the leadership of Bābak, began around 201 (816–17), in al-Maʾmūn's reign; cf. Ṭabarī, III, 1015. See B. Scarcia Amoretti, "Sects and Heresies," 504–6; *EIr*, s.v. "Bābak Ḵorramī" (Ḡ.-Ḥ. Yūsofī).

8. Abū al-Ḥasan Isḥāq was the most distinguished of what might be called the Muṣʿabid line, parallel to the Ṭāhirid line of Ṭāhir Dhū al-Yamīnayn, and was first cousin to ʿAbdallāh b. Ṭāhir. He was *ṣāḥib al-shurṭah*, or governor, of Baghdad and Sāmarrā, and deputy for the Caliph when he was absent from Iraq, for nearly thirty years, until his death in 235 (849–50). Having been one of al-Maʾmūn's right-hand men (see Ṭabarī, III, 1328; p. 214, below), he had taken a prominent part in the opening interrogations of the *Miḥnah*, or Muʿtazilī inquisition; see Ṭabarī, III, 1116, 1121 ff., 1131–32; on his role in general, see E. Herzfeld, *Geschichte der Stadt Samarra*, 107; C. E. Bosworth, "The Ṭāhirids and Arabic Culture," 67–68; M. Kaabi, *Les Ṭāhirides*, I, 315–25.

9. The day during the sequence of Pilgrimage ceremonies when the participants move from Mecca to Minā and ʿArafāt. See M. Gaudefroy-Demombynes, *Le pèlerinage à la Mekke*, 236ff.; *EI*[2], s.v. "Ḥadjdj" (A J. Wensinck [-J. Jomier]).

10. Ṭabarī, trans. Balʿamī, IV, 523; Azdī, *op. cit.*, 415; *Kitāb al-ʿuyūn*, 380; Niẓām al-Mulk, *Siyāsat-nāmah*, 292–93, trans. 233–34 (detailed account with several original details); Ibn al-Athīr, *op. cit.*, VI, 441. Poetry written by Abū Tammām (on whom see p. 92 n. 258, below) in praise of Isḥāq b. Ibrāhīm includes the names of various places in Ādharbayjān and al-Jibāl where clashes with the Khurramiyyah took place, for example, Qurrān and Ashtar; see A. Haq, "Historical Poems in the Diwan of Abū Tammām," 21.

A detailed analysis of this Khurramī rising is given by M. Rekaya in his "Mise au point sur Théophobe," 42–48, emphasizing the need to distinguish this rising in al-Jibāl and Kurdistān from Bābak's parallel movement in Arrān and Ādharbayjān and the important fact that it was the numerous body of refugees fleeing from Isḥāq b. Ibrāhīm's repressions to Byzantine territory who then became the Persian and Kurdish contingent of the Emperor Theophilus's army under their leader Naṣīr/Nuṣayr (Masʿūdī, *Murūj*, VII, 136 = par. 2818; Ṭabarī never gives this name) or Naṣr the Kurd (Michael the Syrian), who became a convert to Christianity and adopted the Greek name Theophobus. He was eventually killed in 225 (839–40) fighting the Muslims in the *thughūr*, or frontier regions, around al-Maṣṣīṣah in Cilicia; see p. 119 n. 334, below. Naṣīr/Nuṣayr's followers formed part of the Byzantine army that attacked Zibaṭrah in 223

In this year Ṣāliḥ b. al-ʿAbbās b. Muḥammad[11] led the Pilgrimage.[12] The people of Mecca made the sacrifice of the ʿĪd al-Aḍḥā on the Friday, and the people of Baghdad on the Saturday.[13]

(837–38) (see Ṭabarī, III, 1234–35; pp. 93–95, below), and it must have been they who shortly afterward, at the battle of Anzen (see Ṭabarī, III, 1242; p. 105 n. 305, below), made up the 2,000 Persian troops mentioned in both the Christian and Arabic sources (these being numbered by Masʿūdī, *Kitāb al-tanbīh*, 169, trans., 230–31, as "several thousands" and specifically described as the Kurds and Persians who had fled from al-Jibāl some five years before). See also J. Rosser, "Theophilus' Khurramite Policy," based entirely on Greek sources and Arabic sources in translation. Rosser fails to distinguish between the various Khurramī revolts but does correctly observe (267) that Isḥāq b. Ibrāhīm's victory in al-Jibāl caused Khurramī elements to flee westward and enter the Byzantine Emperor's service.

11. Member of the ʿAbbāsid family and first cousin of the Caliph al-Mahdī. The Ṣāliḥ al-ʿAbbāsī subsequently mentioned by Ṭabarī, e.g., at III, 1362–63, was however a Turkish soldier, presumably a mawlā of the ʿAbbāsid family, and it was after this last person that the street in Sāmarrā where his palace stood was named. See Yaʿqūbī, *Buldān*, 262, trans., 55; Herzfeld, *op. cit.*, 111.

12. Ibn al-Athīr, *op. cit.*, VI, 442; but, according to Khalīfah b. Khayyāṭ, *Taʾrīkh*, II, 781, it was Sulaymān b. ʿAbdallāh b. Sulaymān b. ʿAlī who led it.

13. This latter day was actually the tenth of Dhū al-Ḥijjah in the year 218.

The Events of the Year 219

(January 16, 834–January 4, 835)

The Rebellion of the ʿAlid Muḥammad b. al-Qāsim at al-Ṭālaqān

Among the events taking place during this year was the rebellion, at al-Ṭālaqān[14] in Khurāsān, of Muḥammad b. al-Qāsim b. ʿUmar b. ʿAlī b. al-Ḥusayn b. ʿAlī b. Abī Ṭālib,[15] summoning people to the cause of "the well-pleasing one from the family of Muḥammad" (*al-riḍā*[16] *min āl Muḥammad*). A considerable number of people there rallied to his side, and military encounters took place in the vicinity of al-Ṭālaqān and the mountains there between him and ʿAbdallāh b. Ṭāhir's[17]

---

14. A town in Khurāsān between Marw al-Rūdh and Balkh, to be distinguished from others of the same name in Ṭukhāristān and on the borders of al-Jibāl and Daylam. See *Ḥudūd al-ʿālam*, 107, 335; Yāqūt, *Muʿjam*, IV, 6–7; Le Strange, *Lands*, 423–24; *EI*[1], s.v. Ṭālaḳān (Cl. Huart).

15. This ʿAlid, a descendant of al-Ḥusayn through the Fourth Imām, ʿAlī Zayn al-ʿĀbidīn (see K. Öhrnberg, *The Offspring of Fatima*, Table 47), is described by Abū al-Faraj al-Iṣfahānī, *Maqātil*, 384, as an adherent of the Jārūdiyyah subsect of the Zaydī Shīʿah (on the Jārūdiyyah, see C. Van Arendonck, *Les débuts de l'Imāmat Zaidite*, 78–90).

16. Or, perhaps, *al-raḍī*.

17. The son of al-Maʾmūn's governor in Khurāsān Ṭāhir Dhū al-Yamīnayn and himself holder of this office in 215–30 (828–45). See Ḳaabi, *op. cit.*, I, 221–91; *EI*[2]

commanders. [In the end] he and his followers were defeated, and he fled, seeking a certain district of Khurāsān whose people had been in correspondence with him. He reached Nasā,[18] where the father of one of his followers lived, and this follower of his at that point went along in order to greet his [the follower's] father. When he met his father, the latter asked him the news, so the man told his father about what had happened to them and how they were making for so-and-so district. The man's father thereupon went to the governor of Nasā and told him about Muḥammad b.
[1166] al-Qāsim's plans. It has been mentioned that the governor gave the father 10,000 dirhams for information that would lead him to Muḥammad b. al-Qāsim. The father accordingly gave him information about Muḥammad b. al-Qāsim's whereabouts.

So the governor went along to Muḥammad b. al-Qāsim, arrested him, placed him in firm custody, and dispatched him to ʿAbdallāh b. Ṭāhir. The latter sent him to al-Muʿtaṣim; he was brought to him on Monday, the fourteenth of Rabīʿ II (April 28, 834) and was then imprisoned, so it has been mentioned, at Sāmarrā in the house of Masrūr al-Khādim al-Kabīr[19] in a narrow cell some three by two cubits only. He remained there for three days and was then transferred to a more commodious place than the previous cell, food was given to him regularly, and a group of persons was appointed and charged with the task of guarding him. When it was the night of the ʿĪd al-Fiṭr (the thirtieth of Ramaḍān 219, the night of October 8–9, 834 and everybody was distracted by the festival and the rejoicings, he devised a stratagem for escaping.

It has been mentioned that he fled from jail by night and that a rope was let down for him from an aperture [in the wall of] the upper part of the house, through which light penetrated to him. When his jailers came next morning with food for his breakfast,

---

s.v. ʿAbd Allāh b. Ṭāhir (E. Marin); *EIr*, s.v. ʿAbdallāh b. Ṭāher (C. E. Bosworth).

18. Or Nisā, a town on the northern fringes of Khurāsān near the beginning of the Qara Qum Desert. See Yāqūt, *Muʿjam*, V, 281–82; *Ḥudūd al-ʿālam*, 103, 326; Le Strange, *Lands*, 394; W. Barthold, *Historical Geography*, 89–90; *EI*[1], s.v. Nasā (V. Minorsky).

19. Eunuch slave of of Hārūn al-Rashīd's who acted as the Caliph's executioner (e.g., for the killing of Jaʿfar b. Yaḥyā al-Barmakī in 187 [803]; Ṭabarī, III, 678–79); see P. Crone, *Slaves on Horses*, 192–93.

he was missing. It has been mentioned that a reward of 100,000 dirhams was offered for whomever might give information that would lead to Muḥammad b. al-Qāsim; the public herald proclaimed this, but no further news was heard of him.[20]

In this year Isḥāq b. Ibrāhīm [b. Muṣʿab] entered Baghdad, [returning] from al-Jibāl, on Sunday, the eleventh of Jumādā I (May 24, 834), accompanied by Khurramī captives and those who had sought a guarantee of security (*al-musta'minah*). It has been said that, in the course of his fighting with the Khurramiyyah, Isḥāq b. Ibrāhīm killed around 100,000, apart from the women and children (taken captive and enslaved).[21]

The Campaign against the Zuṭṭ

In this year, in Jumādā II (June–July 834), al-Muʿtaṣim sent ʿUjayf b. ʿAnbasah[22] to combat the Zuṭṭ,[23] who had been creating [1167]

20. See Yaʿqūbī, *Ta'rīkh*, II, 576; Abū al-Faraj al-Iṣfahānī, *Maqātil*, 382–92; Masʿūdī, *Murūj*, VII, 116–18 = pars. 2799–2800; Gardīzī, *Kitāb zayn al-akhbār*, ed. Ḥabībī, 76; *Kitāb al-ʿuyūn*, 382; Ibn al-Athīr, *op. cit.*, VI, 442–43. Uncertainty about Muḥammad b. al-Qāsim's fate is reflected in stories given by Masʿūdī, including the one that he returned to al-Ṭālaqān and was expected by the Zaydīs to return as a Mahdī after his death; Iṣfahānī regards it as most probable that he escaped to Wāsiṭ.

21. Yaʿqūbī, *Ta'rīkh*, II, 575–76, according to whom Isḥāq b. Ibrāhīm had to be sent out after the rebels had defeated al-Muʿtaṣim's commander Hāshim b. Bānījūr (read thus for the text's Bātījūr, as also at II, 465); on this family of commanders from the upper Oxus region, also called the Abū Dāwūdids, see *EI*[2] Suppl., s.v. Bānīdjūrids (C. E. Bosworth); Ibn al-Athīr, *op. cit.*, VI, 445.

22. Khurāsānian commander of Arab origin, prominent in al-Ma'mūn's reign and commander of the guard (*ṣāḥib al-ḥaras*) for al-Muʿtaṣim but later to be involved in the plot to dethrone the latter, in 223 (837–38); see Ṭabarī, III, 1256–58, 1264–66; pp. 121–23, 130–32, below. According to Yaʿqūbī, *Ta'rīkh*, II, 576, Aḥmad b. Saʿīd (b. Salm b. Qutaybah) al-Bāhilī was first sent against the Zuṭṭ but was defeated; hence the decision to send ʿUjayf. See also Herzfeld, *op. cit.*, 107.

23. Zuṭṭ is an Arabization of the Indian ethnic term Jhāt. Members of this group were transported from India to the Gulf region by the Sāsānid emperors and their numbers reinforced in the Umayyad period by Indian troops whom the governor al-Ḥajjāj b. Yūsuf brought back from Sind and settled in the Baṭā'iḥ or marshlands of lower Iraq. Under al-Ma'mūn, in 205 (820) we hear of a rebellion by the Zuṭṭ, which would be contemporary with that of Bābak and the Khurramiyyah in northwestern Persia and, like that movement, probably directed at the central government and irksome caliphal control (Ṭabarī, III, 1044). Efforts to put an end to their terrorizing of the region of al-Baṣrah were not however successful until this expedition of ʿUjayf's. See Ch. Pellat, *Le milieu baṣrien*, 37–40; *EI*[1], s.v. Zoṭṭ (G. Ferrand).

disturbances on the road to al-Baṣrah. They attacked traffic along the road, carried off the crops from the threshing floors at Kaskar[24] and adjacent districts of al-Baṣrah, and made the roads unsafe. On every one of the postal and intelligence service roads al-Muʿtaṣim set up relays of horsemen (*sikak al-burud*) who could gallop and bring the news; in this way, information would come from ʿUjayf and reach al-Muʿtaṣim the same day. The person appointed by al-Muʿtaṣim to take charge of the expenses and supplies of ʿUjayf's campaigns was Muḥammad b. Manṣūr, Ibrāhīm al-Bakhtarī's secretary.

When ʿUjayf reached Wāsiṭ he pitched his camp with 5,000 men at a village in the district below Wāsiṭ called al-Ṣāfiyah.[25] Then he went to a canal that leads off the Tigris called Bardūdā[26] and remained there until he had blocked it up. It has been said, however, that ʿUjayf pitched his camp at a village in the district below Wāsiṭ called Najīdā and that he sent Hārūn b. Nuʿaym b. al-Waḍḍāḥ,[27] the Khurāsānian commander, to a place called al-Ṣāfiyah with 5,000 men, while ʿUjayf himself proceeded with another 5,000 troops to Bardūdā and remained there until he had blocked it. He furthermore blocked other waterways by means of which the Zuṭṭ used to slip through and issue forth, and thus encircled and put pressure on them from all sides. Among the waterways that ʿUjayf blocked was a canal called al-ʿArūs ("the Bride"). When he had cut their lines of communication, he attacked them and captured 500 of their menfolk, killing an additional 300 men in the battle. He struck off the heads of the

---

24. An ancient settlement on the right bank of the Tigris in lower Iraq, facing al-Ḥajjāj's new garrison town of Wāsiṭ, and also the name of the surrounding district. See Yāqūt, *Muʿjam*, IV, 461; Le Strange, *Lands*, 39, 42–43; *EI*², s.v. Kaskar (M. Streck- [J. Lassner]).

25. Not apparently the al-Ṣāfiyah ("the Pure," e.g., of water) mentioned by Yāqūt, *Muʿjam*, III, 389, as being near al-Nuʿmāniyyah, to the northwest of Kaskar.

26. The Nahr Bardūdā was one of the five navigable waterways by means of which the Tigris below Wāsiṭ flowed into the Baṭāʾiḥ or Great Marshes; see Le Strange, *Lands*, 41.

27. Khurāsānian commander whose father Nuʿaym was, according to Yaʿqūbī, *Buldān*, 256, trans., 45, the first owner of the Turkish slave commander Ashnās, on whom see p. 98 n. 281, below. On Hārun b. Nuʿaym and his family, see further Herzfeld, *op. cit.*, 107, and p. 113 n. 315, below.

prisoners and sent the heads of the whole lot of them to al-Muʿtaṣim's court. Then ʿUjayf remained in his position facing the Zuṭṭ for fifteen days and seized a great many more of them as captives. The chief of the Zuṭṭ was a man called Muḥammad b. [1168] ʿUthmān, with S.m.l.q as his chief executive and in charge of the conduct of warfare. ʿUjayf stayed there, engaged in fighting the Zuṭṭ, for nine months, according to the reports.[28] In this year Ṣāliḥ b. al-ʿAbbās b. Muḥammad led the Pilgrimage.[29]

---

28. Yaʿqūbī, *Ta'rīkh,* II, 576; Ibn al-Athīr, *op. cit.,* VI, 443–44.
29. Khalīfah, *op. cit.,* II, 783.

The Events of the Year 220

(January 5–December 25, 835)

The Deportation of the Captured Zuṭṭ

Among the events taking place during this year was ʿUjayf's entry into Baghdad with the Zuṭṭ and his crushing them to the point that they had sought from him a guarantee of security, which he had granted them. They came forth to him [in surrender] in Dhū al-Ḥijjah of the year 219 (December 834–January 835), on condition that he would guarantee the security of their lives and possessions. They numbered, according to what has been mentioned, 27,000, of whom 12,000 were fighting men. ʿUjayf enumerated them at 27,000 persons, men, women, and children. He put them in boats and went forward with them until he encamped at al-Zaʿfarāniyyah.[30] There he gave his troops a donative of two dīnārs each and remained for a day. He formed up the Zuṭṭ in their skiffs (*zawārīq*),[31] in their full battle order and

30. A village to the southeast of Baghdad and near Kalwādhā; see Yāqūt, *Muʿjam*, III, 141.

31. Sing. *zawraq*. See H. Kindermann, *"Schiff" im Arabischen*, 36–37; Darwīsh al-Nukhaylī, *al-Sufun al-islāmiyyah*, 59–62.

with trumpets, and then he entered Baghdad with them on ʿĀshūrāʾ Day of the year 220 (the tenth of al-Muḥarram [January 14, 835]). Al-Muʿtaṣim was at this moment at al-Shammāsiyyah,[32] in a boat of the type called *zaww*,[33] when the Zuṭṭ passed before him in their battle order, blowing trumpets; the first of them were at al-Qufṣ[34] and the last of them opposite al-Shammāsiyyah. They remained in their boats for three days and then were taken across the river to the eastern side and handed over to the charge of Bishr b. al-Sumaydiʿ, who took them to Khāniqīn.[35] After this they were transported to ʿAyn Zarbah[36] [1169]
in the Byzantine marches (*al-thaghr*). But the Byzantines swept down on them and exterminated them, not a single one escaping.[37] One of their poets said:

O people of Baghdad, die! May your frustrated rage,
 out of longing for *barnī* and *suhrīz* dates,[38] be prolonged!
We are the ones who struck you in open defiance
 and violently and who drove you on like weaklings.
You did not thank God for His previously vouchsafed goodness
 and were not mindful of His benefits, duly extolling [Him].
So summon help from the slaves, made up of the supporters of
 your state (*abnāʾ dawlatikum*),[39]
 of Yāzamān,[40] of Balj and of Tūz,[41]

---

32. The northernmost quarter of East Baghdad, running down to the Tigris banks; see Le Strange, *Baghdad*, 199–216.

33. See Kindermann, *op. cit.*, 36–37; al-Nukhaylī, *op. cit.*, 58–59.

34. A village on the Tigris between Baghdad and ʿUkbarā, famed as a pleasure spot; see Yāqūt, *Muʿjam*, IV, 382.

35. A town on the road linking Baghdad with Ḥulwān and the interior of Persia. See Yāqūt, *Muʿjam*, II, 340–41; Le Strange, *Lands*, 62–63; *EI*², s.v. K͟hāniḳīn (Schwarz).

36. One of the *ʿawāṣim*, or frontier fortresses, guarding al-Jazīrah, Greek Anabarzo, the Crusaders' Anazarbus. See Yāqūt, *Muʿjam*, IV, 177–78; Le Strange, *Palestine*, 387–88; idem, *Lands*, 128–29; *EI*², s.v. ʿAyn Zarba (M. Canard).

37. Balādhurī, *Futūḥ al-buldān*, 171, 375–76; Ibn al-Athīr, *op. cit.*, VI, 446.

38. Superior varieties of dates; see the references given by Pellat in the glossary of terms to his translation of Jāḥiẓ, *Kitāb al-bukhalāʾ*, 313–14, 319.

39. A sarcastic reference to the designations *ahl al-dawla, abnāʾ al-dawla*, etc., for the supporters of the early ʿAbbāsid state; see p. 17 n. 74, below.

40. On chronological grounds, this is unlikely to be the Yāzmān al-Khādim mentioned later by Ṭabarī as active as a military commander under al-Muʿtamid, i.e., some fifty years later.

41. These two names are unidentified, but the name Tūz at least, like Yāzmān, indicates a Turkish slave commander.

Of Shinās (Ashnās), of Afshīn and of Faraj,[42]
those who are conspicuous in silk brocade and pure gold,
Those who wear garments of Chinese silk velvet,[43]
with the seams of their gored fringes fastened to their sleeves,
Those who carry sharp daggers, with their hilts fastened
to unsewn, fine linen belts.
The sons of Bahallah[44] leading the sons of Fayrūz
will slash their skulls with gleaming Indian swords.
[1170] [They are] riders, whose steeds are black and are bedecked with
seashells on their noses' rims (i.e., their steeds are ships with
decorated bows),
With detachments rendered subject to them, in the water,
which are like ebony and *shīz* wood[45] when they are hurled
forward!
Whenever you are eager to seek us out in the depths of our
boundless open sea,
well, beware, for we shall hunt you down like those who trap
birds with snares[46]

---

42. Perhaps Faraj al-Rukhkhajī, a commander of al-Maʾmūn's (Ṭabarī, III, 1044) and governor of Ahwāz in al-Muʿtaṣim's reign (Ibrāhīm al-Bayhaqī, *Kitāb al-maḥāsin*, ed. Schwally, 447 = ed. Ibrāhīm, II, 148), though Faraj was a common euphuistic name for slaves. For the other two commanders mentioned in this hemistich, see pp. 98 n. 281, 14 n. 54, below.

43. *Kamkhān al-Sīn.* This term (also *kamkhā, kimkhā, kamkhāw*) was used in medieval Islamic times to denote Chinese figured silk; see Thaʿālibī, *Laṭāʾif al-maʿārif*, 221, trans., 141; and R. B. Serjeant, *Islamic Textiles*, 69, 218. Thence it passed to medieval western Europe as a term for damask or brocade, *cammoca*; see H. Yule and A. C. Burnell, *Hobson-Jobson*, 484–85, s.v. Kincob.

44. Apparently a reference to Bahallah al-Hindiyyah, wife of the Umayyad governor al-Muhallab b. Abī Ṣufrah and mother of his son Yazīd; see Ṭabarī, II, 1210. Al-Muhallab himself may have been of mawlā origin; see Crone, *op. cit.*, 39. The Zuṭṭ poet is referring to his own people's Indian origins, and, in "the sons of Fayrūz," to the transplantation westward of the Zuṭṭ by the Sāsānids, which gave the Zuṭṭ a Persian as well as an Indian, connection (see p. 7 n. 23, above). It is also notable that Masʿūdī, *Tanbīh*, 355, trans., 455, speaks of a westward migration of the Zuṭṭ into southern Persia after they were driven out of India by famine, possibly to be regarded as a comparatively recent movement.

45. A dark-colored hardwood, perhaps walnut, from which bowls were made; see E. W. Lane, *Arabic-English Lexicon*, s.v. shīz.

46. Following *Addenda et emendanda*, CDVI, with its suggested reading of this dubious last word as *al-maqāfīz*, the plural of a putative *miqfāz* for *miqfās* "trap, snare." The Cairo edition, IX, 11, has the meaningless *al-maʿātīz*.

Or with a rapid and violent snatching, just as
the birds seeking refuge in overhanging river banks are seized by hunters using swift falcons.[47]
Fierce fighting—fighting the Zuṭṭ—you must acknowledge,
is not like just eating *tharīd*[48] or drinking from goblets!
We are the ones who gave war its milk to drink,
and we shall certainly follow it up with the violent onslaught of warriors who fight in the sea.[49]
And we shall indeed assault you with an assault[50] that will make
the Master of the Throne[51] take heart and inspirit the lord of Tīz![52]
So weep for the dates! May God make your eyes flow with tears
on every Day of Sacrifice, every Day of the Breaking of the Fast, and every New Year (*nayrūz*)![53]

---

47. Following *Glossarium* and *Addenda et emendanda*, CCCXVII, DCCLXXIII, and the Cairo edition, IX, 11, with their reading in the second hemistich of *al-diḥal*; and *Glossarium*, CCCXVII, for the interpretation of *al-shanāqīz* as "falcons."

48. A dish of meat minced with bread, grain, or dates, a favorite food of the Quraysh in Mecca at the time of the Prophet. See M. Rodinson, "Recherches sur les documents arabes," 133 and n. 5; Jāḥiẓ, *Kitāb al-bukhalā'*, trans., 320.

49. *Al-kawālīz*; see *Glossarium*, CDLVII.

50. Echoing Qur'ān XCVI: 15.

51. *Rabb al-sarīr*. In the light of M. J. de Goeje's interpretation in *Glossarium*, CCLXXXIX, E. Marin (Ṭabarī, trans. Marin, 8 n. 66) may be correct in regarding this as a reference to Bābak, for possession of such a throne had connotations of power and authority; see p. 57 n. 171, below. But it is equally possible that the allusion is not to him but to the Caucasian ruler known in the Arabic sources (e.g. Balādhurī, *op. cit.*, 196) as the *ṣāḥib al-sarīr*, who ruled over a group of Avars in southern Dāghistān and after whom the region of Sarīr was subsequently named. See *Ḥudūd al-ʿālam*, 161, 447–50; V. Minorsky, *History of Sharvān and Darband*, 97ff.; *EI*[2], s.v. al-Ḳabḳ (C. E. Bosworth).

52. Tīz was the main port of Makrān, probably near the modern Chāhbahār. See *Ḥudūd al-ʿālam*, 123; Le Strange, *Lands*, 329–30. But it is difficult to see who is meant by *ṣāḥib al-Tīz* or what his contemporary fame was.

53. More correctly *nawrūz*, the festival of the beginning of the Persian solar new year, originally at the summer solstice but now on 21 March. This holiday continued to be observed by Islamic princes and viziers in the ancient Sāsānid lands of Persia and Iraq and to be celebrated by exchanges of gifts and other festivities. It came to have practical, as well as ceremonial, significance, in that subsequent caliphs, beginning with al-Mutawakkil, proposed to adopt Nawrūz as the beginning of the solar year for financial and taxation purposes. Al-Muʿtaḍid was the first who actually did so. Hence Ḥamzah al-Iṣfahānī, writing in the fourth (tenth) century, considered it important enough to devote a special section of his work on history and chronology to the correspondences of the date of *nayrūz* with

In this year al-Muʿtaṣim appointed the Afshīn Khaydhar[54] b.
[1171] Kāwūs governor of al-Jibāl and sent him to combat Bābak, this being on Thursday, the second of Jumādā II (June 3, 220). He pitched his camp at the *muṣallā* of Baghdad[55] and then proceeded to Barzand.[56]

The Affair of Bābak and His Outbreak

It has been mentioned that Bābak's (first) rebellion was in the year 201 (816/817) and that the settlement and town that was his headquarters was al-Badhdh.[57] (On that occasion) he put to flight

---

the dates of the Hijrī calendar from A. H. 1 to A. H. 350; see his *Ta'rīkh sinī mulūk al-arḍ wa-al-anbiyā'*, 130–43. See further A. Mez, *Die Renaissance des Islâms*, 400–1, trans., 425–26; D. S. Margoliouth, "The Historical Content of the *Diwan* of Buhturi," 253–54; G. E. von Grunebaum, *Muhammadan Festivals*, 54–55; *EI*², s.v. Nawrūz (R. Levy).

54. Corrected to this reading in *Addenda et emendanda*, DCCLXXIII, the reading also in Yaʿqūbī, *Buldān*, 259, trans., 51, adopted by de Goeje and followed by F. Justi in *Iranisches Namenbuch*, 253, but often assimilated by Arabic copyists to the more familiar Arabic name Ḥaydar. On al-Afshīn, who plays such a dominant role in the affairs of al-Muʿtaṣim's caliphate, see *EI*², s.v. Afshīn (Barthold- [H. A. R. Gibb]) and *EIr*, s.v. Afšīn (C. E. Bosworth); for the circumstances in which he came to enter ʿAbbāsid service, see Barthold, *Turkestan*, 211; and on the title Afshīn, Justi, *op. cit.*, 252–53; and Bosworth and Clauson, "Al-Xwārazmī on the Peoples of Central Asia," 7–8.

55. I.e., the extensive open site usually used for the *ṣalāt*, or public worship, on the great festivals and on other special occasions; see *EI*², s.v. Muṣallā (A. J. Wensinck and R. Hillenbrand). The Baghdad *muṣallā* lay on the eastern bank of the Tigris, in the Shammāsiyyah quarter (on which see p. 11 n. 32, above), near the Baradān cemetery and close to where the highway to Hamadhān, al-Rayy, and Khurāsān passed. In the historical sources for the fourth (tenth) century (e.g., Hilāl al-Ṣābi' and Miskawayh), it is frequently mentioned as the place where discontented troops massed for rioting and hatching plots. See Le Strange, *Baghdad*, 204–5; M. Canard, *Histoire*, 163 and n. 207. For *muṣallā* in its other technical sense of "prayer rug," see Ṭabarī, III, 1327; p. 214 and n. 638, below).

56. A town in Mūqān (on which see p. 19 n. 77, below), hence adjacent to the mountainous center of Bābak's power and a suitable place for al-Afshīn to establish his field headquarters. See Le Strange, *Lands*, 175–76; Schwarz, *op. cit.*, 1094–95; Gh. H. Sadighi, *Les mouvements religieux iraniens*, 252–53 n. 7; *EI*², s.v. Barzand (R. N. Frye).

57. Bābak's capital lay in the modern Qaraja Dagh region, north of Ahar and south of the Araxes, in northern Ādharbayjān. A Tehran archaeological team seems now to have identified the actual fortified site at Qalʿa-yi Jumhūr. See Abū Dulaf, *Second Risalah*, 35–36, 75; Schwarz, *op. cit.*, 970–74, 1126–34; *EI*², Suppl., s.v. al-Badhdh (C. E. Bosworth); *EIr*, s.v. Badd (Ġ.-Ḥ Yūsofī).

forces sent by the central government and killed a number of its commanders. When the supreme power passed to al-Muʿtaṣim, he sent Abū Saʿīd Muḥammad b. Yūsuf[58] to Ardabīl[59] and ordered him to rebuild the strongholds between Zanjān[60] and Ardabīl that Bābak had destroyed and to put armed men in them as garrisons to hold the road, in order to ensure safe passage for those bringing provisions to Ardabīl. So Abū Saʿīd embarked on this and rebuilt the strong points that Bābak had destroyed. In one of his incursions Bābak sent a detachment of troops against him (Abū Saʿīd) under the command of a man called Muʿāwiyah, who then sallied forth, raided some of the neighboring districts, and withdrew to his base. News of this reached Abū Saʿīd Muḥammad b. Yūsuf, so he gathered his forces together and marched out against Muʿāwiyah, to intercept him at some point along the road. [Abū Saʿīd] attacked [Muʿāwiyah], killed a number of his followers, took a number of them captive, and he recovered what Muʿāwiyah had amassed [in the raids]. This was the first reverse that Bābak's partisans had suffered. Abū Saʿīd sent the severed heads [of the fallen enemy] and the prisoners to al-Muʿtaṣim billāh.[61]

The next defeat of Bābak that followed was at the hands of Muḥammad b. al-Baʿīth.[62] This came about because Muḥammad

58. I.e., al-Marwazī (also called al-Thaghrī, presumably because of his experience fighting on the Byzantine marches), in al-Maʾmūn's reign commander under Ḥumayd b. ʿAbd al-Ḥamīd al-Ṭūsī, d. 236 (850–51).

59. A town of eastern Ādharbayjān. See Yāqūt, *Muʿjam*, I, 145–46; Le Strange, *Lands*, 168; Schwarz, *op. cit.*, 1026–47; Barthold, *Historical Geography*, 215–17; *EI*[2], s.v. Ardabīl (R. N. Frye); *EIr*, s.v. Ardabīl (C. E. Bosworth et al.).

60. A town on the road between Ardabīl and Qazwīn. See Yāqūt, *Muʿjam*, III, 152–53; Le Strange, *Lands*, 221–22; Schwarz, *op. cit.*, 729–31; Barthold, *Historical Geography*, 213; *EI*[1], s.v. Zandjān (V. Minorsky).

61. See Rekaya, "Mise au point sur Théophobe," 49–51. Abū Tammām, who addressed eulogies to the commander Abū Saʿīd Muḥammad b. Yūsuf, states in one of his poems that this clash took place behind Sindbāyā in Ādharbayjān (placed by the geographers in the region of al-Badhdh; see Yāqūt, *Muʿjam*, III, 267, and Schwarz, *op. cit.*, 1125–26) and that Muʿāwiyah was able to flee under cover of night, when the encounter must have taken place; see Haq, *op. cit.*, 21–22.

62. Muḥammad's father had been a soldier in the service of the Rawwādids (see p. 17 and n. 68, below) and had established himself in Marand. Muḥammad himself expanded his power at the expense of the Rawwādids and subsequently rebelled against the caliphs; he was defeated only in 235 (849), by al-Mutawakkil's general Bughā al-Ṣaghīr. See R. Mottahedeh, "The ʿAbbāsid Caliphate in Iran," 78;

b. al-Baʿīth was in a strongly defended fortress of his called Shāhī
[1172] ("the Royal")[63] which Ibn al-Baʿīth had seized from al-Wajnāʾ b. al-Rawwād,[64] which was situated on a rocky ridge (*ʿarḍ, ʿurḍ*) approximately two farsakhs long and which fell within the administrative district of Ādharbayjān. He had another fortress in the province of Ādharbayjān called Tabrīz,[65] but Shāhī was the more impregnable of the two. Ibn al-Baʿīth had made peace with Bābak, so that when Bābak's raiding parties went forth they used to halt [at his fortress], and he would give them hospitality and treat them kindly, to the point that they became completely at ease with him and this became an established custom of theirs. On one occasion, Bābak sent out one of his followers called ʿIṣmah,[66] who was one of his senior commanders (*min iṣbahbadhīhi*),[67] with a raiding party. He halted by Ibn al-Baʿīth, and the latter providing ʿIṣmah, according to the custom then current, with sheep and goats, other foodstuffs fitting for guests, and various items of hospitality. He sent a message to ʿIṣmah for him to go up to him, accompanied by his personal guard and leading commanders. ʿIṣmah accordingly went [to Ibn al-Baʿīth], and Ibn al-Baʿīth plied [ʿIṣmah] and his companions with food and drink until he rendered them all drunk, whereupon he pounced on ʿIṣmah, secured him firmly in bonds, and killed those of his companions who were with him. He then ordered [ʿIṣmah] to

---

and Bosworth, "The Ṭāhirids and Ṣaffārids," 101; *EI*², s.v. Marand (V. Minorsky-[C. E. Bosworth]).

63. This lay on an island in Lake Urmiya, though it could be reached on foot when the water level was low. See Le Strange, *Lands*, 160–61; Schwarz, *op. cit.*, 990; *EI*¹, s.v. Urmiya (V. Minorsky). For the descriptive phrase used just below, *ʿarḍuhā/ʿurḍuhā naḥwan min farsakhayn*, the translation suggested by A. Dietrich, in *BiOr*, XI, 35, has been adopted.

64. A member of the Kurdicized Arab family of the Rawwādids, who in the later fourth (tenth) and early fifth (eleventh) centuries dominated Ādharbayjān from Tabrīz. See Minorsky, *Studies in Caucasian History*, 167–69; Bosworth, *Islamic Dynasties*, 88–89; W. Madelung, "Minor Dynasties," 227, 236–39; Bosworth, "Political and Dynastic History," 32–34.

65. Only a few years, later, however, when the geographer Ibn Khurradādhbih wrote (middle third [eighth] century), Tabrīz was in the hands of Muḥammad b. al-Rawwād; see *EI*¹, s.v. Tabrīz (V. Minorsky).

66. Called by Yaʿqūbī, *Taʾrīkh*, II, 577, "al-Kurdī" and lord of Marand.

67. For this ancient Persian term, Middle Persian *spāhpat*, see *EI*², s.v. Ispabadh (C. E. Bosworth).

enumerate each man of [the remainder of] his followers, one by one and by individual name, at which the man in question would be summoned by name, and he would mount [to the fortress], where Ibn al-Baʿīth would give an order and he would be beheaded. [This process continued] until the remainder of them became aware of that trick so that they fled. Ibn al-Baʿīth sent ʿIṣmah on to al-Muʿtaṣim. Abū Muḥammad al-Baʿīth (Muḥammad b. al-Baʿīth's father) had been one of Ibn al-Rawwād's freebooters and desperadoes (*ṣuʿlūk*).[68] Al-Muʿtaṣim interrogated ʿIṣmah about Bābak's territory, and the latter provided him with information about the roads of access into it and the possible modes of fighting there. ʿIṣmah remained in captivity until the reign of al-Wāthiq.[69]

When al-Afshīn arrived at Barzand he encamped there and repaired the fortresses between Barzand and Ardabīl. He stationed Muḥammad b. Yūsuf at a place called Khushsh,[70] and there Muḥammad b. Yūsuf dug a protective trench (*khandaq*).[71] He stationed al-Haytham al-Ghanawī, a commander who originated [1173]
from the people of al-Jazīrah,[72] in a rural district (*rustāq*) called Arshaq,[73] and al-Haytham repaired its fortress and dug a protective trench around it. He stationed ʿAlawayh al-Aʿwar ("the One-Eyed"), one of the commanders of the Abnāʾ,[74] at a fortress

68. Yaʿqūbī, *Taʾrīkh*, II, 577–78, states that al-Muʿtaṣim first sent the Muṣʿabid Ṭāhir b. Ibrahīm b. Muṣʿab, brother of the governor of Baghdad Isḥāq, against Bābak. Muḥammad b. al-Baʿīth, after having married ʿIṣmah's daughter as part of the strategy against him, brought him and his followers in chains to Ṭāhir. Al-Muʿtaṣim was angry because it was Muḥammad b. al-Baʿīth, and not Ṭahir himself, who had been successful; he therefore sent al-Afshīn against the Khurramiyyah. See Sadighi, *op. cit.*, 251–52; Kaabi, *op. cit.*, I, 322. Ibn al-Athīr, *op. cit.*, VI, 447–48, follows Ṭabarī on this point.

69. Al-Muʿtaṣim's son and successor, who reigned as caliph in 227–32 (842–47). Cf. on this episode, Ṭabarī, trans. Balʿamī, IV, 526–27.

70. This place lies roughly midway between Ardabīl and Barzand and is known today as Kushā. See Schwarz, *op. cit.*, 1160–61; Sadighi, *op. cit.*, 25–52.

71. It was the normal practice to dig such trenches when warfare entered a static phase. See R. Levy, *The Social Structure of Islam*, 437–38.

72. Tribes of Qays such as Ghanī (a tribe associated with Bāhilah; see *EI*², s.v. Ghanī b. Aʿṣur [J. W. Fück]) had settled extensively in northern Syria and al-Jazīrah, the homeland of this otherwise unknown commander.

73. Also in Mūqān, between Ardabīl and Barzand. See Yāqūt, *Muʿjam*, I, 152; Schwarz, *op. cit.*, 1164–65.

74. I.e., the descendants of the Khurāsānian supporters of the ʿAbbāsid *daʿwa*, the *ahl Khurāsān* (largely descended from the original Arab tribesmen settled in

near Ardabīl called Ḥiṣn al-Nahr.[75] Groups of travelers and caravans used to set off from Ardabīl accompanied by an escort until they reached Ḥiṣn al-Nahr, and then the commander of Ḥiṣn al-Nahr would escort them to al-Haytham al-Ghanawī. [Al-]Haytham, in turn, would set off with those who had come from his own district until he handed them over to the garrison force at Ḥiṣn al-Nahr, who would escort those travelers coming from Ardabīl until they reached al-Haytham. Under this arrangement the commander of Ḥiṣn al-Nahr was exactly halfway along the road, and he would hand over those in his protection to [al-]Haytham, and the latter would hand over those in his protection to the commander of Ḥiṣn al-Nahr. One commander would go with the one group and the other commander with the other group. If one group arrived at the meeting place before the other, they would not go on beyond that point until the other group arrived. Then each commander would entrust to the other the group of travelers whom he had escorted, so that the one could escort them as far as Ardabīl and the other could escort them to al-Afshīn's camp. Likewise, al-Haytham al-Ghanawī would escort the group under his protection as far as Abū Saʿīd's men, who themselves meanwhile had set forth and halted at the halfway meeting point along the road with their group of travelers. Then Abū Saʿīd and his men would hand over that group to al-Haytham, and the latter would hand over the group accompanying him to Abū Saʿīd's men. Then Abū Saʿīd and his men would escort those in the caravan to Khushsh, while al-Haytham and his men would go back to Arshaq with the
[1174] travelers entrusted to them so that they would arrive with them the next day. Then they would be able to hand them over to

the east since the Umayyad period). Many of these had come west with Abū Muslim and settled above all in Baghdad, though also in other garrison cities of the central and western Islamic lands. In the early years of the previous reign, that of al-Ma'mūn, the Abnā' of Baghdad had been the mainstay of the opposition in Iraq to al-Ma'mūn and his Persian entourage at Marw; but during al-Muʿtaṣim's caliphate their military importance was considerably reduced, as he shifted his dependence to slave troops (see Ṭabarī, III, 1179–81; pp. 27–28, below). On the Abnā', see Crone, *op. cit.*, 65–67; A. Arazi and A. El'ad, "L'epître à l'armée," 52–61.

75. Or Maṣlaḥat al-Nahr, two farsakhs to the northwest of Ardabīl on the Barzand road; see Schwarz, *op. cit.*, 1168.

ʿAlawayh al-Aʿwar and his men, who would convey them to their intended destination. Abū Saʿīd and those accompanying him would proceed to Khushsh and thence to al-Afshīn's camp, where the leader of a caravan from al-Afshīn met him and that leader would receive from him those in the caravan and send them on to al-Afshīn's camp. This arrangement was in constant use.[76]

Whenever any spy came to Abū Saʿīd or any of the garrisons they would dispatch him to al-Afshīn. The latter used not to kill or beat such spies but on the contrary would give them sums of money and gifts and would question them about what sum of money Bābak was accustomed to give them. Thereupon he would double it for them and say, "Act as a spy for us now!"

In this year a battle took place between Bābak and Afshīn at Arshaq, in which al-Afshīn killed a large number of Bābak's followers—it has been said more than a thousand. Bābak fled to Mūqān[77] and from there proceeded to the town of his that was called al-Badhdh.

The Reason for This Battle between al-Afshīn and Bābak

It has been mentioned that the reason for this was that al-Muʿtaṣim sent with Bughā al-Kabīr[78] a sum of money to al-Afshīn for the latter to use as pay for his troops and for expenditure on supplies. Bughā brought that money to Ardabīl, but when he halted there reports about this reached Bābak and his followers, so they prepared to intercept him before he could reach al-Afshīn. The spy Ṣāliḥ came to al-Afshīn and informed him that Bughā al-Kabīr had arrived with a sum of money and that Bābak

---

76. This involved description of the procedure merely shows how al-Afshīn established a relay system, with Ḥiṣn al-Nahr as its central point, to protect Muslim travelers and caravans from Khurramī raids.

77. The low-lying steppe region to the south of the lower course of the Araxes. See Yāqūt, *Muʿjam*, V, 225–26; Le Strange, *Lands*, 175–76; Schwarz, *op. cit.*, 1086–91; *EI*[1], s.v. Mūḳān (V. Minorsky).

78. A Turkish general of successive caliphs in the middle years of this century; he died in 248 (862). He is not to be confused with Bughā al-Ṣaghīr, or al-Sharābī, who was no relation. See Herzfeld, *op. cit.*, 110–11; *EI*[2], s.vv. Bug̲h̲ā al-Kabīr, Bug̲h̲ā al-S̲h̲arābī (D.Sourdel).

and his followers had prepared to intercept him before he could reach al-Afshīn. However, it has also been said that Ṣāliḥ
[1175] approached Abū Saʿīd and that Abū Saʿīd then sent him to al-Afshīn.

Bābak prepared ambushes in various places. Al-Afshīn in turn wrote to Abū Saʿīd, ordering him to employ stratagems to check on the authenticity of the information about Bābak, so Abū Saʿīd and a group of his men sallied forth disguised until they saw the lights and the fires in the places described to them by Ṣāliḥ. Meanwhile, al-Afshīn wrote to Bughā, instructing him to remain in Ardabīl until details of al-Afshīn's plans should come to him. Abū Saʿīd wrote to al-Afshīn, telling him that Ṣāliḥ's information was authentic; hence al-Afshīn promised Ṣāliḥ largesse and heaped favors on him. He then wrote to Bughā with the instructions that Bughā was to give out that he was ostensibly about to set forth on a journey and was to fasten the sum of money on the camels' backs, tie the beasts together and form a file with them, and set out from Ardabīl as if he were heading for Barzand. But when he should arrive at the stronghold (*maṣlaḥah*) of a al-Nahr, or to within about two farsakhs from it, he was to hold back the convoy of animals until those travelers who were accompanying the money should reach Barzand, and then when the caravan had passed on he was himself to return with the money to Ardabīl.

Bughā did that, and the caravan traveled on until it halted at al-Nahr. Bābak's spies went back to him, informing him that the money had been transported and that they had seen it with their own eyes being carried along until it had reached al-Nahr. But in reality Bughā returned to Ardabīl with the money.

Al-Afshīn rode out from Barzand on the afternoon of the day that he had agreed upon with Bughā and at sunset reached Khushsh, where he encamped with his forces outside the protective trench dug by Abū Saʿīd. When morning came he rode off secretly, without having a drum beaten or displaying a banner, and he ordered that the banner should be kept furled and that the troops should keep silent and proceed swiftly on their journey.

[1176] The caravan that set out on that same day from al-Nahr to the vicinity of al-Haytham al-Ghanawī departed; and al-Afshīn traveled from Khushsh, heading for the vicinity of al-Haytham, to meet him along the road. But al-Haytham was unaware of this; hence he and those with him in the caravan pressed onward in the direction of al-Nahr. Bābak deployed his cavalry, foot soldiers, and troops in war formation and proceeded along the road to al-Nahr, imagining that the money would come into his hands. The commander of al-Nahr went out to escort those in his charge as far as al-Haytham, but Bābak's cavalry launched an attack on him, never doubting that the money was with him. The commander of al-Nahr fought with them, but Bābak's partisans killed both him and the troops and travelers who were accompanying him. They seized all the baggage and other things that they had with them and realized that the actual money had eluded them. They further seized the commander of al-Nahr's banner and also the clothing of the garrison of al-Nahr, their *durrāʿahs,*[79] pennants,[80] and caftans,[81] and they donned them and disguised themselves so that they might capture al-Haytham al-Ghanawī and also his companions. They were at this point unaware of al-Afshīn's departure, and they proceeded as if they were the garrison of al-Nahr. But when they arrived they did not know the place where the banner and insignia of the commander of al-Nahr habitually stood and hence took up their position in a different spot.

Al-Haytham arrived and took up his position; but he was disquieted at what he saw, so he sent forward a paternal cousin of his, saying to him, "Go to this detestable character and tell him, 'Why have you halted there?'" Al-Haytham's cousin went along, but when he saw the group of persons he failed to recognize them, even when he drew near to them. Hence he returned to al-Haytham and informed him, "Indeed, I do not recognize these people!" Al-Haytham said to him, "May God confound you! How cowardly you are!" and he sent out five cavalrymen whom he [1177]

79. I.e., a woolen garment that buttoned up the front; see p. 31 n. 120, below. But, according to n. *f* in the text, ms. O has a variant reading, probably *mazāriqahum,* "their short spears or javelins."

80. *Tarrādātihim,* which could have the meaning "lances, javelins"; cf. R. P. A. Dozy, *Supplément,* II, 34; ms. O has the variant form *ṭarāʾidahum,* as if it were the plural of *ṭarīdah.*

81. *Khafāṭīn;* for this garment, see Dozy, *Vêtements,* 162–68.

detached from his entourage. When they went along and drew near to Bābak two men from the Khurramiyyah sallied forth. They encountered the two men and failed to recognize them [as being really ʿAlawayh's men] but gave the latter to understand that they had recognized them [as being ostensibly members of the Muslim caravan]. They galloped back to al-Haytham and told him, "The unbeliever has killed ʿAlawayh and his companions, and they have taken their banners and their clothing."

[Al-]Haytham thereupon rode off and went back and came to the caravan that he had brought along under his escort. He ordered them to ride hard and return, lest they be captured. He himself remained with his troops, traveling with them for a few stages and then halting with them for a while, to divert the attention of the Khurramiyyah away from the caravan and acting as a protective force for them, as it were, until the caravan reached the fortress that was al-Haytham's base; that is, Arshaq. He said to his companions, "Whoever among you will go to the Amīr (al-Afshīn) and to Abū Saʿīd and will inform them of what has happened shall get 10,000 dirhams and a [new] horse to replace his own, and if his horse becomes exhausted, he will get a fresh one, just like the original one, on the spot!" So two of his men set out on sprightly horses at a gallop, while al-Haytham went back inside the fortress.

Bābak, accompanied by his troops, went forward until he halted at the fortress. A seat was set down for him there, and he sat down on an eminence opposite the fortress. He sent a message to al-Haytham, saying, "Clear out of the fortress and depart, for I intend to demolish it." But al-Haytham refused and delivered battle to him instead. Al-Haytham had with him in the fortress 600 foot soldiers and 400 cavalry, and the fortress had a strongly fortified trench, so he attacked Bābak. The latter sat down, in the midst of his followers, and wine was set before him to drink while the battle was raging, as was his custom.[82]

The two horsemen (those sent by al-Haytham) met al-Afshīn at

82. It is unclear whether a practice like this has any connection with the licentiousness attributed to the Khurramiyyah or Khurramdīnān, "devotees of the religion of joy," by their orthodox opponents. See E. M. Wright, "Bābak of Badhdh and al-Afshīn," 49; Scarcia Amoretti, *op. cit.*, 504.

less than a farsakh from Arshaq, and the moment he saw them from afar he said to the commander of his vanguard, "I perceive two riders galloping at full tilt." Then he added, "Beat the drums [1178]
and unfurl and banners, and gallop out toward the two riders." So his men did that; they sped onward, and al-Afshīn said to them, "Shout to the two of them, 'At your service, at your service!'"[83] The troops continued in a single gallop forward, vying in urging their horses onward, their mounts jostling each other, until they came up to Bābak, who was still seated. He did not have a chance to remove himself or to ride away before the cavalrymen and the body of troops reached him, and a closely fought battle, with the two sides locked together, was engaged. Not one of Bābak's foot soldiers escaped, but he himself escaped with a small group of men and withdrew into Mūqān, by which time his companions had become separated from him. Al-Afshīn remained in that place and spent the night there. Then he returned to his encampment at Barzand.[84]

Bābak remained in Mūqān for a certain number of days; then he sent a message to al-Badhdh, and during the night a force of troops, including foot soldiers, came to him. He traveled with them from Mūqān until he reached al-Badhdh. Al-Afshīn, meanwhile, continued to encamp at Barzand.

Some days later, a caravan passed by him (Bābak), going from Khushsh to Barzand, which had with it a man appointed by Abū Saʿīd named Ṣāliḥ Āb-kash, which means "the Water Carrier" (*al-saqqāʾ*).[85] Bābak's general (*iṣbahbadh*) attacked him and seized the caravan, killing those who were in it and those in Ṣāliḥ's force. Ṣāliḥ himself escaped bootless (barefoot) with those who managed to get away, but all the people in the caravan were killed and their goods and possessions plundered. Thus al-Afshīn's army suffered deprivation (literally, "lacked water," *qaḥaṭa*) because of that caravan's being captured from al-Āb-

---

83. *Labbayka, labbayka,* the *talbiyah* or cry—meaningless by Islamic times—of the pilgrims, uttered during the *wuqūf* on ʿArafāt and at other points in the Ḥajj ceremonies. See J. Wellhausen, *Reste,* 79–80; M. Gaudefroy-Demombynes, *Le pèlerinage,* 179–85, 249.

84. Abū Tammām mentions this defeat of Bābak's in his poems; see Haq, *op. cit.,* 22.

85. From Persian *āb kashīdan,* "to draw water."

kash,[86] for it had been carrying supplies and provisions. Al-Afshīn thereupon wrote to the commander of al-Marāghah,[87] ordering
[1179] him to bring supplies and provisions and to send them to him with all possible speed because the troops were suffering from lack of water and food. The commander in al-Marāghah sent to him a huge caravan, having in it about a thousand steers, as well as asses and riding beasts and mules and the like, bearing supplies and provisions and accompanied by a body of troops as escort. But once again a detachment of Bābak's forces, commanded by either Ṭarkhān[88] or Ādhīn,[89] attacked them and treated the whole caravan, from front to end, and everything in it as their lawful plunder, leaving al-Afshīn's men reduced to dire straits. So al-Afshīn wrote to the commander in al-Sīrawān,[90] ordering him to send food, and he (the commander) accordingly dispatched a large quantity of food to al-Afshīn and brought succor to the people in that year. Also, Bughā came to al-Afshīn with money and men.[91]

In this year, in the month of Dhū al-Qaʿdah (October–November 835), al-Muʿtaṣim set out for al-Qāṭūl.[92]

---

86. With an ironical juxtaposition of the opposing concepts in *qaḥaṭa* and *āb-kash*.

87. One of the chief towns of Ādharbayjān, lying to the southeast of Lake Urmiya, and capital of the Arabs after their first invasions of that province. See Yāqut, *Muʿjam*, V, 93–94; Le Strange, *Lands*, 164–65; Schwarz, *op. cit.*, 1005–23; Barthold, *Historical Geography*, 214–15; *EI*², s.v. al-Marāgha (V. Minorsky).

88. It is curious to see what was in origin an ancient, pre-Turkish title of Inner Asian political and tribal structures used by a presumably Iranian (but conceivably Khazar Turkish?) commander of Bābak's. On this title, see Bosworth and Clauson, *op. cit.*, 11–12. According to R. N. Frye, the title Ṭarkhān should be distinguished from a personal name Ṭarkhūn found in early Islamic sources on the history of Central Asia; see "Ṭarxūn-Ṭürxün," 105–29.

89. Literally, "custom, manner; adornment."

90. The chief town of the district of Māsabadhan in al-Jibāl (see p. 2 n. 6, above). See Yāqūt, *Muʿjam*, III, 296–97; Le Strange, *Lands*, 202; Schwarz, *op. cit.*, 466–67.

91. See also Dīnawarī, *op. cit.*, 402–3; Azdī, *op. cit.*, 422; *Kitāb al-ʿuyūn*, 382–83; Ibn al-Athīr, *op. cit.*, VI, 447–51; Sadighi, *op. cit.*, 252–53; E. M. Wright, *op., cit.*, 50–51; S. Nafīsī, *Bābak-i Khurram-dīn*, 67 ff.

92. The name of canals flowing southward from the Tigris at Dūr just north of Sāmarrā, said to have been dug by Anūshirwān and Hārūn al-Rashīd. See Yāqūt, *Muʿjam*, IV, 297–98; Le Strange, *Lands*, 57. Yaʿqūbī, *Buldān*, 256–57, trans., 45–47, gives a detailed account of al-Muʿtaṣim's attempts (apparently following earlier efforts by Hārūn al-Rashīd; see below) to establish a new military

The Reason for al-Muʿtaṣim's Departure for al-Qāṭūl

It has been mentioned from Abū al-Wazīr Aḥmad b. Khālid[93] that he said: Al-Muʿtaṣim sent for me in the year 219 (834) and told me, "O Aḥmad, purchase for me in the vicinity of Sāmarrā land on which I can build a city—for I am afraid lest these troops of the Ḥarbiyyah quarter[94] raise a great clamor and kill my slave retainers (*ghilmānī*)—in order that I may be above them (*ḥattā akūna fawqahum*).[95] But [once I am installed there], if anything emanating from them disquiets me, I shall come upon them by land and by sea until I overcome them." And he further said to [1180]
me, "Take this 100,000 dīnārs." He related: I said, "I'll take 5,000 dīnārs, and whenever I need any additional money I'll send to you and ask for more." He agreed to that. So I went to the place in question and bought Sāmarrā for 500 dirhams from the Christians

---

settlement for his slave troops outside Baghdad, starting in the east-bank suburb of Shammāsiyyah and gradually moving north, after rejecting various sites, to the Qāṭūl Canal, where construction was begun along the canal and the Tigris. It is not completely clear where al-Qāṭūl lay within the general area of the new town of Sāmarrā. See N. al-Asil, "La ciudad de al-Muʿtaṣim en al-Qāṭūl," 339–57 (inconclusive); Herzfeld, *op. cit.*, 71 ff.; J. M. Rogers, "Sāmarrā," 130; A. Northedge and R. Faulkner, "The 1986 Survey Season at Sāmarrā'," 158–60, noting that the site adjacent to al-Qāṭūl, al-Qādisiyyah of Sāmarrā (to be distinguished from the Qādisiyyah near al-Kūfah, site of the great battle between the Arabs and Persians), has been fairly certainly pinpointed within the Sāmarrā complex.

93. Secretary under al-Muʿtaṣim and al-Wāthiq, said by Masʿūdī to have acted briefly as vizier, perhaps without the specific title, at the outset of al-Mutawakkil's reign. See *Murūj*, VII, 197 = par. 2881; Herzfeld, *op. cit.*, 108; D. Sourdel, *Vizirat*, I, 263, 271.

94. I.e., the suburb to the north and northwest of al-Manṣūr's Round City, originally settled in the early ʿAbbāsid period by the caliphs' Khurāsānian troops and subsequently the center of the Abnā'. See Le Strange, *Baghdad*, 107–35; J. Lassner, *The Topography of Baghdad*, index, s.v. Ḥarbiyya; Ṣ. A. al-ʿAlī, *Baghdād*, 165–84.

95. The meaning would appear to be that, by constructing his new military center upstream from Baghdad, at Sāmarrā, the Caliph would be placing a reasonable distance (actually about seventy-five miles) between his Turkish slave guards and their opponents, the Khurāsānian Arab nobility of the Abnā' (who, as mentioned in n. 94, above, formed the main population element in the Ḥarbiyyah quarter of Baghdad). He would be able further to swoop south on the latter from his position upriver. This seems a more probable translation than that in Ṭabarī, trans. Marin, 15: "kill my pages and me on top of them." Nor did Marin realize that here *Ḥarbiyyah* designates a specific group, not the common noun "warriors".

who dwelt in the monastery,[96] and I purchased the site of the Khāqānī garden[97] for another 5,000 dirhams plus a number of other places until I had fully accomplished what I had set out to do. Then I traveled down [the Tigris] with the deeds of sale (*al-ṣikāk*).[98] Al-Muʿtaṣim resolved to move there in the year 220 (835). He set out until, when he drew near to al-Qāṭūl, the pavilions and tents (*al-qibāb wa-al-maḍārib*) were pitched there for him, and all the troops pitched their tents (*al-akhbiyah*).[99] Thereafter he continued to put into practice his intentions, and tents were set up for him until buildings were erected at Sāmarrā in the year 221 (836).[100]

It has been mentioned from Abū al-Ḥasan b. Abī ʿAbbād al-Kātib that Masrūr al-Khādim al-Kabīr said: Al-Muʿtaṣim once asked me, "Where did al-Rashīd use to have his pleasure ground when he grew fed up with staying in Baghdad?" He related: I replied to him, "At al-Qāṭūl." Al-Rashīd had built a city there, the vestiges and walls of which still remained, for he had been afraid of what his troops might do, just as al-Muʿtaṣim feared. But when the people of Syria rose up and rebelled in Syria al-Rashīd

96. There are said to have been no fewer than eight monasteries in the area.

97. Presumably the garden of the Jawsaq al-Khāqānī palace, the modern Qaṣr al-Khalīfah, to the north of the modern town of Sāmarrā. It was named for the Caliph's Turkish general, the Khāqān Abū al-Fatḥ ʿUrtūj, to whom, as to other commanders, a *qaṭīʿah*, or concession of land was granted; see Yaʿqūbī, *Buldān*, 258, trans. 48–50.

98. Sing. *ṣakk*, a commercial, legal, and above all financial term. Here the *ṣikak* brought back by Aḥmad would attest the disbursement of the price paid to the original owners of the land. For the term, see Bosworth, "Abū ʿAbdallāh al-Khwārazmī," 125–26. 127.

99. On the terminology for tents and their components—the nuances in significance of the various types of tent often being obscure today—see *EI*², s.v. Khayma (Ch. Pellat et al.).

100. The bibliography on the foundation of Sāmarrā and the attempts to identify specific buildings within the urban site is very extensive. For the history of Sāmarrā during the fifty odd years of its occupation by the caliphs, see Herzfeld, *op. cit.*, 86–270. For a general consideration of Sāmarrā and its environs as an expression of caliphal self-glorification, see Rogers, *op. cit.*, 119–55. For the most recent excavations on the site, now considerably eroded by urbanization and agricultural development, see Northedge, "Planning Sāmarraʾ"; idem and Faulkner, *op. cit.*, 143–73.

went off to al-Raqqah.[101] He stayed at this latter place, and the city at al-Qāṭūl remained uncompleted.

When al-Muʿtaṣim set out for al-Qāṭūl he left his son Hārūn al-Wāthiq as his deputy in Baghdad.

Jaʿfar b. Muḥammad b. Bawwāzah al-Farrāʾ related to me that the reason for al-Muʿtaṣim's departure for al-Qāṭūl was that his Turkish slave retainers were continually finding (their comrades), one after the other, slain in their quarters. This arose from the [1181] fact that they were rough-mannered barbarians (*ʿujm*)[102] who used to ride their steeds and gallop through the streets and roads of Baghdad, knocking down men and women and trampling children underfoot. As a result, the men of the Abnāʾ would seize them, drag them off their steeds, and inflict wounds on some of them; on occasion, some of them would perish through their wounds. The Turks complained of that to al-Muʿtaṣim, and because of them the general populace suffered. Jaʿfar further mentioned that he saw al-Muʿtaṣim riding back from the *muṣallā* on the day of the Festival of the Sacrifice or that of the Breaking of the Fast, and when he reached the square of al-Ḥarashī[103] he perceived that an old man had planted himself in his path and cried out, "O Abū Isḥāq!" He related: The troops hastened forward to strike him, but al-Muʿtaṣim motioned to them and restrained them from him, saying to the old man, "What do you want?" The old man answered, "May God not recompense you with good for your stay here among us! You have dwelt among us and have brought in these untutored foreigners (*ʿulūj*)[104] and have set them down to dwell in our midst. Through them you have made our children orphans, you have made our womenfolk

101. The main center of the Diyār Muḍar district of al-Jazīrah, which al-Rashīd in effect made his capital during his later years. See Yāqūt, *Muʿjam*, III, 58–60; Le Strange, *Lands*, 101–2; Canard, *Histoire*, 90–91; *EI*[1], s.v. al-Rakka (E. Honigmann).

102. Literally, "those speaking Arabic indistinctly," *aʿjam*.

103. The *murabbaʿah* of (Saʿīd) al-Ḥarashī, which included within it a market and a palace, marked the site of Saʿīd's *qaṭīʿah* in the Mukharrim quarter on the east side of Baghdad. See Le Strange, *Baghdad*, 221–22; Lassner, *op. cit.*, 79, 262–63. Saʿīd stemmed from a Qaysī family prominent as military commanders under both the Umayyads and early ʿAbbāsids; see Crone, *op. cit.*, 144–145.

104. Literally, "stout, coarse-bodied," *ʿilj*, but applied especially to non-Arabs, usually those who were country dwellers.

widows, and you have killed our men!" Al-Muʿtaṣim listened to all of that. He related: Then he went back into his palace and was not seen again out riding until the very same day of the following year. When it was the next year, on exactly the same day, al-Muʿtaṣim went forth and led the people's worship at the celebration of the Festival; however, he did not go back to his residence in Baghdad but turned his steed's face toward the vicinity of al-Qāṭūl and left Baghdad, never to return thither.[105]

In this year al-Muʿtaṣim became angry with al-Faḍl b. Marwān and imprisoned him.

The Reason behind al-Muʿtaṣim's Anger against al-Faḍl b. Marwān and His Imprisoning of the Latter, and the Reason for al-Faḍl's Connection with al-Muʿtaṣim

It has been mentioned that al-Faḍl b. Marwān, who was a man
[1182] from al-Baradān,[106] was connected with one of the financial officials, for whom he used to indite correspondence; he had a beautiful hand. Then he joined one of al-Muʿtaṣim's secretaries

---

105. Al-Muʿtaṣim's prime motive for moving from the ʿAbbāsids' ancestral capital to the new town of Sāmarrā—where there was probably some form of settlement around the monasteries even before al-Rashīd's time—does seem broadly to have been a desire to separate his professional slave troops (Turks, Maghribīs, etc.) from the longer-established Abnāʾ military elements in the Ḥarbiyyah and other parts of Baghdad, as Ṭabarī (followed also by trans. Balʿamī, IV, 523–25; *Kitāb al-ʿuyūn*, 381–82; and Ibn al-Athīr, *op. cit.*, VI, 451–52) states here. It is likewise the motive put forward by the other early sources, including Yaʿqūbī, *Buldān*, 255–64, trans., 44–57; Masʿūdī, *Murūj*, VII, 118–23 = pars. 2801–5; idem, *Tanbīh*, 356–57, trans., 457–58; cf. Herzfeld, *op. cit.*, 88 ff. As D. Ayalon has remarked ("Preliminary Remarks," 53–56), there seems no reason to doubt these assertions. Nor is there any sound reason for adopting the skeptical attitude of Shaban, *op. cit.*, 63, toward the idea that the new troops were proving a rowdy and uncontrollable element in the city of Baghdad itself. See also on the topic of the motive behind the transfer to Sāmarrā, O. S. A. Ismail, "Founding of a New Capital," 3–6; and H. Kennedy, *The Prophet and the Age of the Caliphates*, 158–60, who attempts, on the questions of the legal status and the ethnic origins of the new troops (see also p. 49 n. 159, below), to steer a middle course between the views of Shaban, on the one hand, and those of Crone (*op. cit.*, especially, 78–79) and D. Pipes (*Slave Soldiers and Islam*, especially, 150–58), on the other.

106. A small town on the left bank of the Tigris just north of Baghdad. See Yāqūt, *Muʿjam*, I, 375–76; Le Strange, *Lands*, 32, 50; *EI*², s.v. Baradān (M. Streck-[S. H. Longrigg]).

called Yaḥyā al-Jurmuqānī, and al-Faḍl b. Marwān used to indite letters directly for him. When al-Jurmuqānī died al-Faḍl succeeded to his place,[107] and ʿAlī b. Ḥassān al-Anbārī used then to indite correspondence for al-Faḍl. This arrangement continued until al-Muʿtaṣim attained his high office,[108] with al-Faḍl as his secretary. Then al-Faḍl accompanied al-Muʿtaṣim to al-Maʾmūn's field headquarters and after that went with him to Egypt, where he gathered in the taxes of Egypt. Before al-Maʾmūn's death al-Faḍl returned to Baghdad, where he used to deal with al-Muʿtaṣim's business affairs and used to write down, in al-Muʿtaṣim's name, whatever he himself desired until al-Muʿtaṣim came [to Baghdad] as caliph. From that point on, al-Faḍl became the effective director of the caliphate: All the government departments came under his control, and he stored up all the collected taxes. When Abū Isḥāq [al-Muʿtaṣim] entered Baghdad he ordered al-Faḍl in the first place to give largesse to singers and musicians, but al-Faḍl failed to carry out that order; this made Abū Isḥāq resentful.[109]

Ibrāhīm b. Jahrawayh related to me that Ibrāhīm, who had the cognomen al-Haftī ("the Foolish"), was a jester and buffoon (*muḍḥik*) and al-Muʿtaṣim ordered him to be given a sum of money. He instructed al-Faḍl b. Marwān to pay out that sum to Ibrāhīm, but al-Faḍl would not give him what al-Muʿtaṣim had commanded that he was to get. Some time afterward, al-Haftī was with al-Muʿtaṣim one day—this being after his palace in Baghdad had been built and a garden there had been made for his use—and al-Muʿtaṣim got up and walked around the garden, looking at it and at the various kinds of aromatic herbs and trees growing

107. See Sourdel, *Vizirat*, I, 248 n. 1.

108. I.e., when he became governor in Egypt and suppressed the rebellion there in 214–15 (829–30). See Ṭabarī, III, 1101; Yaʿqūbī, *Taʾrīkh*, II, 567; Ibn al-Athīr, *op. cit.*, VI, 409; A. H. Saleh, "Les Bédouins d'Égypte," 157.

109. On al-Faḍl, who was the first of the many secretaries of Iraqi Christian origin to serve the caliphs during this century, see Sourdel, *Vizirat*, I, 246–53; and *EI*², s.v. al-Faḍl b. Marwān (D. Sourdel). It seems that, as is implied here and in the next anecdote, al-Faḍl endeavored during his three-year vizierate, 218–21 (833–36), to restore financial stability and to satisfy the pay demands of the troops by restricting the caliph's personal expenditure and prodigality. Unusually, after his fall he filled lesser administrative offices under al-Wāthiq and other caliphs, dying in 250 (864) at an advanced age.

there, accompanied by al-Haftī. Meanwhile, al-Haftī—who had been al-Muʿtaṣim's companion since before the caliphate came to
[1183] him[110]—was saying to him, among the pleasantries he was exchanging with the caliph, "By God, your affairs will never prosper!" He related: Al-Haftī happened to be a plumpish person of middle height, whereas al-Muʿtaṣim was a lean man with little flesh on him. Al-Muʿtaṣim would begin to outstrip al-Haftī when they were walking, and when he got ahead of al-Haftī and did not see the latter still with him he would turn to him and say, "Why don't you get a move on?" at the same time urging al-Haftī to catch up with him.

When this sequence of events involving al-Muʿtaṣim and al-Haftī had taken place on several occasions al-Haftī said to him jokingly, "May God guide you in an upright way! I used to visualize myself ambling around with a caliph, but I never saw myself striding along with a courier![111] By God, I am sure your affairs will never prosper!" Al-Muʿtaṣim laughed at all this and said, "Woe on you! Is there anything of success remaining that I have not already attained? Can you say this to me after my having attained the caliphate?" But al-Haftī replied, "Do you really think that you have now attained success? In reality, you have nothing of the caliphate except the mere name! By God, your commands do not go farther than your own ears! The real caliph is al-Faḍl b. Marwān, who issues commands that are immediately put into execution." Al-Muʿtaṣim said to him, "And what command of mine has not been carried out?" Al-Haftī responded, "Two months ago you commanded that I should be given so-and-so, but since that time I have not been given even a single grain[112] of what you commanded." He related: As a result, al-Muʿtaṣim held this in his mind against al-Faḍl until he pounced upon him.[113]

It has been said that the first thing that al-Muʿtaṣim did concerning al-Faḍl when his attitude toward him changed was to

---

110. Following the Cairo edition, IX, 19, *qabla an tufḍiya.*

111. *Fayj*, the Arabized form of Persian *payk*, "messenger, courier."

112. *Habbah*, literally "a grain of corn," but used as a weight—the smallest one distinguished—for gold and silver coins, canonically something like .0445 gr. but varying among different provinces of the Islamic world and at different periods. See W. Hinz, *Islamische Masse und Gewichte*, 12–13.

113. Cf. Herzfeld, *op. cit.*, 93.

appoint Aḥmad b. ʿAmmār al-Khurāsānī[114] as financial controller (*zimām*)[115] over him in regard to the privy-purse expenditure and Naṣr b. Manṣūr b. Bassām as financial controller over him in regard to the land tax and all other taxes collected. And he continued like that.[116]

Muḥammad b. ʿAbd al-Malik al-Zayyāt[117] used to be responsible, just as his father had been responsible in the time of al-Maʾmūn, for the manufacture of the parasol (*al-mushammas*),[118] the large tents (*al-fasāṭīṭ*),[119] and the equipment for swift riding camels (*ālat al-jammāzāt*), and in return for that, he (ʿAbd al-Malik al-Zayyāt) used to write about what Muḥammad b. ʿAbd al-Malik al-Zayyāt was doing (i.e., acted as a spy on his son's activities). Muḥammad b. ʿAbd al-Malik used to wear a black *durrāʿah*[120] and a sword with its belts and fastenings

114. A native of al-Mādhar in lower Iraq, he became chief secretary to al-Muʿtaṣim in Ṣafar 221 (February 836); after al-Faḍl's disgrace, he seems to have acted for a while as vizier, in practice if not in name. See Sourdel, *Vizirat*, I, 252, 253, II, 726.

115. On this term, see Dozy, *Supplément*, I, 601–2. At various epochs under the ʿAbbāsids there was a special *Dīwān al-Zimām/al-Azimmah* to control the accounts of the financial departments. See Herzfeld, *op. cit.*, 106; *EI*², s.v. Dīwān. i. The Caliphate (A. A. Duri).

116. Cf. Sourdel, *Vizirat*, I, 252.

117. Literally, "the dealer in oil" (*zayt*); hence the reference below to Muḥammad b. ʿAbd al-Malik as a trader or tradesman (*tājir*).

118. I.e., the *miẓallah*, Persian *chatr*, which was one of the insignia of royal power. See *EI*², s.v. Miẓalla (C. E. Bosworth et al.); Bosworth, *Ghaznavids*, index s.vv. *chatr, chatr-dār*.

119. *Fusṭāṭ*, from Late Latin *fossatum*, "trench (and rampart)," originally denoted the armed camps of earliest Islam (as in the name Fusṭāṭ for the Arabs' new center in Egypt after transfer of the capital from Alexandria); see *Glossarium*, CDIII. The term seems then to have come to denote the large tents that must have been a feature of these camps in their early stages; see Dozy, *Supplément*, II, 266.

120. The *durrāʿah*, a robe that seems to have had a slit fastened with buttons in the front, was worn on ceremonial occasions by the ʿAbbāsid caliphs from the time of al-Manṣūr to the mid-third (ninth) century, when it was replaced by a shorter jacket (*qabāʾ*) of Persian origin. It was also worn by civilian and military members of the ruling elite, as distinct from the religious classes (for whom the *ṭaylasān* was regarded as the distinguishing garment; see p. 192 n. 553, below) and the lower classes. Cf. the geographer Maqdisī's use of the term *ahl al-durrāʿah*, cited in Mez, *op. cit.*, 75, trans., 83–84, and his experience of the greater prestige conferred by the wearing of a *durrāʿah*, cited in D. A. Agius, *Arabic Literary Works*, 217–20; for information on the garment in general, see Dozy, *Vêtements*,

[1184] whenever he was present at court. Al-Faḍl b. Marwān said to him, "You're only a trader; what right have you to wear black and carry a sword?" So Muḥammad had to stop wearing these. When Muḥammad had done this al-Faḍl moved against him by bringing his accounts to the attention of Dulayl b. Yaʿqūb al-Naṣrānī,[121] and then he arraigned him. But Dulayl acted kindly in the matter of Muḥammad and did not confiscate anything from him. Muḥammad offered Dulayl presents, but the latter refused to accept anything at all from Muḥammad.[122]

When it was the year 219 (834)—or, it has been said, (2)20 (835), but in my opinion this is a mistake—al-Muʿtaṣim set out toward al-Qāṭūl, intending to undertake building operations at Sāmarrā. But the excessively high level of the Tigris waters deflected him from this, and he was unable to continue his move; hence he turned back to Baghdad and to al-Shammāsiyyah. Then he set out again after that. When he reached al-Qāṭūl in Ṣafar (February–March 834) he showed his anger at al-Faḍl b. Marwān and his household and ordered them to give an accounting of what had passed through their hands. Al-Faḍl was arrested, as the object of [al-Muʿtaṣim's] anger regarding the conduct of his accounts. When al-Muʿtaṣim had completed this accounting process he made no further investigation into his affairs, but he ordered him (al-Faḍl) to be imprisoned and conveyed to his house at Baghdad in the street of the Maydān.[123] He further imprisoned al-Faḍl's associates and appointed in his place Muḥammad b. ʿAbd al-Malik al-Zayyāt.[124] He jailed Dulayl and exiled al-Faḍl to

177–81; idem, *Supplément*, I, 434. At this point in Ṭabarī's *History* al-Faḍl b. Marwān is ridiculing Muḥammad b. ʿAbd al-Malik's pretensions to membership in the secretarial class. Black was, of course, the official ʿAbbāsid color (whence the name *al-Musawwidah*, "wearers of black," applied to their partisans at the time of the ʿAbbāsid Revolution). See Hilāl al-Ṣābi', *Rusūm dār al-khilāfah*, 91–92, trans., 74; Mez, *op. cit.*, 80, trans., 89; F. Omar, *ʿAbbāsiyyāt*, 148–49.

121. A Christian official who was later secretary to the Turkish general Bughā al-Ṣaghīr; see Sourdel, *Vizirat*, I, 256, 304.

122. *Ibid.*, 255–56.

123. Naturally, there were many squares and open places (*mayādīn*) in Baghdad, but it is unclear which particular one is meant here.

124. According to Ibrāhīm al-Bayhaqī, *op. cit.*, ed. Schwally, 567 = ed. Ibrāhīm, II, 332–33, when al-Faḍl was disgraced and imprisoned, he was made to disgorge (*istiʿdā'*) 1.6 million *dīnārs*.

a village called al-Sinn[125] on the road to al-Mawṣil, where he thenceforth remained. Muḥammad b. ʿAbd al-Malik now acted as vizier and secretary, and the greater part of the building operations that al-Muʿtaṣim undertook at Sāmarrā, both on the eastern and western banks [of the Tigris], passed through his hands. He continued to enjoy his high position until al-Mutawakkil became caliph and then killed Muḥammad b. ʿAbd al-Malik.[126]

It has been mentioned that when al-Muʿtaṣim appointed al-Faḍl b. Marwān as his vizier the latter came to occupy a position so close to al-Muʿtaṣim's heart that no one could hope to gain his attention, much less to dispute with him or to thwart him [1185]
regarding his commands and prohibitions, his requirements and decisions. This continued to be his manner of acting and his exalted status until overconfidence and a sense of his own great prestige impelled him to oppose al-Muʿtaṣim in regard to certain of the latter's commands and to refuse him money that he was needing for his important affairs.

It has been mentioned from Ibn Abī Duwād[127] that he said: I used to be present at al-Muʿtaṣim's court sessions, and I often used to hear him say to al-Faḍl b. Marwān, "Bring me so-and-so amount of money," and al-Faḍl would reply, "I haven't got it," at which al-Muʿtaṣim would say, "Then devise some means or other of procuring it!" Al-Faḍl would answer, "Where am I going to be

---

125. At the junction of the Tigris and Lower Zāb rivers, about halfway between al-Mawṣil and Sāmarrā. See Yāqūt, *Muʿjam*, III, 268–69; Le Strange, *Lands*, 90–91.

126. Ibn al-Zayyāt was to serve al-Muʿtaṣim as his second vizier, in 221–27 (838–42), and his successor al-Wāthiq as his first vizier, in 227–32 (842–47). He also briefly served al-Mutawakkil in 232–33 (847) until he was executed, after having been tortured in an instrument of his own devising, a spiked cylinder similar to the Nuremburg Iron Maiden. He left behind him a reputation for harshness and cruelty. See Sourdel, *Vizirat*, I, 254–69; *EI*², s.v. Ibn al-Zayyāt (D. Sourdel).

127. Chief judge under al-Muʿtaṣim and the guiding spirit behind the Muʿtazilī inquisition, or *miḥnah*, established by al-Maʾmūn toward the end of his reign. His influence on al-Muʿtaṣim seems to have been as great as that of the Caliph's viziers, and in fact he grew increasingly hostile to Ibn al-Zayyāt (Sourdel, *Vizirat*, I, 258–60, 265, 269). See the extensive biography in al-Khaṭīb al-Baghdādī, *Taʾrīkh Baghdād*, IV, 141–56 no. 1825; *EI*², s.vv. Aḥmad b. Abī Duʾād (K. V. Zettersteen and Ch. Pellat), Miḥna (M. Hinds).

able to light upon such a sum, who will give me this amount of money, and with whom shall I find it?" That used to displease al-Muʿtaṣim, as I could discern from his face. When al-Faḍl had behaved thus on several occasions I rode over to him one day and said to him, after having sought a private word with him, "O Abū al-ʿAbbās, people are coming between us with what I dislike and you dislike, too. You are a man whose character I have well understood, but those who come between us understand it equally. If I am compelled to take action against you[128] justifiably, then set it down as devoid of real animus (do not hold it against me). Despite that, I shall not cease giving you sincere advice and doing what is incumbent upon me to perform or justly owed to you. Now I have often observed you returning the Commander of the Faithful a brusque answer that sears him and pierces his heart. A ruling authority (*sulṭān*)[129] will not tolerate this even in his own son, especially when it happens frequently and in an abrupt manner." He asked, "O Abū ʿAbdallāh, what exactly is this?" I replied, "I have often heard him say to you, 'We need such-and-such an amount of money for expending on so-and-so matter,' and you retort, 'And who will give me this sum?' This sort of thing is what caliphs will not tolerate." He
[1186] said, "But what, then, am I to do when he demands from me what I don't have?" I said, "Be prepared to say, 'O Commander of the Faithful, we will devise some means or other for getting that,' and you will secure for yourself a delay of a few days until he is prepared, and then you will take to him part of what he seeks and put him off in regard to the remainder." He replied, "Yes, I'll do that, and I'll adopt the procedure that you advise me." He related: Yet, by God, it was as if I had been urging him on to refuse [even more], for, when the caliph once more repeated to him his

128. Following the voweling of the Cairo edition, IX, 21, *fa-idhā ḥurriktu fīka.* The passage is, however, difficult; one might read *fa-idhā ḥarrakat fīka,* with the word "character" (*akhlāqaka*) considered as the subject of the verb and with a meaning like "if it stirs up in you a charge [against me], then consider it false, and on that basis, I shall not cease . . . ."

129. Or perhaps this is an early instance of the abstract noun in its later sense of "the holder of power > ruler," as *sulṭān* is at least personified here as having a son; see *EI*[1], s.v. Sulṭān (J. H. Kramers).

demand with the same words, al-Faḍl returned an answer of the same sort as the caliph resented.

He related: When al-Muʿtaṣim had endured this treatment on several occasions al-Faḍl came into his presence one day bearing a bunch of freshly plucked narcissus. Al-Muʿtaṣim took them and toyed with them, and then he said, "O Abū al-ʿAbbās, may God preserve you alive!" Al-Faḍl took them in his right hand, and al-Muʿtaṣim drew his seal ring from the finger of al-Faḍl's left hand, saying to him in a low voice,[130] "Give me my seal ring," and then pulled it from al-Faḍl's hand and placed it in Ibn ʿAbd al-Malik's hand.[131]

In this year Ṣāliḥ b. al-ʿAbbās b. Muḥammad led the Pilgrimage.[132]

---

130. Or perhaps "in words full of hidden meaning," *bi-kalām khafī.*

131. *Kitāb al-ʿuyūn,* 383–84; Ibn al-Athīr, *op. cit.,* VI, 453–54; Herzfeld, *op. cit.,* 93–94. According to Masʿūdī, *Tanbīh,* 356, trans., 456, al-Muʿtaṣim's seal had the motto "Glory to God, Who has no equal, Creator of all things," but, according to *Kitāb al-ʿuyūn,* 410, the motto was "God is the Trusted One of Muḥammad b. al-Rashīd, and in Him he believes." See the discussion on the caliphs' seals in Herzfeld, *op. cit.,* 156–57.

132. Khalīfah, *op. cit.,* II, 784; Azdī, *op. cit.,* 424; Ibn al-Athīr, *op. cit.,* VI, 454.

The Events of the Year

221

(December 26, 835–December 13, 836)

Among the events taking place during this year was the battle that took place in the vicinity of Hashtādsar[133] between Bābak and Bughā al-Kabīr, in which Bughā was defeated and his camp laid open to plundering. Also in this year al-Afshīn fell upon Bābak and defeated him.

[1187] *The Clashes of Bughā al-Kabīr and al-Afshīn with Bābak, and the Reasons behind Them*

It has been mentioned that Bughā al-Kabīr reached al-Afshīn with the money which has previously been mentioned and that al-Muʿtaṣim also sent with him to al-Afshīn pay for the troops accompanying him and for his own expenses. Furthermore, Bughā reached him with the troops for al-Afshīn that were being sent

133. In Persian literally "eighty peaks." This must have lain in the mountain region of northern Ādharbayjān; see Schwarz, *op. cit.*, 990–91. It may well be, as the editor Houtsma conjectured, the name that lies behind the very corrupt rendering (*Sādār.s.b* ?) of the name of the place where al-Afshīn is said by Yaʿqūbī, *Taʾrīkh*, II, 578, to have established himself; see also Herzfeld, *op. cit.*, 139 n. 3.

out with him [as reinforcements]. Al-Afshīn was thus able to pay the money to his troops, and after the New Year celebrations he fitted out his troops in readiness and sent Bughā with a force to circle round Hashtādsar and encamp at the Trench of Muḥammad b. Ḥumayd[134] and excavate it further, strengthen it, and station himself there. Bughā set out and made his way to the Trench of Muḥammad b. Ḥumayd. Al-Afshīn left Barzand, and Abū Saʿīd left Khushsh in search of Bābak. They met up at a place called Darwadh.[135] There al-Afshīn dug a trench and built a rampart round it, and he and Abū Saʿīd, together with those volunteers (*muṭṭawwiʿah*)[136] who had joined his forces, encamped within the perimeter of the trench. Between him (or: it) and al-Badhdh was six miles.

Bughā now made his preparations and took with him traveling provisions of a different kind from those about which al-Afshīn had written to him and a kind that he had not ordered him to take. He circled round Hashtādsar until he entered the settled area (*qaryah*) of al-Badhdh[137] and halted in its center, remaining there for one day. Then he sent out 1,000 men as a foraging party (*ʿallāfah*). But one of Bābak's detachments came out and put to plunder the foraging party, killing all those who resisted them

---

134. Muḥammad b. Ḥumayd al-Ṭūsī was the grandson of ʿAbd al-Ḥamid al-Ṭāʾī, one of the leaders of the ʿAbbāsid *daʿwah*; the family seems subsequently to have kept up its links with and residence in Khurāsān. See Crone, *op. cit.*, 174–75; Arazi and El'ad, *op. cit.*, 61 n. 79. Muḥammad had been killed at Hashtādsar in 214 (829) by Bābak's army, after he had constructed this defensive *khandaq*. See Ṭabarī, III, 1101; *Kitāb al-ʿuyūn*, 373–74; Niẓām al-Mulk, *op. cit.*, 291–92, trans., 233; Ibn al-Athīr, *op. cit.*, VI, 412–13; Schwarz, *op. cit.*, 971–72, 1167–68.

135. Apparently the Dū al-Rūd mentioned by Ibn Khurradādhbih, al-*Masālik wa-al-mamālik*, 121, as one farsakh from al-Badhdh but here placed by Ṭabarī at six miles' distance. It would appear to be the D.r.w.dh al-Rūdh of Yaʿqūbī, *Taʾrīkh*, II, 578 (reading the defective text thus). See Schwarz *op. cit.*, 1131; Sadighi, *op. cit.*, 254 n. 3.

136. I.e., those irregular troops who were not originally registered on the *dīwān*, hence in receipt of *ʿaṭāʾ* or salary, but who joined up with the professional forces and received a share of captured plunder; see Levy, *op. cit.*, 415. On the role of volunteers and *ghāzīs* in the society and affairs of Transoxania and Khurāsān see Barthold, *Turkestan*, 214–15. Men from these regions almost certainly would have followed al-Afshīn from the eastern Islamic provinces to the campaigns against Bābak here in Ādharbayjān.

137. If the recent identification of the site of al-Badhdh (see p. 14 n. 57, above) is correct, this must have been the urban area in the valley around the approximately 8,000-foot-high mountain on which Bābak's citadel and residence were situated.

and taking prisoner all whom they could. Bābak's force selected some of the captives and sent two men, who were especially close
[1188] to al-Afshīn, from among them and instructed them, "Go to al-Afshīn and inform him about what has befallen your comrades." The two men hove in sight, and the chief of the force of watchmen placed on the mountaintops (*al-kuhbāniyyah*)[138] spotted them. He waved the signal flag, and at that the troops in the encampment shouted "To arms, to arms!" and rode out in the direction of al-Badhdh. The two men, reduced to a state of nakedness, met them. The commander of the vanguard took them and brought them to al-Afshīn, and they told him about the calamity that had befallen them, and al-Afshīn commented, "Bughā did something without authorization from us."

Bughā returned to the Trench of Muḥammad b. Ḥumayd in something resembling a rout and wrote to al-Afshīn, telling him about it and asking him for reinforcements, explaining that his army had been shattered. Al-Afshīn sent to him his brother al-Faḍl b. Kāwūs, Aḥmad b. al-Khalīl b. Hishām,[139] Ibn Jawshan, Janāḥ al-Aʿwar al-Sukkarī, the commander of al-Ḥasan b. Sahl's[140] police guard (*shurṭah*), and one of two brothers, kindred of al-Faḍl b. Sahl.[141] They circled round Hashtādsar, and the troops in Bughā's camp were inspirited by their approach. Then al-Afshīn wrote to Bughā, informing him that he himself would lead out an expedition against Bābak on a day that he specified to him and ordering Bughā also to lead [another] expedition on that same day to attack Bābak from both sides.

---

138. See *Glossarium*, CDLXI, literally "mountain keepers." According to Herzfeld, *op. cit.*, 141 n. 2, the term stems from Middle Persian **kōhbān* < Old Persian **kaufa-pāna* "mountain guard, watcher". There is nothing in Ṭabarī or in any other source to support Shaban's conjecture, *op. cit.*, 66–67, that these mountain watchmen were from al-Afshīn's native province of Ushrūsanah; it is more probable that they were recruited on the spot in Ādharbayjān, as experts on the local terrain and conditions.

139. Later to be involved in the conspiracy to depose al-Muʿtaṣim in favor of al-ʿAbbās b. al-Maʾmūn; he was punished by death at Sāmarrā. See Ṭabarī, III, 1260–67 (pp. 125–33, below).

140. I.e., al-Maʾmūn's old commander and secretary, and the Caliph's father-in-law through his marriage to Būrān; see *EI*², s.v. al-Ḥasan b. Sahl (D. Sourdel).

141. I.e., al-Ḥasan's brother and vizier to al-Maʾmūn; see *EI*², s.v. al-Faḍl b. Sahl b. Za<u>dh</u>ānfarū<u>kh</u> (D. Sourdel).

Al-Afshīn accordingly went forth on the specified day from Darwadh intending to attack Bābak; and Bughā set out from the Trench of Muḥammad b. Ḥumayd, ascended to Hashtādsar, and encamped within hailing distance[142] at the side of Muḥammad b. Ḥumayd's grave.[143] But a cold wind and violent rain raged, and the troops were unable to hold the position on account of the excessive cold and strong wind, so that Bughā returned to his camp.

The next morning, after Bughā had already gone back to his camp, al-Afshīn fell upon Bābak's troops; he put Bābak to flight, [1189]
captured his camp, his tent, and also a woman who was with him in the camp. He then established himself in Bābak's encampment.

In the morning Bughā again got his forces ready and went up to Hashtādsar, but he found that the force that had been established opposite him at Hashtādsar had already gone back to join Bābak; so Bughā pushed on to the place where the force had been, finding there, however, only simple utensils and pieces of clothing. He descended from Hashtādsar toward al-Badhdh, and on the way found a man and a youth sleeping. Dāwūd Siyāh,[144] the commander of Bughā's vanguard, seized them and interrogated them. They related that an envoy from Bābak had come to them on the night in which Bābak had fled in defeat and had ordered them to meet up with him at al-Badhdh. The man and youth were both drunk, and sleep had overcome them, so that they had no other information except this. This incident took place before the afternoon worship. At this point Bughā sent a message to Dāwūd Siyāh, saying, "We are now in the midst of the place with which we are already familiar (he meant the place where they had been the first time). It is now evening, and the infantrymen are tired out; so look for a naturally defensible mountain that will accommodate our army, so that we may encamp there tonight." Dāwūd Siyāh sought for such a site. He ascended one of the

142. *ʿAlā daʿwah. Addenda et emendanda*, DCCLXIII, suggest the possible reading *ʿalā raghwah* "on a rocky area."

143. A possible reading from ms. O, signaled in n. *p* of the text, is "Trench" (*khandaq*, instead of *qabr*), this being followed in Ṭabarī, trans. Marin, 23.

144. I.e., in Persian "the Black One."

mountains and made for its summit and from there looked down. He saw al-Afshīn's banner and his encampment almost opposite and said, "This will be our place until early next morning, and at that time we will swoop down upon the unbelievers (i.e., Bābak and his followers), if God wills."

However, during that night clouds came down upon them, accompanied by cold and rain and heavy snow, so that when morning arrived no one was able to descend the mountain to fetch water or to water the riding beasts because of the intense cold and excessive snow. The heavily overcast sky and the mist were such that it was as if they were still in the night. At the third day the troops said to Bughā, "The provisions that we had with us
[1190] are now exhausted, and the cold has been harmful for us. So go down, whatever course of action is to be adopted, whether for us to return or to press on toward the unbeliever." The days remained misty; Bābak harried al-Afshīn by night and hammered his army so that al-Afshīn disengaged his forces and withdrew into his encampment.

Bughā then beat his drums and went down, still seeking to reach al-Badhdh, until he reached the plain. There he saw the sky clear and the terrain passable everywhere, except for the mountaintop where he had been. Bughā now deployed his troops in battle formation, with a right wing, a left wing, and a vanguard, and moved forward in the direction of al-Badhdh, never doubting that al-Afshīn was in his encampment. He proceeded onward until he came to the side of the mountain of al-Badhdh, and there only a half-mile ascent remained between where he was and the point where he would be overlooking the houses of al-Badhdh. In his vanguard were a number of soldiers, including a youth (or slave, *ghulām*) of Ibn Baʿīth's, who had relatives in al-Badhdh. Scouts of Bābak's met them, and the youth recognized one and said to him, "So-and-so!" The man replied, "Who's this here?" So the youth named to the man those of his kinsmen who were with him. The man said, "Draw near, and let me speak with you!" So the youth went up to him, and the man said, "Go back, and tell the person in charge to withdraw, for we have attacked al-Afshīn by night, and he has fled to his defensive trench, and against you, moreover, we have prepared two armies. Hence return quickly, and you may be able to escape!"

The youth went back and informed Ibn al-Baʿīth about all this. He named the man to him, and Ibn al-Baʿīth knew the man in question; so he informed Bughā about this. Bughā halted and took counsel with his companions. One of them expostulated, however, "This is a fraud, this is a trick, there can't be anything in it!" At this, one of the mountain watchman said, "This is a mountaintop with which I am familiar! Anyone who ascends to its summit will be able to see al-Afshīn's camp." Bughā, al-Faḍl b. [1191]
Kāwūs, and a group of their men who were agile and nimble climbed up and were able to look down on the place; but they could not discern al-Afshīn's camp there and were convinced that he had moved away. They consulted together again and came to the opinion that the troops should go back in the early part of the daytime before the night enveloped them. Bughā ordered Dāwūd Siyāh to return, and he set out, traveling swiftly and avoiding the road by which he had previously approached Hashtādsar, fearful of the defiles and mountain tracks. Instead, he took the road that he had taken the first time, circling round Hashtādsar, as there were no defiles along it except at one place. He traveled with the troops and sent the infantrymen on ahead. The latter threw away their spears and weapons along the road (i.e., to travel more swiftly), and a great fear and terror came over them.

Bughā, al-Faḍl b. Kāwūs, and a group of the commanders traveled in the rear guard. Bābak's scouts appeared, and, whenever Bughā's troops went down a mountain slope, Bābak's scouts went up it (to spy on them). Sometimes the scouts came into their sight and sometimes they were out of their view; and the scouts, comprising about ten horsemen in all, were following the army's tracks until the period between the noon and afternoon worships (i.e., the early afternoon). Bughā dismounted to do the minor ablutions and perform the worship. Bābak's scouts drew near them and came out into the open within their field of vision. Bughā performed the worship and stood there, within their sight, and when they saw him they halted. Bughā was afraid for his army, lest the scouts should fall upon it from one side and a further body of Bābak's forces should encircle them in some of the mountains and defiles. He sought the advice of those who were with him and said, "I am not sure that these people have not planned a diversionary attack that will prevent us from

[1192] continuing along the road, and then they will send forward their forces to seize the defiles against our own troops."

But al-Faḍl b. Kāwūs told him, "These people do not fight by day, but only by night, and one need fear for our troops only at night; so send to Dāwūd Siyāh [a message telling him] to speed up his march and not to halt, even if it should not be midnight before he gets through the defile. Meanwhile we will wait here, for as long as the enemy forces continue to keep us in their view, they will not go onward. In that way, we shall delay them and keep them off to some extent until darkness falls. Then, when it is dark, they will not know our position, and our troops will go forward and pass through one by one; and, if the defile is closed against us, we will reach safety by means of the Hashtādsar road or some other route."

Someone else, however, gave Bughā advice and pointed out, "The army has become divided into separate groups, and its front portion will not be able to join up with the rear portion. Moreover, the troops have thrown down their weapons, although money and arms still remain on the mules. There is no one with this money and arms, and we cannot be sure that someone may not make a dash for it and seize the money and the captive," meaning Ibn Jawīdhān,[145] who was a prisoner with them and by means of whom they sought to ransom a secretary of ʿAbd al-Raḥmān b. Ḥabīb who had been captured by Bābak.

When the [additional factors of the] money, arms and captive were mentioned to Bughā, he decided to encamp with his troops; and he sent a message to Dāwūd Siyāh saying, "Wherever you see an easily defensible mountain, encamp there." Dāwūd turned aside and went obliquely up the side of a mountain, but there was no place on it for the troops to rest because of its excessively steep slopes. Dāwūd nevertheless pitched his camp and put up a tent for Bughā on the flank of the mountain in a spot that resembled a

145. Clearly the son of the leader of the Khurramī movement in its pre-Bābak phase, Jawīdhān b. Shahrak or Sahl (the latter in Ṭabarī, III, 1015), whose wife Bābak married after Jawīdhān had been killed in battle, thus consolidating his own role as the new leader of the sect. It would seem that Bābak was able to set aside any claims in leadership that Jawīdhān's son might have had. See E. G. Browne, *Literary History*, I, 324–28; Sadighi, *op. cit.*, 242–45; E. M. Wright, *op. cit.*, 45–47; Scarcia Amoretti, *op. cit.*, 505, 517–18.

walled enclosure with no path into it. Bughā arrived and halted and made the troops encamp, for they were weary and tired, and their provisions were exhausted. They passed the night deployed ready for action and on guard against the direction of the slope; but the enemy came upon them from another direction and went up the mountainside until they reached Bughā's tent. They [1193] surrounded and attacked the tent and fell upon the army by night. Bughā fled on foot and escaped safely. Al-Faḍl b. Kāwūs was wounded; Janāḥ al-Sukkarī, Ibn Jawshan, and one of the two brothers who were kindred of al-Faḍl b. Sahl were killed. Bughā had indeed fled from the camp on foot, but he found a mount and rode on it, passing by Ibn al-Ba'īth. He made the latter go up [with him] to above Hashtādsar until he brought him down to Muḥammad b. Ḥumayd's camp (i.e., his Trench), which they reached in the middle of the night. The Khurramiyyah seized the money, the encampment, and the weapons and rescued the prisoner Ibn Jawīdhān; but they did not pursue the [Muslim] troops, and these last made their way, routed and in disarray, till they came to Bughā, who was within the Trench of Muḥammad b. Ḥumayd.

Bughā remained within the Trench of Muḥammad b. Ḥumayd for fifteen days. Then a letter reached him from al-Afshīn, ordering him to return to al-Marāghah and to send back the reinforcements that he had sent to strengthen him. Bughā proceeded to al-Marāghah, while al-Faḍl b. Kāwūs, together with all those of al-Afshīn's troops who had gone with him, rejoined al-Afshīn. The latter allocated to them their winter quarters for that year until the spring of the following year arrived.[146]

In this year one of Bābak's commanders called Ṭarkhān was killed.

The Killing of Bābak's Commander Ṭarkhān

It has been mentioned that this Ṭarkhān held a prominent position in Bābak's entourage, being one of his commanders.

146. Ya'qūbī, *Ta'rīkh*, II, 578–79; Dīnawarī, *op. cit.*, 403; Azdī, *op. cit.*, 422; *Kitāb al-'uyūn*, 382–85; Ibn al-Athīr, *op. cit.*, VI, 456–59; Sadighi, *op. cit.*, 254–55; E. M. Wright, *op. cit.*, 52; Nafīsī, *Bābak-i Khurram-dīn*, 104–8.

When the winter of this year set in he sought permission from Bābak to pass the winter in a village of his in the vicinity of al-Marāghah. Al-Afshīn, meanwhile, was lying in wait for him
[1194] and hoping to capture him because of his high position with Bābak. Bābak accordingly gave Ṭarkhān permission, so he went off to his village in the neighborhood of Hashtādsar to spend the winter. Al-Afshīn now wrote to Turk, the mawlā of Isḥāq b. Ibrāhīm b. Muṣʿab, who was then at al-Marāghah, ordering him to make a nocturnal raid on that village—which he described to him—with the aim of either killing Ṭarkhān or else sending him back to al-Afshīn as a prisoner. Turk therefore mounted a nocturnal raid against Ṭarkhān. He went to him in the middle of the night, killing him, and sending his head to al-Afshīn.[147]

In this year, Ṣūl Er-tigīn and people from his country arrived in fetters. The fetters were struck off them, and they were transported on mounts, there being about 200 men all told.[148]

In this year, al-Afshīn became angry with Rajāʾ al-Ḥiḍārī[149] and sent him forward in fetters.

---

147. Ibn al-Athīr, *op. cit.*, VI, 459; Sadighi, *op. cit.*, 255; Nafīsī, *Bābak-i Khurram-dīn*, 108.

148. Ibn al-Athīr, *op. cit.*, VI, 460. The occasion of this event is otherwise unknown but appears related to the bringing into caliphal service—probably after defeat in a revolt or as the result of a punitive expedition into the steppes—of a member of the ancient Iranized Turkish rulers of the Gurgān and Dihistān steppes to the southeast of the Caspian Sea, who had the family or tribal name of Chöl, Arabized to Ṣūl, and a band of his retainers. The correct form of the man's name is more likely that given in the text n. *e*, from ms. O, Ṣūl-Tigīn "Ṣūl the Prince." A Ṣūl is mentioned as *dihqān* of Gurgān and Dihistān in 97 (715–16); see Ṭabarī, II, 1320. The famous family of Arabic littérateurs in the third-fourth (ninth-tenth) centuries, that of al-Ṣūlī, was descended from this local dynasty. See J. Marquart, *Ērānšahr*, 73; Barthold, *History of the Turkman People*, 87–88. At all events, Ṣūl-Tigīn now rapidly achieved favor with al-Muʿtaṣim, for he is mentioned in Ṭabarī, III, 1313 (p. 194, below) as governor of Damascus in 226 (840–41).

149. Ibn al-Athīr, *op. cit.*, VI, 460. Ḥidār (thus vocalized explicitly in Ibn al-Athīr, *pace* Caskel's spelling Ḥadār) b. Ḥarb b. ʿĀmir were a clan of the South Arabian tribe of al-Ashʿar b. Udad; see Ibn al-Kalbī, *Jamharat al-nasab*, I, Tafel 273, II, Register, 290. The cause of Rajāʾ's digrace is not specified here but cannot have been permanent; he was sent against the rebel al-Mubarqaʿ in Syria and Palestine in 227 (841–42); Ṭabarī, III, 1320–22 (pp. 204–6, below), and again in 240 (854) he or his son Muḥammad was recommended to be sent against rebels in the Syrian town of Ḥimṣ. He died in 244 (858–59), according to Ibn ʿAsākir, *Tahdhīb*, V, 312.

In this year, Muḥammad b. Dāwūd b. ʿĪsā b. Mūsā b. Muḥammad b. ʿAlī b. ʿAbdallāh b. ʿAbbās led the Pilgrimage, he being at that time governor of Mecca.[150]

---

150. Khalīfah, *op. cit.*, II, 885; Azdī, *op. cit.*, 424; Ibn al-Athīr, *op. cit.*, VI, 460.

The Events of the Year 222

(December 14, 836–December 2, 837)

Among the events taking place during this year was al-
1195] Mu'taṣim's sending Ja'far b. Dīnār al-Khayyāṭ[151] to al-Afshīn as a reinforcement for the latter and then his sending Aytākh[152] subsequently to follow him, accompanied by 30 million dirhams as pay for the army and for supplies and expenses.

In this year a battle took place between the forces of al-Afshīn and one of Bābak's commanders called Ādhīn.

The Engagement between al-Afshīn's Forces and Bābak's Commander Ādhīn and Its Causes

It has been mentioned that, when the winter of 221 (835/836) was over and spring came along and the year 222 had begun,

151. Ja'far had fought on the Byzantine frontier (Ṭabarī, III, 1103) and was to be governor of Yemen 224–25 (839–40) (Ṭabarī, III, 1300, 1302–3 [pp. 174, 179, below]) and military governor over the Pilgrimage route during the years 239–43 (853–57; Ṭabarī, III, 1420, 1422, 1433, 1435, 1436). See Herzfeld, *op. cit.*, 108.

152. Aytākh al-Khazarī, often called al-Ṭabbākh ("the cook") because he had originally been a domestic slave in the kitchens, achieved high favor as commander of the caliphal guard in Sāmarrā under al-Mu'taṣim, but was killed by

al-Mu'taṣim sent to al-Afshīn certain reinforcements and money, all of which reached the latter when he was at Barzand. Aytākh handed over to al-Afshīn the money and the troops who had accompanied him and set off homeward, but Ja'far al-Khayyāṭ remained with al-Afshīn for some time.[153] Then al-Afshīn moved on when the time of year made movement possible and came to a place called Kalān Rūdh, where he dug a defensive trench and rampart (*khandaq*). He wrote to Abū Sa'īd, who journeyed from Barzand to a spot opposite him on the fringes of the rural district of Kalān Rūdh—which means (in Persian) "Great River"[154]—so that a distance of three miles separated the two of them. Abū Sa'īd established a camp within a defensive trench and remained at Kalān Rūdh for five days. Then someone came to him and informed him that a certain one of Bābak's commanders called Ādhīn had encamped opposite al-Afshīn and had sent his family up into a mountain that overlooked Rūdh al-Rūdh,[155] saying, "I won't entrench myself in a defensive position from the Jews"—he meant the Muslims[156]—"and I won't place my family within a fortified position!" This was because Bābak had said to him, "Place your family within a fortified position!" But Ādhīn had replied, "I protect myself from the Jews? By God, I'll never place my family within any fortified position!" Hence he moved them to this mountain. [1196]

Al-Afshīn sent Ẓafar b. al-'Alā' al-Sa'dī and al-Ḥusayn b. Khālid

---

al-Mutawakkil in 235 (849–50). See Ṭabarī, III, 1384–87; EI^2 Suppl. s.v. Aytākh al-Turkī (Ed.). The etymology of the name is presumably Turkish "moon-like."

153. In the fairly compressed account of Dīnawarī, *op. cit.*, 403 (cf. 404), it is mentioned that around this time al-Afshīn sent forward Ja'far b. Dīnār and his own deputy Yūbārah (?) to dig this new defensive trench; the latter name—whatever its true form may be—appears only later in Ṭabarī, III, 1225–26 (p. 79, below), in the account of Bābak's extradition from Armenia, as Būzbārah; the reading of the name in parallel and later sources, e.g. Mas'ūdī, *Murūj*, VII = par. 2809, is equally uncertain.

154. Glossed here in the text as Arabic *nahr kabīr*.

155. Described by Ibn Khurradādhbih, *op. cit.*, 121, as the site of al-Afshīn's third camp, only one farsakh from al-Badhdh.

156. Hereby setting off his own group of the Khurramiyyah, a body within the ancient Iranian religious tradition, from the Muslims, with their Semitic religious background, shared by the Jews. Ādhīn's contemptuous reference to his opponents as Jews was to be echoed by Bābak when the Armenian prince Sahl b. Sunbāṭ betrayed him to al-Afshīn; see Ṭabarī, III, 1226 (pp. 80–81, below); Sadighi, *op. cit.*, 265; E. M. Wright, *op. cit.*, 51, 53–54.

al-Madāʾinī, two of Abū Saʿīd's commanders, with a force of cavalrymen and mountain guards. They traveled all through the night from Kalān Rūdh until they descended into a defile so narrow that even a single rider could pass through it only with great effort. Most of the troops led their mounts; and they squeezed through, one man behind the other, for al-Afshīn had ordered them to travel to Rūdh al-Rūdh before the break of dawn. [He also ordered] the mountain guards to cross on foot, because it was impossible for cavalrymen to maneuver there, and to climb up the mountain. They reached Rūdh al-Rūdh before daybreak. At this point, he (Ẓafar b. al-ʿAlāʾ) ordered the cavalrymen who had approached to dismount and go on foot and to remove their clothing. So all the cavalrymen dismounted and crossed [the river] on foot, accompanied by the mountain guards, en masse, and they went up the mountainside. There they seized Ādhīn's family and some of his children and brought them back across the river.

The news about the seizure of his family reached Ādhīn. It happened that al-Afshīn had been fearful lest, when this force of troops on foot pressed onward and entered the defile, the defile be closed against them. Hence he ordered the mountain guards to take banners with them and to station themselves on the peaks of the loftiest mountains in places from which they could look down on Ẓafar b. al-ʿAlāʾ and his forces; and, if they should see anyone about whose behavior they were suspicious, they were to wave the banners (i.e., as a signal). The mountain guards accordingly passed the night on the mountaintops.

When Ibn al-ʿAlāʾ and al-Ḥusayn b. Khālid returned with those members of Ādhīn's family whom they had captured and when they had gone some way along the road, before they were to reach the defile, Ādhīn's foot soldiers swept down on them and engaged them in fighting before they could enter the defile. Men on both
[1197] sides were slain, but they rescued some of the women [from being massacred]. The mountain guards, whom al-Afshīn had deployed, saw them. Ādhīn had sent two bodies of troops, one to engage the Muslims in battle and one to seize the defile and hold it against them.[157] Thus, when the mountain guards waved their flags [as a

157. Following the text (and that of the Cairo edition, IX, 30), which seems better than the suggestion in *Addenda et emendanda*, DCCLXXIII.

signal], al-Afshīn sent Muẓaffar b. Kaydar with a squadron (*kurdūs*)[158] of his troops, and these last galloped off. He also sent Abū Saʿīd behind al-Muẓaffar and then, to follow them both, the Bukhārā-khudāh,[159] and these all met up together. When Ādhīn's foot soldiers who were above the defile looked down on them, they descended and joined forces with their comrades. Ẓafar b. al-ʿAlāʾ and al-Ḥusayn b. Khālid, together with the troops who were with them, escaped; none of them was killed except those

158. Defined as a small detachment of troops, especially of cavalry but possibly also of infantry, numbering some forty to fifty men, hence smaller than a *katībah* (see *WbKAS*, I, 122–23). Ṭabarī, II, 1941, 1944, mentions the adoption by Marwān b. Muḥammad (sc. the last Umayyad Caliph Marwān II) of the military formation of *karādīs*, compact bodies of troops as opposed to the traditional Arab formation of lines of soldiers (*ṣufūf*). S. Fraenkel, *Die aramäische Fremdwörter*, 239, suggested a derivation of the word *kurdūs* from the Greek plural *choortis*, ultimately from Latin *cohortes*. Hence some authorities have held that Marwān took over this military formation from the Byzantines in the course of his warfare with them along the eastern Anatolian frontier (cf. Wellhausen, *Das arabische Reich*, 232–33, trans., 371–73; Herzfeld, *op. cit.*, 141 n. 1; *EI*², s.v. Ḥarb. ii. The Caliphate [Cl. Cahen]), but it is probable that it was used before then. Poets of a somewhat earlier period, such as Aʿshā Qays and Jarīr, used the word in their poetry, and Levy, *op. cit.*, 430, noted that it is used by Ṭabarī, I, 2091 ff., in connection with the Battle of Yarmūk against the Byzantines.

159. This is the first mention by Ṭabarī of this Iranian prince, the hereditary local ruler of Bukhārā, as one of al-Afshīn's leading commanders, and it is an indication of the strength and importance of Iranian elements from Transoxania within the ʿAbbāsid army side by side with the Turkish *ghilmān*. With the final subjugation and Islamization of Transoxania and adjacent regions, the local Soghdian, Khwārazmian, and other free Iranian peoples were recruited in large numbers by the caliphs, thus providing a fresh wave of easterners, *mashāriqah*, after the Khurāsānians of the first ʿAbbāsid decades. They seem often to have been led by their own local princes, of whom al-Afshīn and the Bukhārā-khudāh are of course good examples. Thus we find mentioned in the historical sources "the men of Farghāna," *al-Farāghinah*, "the men of Ushrūsanah," *al-Ushrūsaniyyah*, and "the men of Ishtīkhān," *al-Ishtīkhaniyyah* (not *al-Ishtīkhāniyyah*; cf. Ṭabarī, III, 1362) as distinct units. Ishtīkhān was the district north of Samarqand, to which the local rulers of Soghdia, the Ikhshīds, had moved their capital in the second (eighth) century, after the Arabs' occupation of Samarqand; see Le Strange, *Lands*, 466; Barthold, *Turkestan*, 95–96. At Sāmarrā these Iranian units were allocated land grants, *qaṭāʾiʿ*, adjacent to those of the Turks, as Masʿūdī expressly states (*Murūj*, VII, 122 = par. 2805). Indeed, Yaʿqūbī, in his detailed survey of Sāmarrā and also of its component parts, mentions quarters inhabited by people from Balkh, Marw, Khuttal, Bukhārā, Isfījāb, Kābul, Khwārazm, Soghdia, Fāryāb, Ishtakhanj, etc. (*Buldān*, 248–49, 259, 262–63, trans., 30–31, 52, 54–55). Shaban is right in emphasizing that al-Muʿtaṣim's new armies included a considerable proportion of these Iranian troops from the northeastern fringes of the Islamic world (*op. cit.*, 62–64). It is equally true that these soldiers were freemen, who entered the ʿAbbāsid service of their own accord, for reasons of personal advancement, and not as slaves. But to deny, as Shaban does (63–66), that there

killed in the first engagement. They all eventually reached al-Afshīn's encampment, accompanied by some of the womenfolk whom they had captured.[160]

In this year, Bābak's capital, al-Badhdh, was captured. The Muslims entered it and treated it as lawful plunder (i.e., sacked it). This was on Friday, the twentieth of Ramaḍān of this year (26 August 837).[161]

The Capture of al-Badhdh, How It Was Achieved, and the Reasons for This

It has been mentioned that, when al-Afshīn resolved to advance toward al-Badhdh and depart from Kalān Rūdh, he began to creep

---

were any appreciable numbers of Turks in the new ʿAbbāsid armies and that there were any slave elements at all is perverse and ludicrous. The undoubted presence of Turks is shown, if by nothing else, by the frequency of Turkish names among the leading commanders of the third (ninth) and fourth (tenth) centuries: Bughā, Aytākh, Unūjūr, Minkajūr, Adgutigīn, Bektimūr, Yināl, etc.. There is no obvious cultural process by which Iranians would have adopted Turkish names; rather, the reverse (cf. perhaps Ash[i]nās, the commander of al-Ma'mūn and al-Muʿtaṣim, whose name is explained by Ṭabarī, III, 1017, as derived from Persian *shinākhtan* "to recognize, know"). Furthermore, the slave origins of these commanders is shown by the use of such terms as *waṣīf* and *khādim* (for which see pp. 99 n. 293, 134 n. 375, below; Ayalon, "On the Eunuchs in Islam." 74–89) and by the presence of commanders known to have been eunuchs (Yāzmān, Mu'nis al-Muẓaffarī, etc.); it is most unlikely that free Iranians would willingly have consented to be castrated. Nor would Jāḥiẓ have thought it worthwhile to compose a lengthy epistle on the virtues of the Turks as the fighting race par excellence if these troops had not loomed large in the public eye. On the Turkish element of the ʿAbbāsid army, see also Ayalon, "Military Reforms," 29–33; Ismail, "Muʿtaṣim and the Turks," 14–15, 17.

The personal name of the Bukhārā-khudāh is not given by Ṭabarī, but he was probably the grandson of the Bunyāt b. Tughshādah, killed in 166 (782–83), whose line continued to rule the city-state of Bukhārā until the time of the Sāmānid Ismāʿīl b. Aḥmad in the later third (ninth) century (Narshakhī, *Ta'rīkh-i Bukhārā*, 10–11, trans., 11). Dīnawarī, *op. cit.*, 403, and Yaʿqūbī, *Ta'rīkh*, II, 580, actually name him as Muḥammad b. Khālid; if this is correct, it shows that these rulers had by now adopted fully Islamic, rather than indigenous Iranian, names.

Finally, one may note that the Bukhārā-khudāh (with the name written corruptly but recognizably) appears as a patron of the poet al-Masdūd in the time of the Caliph al-Muntaṣir, sc. 247–48 (861–62); see Abū al-Faraj al-Iṣfahānī, *Kitāb al-aghānī*, XXI, ed. Brünnow, 258 line 14. This may well be the same Bukhārā-khudāh as the one involved here against Bābak, or it may be his son.

160. Ṭabarī, trans. Balʿamī, IV, 527–33; *Kitāb al-ʿuyūn*, 385; Ibn al-Athīr, *op. cit.*, VI, 461–62.

161. Actually a Sunday.

forward a little at a time, in a manner different from his steady advance on earlier occasions, to the places where he had previously encamped. He would advance for four miles and then encamp in a spot on the road leading to the defile that goes down to Rūdh al-Rūdh, not digging a defensive trench but pitching his camp inside a protective belt of caltrops (*al-ḥasak*).[162] Al-Muʿtaṣim wrote to him, ordering him to station his troops in squadrons that would take turns on guard duty [during the day], [1198]
mounted on their horses, just as the army would normally patrol [the encampment] by night; some of the troops were to remain in camp, and others were to remain mounted on their steeds about a mile away, just as the army would normally patrol [the encampment], but night and day for fear of any nocturnal attack. In this fashion, if any sudden disaster should assail them, the troops [of the cavalry] would be deployed in battle formation, and the infantry would be in the encampment.

However, the troops raised an outcry because of their exhaustion and said, "How long are we going to be stuck here in the defile when we could be out on the open plain? Between us and the enemy are four farsakhs, yet we are behaving just as if the enemy were directly facing us! We have become an object of shame in the eyes of the people and the spies who pass between us and the enemy within this four farsakhs' intermediate zone, and we behave as if we were nearly dead of fright. Let us advance, whether the outcome be for us or against us!"

Al-Afshīn replied, "By God, I know full well that what you say is right. But the Commander of the Faithful has ordered me to do this, and I have no choice but to implement it." Not long after that, a letter came to him from al-Muʿtaṣim, commanding him to remain on his course of action by night, just as he was already doing. So he continued thus for several days and then went down with his close retainers till he halted at Rūdh al-Rūdh. He proceeded onward until he found himself overlooking the spot where there was the rocky area[163] at which Bābak had attacked

162. For this term, see Dozy, *Supplément*, I, 286.

163. *Al-rakwah*, following *Glossarium*, CCLXX (cf. Ṭabarī, III, 1188 (p. 39 n. 142, above). *Glossarium*, however, also mentions a possible translation "pool," following the *Glossaire* to Ibn Khurradādhbih, *op. cit.*, 4.

him the previous year. He examined the place and found there a squadron of the Khurramiyyah, but they did not attack him, nor did he attack them. One of (or: some of) the indigenous non-Arab population (*baʿḍ al-ʿulūj*) said to him, "What's the matter with you? You move forward and then come to a halt! Aren't you ashamed of yourselves?" Nevertheless, al-Afshīn ordered that they should not attack them (the Khurramiyyah)[164] and that no one should march out and give them battle. He remained there confronting the enemy until nearly noon and then returned to his encampment. He stayed in it for two days, and then he went
[1199] down the slope again with a larger force than he had gone down with on the first occasion. He ordered Abū Saʿīd to go forward and confront the enemy in the same manner in which he had confronted them on the first occasion but not to provoke them and not to launch an assault on them.

Al-Afshīn remained at Rūdh al-Rūdh. He ordered the mountain guards to climb up to those mountaintops that they deemed to be naturally defensible, so that they might then report back in person to him about them and might choose for him places on the mountaintops in which the infantrymen could fortify themselves. Hence they chose for him three mountains where there had in the past been fortifications that were now in ruins; and al-Afshīn learned of them. He next sent for Abū Saʿīd, who came back to him on that very same day. When two days had elapsed al-Afshīn went down from his camp to Rūdh al-Rūdh, taking with him the *kilghariyyah*,[165] that is, the pioneer and labor corps, who brought with them skins filled with water and also dry biscuit (*kaʿk*).[166] When they reached Rūdh al-Rūdh he sent Abū Saʿīd

164. The text here and in the Cairo edition, IX, 31, gives *yajīʾūhum*, which seems preferable to the possible emendation *yujībūhum* of *Addenda et emendanda*, DCCLXIII, with the translation "that they should not make any response to them."

165. This word is stated in *Glossarium*, CDLVII, and *WbKAS*, I, 320, to be from Persian *gilghar*, but the Persian lexica (Vullers; Steingass) do not list this word with any appropriate meaning. It would in fact appear to derive from Persian *gil-kār* "one who works with clay; e.g., clay bricks in building."

166. A kind of dry bread or biscuit, particularly associated with Egypt (where the Greek geographer Strabo mentions *kakeis*; Coptic *caace, kake*) and used as iron rations by pilgrims and other travelers across deserts and difficult terrain. See Dozy, *Supplément*, II, 474; BGA, IV, 341; *WbKAS*, I, 234–35. On the Persian form

forward, ordering him to stand up against the enemy once more in the same manner as he had ordered him on the first day. He ordered the laborers to transport rocks and fortify the roads that led to those three mountains until they resembled fortresses. He gave further commands, and along every road behind those rocks he had a trench dug, right up to the top of the mountain, leaving [free] only a single way up the each mountaintop. Then he instructed Abū Saʿīd to return; the latter returned, and al-Afshīn also went back to his encampment.

He related: When it was the eighth day of the month and the stronghold had been rendered well fortified al-Afshīn issued biscuit and *sawīq*[167] [as provisions] for the foot soldiers and provisions and barley for the cavalry. He appointed men to guard his encampment, and the rest of the troops went down. He ordered the foot soldiers to ascend to the tops of those mountains and take up with them water and all that they would need there; [1200]
and they in fact did this. He encamped in the vicinity and sent Abū Saʿīd to confront the enemy as previously, at the same time ordering his troops to descend with their weapons at the ready but that the cavalry were not to take the saddles of their mounts. Then he delimited the trench and ordered the laborers to get to work on it, setting over them overseers who would urge them on, and he and the cavalry dismounted. They halted in the shade beneath the trees, letting their mounts pasture. When he had led the afternoon worship, he ordered the laborers, together with the foot soldiers, to ascend to the mountaintops that he had fortified, and he ordered the foot soldiers to stay on their guard and not to go to sleep on the mountaintops but to let the laborers on the mountaintops sleep. He ordered the cavalry to mount their steeds at the gleam of dawn and formed them up into squadrons that he stationed one in front of the other, with the distance of a bowshot between each squadron. He gave the command to all the

kāk, see A. Siddiqi, *Studien über die persischen Fremdwörter*, 71. The trade of the *kaʿki*, or baker of *kaʿk*, was recognized in medieval Cairo; see S. D. Goitein, *A Mediterranean Society*, I, 114.

167. A dish made from flour and then a soup thickened with flour and other ingredients. See Thaʿālibī, *op. cit.*, 10, trans., 41 and n. 20; *EI*², s.v. Sawīk (J. Ruska).

squadrons, "Make sure that each one of you pays no attention to the other, so that each person guards what is near him. Even if you hear any loud noise, let none of you pay any attention to anyone else; each squadron is to be responsible only for what is near it, without being heedful to any loud noise."[168]

The squadrons of cavalry remained mounted [at the ready] until dawn, while the foot soldiers were keeping guard on the mountaintops. Al-Afshīn ordered the foot soldiers that, if they became aware of anyone in the course of the night, they were not to concern themselves with it. Rather, each group of them was to remain in the assigned position and guard its particular mountain and trench; and no one was to pay any attention to anyone else.

They continued in this way until daybreak. Then he ordered someone to get the cavalrymen and the foot soldiers to come to a
[1201] mutual agreement concerning the night (i.e., for dividing it into periods of guard duty and sleep); then [later] he would consider their situation. They spent the next ten days excavating the trench, and on the tenth day he took up his position in it. Then he divided it among the troops and ordered the commanders to send for their baggage and that of their men, so that they would fight to better advantage (literally, "by way of bringing them comfort and support," *ʿalā rifq*).

[At that point] an envoy from Bābak came to him, bearing cucumbers (*qiththāʾ*), melons and [other kinds of] cucumber (*khiyār*), explaining to al-Afshīn that it was known that he was suffering hardship in those days and that he and his troops were having to exist on biscuit and *sawīq* alone; hence Bābak wished to show kindness to him by means of these gifts. Al-Afshīn replied to the envoy, however, "I am certainly aware of what my brother intends with this! He only wishes to get a look at the army, but I am indeed most worthy of receiving his benevolence and satisfying his desire, for he has truly observed that I am having a hard time." He also told the envoy, "As for you, you must definitely go up in order to view our encampment; you have already seen what there is here [in front of us], and now you will

168. As Marin observed, Ṭabarī, trans. Marin, 32, n. 175, the text is disturbed here, and any translation is conjectural.

see what is behind us too." He thereupon gave orders that the envoy was to be provided with a mount and taken up [the mountain] until he should see the trench and likewise the trenches of Kalān Rūdh and Barzand; that he should have a good look at all three of them and study them carefully and should have nothing of the military arrangements concealed from him, so that he might fully inform his master. All this was done for the envoy until he reached Barzand, and then al-Afshīn had him sent back to his own presence. Al-Afshīn now set him free, saying, "Go and give Bābak my greetings!"

Some of the Khurramiyyah used to interfere with those who were bringing supplies to the army (to that of al-Afshīn). This was done once or twice, but after that the Khurramiyyah came in three squadrons until they drew near to the ramparts of al-Afshīn's trench, all the time shouting. Al-Afshīn ordered that none of his troops should speak [to them], and this they did for two or three nights running. They (the Muslim troops) began to gallop their steeds behind the ramparts on several occasions until, [1202] when the Khurramiyyah were familiar [with that noise], al-Afshīn got ready against them four squadrons of cavalrymen and foot soldiers—the latter being archers—and established them in ambushes against the Khurramiyyah within the valleys, placing lookouts above them. When the Khurramiyyah came down at the time they had usually swept down on each previous occasion, shouting and yelling as was their wont, al-Afshīn unleashed against them the cavalry and foot soldiers who had been [previously] deployed, and these blocked the Khurramiyyah's way of retreat. Al-Afshīn further launched against them two squadrons of foot soldiers in the middle of the night. The Khurramiyyah realized that the mountain pass had been blocked against them, so they scattered along a number of tracks until they began to ascend the mountains. They passed along and never returned to what they had been doing before. Al-Afshīn's troops came back to the trench at Rūdh al-Rūdh from the pursuit at the time of the morning worship, without however having overtaken a single one of the Khurramiyyah.

Once every week al-Afshīn used to have the drums beaten at midnight and would go out with candles and naphtha torches

(*al-naffāṭāt*)[169] to the gate of the trench. Meanwhile, each one of his troops knew his own squadron, whether he was on the right wing or the left wing, and they would go forth and then wait in their positions and places. Al-Afshīn also used to carry large black banners, twelve of them, which he transported on mules, rather than on horseback, lest the banners should wave, placing them [instead] on twelve mules. His large drums numbered 21 and his smaller banners around 500. His troops would wait, each section arranged in its place, from the first quarter of the night until, when dawn first gleamed, al-Afshīn rode forth from his tent. The
[1203] muezzin would give the call to worship in his presence, and al-Afshīn would perform the worship. Then the troops would perform the worship at daybreak. Al-Afshīn would thereupon order the drums to be beaten, and he would move slowly forward. His signals for moving and halting were the beating and silencing of the drums because of the great number of troops who were traveling in the mountains and on the narrow paths in their military formations. Whenever they came to a mountain they would ascend it, and when they descended into a valley they would proceed onward through it, unless it was an inaccessible mountain, impossible either to ascend or descend, in which case they would rejoin the army units and return, when they came to a mountain, to their military formations and positions. The signal for moving forward was the beating of drums, but if al-Afshīn wanted the army to halt he silenced the drums, and the troops would stop, the whole lot of them, in every part of the mountain or valley or wherever they might be. Al-Afshīn advanced by slow stages, and, whenever one of the mountain guards came to him with a piece of information, he halted for a brief while. He traversed those six miles between Rūdh al-Rūdh and al-Badhdh between the gleaming of dawn and high noon. When he wished to ascend to the area of rocky ground where the battle had taken place the previous year, he left the Bukhārā-khudāh at the top of the mountain slope with 1,000 cavalrymen and 600 foot soldiers to guard the road for him and block the road against any of the Khurramiyyah who might sally forth.

---

169. Clearly with this meaning, here, whereas in Ṭabarī, III, 1215 (p. 68, below), *naffāṭah* has the sense of "naphtha-hurling weapon."

When Bābak became aware that the [Muslim] army was closing in upon him, he sent one of his detachments of troops, consisting of foot soldiers, to a valley below the mountain slope on top of which was the Bukhārā-khudāh, and they lay in ambush for anyone who might intend to block the road against him (i.e., against Bābak). Al-Afshīn had stationed the Bukhārā-khudāh to [1204]
hold this mountain track to which Bābak had sent his military force in order to seize it against al-Afshīn. The Bukhārā-khudāh was to stand fast there for as long as al-Afshīn was entering al-Badhdh across the stretch of rocky ground. Al-Afshīn had ordered the Bukhārā-khudāh to station himself in a valley resembling a defensive trench, which lay between him and al-Badhdh. He also ordered Abū Saʿīd Muḥammad b. Yūsuf to cross that valley with a squadron of his troops. He ordered Jaʿfar al-Khayyāṭ, moreover, to station himself with a squadron of his troops; and he ordered Aḥmad b. al-Khalīl to take up his position with another squadron. Thus in that part of the valley there would be three squadrons on the outskirts of the houses of Bābak's people (i.e., of the urban area of al-Badhdh).

Bābak had sent out a military force under Ādhīn, who stationed himself on a hill opposite these three squadrons [of al-Afshīn's troops] outside al-Badhdh, lest any of al-Afshīn's forces approach the gate of the town. Al-Afshīn was intending to make for the gate of al-Badhdh and was ordering his troops to cross but then just halt and not engage Bābak's forces in battle. When Bābak realized that al-Afshīn's troops had moved out of the trench and were aiming toward him, he split his men up into ambush groups, retaining with him only a small number of men. Al-Afshīn got knowledge of this but did not know the places where the ambushes had been laid. Then the information came to him that the Khurramiyyah had come out en masse and that only a handful of his men remained with Bābak.

When al-Afshīn had gone up to that position, a leather mat (*naṭʿ*)[170] was spread out for him and a seat (*kursī*)[171] set up for [1205]

170. This term is also used for a leather mat with drawstrings round the edges, which could be used at beheadings as a receptacle for the severed heads.

171. For the *kursī*, originating from the Iranian cultural sphere, see Sourdel, "Questions de cérémonial," 130–31; J. Sadan, *Mobilier*, 92–94, 123 ff.; *EI*², s.v.

him. He sat on a hillock that overlooked the gate of Bābak's fortress, with the troops drawn up in their [cavalry] squadrons; he ordered those who were with him on this side of the valley to dismount from their steeds and likewise those on the other side with Abū Saʿīd, Jaʿfar al-Khayyāṭ, and his men. Aḥmad b. al-Khalīl, however, did not dismount because of his close proximity to the enemy, and his troops remained in place and on the backs of their mounts. Al-Afshīn now divided up the mountain-guard foot soldiers in order to search the valleys, because he was eager to find the places where the enemy was lurking in ambushes and thus be aware of them.

This was al-Afshīn's procedure [each day] in carrying out this work of searching until afternoon; the Khurramiyyah would be with Bābak, drinking wine (*nabīdh*),[172] playing on reed pipes (*surnāyāt*),[173] and beating drums until, when al-Afshīn had performed the noon worship, he would go forward and then go down to his trench at Rūdh al-Rūdh. Abū Saʿīd would be the first to descend, followed by Aḥmad b. al-Khalīl and then Jaʿfar b. Dīnār. Then al-Afshīn would come back again. This coming and going of al-Afshīn used to infuriate Bābak, so that, when he was on the point of returning, the Khurramiyyah would strike their cymbals (*ṣunūj*)[174] and blow their trumpets (*būqāt*)[175] in a mocking fashion. The Bukhāra-khudāh, meanwhile, would re-

---

Kursī (Cl. Huart and J. Sadan). It was often regarded as a symbol of power, like a throne; cf. the Chair of ʿAlī, covered in silk and brocade, which was the focus of circumambulation and was carried into battle like the Hebrews' Ark of the Covenant during the revolt of al-Mukhtār in 66–67 (685–87); Ṭabarī, II, 702–6.

172. Originally date wine and as such allowed for medicinal use by certain of the Islamic law schools, but the term often becomes a generalized designation for wine. See *EI*[1], s.v. Nabī<u>dh</u> (A. J. Wensinck); EI[2], s.v. <u>Kh</u>amr. 1. Juridical Aspects (A. J. Wensinck).

173. On this small reed pipe, the name of which is also found in the form *suryānay*, see *EI*[2], s.v. Mizmār (H. G. Farmer); it came to be used especially in military bands; see Farmer, *History of Arabian Music*, 154, 208.

174. Sing. *ṣanj(ah)*, another name for the *jank*, pl. *junūk* (< Persian *chang*), a term used both for the harp or lyre and for the cymbals; in both senses it was derived by the Arabs from Sāsānid Persian music. See Dozy, *Supplément*, I, 845; Farmer, *op. cit.*, 16, 18, 74, 155; for the philological aspects of the varying Persian and Arabic forms, see Siddiqi, *op. cit.*, 72, 73.

175. Sing. *būq*, essentially a military band instrument; see *EI*[2], s.v. Būḳ (H. G. Farmer).

main on the mountain slope where he was stationed until all the troops had passed him and only then would return in their tracks. One day the Khurramiyyah became tired of the position of stalemate (*mu'ādalah*) and the process of searching being carried out against them. So, [when] al-Afshīn returned, according to his custom, and the squadron returned one after the other and Abū Sa'īd crossed the valley as also Aḥmad b. al-Khalīl and some of Ja'far al-Khayyāṭ's troops, the Khurramiyyah opened the gate of their defensive trench and rampart, and ten of their cavalrymen rode forth and attacked those of Ja'far al-Khayyāṭ's men who had [1206]
remained in that place. A clamor broke out among the [Muslim] army, and Ja'far, on his own initiative, came back with a squadron of his troops and charged those [Khurramī] cavalrymen until he drove them back to the gate of al-Badhdh. Further clamor nevertheless continued within the army, and at this point al-Afshīn returned, while Ja'far and his troops were fighting on that side, a number of Ja'far's men having previously gone forth (i.e., to join him). Bābak rode forth with a number of his cavalrymen, neither side—al-Afshīn's or Bābak's—having any infantrymen with them. Each side in turn would lead assaults on the other side; and men on both sides suffered wounds. Al-Afshīn went back, and the leather mat was laid down for him and the seat set up. He then sat down in the place which had been his wont, all the time blazing with anger against Ja'far, who, he kept saying, "has spoiled my deployment of the troops and my intended plans."

The clamor rose higher. Abū Dulaf[176] had with him, in a squadron, a group of volunteers from al-Baṣrah and others also. When these volunteers saw that Ja'far was engaged in battle, they went down, without any order from al-Afshīn, and crossed to that side of the valley[177] until they reached the flank of al-Badhdh.

---

176. I.e., Abū al-Qāsim b. 'Īsā al-'Ijlī, lord of Karaj in al-Jibāl, famed not only as a warrior, the beau ideal of an Arab knight, but as a Maecenas and littérateur himself; see Herzfeld, *op. cit.*, 139–40; *EI*², s.v al-Ḳāsim b. 'Īsā (J. Bencheikh). Abū Dulaf's contingent of volunteers from lower Iraq would be mainly Arabs, and there seems in fact to have been hostility between him, as a representative of Arab influence at the caliphal court, and the Iranian al-Afshīn; see further Ṭabarī, III, 1308 (p. 186 and n. 529, below).

177. Strict grammar requires *jānib al-wādī dhālika*, rather than *dhālika jānib al-wādī*, as given in the text; the variant in n. *1*, from two of the manuscripts,

They kept close to it (i.e., to the side of the valley), marked out tracks up it, and almost climbed to its top and entered the town. Jaʿfar sent a message to al-Afshīn, "Send me reinforcements of 500 foot soldiers, archers, for I hope to enter al-Badhdh, if God wills, and I do not see facing me more than this single squadron of troops that you yourself can see," meaning Ādhīn's squadron. But al-Afshīn sent back the reply, "You have already ruined my
[1207] intended plan, so extricate yourself little by little and save your troops, and come back." Clamor broke out among the volunteers when they came up against al-Badhdh. The Khurramī troops whom Bābak had sent out to man the ambushes thought that the battle had become firmly interlocked so they rushed forward and rose from under the Bukhārā-khudāh's force, while another group of ambushers rose up from beyond the rocky tract where al-Afshīn had been sitting. The Khurramiyyah rushed around, while the troops stationed above them made no move, for al-Afshīn commented, "Praise be to God Who has revealed to us the enemy's places!"

Then Jaʿfar and his troops and the volunteers returned, and he went to al-Afshīn and told him, "My master the Commander of the Faithful sent me solely to the military compaign that you see and did not send me to sit down here. You hindered me in the very hour of my need—a mere 500 foot soldiers would have been sufficient for me to enter al-Badhdh or to penetrate into Bābak's residence [there], for I had perceived what forces lay before me." Al-Afshīn answered him, "Don't look at what lies before you; just look at what is behind you and at how they launched an assault on the Bukhārā-khudāh and his men." Al-Faḍl b. Kāwūs said to Jaʿfar al-Khayyāṭ, "If the decision had been yours, you wouldn't have been able to get up to this place where you are now standing so that you might say, 'I would have done this' or 'I would have done that'!" Jaʿfar replied to him, "[You call] this war, when here we are standing waiting for whoever may come!" Al-Faḍl told him, "If this were not the Amīr's council, I would teach you on the spot how to behave!" but al-Afshīn called out to them both, and they desisted.

---

leads one to suspect that the correct reading is probably *dhālika al-jānib li-al-wādī*, though it would make no difference to the essential meaning.

Al-Afshīn ordered Abū Dulaf to recall the volunteers from the wall (i.e., of al-Badhdh); hence Abū Dulaf said to them, "Come back!" But one of the volunteers came back bearing a stone and [1208]
said, "Are you going to send us back now? I have taken this stone from the town wall!" But Abū Dulaf told him, "Return instantly, and when you get back you will realize who is straddling your road (i.e., your way of retreat)," meaning by this the force [of the Khurramiyyah] that had leaped upon the Bukhārā-khudāh from behind the [Muslim] troops.

Then al-Afshīn said to Abū Saʿīd in Jaʿfar's presence, "May God grant you a goodly recompense, both on your own account and on behalf of the Commander of the Faithful! I never knew that you were so knowledgeable about matters concerning those troops and their management! And does not every person old enough to shave his head say that halting in a place that he needs is better than giving battle in a place that he does not need? If those of the enemy who were beneath you had risen up"—and he pointed to those in the ambush below the mountain—"what do you think would have been the state of these volunteers, who have what beats under their shirts (i.e., who are far from stout-hearted)? What would have been their condition, and who would have got them together again? Praise be to God, Who has delivered them safely! Now wait here and do not move until no one is left here."

Al-Afshīn went back, and it was his custom when preparing to return that the flag of the squadrons, his cavalrymen, and his foot soldiers should be lowered, while the last squadron would wait, so that between him and it was the distance of an arrow shot. He would not go near the mountain slope or the defile until he could see that all the men in the squadron in front of him had passed through and the road was then clear for him. After that he would approach and would go down with his cavalrymen and his foot soldiers, together with the last squadron, and would continue thus. He had previously instructed each squadron behind whom it was to return and [had instructed them] that not a single man was to go on ahead of his companions or dawdle behind. This was to be the procedure until all the squadrons had passed through and no one remained behind except the Bukhārā-khudāh; then [1209]
the Bukhārā-khudāh himself was to go down, abandoning the mountain slope. On that day the Bukhārā-khudāh went back in

this same manner; Abū Saʿīd was the last to return, and, whenever the troops passed by the place where the Bukhārā-khudāh was stationed and saw the spot where the ambushers were concealed, they realized what was in store for them. Then those of the indigenous population (*al-aʿlāj*) who wanted to capture the place that the Bukhārā-khudāh was holding dispersed and returned to their positions.

Al-Afshīn remained in his trench at Rūdh al-Rūdh for several days. At that point the volunteers complained to him about their straitened circumstances in regard to fodder, provisions, and living expenses (*nafaqāt*).[178] He answered them, "Whoever of you endures patiently, let him endure patiently, and whoever cannot endure, well, the road is wide open, so let him go back in peace. I have with me the Commander of the Faithful's army (*jund*), and those who are in receipt of regular pay allowances (*arzāq*)[179] from him will stay with me in heat and cold; I am not going to leave this place until the snow falls."

The volunteers went back but were murmuring among themselves, "If only al-Afshīn had left Jaʿfar and us alone, we would have captured al-Badhdh; this man wants only to procrastinate." This talk, and all the other lengthy words of the volunteers, reached al-Afshīn. They bandied these words around with their tongues and asserted that al-Afshīn did not want to march out

---

178. Volunteers, as noted, p. 37 n. 136, above, were not paid regular salaries by the *dīwān al-jaysh* (cf. n. 179, below) but attached themselves to the regular forces, either from motives of religious enthusiasm (hence as *ghuzāt* or *mujāhidūn*) or from sheer love of plunder (see Levy, *op. cit.*, 414–15. Both motives were doubtless present in the volunteer element of al-Afshīn's forces, and both may have contributed to the disenchantment and impatience with al-Afshīn's cautious generalship expressed here. The problems of supplying themselves with food and other necessities were beginning to outweigh the prospects of martyrdom fighting the infidel Bābak or, more probably, the hopes of finding rich plunder within al-Badhdh. Hence, as appears below, faced with the onset of winter and no immediate prospect of victory, some of the volunteers were starting to melt away homeward. In general, keeping an army together in the field for a long period was as much a problem for medieval Islamic commanders as for their medieval Christian counterparts.

179. The regular soldiers, those in receipt of salaries (*rizq/razqah*, *ʿaṭāʾ*), were accordingly known as *murtaziqah*. On such terms as *jund* and *razqah*, see W. Hoernerbach, "Zur Heeresverwaltung der ʿAbbāsiden," 278 ff.; Levy, *op. cit.*, 414–15; Bosworth, "Abū ʿAbdallāh al-Khwārazmī," 144–45; *EI*², s.v. Djaysh. i. Classical (Cl. Cahen).

against the enemy but only wanted to prolong matters as far as possible, until one of them stated that he had seen in a dream the Messenger of God, who said to him, "Tell al-Afshīn, 'If you make war on this fellow (Bābak) and exert yourself in hunting him down, [then well and good!]. But if not, I will order the mountains to rain down stones on you!'" As a result, the troops talked about that openly in the encampment, as if the man who had seen the dream had been divinely inspired (*mastūr*).[180]

[When he learned of this,] al-Afshīn sent a message to the leaders of the volunteers and had them brought before him. He told them, "I would like you to show me this man, for people see in dreams remedies and solutions to problems (*abwāb*)."[181] So they brought the man to him, together with a group of other people. Al-Afshīn greeted him, put him at his ease, and brought him near, saying to him, "Tell me your dream; don't be [1210]
embarrassed or ashamed, but just relate it." The man said, "I saw in my dream so-and-so and so-and-so." Al-Afshīn replied, "God knows everything before anyone else and [knows] what is wanted of these people. If God, He is blessed and exalted, wanted to command the mountains to pelt anyone [with stones], then He would pelt the unbeliever (Bābak) and relieve us of the trouble of dealing with him. How could He stone me and thereby allow me to relieve Him of the trouble of dealing with the unbeliever? [On the contrary, if He wanted to stone anyone,] He would be stoning Bābak and would not need me to make war on him! I know that nothing is concealed from God, He is mighty and exalted, and that He is the One who knows the secrets of my heart and what I intend to do with you, O wretches!"

One of the volunteers, who had a reputation for piety, said, "O Amīr, do not deprive us of [a chance of] martyrdom, if an opportunity for it has now come to hand! We only intended and sought God's reward and His favor. So leave us alone until we can advance, after receiving your permission, and it may be that God will grant us the victory." Al-Afshīn replied, "Indeed, I perceive

180. Literally, "veiled," but here in the sense of "humble, self-deprecating, hidden from public view" > "pious, ascetic, having outstanding spiritual gifts." See *Glossarium*, CCLXXXVI; Dozy, *Supplément*, I, 633.

181. For this sense of *bāb*, see *Glossarium*, CXLIV.

that the object of your intention is now close at hand, and I believe that God does in fact desire this course of action and that it will be successful, if He so wills. You and the rest of the troops have now an intense desire for engaging battle. God knows best that this was not my original view, but it has now at this point become that after hearing your words. I hope that He desires this course of action and that it will be successful. Go forth, with God's blessing, on whichever day you think best, so that we may rise up and assail them. There is no strength and no power except through God!"

The soldiers went away rejoicing and passed on the good news to their comrades. Those who had wanted to go back remained, and those who were still in the vicinity, having actually gone back some days' distance [only] but who then heard about the decision, now returned. Al-Afshīn named an appointed day to the troops and ordered the regular troops (*al-jund*), the cavalry, the infantry, and all the other warriors to get ready; and he made it
[1211] clear that he was intending to fight, without any doubt. He set out bearing money and provisions; not a mule remained in the encampment that did not carry a litter for transporting the wounded. He brought with him physicians and supplies of biscuit, *sawīq*, etc., and everything that he might possibly need. The troops moved forward slowly until they went up to al-Badhdh,[182] leaving the Bukhārā-khudāh in the position on the mountain slope where he had previously stationed him. Then the leather mat was spread out and the seat set up for him, and he seated himself on it, as was his wont.

He said to Abū Dulaf, "Tell the volunteers to concentrate their efforts and confine themselves to whatever sector is easiest for them," and he said to Jaʿfar, "You have the whole army at your disposal, including the archers and the naphtha throwers (*al-naffāṭūn*);[183] and if you need extra men, I will transfer them to you. So take all necessary items and whatever you need, and go

182. According to Yaʿqūbī, *Ta'rīkh*, II, 578, this slow advance (verb *zaḥafa*) took place on Thursday, the ninth of Ramaḍān (August 15, 837).

183. On these troops, also called *zarrāqūn* "those who hurl, throw (missiles)," see Levy, *op. cit.*, 439; *EI*², s.vv. Bārūd. i. General (G. S. Colin), Ḥiṣār. iii. Persia (C. E. Bosworth).

forth, with God's blessing! Proceed to any place (i.e., in the battle front) you choose." Ja'far replied, "I intend to make for the place where I was before." Al-Afshīn said, "Make your way there, then." He summoned Abū Sa'īd and said to him, "Stay here with me, you and all your troops, and don't let any one of you leave!" He summoned Aḥmad b. al-Khalīl and said to him, "You and your troops stay here, and let Ja'far and all the men with him cross. If he requires any more [foot] soldiers or cavalry, we will assist him with these reinforcements and send them to him." He now sent forward Abū Dulaf and his troops, comprising the volunteers, and they dropped down into the valley and then went up to the walls of al-Badhdh from the place where they had gone up to them on that previous occasion and took up a position against the wall, just as they had done on that day.

Ja'far launched an attack until he reached right up against the gate of al-Badhdh, exactly as he had done on that first occasion. [1212] He halted there, and the unbelievers held him up for a substantial while. So al-Afshīn sent a man with a purse (*badrah*)[184] of dīnārs, saying to him, "Go to Ja'far's men and ask who was in the van of the battle, and then pour out a handful of coins for him." He handed over a second purse to another one of his men, telling him, "Go to the volunteers, taking with you this money, neck chains, and bracelets (*aṭwāq wa-aswirah*),[185] and tell Abū Dulaf to reward each of the volunteers and the others whom he sees fighting well." Then he summoned the chief cellarer (*ṣāḥib al-sharāb*)[186] and said to him, "Go and take up a position with the troops in the midst of the fray so that I can see you with my own eyes, and take with you *sawīq* and water in case the troops become thirsty and have to return." He did likewise regarding water and *sawīq* for Ja'far's troops. Then he summoned the

184. Conventionally a *badrah* contained 10,000 dirhams.

185. Gold neck chains and arm bracelets were often conferred, together with robes of honor (*khila'*), on successful commanders. See Hilāl al-Ṣābi', *op. cit.*, 93–94, trans., 75–76; Mez, *op. cit.*, 131 n. 2, trans., 133 n. 1; Sourdel, "Questions de cérémonial," 143.

186. Cellarers, in charge of the provision of wine and drinking vessels, were employed by private individuals (see Mez, *op. cit.*, 376–77, trans., 398). The post of cellarer to the Caliph at this time was held by a high-ranking Turkish slave commander; slightly later it was held by Bughā al-Ṣaghīr, also called al-Sharābī (see *EI*[2], s.v. Bu<u>gh</u>ā al-Ṣa<u>gh</u>īr [D. Sourdel]).

commander of the pioneer and labor corps (*ṣāḥib al-kilghariyyah*), instructing him, "Whichever person of the volunteers whom you see in the thick of the fighting, with a battle-ax in his hand, will get fifty dirhams from me," and he handed over to him a purse of dirhams. He did likewise for Jaʿfar's troops and sent to them the pioneer and labor corps, with their battle-axes in their hands. He also sent to Jaʿfar a chest containing neck chains and bracelets and told him, "Hand over these to whomever you wish of your troops, this being in addition to what they are due to receive from me (i.e., their regular pay) and the increased amount of pay allowances that they have been guaranteed from me, plus the letters (i.e., of commendation for bravery) containing their names that are to be sent to the Commander of the Faithful."

For a long while the battle at the gate was closely interlocked. Then the Khurramiyyah opened the gate to sally forth to attack
[1213] Jaʿfar's men and pushed them back from the gate. They also assailed the volunteers from another quarter; they captured two of their standards, hurled the volunteers back from the walls, and inflicted wounds on them with rocks to the point that they made appreciable marks on the Muslims, so that the latter were unable to sustain the fighting and had to stop. Jaʿfar cried out to his men, and about a hundred of them rushed forward and knelt behind the shields with which they were equipped, halting up against the enemy, with both sides refraining from fighting, neither side advancing upon the other. They continued like that until the [Muslim] troops performed the noon worship.

Al-Afshīn had brought up ballistas (*ʿarrādāt*)[187] and he set one of these up near Jaʿfar at the gate and another on the side of the valley in the vicinity of the volunteers. Jaʿfar fought to defend the ballista that was near him, the ballista being in the area between the two opposing sides for a lengthy period; but then Jaʿfar's troops got it free after strenuous efforts, dragged it away, and brought it back into their own camp. The troops on both sides

187. In antiquity the ballista (Greek *onagros*) was a kind of torsion artillery and probably tension artillery also. In Islam the *ʿarrādah* was generally a smaller instrument than the *manjanīq* (though the terms seem at times to have been interchangeable), and until the Crusading period they were of the beam-operated traction type, the trebuchet. See *EI*², s.vv. ʿArrāda (Cl. Cahen), Mandjanīḳ (D. R. Hill).

continued in positions against each other, refraining from (hand-to-hand) fighting, but with arrows and stones flying to and fro between them, Bābak's troops being on the walls and at the gate and Jaʿfar's hundred warriors sheltering beneath their shields. Then later the two sides fought with each other.

When al-Afshīn observed that, he feared lest the enemy become emboldened against his troops. So he sent on ahead the foot soldiers whom he had marshaled, and they took up their stand in the same place as the volunteers. He sent to Jaʿfar a squadron containing infantrymen, but Jaʿfar said, "I have not been adversely affected by shortage of men; I have ample troops[188] with me, but I don't discern any place where they can advance and fight. Here there is space only for one or two men to maneuver. They have been reduced to a standstill in this spot, [1214] and fighting has ceased." [On hearing that,] al-Afshīn sent a message to him, "Return, with God's blessing"; hence Jaʿfar returned.

Al-Afshīn sent the mules that he had brought with him, with litters on their backs, and the wounded and those incapacitated by the stones and unable to walk were placed on them. He ordered the troops to turn back, so they returned to their trench at Rūdh al-Rūdh. The troops despaired of victory in that year, and the greater part of the volunteers departed.

Two weeks later al-Afshīn got his forces ready. When it was the middle of the night he aroused the infantrymen archers, amounting to about 1,000 men, and to each one of them he gave a waterskin and some biscuit, while to some of them he gave black banners and such things. He dispatched them at sundown, sending guides with them. They traveled all the night through unknown, difficult mountains, avoiding the roads, until they made their way round and came up behind the hill on which Ādhīn was stationed, this being [in fact] a lofty mountain. Al-Afshīn ordered them not to let their presence be known to anyone until they saw al-Afshīn's banners, had performed the morning worship, and had seen battle raging; then they were to mount those banners on their spears, beat the drums, go down from above the mountain, and hurl arrows and rocks at the

188. *Rijāl firah*; the Cairo edition, IX, 41, has *rijāl furh* "skilled troops."

Khurramiyyah. If, however, they did not see al-Afshīn's banners, they were not to move until information from him reached them.

They did that and reached the crest of the mountain at daybreak; they had filled those waterskins with water from the wadi and had traveled to the top of the mountain. When a certain night came round, al-Afshīn sent a message to his commanders that they were to get ready with their weapons, for he himself intended to ride out at dawn. At some point in the night he sent
[1215] Bashīr al-Turkī and several commanders from the Farghānan troops[189] who were with him and ordered them to move onward until they reached the point below the hill in the lowest part of the wadi from which they had carried away their water, this spot being below the mountain where Ādhīn was. Al-Afshīn had previously become aware that the unbelievers hid in ambush below that mountain whenever troops approached it. Bashīr and the Farghānan troops made for that place, where he knew that the Khurramiyyah had a force lying in ambush. Bashīr and his troops traveled through part of the night, with the greater part of the troops in the camp being unaware of their movement. Then Bashīr sent word to his commanders that they were to get ready for riding forth with their weapons because the Amīr was going to thrust forward at daybreak.

Accordingly, when daybreak came, al-Afshīn sallied forth, taking with him the troops, naphtha throwers (*al-naffāṭīn*),[190] naphtha-hurling weapons (*al-naffāṭāt*), and torches (*al-shamʿ*, literally "wax candles"), just as he had previously done. He performed the dawn worship, and he beat the drum and rode out until he reached the place where he used to halt each time, and the leather mat was spread out for him and his seat set out for him, as was his usual practice.

The Bukhārā-khudāh was meanwhile waiting on the mountain slopes where he used to have his position each day. But on that

---

189. I.e., from the region of Farghānah, the valley of the upper Syr Darya or Jaxartes, the later khanate of Khokand. See Yāqūt, *Muʿjam*, IV, 253; Le Strange, *Lands*, 447–80; Barthold, *Turkestan*, 155–65; for the Farghānan troops in the caliphal service, see p. 49 n. 159, above.

190. Here *naffāṭ* is used as military term; in a civilian context it denotes a person concerned with the processing or refining of petroleum. See Goitein, *op. cit.*, 85.

particular day al-Afshīn sent the Bukhārā-khudāh forward in the vanguard with Abū Saʿīd, Jaʿfar al-Khayyāṭ, and Aḥmad b. al-Khalīl. The troops were unfamiliar with this battle formation at that time, and al-Afshīn ordered them to approach the hill where Ādhīn was, in order to encircle it, although previous to that particular day he had been forbidding them to do so. The troops went onward, led by these four commanders named above until they surrounded the hill. Jaʿfar al-Khayyāṭ was near the gateway of al-Badhdh, Abū Saʿīd was next to him, the Bukhārā-khudāh was next to Abū Saʿīd, and Aḥmad b. al-Khalīl b. Hishām was next to the Bukhārā-khudāh. They came together in an encircling formation round the hill, and the confusion and uproar from the lower part of the valley was great. The troops hidden in [1216]
ambush below the hill where Ādhīn was stationed had suddenly leaped out upon Bashīr al-Turkī and the Farghānan troops. They fought with them for some time, and the conflict became confused. The troops in the [Muslims] camp heard the uproar and became stirred up for action, so al-Afshīn ordered his heralds to proclaim, "O troops, this is Bashīr al-Turkī and the men of Farghānah whom I sent on ahead, and they have as a result stirred up an enemy ambush [into showing their position], so do not get overexcited!"

When the infantrymen archers who had advanced to the crest of the mountain heard this, they raised the banners just as al-Afshīn had commanded them. The troops then saw banners coming from a lofty mountain, black banners, there being about a farsakh between the army and the mountain. They themselves were descending Ādhīn's mountain from above Ādhīn's forces, since the banners had been raised, and began to go down with the aim of attacking Ādhīn. When the soldiers in Ādhīn's army spied them, Ādhīn sent some of the Khurramī infantrymen who were with him against the enemy. When the Muslim troops saw them, they filled them with fear, but al-Afshīn sent a message to the Muslim troops, saying, "Those [descending the mountain] are our own troops, who will reinforce us in the struggle against Ādhīn." With that, Jaʿfar al-Khayyāṭ and his men attacked Ādhīn and his followers until they advanced right up to them. But then Ādhīn's forces mounted a strong counterattack against the Muslims and hurled Jaʿfar and his men back down to the valley. A man who

was one of those fighting in the vicinity of Abū Saʿīd, one of his own warriors called Muʿādh b. Muḥammad or Muḥammad b. Muʿādh, then led a further assault on the Khurramiyyah with a band of troops, but behold, beneath their horses' hooves pits had been dug out (i.e., by the Khurramiyyah), into which the horses' forelegs stumbled, so that Abū Saʿīd's cavalrymen fell into them
[1217] one after the other. At that point al-Afshīn sent the pioneers and labor corps to prise out [the stones from] the walls of their dwelling places[191] and to fill up those pits with them, which they did, and then the Muslim troops made a concerted attack on the Khurramiyyah. Ādhīn had got ready on the mountaintops carts (or trolleys, *ʿajal*) loaded with rocks, and when the Muslim troops attacked him he pushed the carts toward them and released them onto the troops so that they rolled down. Then the troops attacked from every side.

When Bābak saw that his followers had been surrounded, he left al-Badhdh by means of the gate nearest to al-Afshīn—there being a mile's distance between this gate and the hill on which al-Afshīn was—and approached, accompanied by a band of his partisans, inquiring for al-Afshīn.[192] Abū Dulaf's followers demanded, "Who is this?" They replied, "This is Bābak seeking al-Afshīn." Abū Dulaf sent word to al-Afshīn, informing him of that, who thereupon dispatched a man who knew Bābak. This man looked at Bābak, returned to al-Afshīn, and told him, "Yes, he is indeed Bābak!" Hence al-Afshīn rode off to where he could have speech with Bābak and his companions; meanwhile, the battle had become confused and interlocked in Ādhīn's sector of the front. Bābak said to al-Afshīn, "I seek a safe-conduct from the Commander of the Faithful." Al-Afshīn replied, "I have already offered you this, and it is available whenever you want it."[193] Bābak said, "I want it now, on condition that you allow me a

191. Presumably of the rough shelters that the Muslim troops had constructed within their lines.

192. According to Dīnawarī, *op. cit.*, 404, Bābak first sent a representative, one Mūsā al-Aqṭaʿ, to inquire about the possibility of a meeting.

193. As Marin notes, Ṭabarī, trans. Marin, 43 n. 208, these words and what follows seem to point to some previous communication between al-Afshīn and Bābak, as also hinted at in correspondence adduced in al-Afshīn's subsequent trial ("I exerted myself to avert death from him," Ṭabarī, III, 1311; p. 191, below); cf. Sadighi, *op. cit.*, 260, 293. Yaʿqūbī, *Taʾrīkh, II*, 579, regards Bābak's approaches and

period of time in which I can get together mounts for my household and equip myself for traveling." Al-Afshīn told him, "By God, I have already given you advice more than once, but you didn't take my advice; I am now giving you up-to-the-moment advice—it is better for you to come forth today with your safe-conduct than tomorrow!" He answered, "O Amīr, I accept this and will follow this course [forthwith]!" Al-Afshīn then said to him, "Now send the hostages about whom I asked you [1218] previously." He replied, "Yes, but so-and-so and so-and-so are on that hill (i.e., where Ādhīn was fighting), so order your troops to hold back."

He related: Al-Afshīn's envoy went to bring the troops back and was told that the banners of the Farghānan troops had already entered al-Badhdh and that the troops had scaled the strongholds there. He therefore rode on, shouting to the troops [to follow him]. Then he entered, and they entered, too, and the troops went up with their banners over Bābak's strongholds. However, Bābak had set ambushes in his strongholds—there being four of these—the men in ambush totaling 600, and the Muslim troops encountered them. They climbed to the tops of the fortresses with the banners, and the streets and public square of al-Badhdh were thronged with people. Those partisans of Bābak lying in ambush threw open the gates of the fortresses, and foot soldiers poured forth, combating the Muslim troops. Meanwhile, Bābak traveled onward until he came to the valley near Hashtādsar.

Al-Afshīn and all his commanders were fully occupied with the fighting at the gates of the fortresses, and the Khurramiyyah fought on strenuously. He brought up the naphtha throwers, and they began to pour naphtha and fire over the Khurramiyyah, while the troops were pulling down the fortresses until the Khurramī soldiers were killed to the last man. Al-Afshīn took captive Bābak's children and those members of their families who were with them in al-Badhdh.[194] Finally, evening came on, so

---

seeking of *amān* here as simply procrastinating measures so that he could fortify al-Badhdh more securely against the Muslims.

194. According to Yāqūt, *Irshād*, I, 369, al-Muʿtaṣim subsequently had in his harem a daughter of Bābak's, together with daughters of Māzyār and the *patricius* of ʿAmmūriyyah, or Amorion, Yaʿqūbī, *Taʾrīkh*, II, 579, states that al-Afshīn's forces released 7,600 Muslim captives from al-Badhdh.

al-Afshīn gave orders for the return, so the troops returned [to their camp], all the [survivors of the] Khurramiyyah being [still] in their houses. Al-Afshīn himself returned to the defensive trench at Rūdh al-Rūdh.[195]

It has been mentioned that, when Bābak and those followers of his who had gone with him into the valley learned that al-Afshīn had returned to his defensive trench, they returned to al-Badhdh. They carried off all the travel provisions they could transport and bore away their personal possesions; then they went into the valley near Hashtādsar. The next morning al-Afshīn set out until he reentered al-Badhdh. He halted in the town; he ordered the
[1219] fortresses to be demolished and sent foot soldiers to patrol the outer fringes of the town, but they did not find there a single member of the indigenous population (*al-ʿulūj*). He sent up the pioneer and labor corps, and they pulled down and set fire to the fortresses, spending three days on that until he had destroyed by fire Bābak's treasuries and fortresses. He did not leave a single house or fortress in al-Badhdh without burning down or demolishing it.[196] After that al-Afshīn went back and learned that Bābak had slipped away with a group of his followers. Hence he wrote to the rulers of Armenia and its local princes (*baṭāriqihā*),[197] informing them, "Bābak, together with a number of his partisans, has fled and has gone to a certain valley, and from there has set out in the direction of Armenia and will pass by you." He ordered each one of them to guard his own district

195. Yaʿqūbī, *Taʾrīkh*, II, 578–79; Dīnawarī, *op. cit.*, 403–4; Masʿūdī, *Murūj*, VII, 123–24 = par. 2806; Ṭabarī, trans. Balʿamī, IV, 533–39; Azdī, *op. cit.*, 425; *Kitāb al-ʿuyūn*, 385–87; Niẓām al-Mulk, *op. cit.*, 293–95, trans., 234–35; Ibn al-Athīr, *op. cit.*, VI, 462–71; Sadighi, *op. cit.*, 256–61; E. M. Wright, *op. cit.*, 51–52; B. Spuler, *Iran in früh-islamischer Zeit*, 61–63; Nafīsī, *Bābak-i Khurramdīn*, 109–17; Kennedy, *op. cit.*, 166.

196. The poetic eulogies on al-Afshīn's victory (by Abū Tammām, al-Buḥturī, and al-Ḥusayn b. al-Ḍaḥḥāk, the verses of the last being given by Ṭabarī at III, 1256 [pp. 120–21, below]), imply that the Khurramī population of al-Badhdh, or that part of it that had not yet fled, was massacred en bloc. Haq notes (*op. cit.*, 23) that this particular author refers in his verses not only to the final capitulation of al-Badhdh but also to various other skirmishes and engagements of the previous two years not apparently mentioned by Ṭabarī.

197. *Baṭrīq/biṭrīq* is the normal Arabic rendering of the Byzantine title *patricius*; see Bosworth, "Al-Khwārazmī," 30–32. Here it is used for the Christian princes of Armenia, who could be considered equivalent in status and rank to the Byzantine nobles and generals bearing the title *patricius*.

carefully and not to let anyone travel through it without first seizing him and ascertaining his identity.

Spies came to al-Afshīn and informed him of Bābak's hiding place in valley. It was a valley filled with thick vegetation and trees, with Armenia on one side and Ādharbayjān on the other. Cavalry could not penetrate into it, nor could anyone hiding there be seen on account of the density of its trees and watercourses. It was indeed one big jungle-like thicket, and this valley was in fact called a "thicket" (*ghayḍah*).[198] Al-Afshīn sent to every place to ascertain whether there was any road going down from that place into that thicket or whether [if there were such a road] Bābak could get out by that road. On every road in every locality in those parts he posted a detachment of troops, comprising between 400 and 500 warriors, and he sent with them the mountain guards to provide them with information about the road; and he ordered them to guard the road by night, lest anyone leave by it. At the same time he sent to each one of these detachments of troops provisions from his own army camp. These detachments amounted to fifteen in all.

They remained thus until there arrived a letter from the [1220]
Commander of the Faithful al-Muʿtaṣim, sealed in gold and containing a safe-conduct (*amān*) for Bābak. Thereupon al-Afshīn summoned those [former] partisans of Bābak who had sought protection (*ista'mana*) from him, among whom was one of Bābak's grown-up sons, the eldest of his sons in fact. Al-Afshīn said to him and the other captives, "This is something which I had not expected from the Commander of the Faithful and had not been hopeful of him regarding it, that he should write a safe-conduct for Bābak when the latter is in this present situation.[199] Now which of you will take it and convey it to Bābak?" But none of them dared to undertake it, and one of them protested, "O Amīr, none of us would venture to confront him with this!" "Woe to you," al-Afshīn answered him, "surely he will rejoice at this?" The man replied, "May God guide the Amīr

198. Presumably this was part of the low-lying Kur valley.

199. Following here the suggested translation of H. Ritter, "Autographs," 158, which makes unnecessary Marin's surmise, Ṭabarī, trans. Marin, 45 n. 213a, that al-Afshīn was alarmed at the arrival of the Caliph's safe-conduct, in the light of his own previous connivance at Bābak's escape.

in an upright way! We know better than you about this matter." Al-Afshīn said, "Even so, you must ineluctably submit yourselves to me completely and must deliver this letter to him."

At that, two men from among them got up and said to him, "Give us a guarantee that you will provide for our families"[200] (i.e., if anything unpleasant should happen to us), so al-Afshīn gave them the required guarantee. The two men took the letter, set out, and kept on going round in the thicket until they came upon Bābak. Bābak's son sent a letter [also] with the two envoys, informing him of the new situation and asking him to come back and take up the safe-conduct, for this would be the safest and best course for him.

The two men delivered to Bābak his son's letter, which he read. Then he said, "What have you been doing?" They replied, "Our families and children were taken captive on that night, and we did not know where you were in order that we might join you. We were in a place where we feared that they would capture us, so we sought a guarantee of protection." Bābak said to the man who had brought the letter, "I know nothing of this. But you, O son of a whore, how have you dared to do this, to come to me from that son of a whore," and he seized the man, cut off his head, and fastened the (caliph's) letter to his breast, still sealed, never having broken the seal. Then he said to the other man, "Go and
[1221] ask that son of a whore"—he meant his own son—"how it is that he writes to me thus?" And he wrote back to him in these terms, "If you were to join up with me and follow in the way of the movement to which you belong (*daʿwataka*, i.e., the movement of the Khurramiyyah) until one day you succeeded to power, you would indeed be my son, but at this point I am certain about the corruption of your mother, the whore. O son of a whore, it may be that I shall live [a long time] after this, but it will have been as one bearing the name of this ruling position, and, wherever I am or wherever I am spoken of, it will be as a king. You [on the other hand] come from a stock that is devoid of good characteristics, and I bear witness that you are no son of mine, for it is better to live for just a single day as a ruler than to live for forty years as an abject slave." With that, he left his place of concealment and sent

200. Following *Addenda et emendanda*, DCCLXXIII, *tujrī ʿalā ʿiyālātinā.*

three men with al-Afshīn's envoy to escort him up to a certain spot. Then they rejoined Bābak.

Bābak remained in that thicket until his provisions were exhausted, and then he went out at a place adjoining a road on which some troops were stationed on guard. The place where this road ran was a mountain devoid of water; hence the detachment of troops was unable to stay on the road because of its distance from water and had to turn away from the road to a spot near which water was available. They had, however, stationed two mountain guards and two cavalrymen at the side of the road to guard it, there being about a mile and a half between the road and the main body of troops. Each day two cavalrymen and two mountain guards took turns in patrolling the road. One day, around midday, they were engaged on this duty when Bābak and his companions came forth; they saw no one and did not observe the two cavalrymen and the two mountain guards and imagined that there were no troops there. Accordingly, Bābak and his two brothers ʿAbdallāh and Muʿāwiyah,[201] together with his mother and one of his wives called Ibnat al-Kalandāniyyah, set out. The whole group went forth, leaving the road and heading for [1222]
Armenia.

The two cavalrymen and the two mountain guards saw them and sent a message to the main body of troops, which was under the command of Abū al-Sāj,[202] "We saw a group of horsemen passing by, but we do not know who they are." The troops thereupon mounted and rode off and observed them (Bābak's party) from afar, Bābak's group having halted at a spring of water to eat their midday meal. When they spotted the Muslim troops the unbelievers rose up in great haste. Bābak and those with him rode off and managed to escape, but Muʿāwiyah, Bābak's mother, and the wife who was with him were captured. One of Bābak's

---

201. Somewhat surprisingly, the Islamic names of Bābak's brothers are used here. We learn Bābak's own one, al-Ḥasan, only from Masʿūdī, *Murūj*, VII, = par. 2812 (given in several manuscripts as al-Ḥusayn).

202. I.e., Abū al-Sāj Dīwdād b. Yūsuf Dīwdast, an Iranian commander from the Transoxanian region (in fact, like al-Afshīn himself, from Ushrūsanah), who subsequently served the caliphs in various governorships until his death in 266 (879–80); his sons Muḥammad and Yūsuf became governors of Ādharbayjān and Armenia and founded a virtually autonomous short-lived ruling line there. See Madelung, "Minor Dynasties," 228–32; *EI*[1], s.v. Sādjids (Cl. Huart).

slave retainers (*ghulām*) escaped with him also. Abū al-Sāj sent Muʿāwiyah and the two women back to his army camp. Bābak pressed onward in the direction that he intended until he came to the mountains of Armenia,[203] traveling through them clandestinely. He was in urgent need of food, but all the Armenian nobles had set watchmen and guards over their neighborhoods and outlying districts and had instructed their guard posts (*masāliḥ*) not to let anyone pass without seizing him so that they might establish his identity. Hence all the guard-post commanders were on the alert.

Bābak was stricken with hunger. He looked down from an eminence and noticed a ploughman ploughing one of his acres (*faddān*)[204] in a certain valley, so he said to his slave retainer, "Go down to this ploughman and take with you dīnārs and dirhams, and if he has bread with him take it and give him the money (i.e., in exchange)." The ploughman had a companion who had gone aside to fulfill a need of nature. The slave went down to the ploughman, and the latter's companion observed him from a distance; he stood there apart, waiting, fearful of the slave's going up to his companion and watching what his companion would do. The slave handed something over to the ploughman; the ploughman came forward and, taking some bread, handed it over to the slave. His companion was meanwhile standing there watching him and imagined that the slave had seized the bread from the ploughman by force, not realizing that he had given the ploughman something in return. He ran off to the guard post and told them that a man bearing a sword and weapons had come to them and that he had taken the bread of his companion who was in the valley.

The commander of the guard post rode out, and, as this was in
[1223] the mountains of Ibn Sunbāṭ, he sent information about this to
Sahl b. Sunbāṭ,[205] who thereupon rode off in haste, with a group

---

203. As Bābak later entered the territory of Sahl b. Sunbāṭ, he must have been heading northwest toward the upper reaches of the Kur River in the Western part of the modern Azerbaijan Soviet Socialist Republic; see n. 205, below.

204. In medieval times this measurement of area was around 6,000–6,400 square meters. See Hinz, *op. cit.*, 65; *EI*[1], s.v. Faddān (Cl. Huart); *EI*[2], s.v. Misāḥa. 1. In the Central Islamic Lands (C. E. Bosworth).

205. Sahl b. Sunbāṭ (Armenian Smbat), from a local Armenian family of eastern Transcaucasia, lord of Shakkī (Shakʿē) to the north of the upper reaches of the Kur

of his retainers, until he came to him. When he reached the ploughman, the slave was still with him, and he said to the man, "What's happening here?" The ploughman replied, "This is a person who was passing by me and asked me for bread, so I gave him some." Ibn Sunbāṭ thereupon said to the slave, "Where is your master?" and he replied, "Over there," inclining his head in the direction of Bābak. Ibn Sunbāṭ followed him and came up with Bābak, who was descending [the mountain]. When he saw his face, he recognized him. Ibn Sunbāṭ dismounted from his horse in deference to Bābak and drew near to him on foot, kissing his band. Then he said to him, "Alas, my lord, where are you heading?" Bābak replied, "I am heading for the Byzantine lands," or some other place that he named. Ibn Sunbāṭ said, "You will not find any place or any person who is more conscious of your rights or more deserving that you should stay with him than myself. You know my position; there is no contact between me and the central power (*al-sulṭān*, i.e., the central power of Islam, meaning the caliphate), and you will not be coming into the presence of one of that power's adherents. You are well acquainted with my personal affairs, my country, and all the local princes here; indeed, they are people of your own house, for sons have come to you by them!" By that he meant that, whenever Bābak learned of a beautiful daughter or sister of one of the nobles, he would send a message to that noble, seeking her [in marriage]. If the noble in question sent her to Bābak, [all well and good]; but, if not, Bābak

---

River and an important figure in the affairs of Arrān (Armenian Aɫvan-kʿ, classical Caucasian Albania), is mentioned in both Armenian and Arabic sources; it may be that Ibn Sunbāṭ (Armenian Smbatean) was a family name, rather than a direct patronymic. He came into prominence after 205 (820–21) and was involved in resistance against the Arabs' attempts to extend their influence in Arrān (see p. 78, n. 208, below). Then, after the fall of al-Badhdh, Bābak, hoping for asylum with Sahl, fled north into Arrān by a route that cannot be determined exactly from the vague itinerary in Ṭabarī's account. The two leaders, Sahl and Bābak, shared a common hostility to the Arabs, but in the event Sahl decided to conciliate them and to surrender Bābak, as detailed below. He must have enjoyed the Caliph's favor for about fifteen years, until ca. 238 (852–53), when Bughā al-Kabīr, the new governor of Ādharbayjān and Arrān, is reported in Armenian sources to have deported him, along with many local Armenian princes; in Ṭabarī's list of these deportees (III, 1416), however, it was Sahl's son Muʿāwiyah, "*baṭrīq* of Arrān," who was deported in this group. Ṭabarī (III, 1232 [pp. 89–90, below]) also mentions Muʿāwiyah as having escorted Bābak to al-Afshīn. See Marquart, *Osteuropäische und ostasiatische Streifzüge*, 412–14, 422–23; Minorsky, "Caucasica," 505–10; *EI*[2], s.v. Arrān (R. N. Frye); *EIr*, s.v. Arrān (C. E. Bosworth).

would swoop down on him in a night raid and seize her, together with all the noble's possessions, etc., and take everything back to his own land by force.

Ibn Sunbāṭ then said to Bābak, "Come and stay with me in my fortress, for indeed it is your own house and I am your slave. Spend this winter here and then consider your future course of action." Bābak was suffering from hardship and fatigue, so he relied on Sahl b. Sunbāṭ's words and told him, "It is not good that both myself and my brother should be in the same place, for if anyone should stumble upon one of us, then [if we have separated] the other would be preserved alive; but I will stay here with you and my brother ʿAbdallāh will go to Ibn Iṣṭifānūs,[206] for
[1224] we do not know what might happen, and we have no successor who could then continue to uphold our cause."[207] Ibn Sunbāṭ said to him, "Your sons are many!" But Bābak answered, "There is not one of them who is any good," and he resolved upon sending his brother to Ibn Iṣṭifānūs's fortress, for he trusted him. So at that point he went with Ibn Sunbāṭ to his fortress, and when it was morning ʿAbdallāh proceeded to Ibn Iṣṭifānūs's fortress, while Bābak remained with Ibn Sunbāṭ.

Ibn Sunbāṭ wrote to al-Afshīn, informing him that Bābak was with him in his fortress. Al-Afshīn wrote back to Ibn Sunbāṭ, "If this news is true, then you will have something coming to you from me and from the Commander of the Faithful, may God strengthen him, which you will like very much!" And he wrote promising Ibn Sunbāṭ a handsome recompense. Al-Afshīn gave a description of Bābak to one of his intimates whom he trusted and sent him to Ibn Sunbāṭ, and he wrote to the latter that he had sent to him one of his intimate circle, with the aim that he should see Bābak in order to report back to al-Afshīn (i.e., with the identification).[208]

---

206. The full name of Ibn Iṣṭifānus appears in the list of Armenian princes deported by Bughā al-Kabīr in 238 (852–53; Ṭabarī, III, 1416) as ʿĪsā b. Yūsuf b. Ukht Iṣṭifānus, which Minorsky interpreted as a nephew of Iṣṭifānus (Armenian Step'annos), born to Yūsuf of a sister of Iṣṭifānus. His principality must have lain to the south of the Kur River valley in Arrān; according to Ṭabarī, III, 1232 (p. 90, below), it was in the region of Baylaqān. See Minorsky, "Caucasica," 512–14.

207. Bābak was obviously not wholly certain of Sahl's good faith in offering him shelter.

208. Yaʿqūbī, *Taʾrīkh*, II, 579 (cf. also Balādhurī, *op. cit.*, 211), records that, when al-Afshīn first arrived an Ādharbayjān to take charge of the war against

Ibn Sunbāṭ did not wish to arouse Bābak's suspicions, so he said to the man, "You won't be able to see him except at the times when he is occupied with eating his food. He has his midday meal [with me], so, when you see us calling for the meal, put on the clothes of the cooks in our household, the garb of the indigenous people hereabouts, and come forward as if you were bringing in food or presenting something. He will be preoccupied with the food, and you can look closely at him as much as you want; then go back and report it to your master." The man accordingly did that at the mealtime. At that point Bābak raised his head and looked at him but failed to recognize him, saying, "Who is this man?" Ibn Sunbāṭ answered him, "He is a man from the people of Khurāsān, who came to join us some time ago, a Christian," and [1225]
he made the Ushrūsanī understand what he was saying. Then Bābak said to the man, "How long have you been here?" He replied, "Since the year so-and-so." Bābak said, "How did you come to remain here?" He replied, "I got married here." Bābak exclaimed, "You have spoken truly! When a man is asked, "Where do you come from?' he replies, 'From where my wife comes!"

The man then went back to al-Afshīn with the information and described to him everything that he had seen there of Bābak. Al-Afshīn sent Abū Saʿīd and Būzbārah[209] to Ibn Sunbāṭ with a letter to him and ordered that, when they came to a certain road, they should forward his letter to Ibn Sunbāṭ with one of the indigenous people. He further ordered them not to disobey Ibn Sunbāṭ in whatever instructions he might give them. They did that. Ibn Sunbāṭ wrote to them both, telling them to stay in a certain place, which he named and described to them, until his envoy should come to them. They therefore remained fixed in the location that he had described to them, and Ibn Sunbāṭ sent supplies and provisions to them until Bābak was moved to go forth hunting. Ibn Sunbāṭ said to him, "Here is a valley with sweet and fragrant air, and you are enveloped in care within the

---

Bābak, Sahl had been in revolt in Arrān; al-Afshīn had sent against him the governor whom he had appointed over Armenia, Muḥammad b. Sulaymān al-Azdī al-Samarqandī, but the latter was defeated by Sahl. Sahl's extradition of Bābak may accordingly be viewed as an attempt—successful as it turned out—to regain favor with the caliphal authorities.

209. See p. 47 n. 153, above.

bowels of this fortress! Why don't we go out, taking with us a falcon and sparrow hawk and other necessary equipment, and we'll dispel our cares and divert ourselves till the midday mealtime by hunting." Bābak answered, "Just as you wish."

Ibn Sunbāṭ put this intention into execution, so that they rode out together the next morning. He wrote to Abū Saʿīd and Būzbārah informing them of what he had resolved upon and instructing them to meet him with their military forces, one on one side of the mountain and the other on the other side. [He
[1226] further instructed them] to journey clandestinely at the time of the dawn prayer. Then, when his messenger should come to them, they were to take up a vantage point overlooking the valley, and when they saw them they were to come down into the valley and capture them. When Ibn Sunbāṭ and Bābak rode out the next morning, the former sent a messenger to Abū Saʿīd and another one to Būzbārah, and to each messenger he said, "Take this [group of men] to such-and-such a place, and take this [group of men] to such-and-such a place; then assume a position overlooking us, and, when you see us both, shout 'There they are! Seize them!'" He wished [by means of this stratagem] to throw Bābak into confusion, so that he might say, "This group of cavalrymen has come toward us and will capture us!"—not wanting to hand Bābak over to them [directly] from his own residence.

The two messengers came to Ibn Saʿīd and Būzbārah and proceeded with them until they reached a vantage point over the valley. Lo and behold, there they found themselves in the presence of Bābak and Ibn Sunbāṭ! They looked down at Bābak, and then they and their men descended to him, one from one side and the other from the other side, and seized both of them, together with their sparrow hawks. Bābak was wearing a white *durrāʿah*, a white turban, and short boots and is said to have had a sparrow hawk on his hand. When he saw that the troops had surrounded him, he stopped and looked at the two leaders, who told him, "Dismount!" He replied, "Who are you both?" One of them replied, "I am Abū Saʿīd," and the other replied, "I am Būzbārah." Bābak said, "All right then," bent his leg, and dismounted. Ibn Sunbāṭ was meanwhile watching him. Bābak raised his head toward him and reviled him, saying, "Indeed, you have sold me to the Jews[210] merely for a trifling amount. If you wanted money and had asked me for it, I would have given you much more than these are giving you!" Abū Saʿīd said, "Mount again and ride on!" Bābak replied, "So be it!"

They conveyed him thus and brought him to al-Afshīn. When Bābak drew near to the camp, al-Afshīn went up to Barzand, and a [1227]
tent was pitched for him there. He ordered the troops to form two lines, and he himself sat down within a tent or booth (*fāzah*).[211] They brought in Bābak, and al-Afshīn commanded that they should not let anyone of the Arabs[212] enter between the two lines, out of fear lest someone whose comrades Bābak had killed or upon whom he had wrought great misfortune might kill or wound Bābak. A large number of women and children had already come to al-Afshīn, relating that Bābak had taken them captive and that they were of freeborn status, either from the Arabs or from the (Persian) *dihqāns*. So an extensive enclosure was set aside in which he installed them and issued to them allowances of bread. He instructed them to write to their next of kin, wherever they might be, and he handed them over to anyone who might come along and recognize a woman, a boy, or a girl and then bring forward two witnesses testifying that he really did know them or that they were women of his household or kindred. People came along and took away a large number of them, but a considerable number of them were left behind, still waiting for their relatives.[213]

---

210. I.e., the Muslims; see p. 47 n. 156.

211. This term recurs at III, 1261 (p. 126, below), where it has the sense of a tent or booth within a larger tent or pavilion, as noted in *Glossarium*, CDVIII. This meaning is confirmed by the detailed description in Jahshiyārī, *Kitāb al-wuzarāʾ*, 221, of Hārūn al-Rashīd's encampment at Ṭūs in Khurāsān just before his death there. He held public audience in a large, black-silk tent or pavilion (*miḍrāb*), apparently rectangular, for in the corners there were four canopies or cupolas (*qibāb*), also covered in black silk; the whole tent was 400 *dhirāʿs* around. Within this, the Caliph sat in a black silk *fāzah* in the center of the *miḍrāb*, the supporting columns of which were also black. The rendering "large two-poled tent" in Ṭabarī, trans. Marin, 51 and n. 233, based on Lane, does not therefore seem appropriate. Cf. Sourdel, "Questions de cérémonial," 128.

212. Thus in the text and in that of the Cairo edition, IX, 50. But one could read with ms. C *gharīb*[an] "any stranger" for *ʿarabiyy*[an]; *gharīb*[an] is preferred in Ṭabarī, trans. Marin, 51 nn. 233–34.

213. The restoration of the former captives to their families is referred to by Abū Tammām in his poetry; see Haq, *op. cit.*, 23.

On that day when al-Afshīn ordered the troops to form up in lines, there being a distance of half a mile between him and Bābak, the latter was made to dismount and walk between the two lines in his *durrāʿah,* turban, and boots until he reached al-Afshīn and stood before him. Al-Afshīn scrutinized him and said, "Take him down to the army camp"; so they rode down with him. But, when the women and boys in the enclosure saw him, they beat their faces, cried out, and wept until their voices rent the air. Al-Afshīn said to them, "Last night you were crying out, 'He made us captive!' yet today you are weeping for him, may God curse you!" They answered, however, "He used to treat us
[1228] well!" Al-Afshīn then gave orders, and Bābak was placed in a house, with al-Afshīn then appointing some of his men as guards over him.

Bābak's brother ʿAbdallāh, at the time when Bābak was staying with Ibn Sunbāṭ, went to [the stronghold of] ʿĪsā b. Yūsuf b. Istifānūs.[214] When al-Afshīn had seized Bābak and had brought him to his army camp and set guards over him, he was informed of ʿAbdallāh's whereabouts: that he was in fact staying with Ibn Iṣṭifānūs. Hence al-Afshīn wrote to this last asking him to send ʿAbdallāh to him, so Ibn Iṣṭifānūs duly dispatched ʿAbdallāh to him. When he came into al-Afshīn's hands, al-Afshīn imprisoned him in the same house with his brother (with Bābak), setting a group of men to stand guard over them both. He wrote to al-Muʿtaṣim about his capture of Bābak and his brother, and al-Muʿtaṣim wrote back, ordering him to bring them both to him. When al-Afshīn was on the point of traveling back to Iraq, he sent a message to Bābak, saying, "I am about to set off, taking you along, so have a last look at whatever you wish in the land of Ādharbayjān." Bābak answered, "I long to see my own town again." So al-Afshīn sent an escort of men with him on a moonlit night to al-Badhdh, and Bābak roamed around in it and looked at the slain and the houses until dawn; then the escort brought him back to al-Afshīn. The latter had consigned Bābak to the custodianship of one of his retainers, but Bābak sought from al-Afshīn to be relieved of that man. Al-Afshīn said to him, "Why

---

214. For the more probably correct filiation of this name, see p. 78 n. 206, above.

do you seek to be relieved of him?" Bābak replied, "He comes [to me] with his hands full of the foul reek of meat and then sleeps at my head, and the smell from his hands discommodes me." So al-Afshīn removed the man. Bābak came to al-Afshīn in Barzand on the tenth of Shawwāl (15 September 837), [escorted] between Būzbārah and [Abū al-Sāj] Dīwdād.[215]

In this year Muḥammad b. Dāwūd led the Pilgrimage.[216]

---

215. Dīnawarī, *op. cit.*, 404–5; Ya'qūbī, *Ta'rīkh*, II, 579; Mas'ūdī, *Murūj*, VII, 124–27 = pars. 2807–9; Ṭabarī, trans. Bal'amī, IV, 539–44; *Kitāb al-'uyūn*, 387–88; Ibn al-Athīr, *op. cit.*, VI, 471–75; Sadighi, *op. cit.*, 265; Spuler, *op. cit.*, 63–64; Nafīsī, *Bābak-i Khurram-dīn*, 40.

216. Khalīfah, *op. cit.*, II, 786; Ibn al-Athīr, *op. cit.*, 476. One might have expected to have found here, among the miscellaneous events that Ṭabarī often inserts at the end of the entry for each year, mention of a plague of rats (or mice, *fa'r*) that infested the districts of Sarakhs and Marw al-Rūdh in northern Khurasan during this year and even affected the crops adversely; it is mentioned on the authority of Ṭabarī by Ḥamzah al-Iṣfahānī, *op. cit.*, 144, under this year.

The
[1229] Events of the Year

223
(December 3, 837–November 22, 838)

Al-Afshīn's Bringing of Bābak and His Brother to al-Muʿtaṣim at Sāmarrā and Their Execution

It has been mentioned that al-Afshīn reached al-Muʿtaṣim at Sāmarrā with them on the night of Thursday (i.e., the night of Wednesday–Thursday), the third of Ṣafar (4 January 838) and that al-Muʿtaṣim used [at this time] to send to al-Afshīn, on every day from the moment when he set off from Barzand until he reached Sāmarrā, a horse and a robe of honor.[217] [It is further mentioned] that, because of his concern over the matter of Bābak and over getting news about him and because of the bad state of the road on account of snow and other things, al-Muʿtaṣim stationed sleek, swift horses (*khayl muḍammarah*) along the road from Sāmarrā to the pass leading to Ḥulwān.[218] At the start of each

217. The standard awards for victorious generals (robes of honor, jeweled sword, standards, horses, gold collars and armbands, etc.) are mentioned by Hilāl al-Ṣābiʾ as having been given to al-Afshīn by the Caliph; *op. cit.*, 93–94, trans. 75 (read al-Muʿtaṣim for al-Muʿtaḍid); in Masʿūdī, *Murūj*, VII, 127–28 = par. 2810, there is a detailed description of the gifts heaped on al-Afshīn when he reached Sāmarrā.

218. Ḥulwān was on the borders of Iraq and al-Jibāl, where the highway to

farsakh was specially stationed a horse with a rapid rider (*mujrī*), who would gallop with the news, so that he might relay it personally to another man [similarly stationed], placing it in the latter's hand directly from his own. In the stretch from beyond Ḥulwān to Ādharbayjān they had stationed mounts from al-Marj;[219] these were ridden for a day or for two days and then would be exchanged for new mounts that were then dispatched onward, and slaves from the personnel at al-Marj would travel on their backs, each mount being stationed at the beginning of each [new] farsakh. He (al-Muʿtaṣim) posted for them watchmen (*dayādibah*)[220] on the mountaintops by night and day and ordered them to cry out when news came to them (i.e., of the approach of one of the relays). When the person who was near the shouting heard the noise, he got himself ready, but his opposite number who had shouted was not to go to him until the other was waiting for him on the road; then he would take the dispatch bag (*kharīṭah*).[221] In this way, the mail bag used to reach Sāmarrā from al-Afshīn's army camp in four days or less.

When al-Afshīn reached Qanāṭir Ḥudhayfah,[222] there met him Hārūn b. al-Muʿtaṣim (al-Wāthiq) and members of al-Muʿtaṣim's household. When al-Afshīn brought Bābak to Sāmarrā, he lodged the latter in his own palace at al-Maṭīrah.[223] During the middle of [1230]

Khurāsān left the plain and entered the mountains; the Paytak Pass over the Zagros Mountains leading to Hamadhān lay to the east of the town. See Yāqūt, *Muʿjam*, II, 290–93; Le Strange, *Lands*, 191–92; Schwarz, *op. cit.*, 673–83; Barthold, *Historical Geography*, 198–99; *EI*², s.v. Ḥulwān (L. Lockhart).

219. Sc. Marj al-Qalʿah "Meadow of the Fortress," a fertile grazing ground at the head of the Ḥulwān Pass, ten farsakhs from Ḥulwān itself, where, according to Yaʿqūbī, *Buldān*, 270, trans., 68, the caliphal studs were kept. Obviously these studs were drawn upon, as stated here, for the use of the postal and intelligence couriers. See Yāqūt, *Muʿjam*, V, 101; Marquart, *Untersuchungen*, II, 159–60; Le Strange, *Lands*, 191–92; Schwarz, *op. cit.* 491–92.

220. Arabic broken plural of Persian *dīda-bān*. The task of these men must have been similar to that of the *kūhbāniyyah* mentioned earlier, in the account of the campaign against Bābak, e.g., at Ṭabarī, III, 1188 (see p. 38, above); cf. Herzfeld, *op. cit.*, 142 n. 1.

221. According to Hilāl al-Ṣābiʾ, the official *kharāʾiṭ* were of black silk brocade secured by a drawstring with a sealed tassel made of either ambergris and musk or of black clay mixed with ambergris; *op. cit.*, 127, trans., 103.

222. These bridges, named after the Companion Ḥudhayfah b. al-Yamānī al-ʿAbsī, who had encamped there during the conquest of Iraq from the Sāsānids, lay in the Sawād of Baghdad, according to Yāqūt, *Buldān*, IV, 400.

223. This lay some two miles to the south of the modern city of Sāmarrā and was, according to Yāqūt, *Buldān*, V, 151–52, a pleasure ground (*mutanazzah*) for

the night Aḥmad b. Abī Duwād came in disguise and saw and spoke with Bābak; then he went back to al-Muʿtaṣim and described Bābak to him. Very soon thereafter al-Muʿtaṣim rode forth to Bābak between the two walls of al-Ḥayr,[224] went into Bābak's presence disguised, and scrutinized him at length, without Bābak's recognizing him.

The next morning al-Muʿtaṣim sat in state to receive Bābak, this being either Monday or Thursday.[225] The troops were drawn up in lines [along the road] from the Bāb al-ʿĀmmah[226] to al-Maṭīrah, and al-Muʿtaṣim wished to display Bābak publicly and show him to the populace at large. He therefore asked, "On what sort of mount should this fellow be placed, and how can he best be shown off?" Ḥizām[227] told him, "O Commander of the Faithful, there is nothing better for displaying [someone] than an elephant!" Al-Muʿtaṣim commented, "You have spoken truly," and ordered the elephant to be gotten ready.[228] He gave further orders concerning Bābak, and he was dressed in a short coat

---

Baghadad and Sāmarrā, first laid out in al-Maʾmūn's reign. Subsequently, al-Muʿtaṣim allotted it to al-Afshīn, and around it were the land grants to his Ushrūsanī troops (Yaʿqūbī, *Buldān*, 259, trans., 51). After his fall it passed to the general Waṣīf and then to a son of al-Mutawakkil's. The actual site of al-Maṭīrah and even that of al-Afshīn's palace have now been identified with reasonable certainty as lying in the modern area of Jubayriyyah. See Herzfeld, *op. cit.*, 101; Northedge, "Planning Sāmarrāʾ," 118–21; idem and Faulkner, *op. cit.*, 145.

224. Literally, "the enclosure"; see Herzfeld, *op. cit.*, 100–1, and *EI*², s.v. Ḥāʾir (J. Sourdel-Thomine). Yāqūt, *Buldān*, II, 328, states that this was a palace at Sāmarrā on which al-Mutawakkil spent a vast amount of money, but it clearly antedates that Caliph. It is mentioned at length by Yaʿqūbī, *Buldān*, 258 ff., trans., 50 ff., as an area with many estates allotted to the Turkish generals, where al-Mutawakkil subsequently built a large congregational mosque.

225. According to Yaʿqūbī, *Buldān*, 261, trans., 53 (cf. Sourdel, "Questions de cérémonial," 126), Mondays and Thursdays were the days when the caliphs at Sāmarrā held public audience in the Dār al-ʿĀmmah. Masʿūdī, *Murūj*, VII, 129 = par. 2811, fixes the precise date of the reception of Bābak as Thursday, the second of Ṣafar, 223 (January 3,838).

226. On the "Public Gate," see n. 232, below.

227. Ḥizām b. Ghālib, Khurāsānian commander who, with his brother Yaʿqūb, was in charge of the caliphal stables at Sāmarrā and to whom a land grant was allotted in the area of al-Maṭīrah. See Yaʿqūbī, *Buldān*, 260, trans., 52; Herzfeld, *op. cit.*, 107.

228. Masʿūdī, *Murūj*, VII, 127 = par. 2810, describes the sumptuous coverings of this gray elephant, which had been a present from an Indian prince.

(*qabā'*)[229] of satin brocade and a round cap (*qalansūwah*)[230] of sable fur; he was completely alone. Muḥammad b. ʿAbd al-Malik al-Zayyāt[231] recited,

The elephant has been painted and adorned with dyestuff, as is
the custom with such a beast,
for it is bearing the devil from Khurāsān.
The elephant does not have its limbs painted and adorned
except for a very momentous person (or: for a very momentous occasion, *dhī sha'nⁱⁿ min al-shān*).

The people watched Bābak intently from al-Maṭīrah to the Bāb al-ʿĀmmah, and then he was brought into the Public Audience Chamber (*Dār al-ʿĀmmah*) before the Commander of the Faithful.[232] The latter summoned a butcher to cut off his hands and feet. But then he ordered [instead] Bābak's own executioner

229. This coat or jacket, regarded as a Persian garment, in contrast to the Arab *durrāʿah,* was increasingly worn by the caliphs from the mid-third (mid-ninth) century onward; see Dozy, *Vêtements,* 352–62.

230. This headgear (often qualified as *ṭawīlah* "tall" or *ruṣāfiyyah,* from the type of fabric used for it) was worn by the caliphs and by the learned classes, often in conjunction with a turban (*ʿimāmah*). See Dozy, *Vêtements,* 365–71; idem, *Supplément,* II, 401; Herzfeld, *op. cit.,* 142–43 n. 5; Sourdel, "Questions de cérémonial," 133–34; *EI*[1], s.v. Ḳalansuwa (W. Björkman). Herzfeld saw in its use by the caliphs a reminiscence of the Achaemenid emperors' *kyrabasia* mentioned by Aristophanes. The word *qalansūwah* is clearly non-Arabic, but its origin is unclear; as Herzfeld implies, it does not seem to be derived from New Persian *kalāh* "hat."

231. I.e., the vizier; see pp. 31–33 and nn. 117, 126, above. In his time, Ibn al-Zayyāt had in fact a considerable reputation as a poet and *adīb,* leaving behind a *dīwān* of poetry that has survived, though so far unpublished; Sezgin, *GAS,* II, 576–77.

232. It is clear from this passage that there was a distinction between the Public Gate, presumably a monumental edifice, and the Public Audience Chamber, which would be part of the palace complex—in this case, the Jawsaq al-Khāqānī, the modern Qaṣr al-Khalīfah (see Herzfeld, *op. cit.,* 95–99, 104–6)—but would lie before the inner, private parts of the palace. In the Public Audience Chamber, as noted, p. 86 n. 225, above, the Caliph held open sessions on Mondays and Thursdays, and the texts make clear that visitors and suppliants had to traverse a series of courtyards and rooms before reaching it. Sourdel has affirmed, in "Questions de cérémonial," 126–28, that the triple-arched *īwān* of the Jawsaq al-Khāqānī, which still stands, was an ideal place for the Caliph to hold audience, but there is no reason to equate it, as did Herzfeld, with the Public Gate, the site of which remains unclear.

to be brought in, so the chamberlain went out by the Bāb
[1231] al-ʿĀmmah, at the same time calling out "Nūdnūd!"—this being the name of Bābak's executioner—and the cry of "Nūdnūd!" rose up until he actually appeared. He came into the Public Audience Chamber, and the Commander of the Faithful ordered him to cut off Bābak's hands and feet. He did this, and Bābak fell to the ground. Then the Commander of the Faithful ordered him to be slaughtered (or: to be ripped open, *bi-dhabḥihi*), and one of the two of them (i.e., either the butcher originally summoned or Nudnūd) slit open his belly. Then he sent Bābak's head to Khurāsān[233] and gibbeted his trunk[234] in Sāmarrā at al-ʿAqabah (literally, "the rise, slope"), a place well known for its pieces of timber.[235]

Al-Muʿtaṣim further ordered that Bābak's brother ʿAbdallāh should be sent with Ibn Sharwīn al-Ṭabarī[236] to Isḥāq b. Ibrāhīm (al-Muṣʿabī), his deputy in the City of Peace; and he commanded

233. Ṭabarī, trans. Balʿamī, IV, 545, adds the detail (from a local tradition?) that ʿAbdallāh b. Ṭāhir had it paraded around the towns of Khurāsān and then finally exhibited on a pole at Nīshāpūr.

234. *Wa-ṣalaba badanahu.* Although *ṣalb* and *taṣlīb* can literally mean "crucifixion" (see *Glossarium*, CCCXXVI), they often refer to the impalement or gibbeting of a corpse (or a victim still alive?) on a post or beam; see Herzeld, *op. cit.*, 143n. 1.

235. Masʿūdī, *Murūj*, VII, 129–31 = par. 2812, gives a different version of Bābak's mutilation and execution. See also Dīnawarī, *op. cit.*, 405; Tanūkhī, *Nishwār al-muḥāḍarah*, I, 147–48 (anecdote on Bābak's fortitude); Ṭabarī, trans. Balʿamī, IV, 544–45; Azdī, *op. cit.*, 426; *Kitāb al-ʿuyūn*, 388; Niẓām al-Mulk, *op. cit.*, 295, trans., 235–36; Ibn al-Athir, *op. cit.*, VI, 477–78; Browne, *op. cit.*, I, 329; Sadighi, *op. cit.*, 265–67; E. M. Wright, *op. cit.*, 54–55; Nafīsī, *Bābak-i Khurram-dīn*, 141–44; Frye, *Golden Age*, 115. Yaʿqūbī, *Buldān*, 260, trans., 52, locates Bābak's gibbet on the main avenue leading from al-Maṭīrah to the Nahr Isḥāq b. Ibrāhīm, along which lay the land grants of the Khurāsānian commanders, just before the great market and the Old Mosque, later to be replaced by al-Mutawakkil's *jāmiʿ* (see p. 86 n. 224, above); cf. Herzfeld, *op. cit.*, 103, 143. The post in Sāmarrā on which Bābak's corpse was gibbeted was still known for this more than thirty years later, as appears from Abū al-Faraj al-Iṣfahānī, *Aghānī*, XXI, ed. Brünnow, 258, *shajarat Bābak*; Masʿūdī, *Murūj*, VII, 131 = par. 2813, says that the spot was still known as *khashabat Bābak* in his own time, a century later, when Sāmarrā was much reduced in population.

236. This name was frequent among the Bāwandids of the mountainous region of Ṭabaristān, so that their homeland became known as Jabal Sharwīn, but at this time the head of the family was Qārin b. Shahriyār b. Sharwīn. He is nevertheless probably the person referred to here, "Ibn Sharwīn" being a dynastic, rather than a personal, name. See Ibn Isfandiyār, *Taʾrīkh-i Ṭabaristān*, 147 ff; H. L. Rabino di Borgomale, "Les dynasties du Māzandarān," 412–13.

the latter to decapitate ʿAbdallāh and to do to him what had been done to his brother and then to gibbet him. When al-Ṭabarī brought ʿAbdallāh to al-Baradān, he halted with him in the palace there. ʿAbdallāh, Bābak's brother, said to Ibn Sharwīn, "Who are you?" Ibn Sharwīn replied, "The ruler of Ṭabaristān." ʿAbdallāh exclaimed, "Praise be to God, Who has fittingly brought for me a man from the *dihqān* class to take charge of my execution!" But Ibn Sharwīn replied, "It is in fact this fellow who is going to be in charge of killing you," for he had with him Nūdnūd, who had killed Bābak. ʿAbdallāh commented, "You are my social equal and compatriot (*ṣāḥibī*), but this fellow is a mere barbarian (*ʿilj*)! Now tell me, were you ordered to allow me any food or not?" He replied, "[Ask for] whatever you like!" ʿAbdallāh said, "Rustle up for me some *fālūdhajah*!"[237] He related: Ibn Sharwīn gave orders, and some *fālūdhajah* was put together for him in the middle of the night, and he ate till he was fully sated. Then he said, "O Abū so-and-so, tomorrow morning you will know that I am a true *dihqān*, if God wills!" Then he asked, "Could you give me some *nabīdh* to drink?" He replied, "Yes, but not a lot." ʿAbdallāh said, "I shan't, indeed, drink a lot." He related: Ibn Sharwīn called for four *raṭls*[238] of wine, and ʿAbdallāh sat down and drank them at a leisurely pace until it was almost dawn. Then he (Ibn Sharwīn) set off at dawn and brought ʿAbdallāh to the City of Peace and to the head of the bridge. Isḥāq b. Ibrāhīm ordered his hands and feet to be cut off, but ʿAbdallāh did not utter a sound or speak during this. Isḥāq b. Ibrāhīm ordered his corpse to be gibbeted, so it was gibbeted at the City of Peace on the eastern side [of the city] [1232]
between the two bridges.[239]

It has been mentioned from Ṭawq b. Aḥmad that when Bābak fled he went to Sahl b. Sunbāṭ. Al-Afshīn then sent Abū Saʿīd and Būzbārah, who assumed custody of Bābak from Sahl. Sahl sent

237. A sweetmeat confected of starch, honey, and nuts. See Jāḥiẓ, *Kitāb al-bukhalāʾ*, 203, trans., 292 (cf. 314, noting that it was a dish originally favored by the Persians and their emperors; Rodinson, *op. cit.*, 148).

238. A *raṭl* was a measure of weight; the Iraqi *raṭl* was considered canonical and at *ca.* 130 dirhams was the equivalent of 406.25 gr. See Hinz, *op. cit.*, 31.

239. Masʿūdī, *Murūj*, VII, 131 = par. 2813; Azdī, *op. cit.*, 426; *Kitāb al-ʿuyūn*, 388; Ibn al-Athīr, *op. cit.*, VI, 478; Browne, *op. cit.*, I, 329–30; Sadighi, *op. cit.*, 267–68; E. M. Wright, *op. cit.*, 55.

his own son Muʿāwiyah with Bābak to al-Afshīn; the latter thereupon ordered 100,000 dirhams for Muʿāwiyah and a million dirhams for Sahl, eliciting this for him from the Commander of the Faithful, plus a richly jeweled belt and a crown denoting princely rank (*tāj al-baṭraqah*), and this was how Sahl acquired the status of prince.[240] [It is also mentioned from Ṭawq that] the person with whom ʿAbdallāh, Bābak's brother, took refuge was ʿĪsā b. Yūsuf, known as Ibn Ukht Iṣṭifānūs, ruler of al-Baylaqān.[241]

It has been mentioned from Muḥammad b. ʿImrān,[242] ʿAlī b. Murr's secretary, that he said that ʿAlī b. Murr told him, on the authority of one of the vagabond desperadoes (*al-ṣaʿālīk*) called Maṭar, who said: "O Abū al-Ḥasan, by God, Bābak was my son!" I said, "How was that?" He replied, "We were with Ibn al-Rawwād,[243] and Bābak's mother was B.r.w.m.y.d[244] the one-eyed, one of Ibn al-Rawwād's indigenous population. I used to lodge with her. She was strong and healthy;[245] hence she used to act as my servant and launder my clothes. One day my eye fell on her, and I leaped upon her with the lust such as one feels when traveling and a long away from home, and I left the seed of Bābak firmly implanted in her womb.[246] Then," he went on to relate, "we went away after that for some time. But then we came back,

---

240. Azdī, op. cit., 425; *Kitāb al-ʿuyūn*, 388; E. M. Wright, *op cit.*, 55.

241. "Ibn Ukht Iṣṭifānūs" pertains to the paternal name Yūsuf; cf. Ṭabarī, III, 1224 (p. 78 and n. 206, above). Baylaqān (Armenian Pʿaytakaran) lay in the steppe between the Araxes and Kur Rivers. See Yāqūt, *Muʿjam*, I, 533; Le Strange, *Lands*, 178; Schwarz, *op. cit.*, 1144, 1296–98; Barthold, *Historical Geography*, 228; *EI*[2], s.v. Baylaḳān (D. M. Dunlop); *EIr*, s.v. Baylaqān (C. E. Bosworth).

242. This name seems fairly common. This person cannot be, on obvious chronological grounds, the official of al-Manṣūr mentioned in Ṭabarī, III, 172–73, 191; nor, as apparently a humble secretary, is he likely to be the Muḥammad, son of ʿImrān b. Mūsā b. Yaḥyā al-Barmakī, who was arrested and mulcted by al-Wāthiq in 227 (841–42) after his father had been killed (Ibn al-Zubayr, *Kitāb al-dhakhāʾir*, 185 no. 239).

243. See Ṭabarī, III, 1172 (p. 16 and n. 64, above).

244. The putative *b* and *y* here are written without dots. According to *Addenda et emendanda*, DCCLXXIII–DCCLXXIV, following the parallel passage in the autograph ms. of Dhahabī's *Kitāb duwal al-Islām*, a probable reading would be "was (known as) Rūmiyyah"; the Cairo edition, IX, 54, however, vocalizes it as T.r.tūmīdh.

245. *Miṣakkah*; the normal meaning of the word seems to fit the context perfectly well, *pace* de Goeje, in *Glossarium*, CCCXXVI, "knock-kneed" = *aṣakk*.

246. An alternative reading for *fa-aqrartuhu* in the text might be *fa-aqarrat-hu* "she was left pregnant with him (quickening in her womb)."

and behold, she had given birth to the child. I lodged in another house, and she came to me one day and said, 'When you made me pregnant, you used to stay here with me, but now you cast me aside,' and she revealed that her son was mine. I told her, 'By God, if you mention my name, I'll assuredly kill you!' She therefore let me alone, but by God, he [really] is my son!"[247]

During the period of his confrontation with Bābak, al-Afshīn was paid, in addition to the pay allowances for the troops, costs of provisions, lodging, and such for extraordinary expenses (*al-arzāq wa-al-anzāl wa-al-ma'āwin*), 10,000 dirhams for every day he [1233]
rode forth [against the enemy] and 5,000 for each day when he did not ride forth.[248]

The total number of people whom Bābak killed in a period of twenty years was 255,000 and he defeated Yaḥyā b. Mu'ādh,[249] 'Īsā b. Muḥammad b. Abī Khālid,[250] Aḥmad b. al-Junayd (whom he took prisoner[251]), Zurayq b. 'Alī b. Ṣadaqah,[252] Muḥammad b. Ḥumayd al-Ṭūsī,[253] and Ibrāhīm b. al-Layth.[254] Together with

---

247. This is a folkloric, even legendary, story intended to affirm the plebeian and bastard origins of Bābak; a parallel story is given, on the authority of one Wāqid b. 'Amr al-Tamīmī, author of *Akhbār Bābak*, by Ibn al-Nadīm, *Kitāb al-fihrist*, 406–7, trans., II, 818–22. Dīnawarī, *op. cit.*, 402, identifies Bābak's father as Muṭahhar b. Fāṭimah bt. Abī Muslim and says that a subsect of the Khurramiyyah called the Fāṭimiyyah were attached to him. As Dīnawarī wrote in the last decades of the third (ninth) century weight should perhaps be given to this filiation, which would accord with Bābak's brother 'Abdallāh's satisfaction that his death was to be at the hands of a Persian nobleman, *dihqān*, the prince of Ṭabaristān Ibn Sharwīn, and not at the hands of a low-class barbarian; see Ṭabarī, III, 1231 (p. 89, above). On the question of Bābak's antecedents and early life, see Browne, *op. cit.*, I, 323–28; Sadighi, *op. cit.*, 239 ff.; E. M. Wright, *op. cit.*, 45–48.

248. Ibn al-Athīr, *op. cit.*, VI, 438.

249. Khurāsānian commander who, according to Ṭabarī, III, 1039, engaged in an indecisive battle with Bābak in 204 (819–20); see Crone, *op. cit.*, 184.

250. He had been apointed governor of Armenia and Ādharbayjān, with special responsibility for carrying on the war against Bābak, in 205 (820–21); see Ṭabarī, III, 1044.

251. This is recorded in Ṭabarī, III, 1072, under the year 209 (824–25).

252. Properly, it seems, Ṣadaqah b. 'Alī, known as Zurayq, given thus in Ṭabarī, III, 1072, where he is said to have been appointed governor of Armenia and Ādharbayjān by al-Ma'mūn in 209 (824–25); see Ṭabarī, trans. Bosworth, *Reunification*, 144 and n. 423.

253. See p. 37 n. 134, above.

254. Appointed governor of Ādharbayjān in 209 (824–25) after the capture of Aḥmad b. al-Junayd; see Ṭabarī, III, 1072, trans. Bosworth, *Reunification*, 144 and n. 424.

Bābak there were captured 3,309 persons (of Bābak's partisans); and out of the Muslim women and children who had fallen into his hands, 7,600 were rescued. The number of the sons of Bābak who fell into al-Afshīn's hands amounted to seventeen, together with twenty-three daughters and daughters-in-law.[255]

Al-Muʿtaṣim presented al-Afshīn with a crown (*tawwaja*),[256] girded him with two jeweled belts (*wishāḥayn*), and presented him with 20 million dirhams, 10 million of which he kept as a personal gift and the other 10 million of which he was to distribute among his troops. Al-Muʿtaṣim appointed him governor of Sind, and he had poets brought in to praise him and ordered presents for them.[257] This was on Thursday, the thirteenth of Rabīʿ II (March 14, 838). Among the poetry eulogizing him were the words of Abū Tammām al-Ṭāʾī:[258]

The stout warriors subdued (*badhdha*) al-Badhdh and it was buried;
no dweller is left there but the wild beasts.
This sword [of ours] has been vouchsafed this endurance in battle only so that this faith (Islam) could be exalted.
Al-Badhdh was formerly a virginal (unbreached) seat of power, but there deflowered it
[1234] with a sword the stallion of the East, al-Afshīn.
And he rendered it once more a place in whose midst the foxes howl,

255. Ibn al-Athīr, *op. cit.*, VI, 45–48; E. M. Wright, *op. cit.*, 55–56.

256. Somewhat surprisingly, the wearing of a crown was not common caliphal practice at this time (although it became so later, in the fourth [tenth] century). Crowns tended to be regarded as Iranian, rather than Arab, emblems of authority and were bestowed, as here, on successful generals. The grant to al-Afshīn seems to be the first attested occasion for this, but in the next two or three decades Ashnās, Bughā al-Ṣaghīr, and others received them from their masters. See Mez, *op. cit.*, 131 and n. 2, trans., 133 and n. 1; Herzfeld, *op. cit.*, 143, 145–46; Sourdel, "Questions de cérémonial," 134, 143–44. Masʿūdī, *Murūj, VII*, 132–33 = par. 2815, is more detailed here than Ṭabarī: al-Afshīn received a *tāj* of gold set with jewels and an *iklīl* with rubies and emeralds within gold-filigree work.

257. Dīnawarī, *op. cit.*, 405; Masʿūdī, *Murūj*, VII, 132–33 = par. 2815; Azdī, *op. cit.*, 426; *Kitāb al-ʿuyūn*, 388; Ibn al-Athīr, *op. cit.*, 45–48; Sadighi, *op. cit.*, 268; E. M. Wright, *op. cit.*, 55.

258. The great poet and compiler of the anthology entitled *Ḥamāsah*, who died in 231 (845). See *GAS*, II, 551–58, IX, 299–300; *EI*², s.v. Abū Tammām (H. Ritter).

as it had been in past times, when it was a thicket for wild beasts.
There rained down on it from the skulls of its people
continuous downpours (i.e., of blood), shed by necks and skulls.
It was a miserable desert waste before the lifeblood flowed,
and then it became transformed through it (i.e., the sword) into a place of running springs.[259]

The Byzantine Emperor's Attacks on the Muslims at Zibaṭrah and Malaṭyah

In this year Theophilus son of Michael,[260] the ruler of the Byzantines, fell upon the inhabitants of Zibaṭrah,[261] taking them captive and devastating their town. He proceeded immediately to Malaṭyah[262] and launched attacks on its people and successively on the people of various of the fortresses held by the Muslims. He enslaved Muslim women—over a thousand of them, it is said—and made an example of those Muslim men who fell into their hands, putting out their eyes with hot irons and cutting off their ears and noses.[263]

---

259. Abū Tammām, *Dīwān*, III, 316–22 no. 166, these being the opening six verses of a *qaṣīdah* of thirty-six verses. Cf. Masʿūdī, *Tanbīh*, 170, trans., 231, citing other verses from this poem. Among what must have been a plethora of panegyrics composed on this occasion of Bābak's being brought to Sāmarrā, Dīnawarī, *op. cit.*, 405, cites three from a *qaṣīdah* addressed to al-Muʿtaṣim; they were composed by Isḥāq b. Khalaf (d. *ca.* 230 [844–45]), a Shīʿī poet of al-Muʿtaṣim's circle, often known as Ibn al-Ṭabīb al-Ṭunburī (see *GAS*, II, 575).

260. Second ruler of the Amorian dynasty, successor of Michael II the Stammerer (829–42). See A. A. Vasiliev, *Byzance*, 89–190; M. V. Anastos, "Iconoclasm and Imperial Rule," 103–4.

261. A fortress in the *thughūr* of al-Jazīrah, the Greek Sōzopetra. See Yāqūt, *Muʿjam*, III, 130–31; Le Strange, *Palestine*, 553–54; idem, *Lands*, 128; Vasiliev, *Byzance*, 138 nn. 4, 5; E. Honigmann, *Die Ostgrenze des byzantinischen Reiches*, index s.v.

262. A fortress of southeastern Anatolia, now a provincial capital of modern Turkey, the classical Melitene. See Yāqūt, *Muʿjam*, V, 192–93; Le Strange, *Palestine*, 499–500; idem, *Lands*, 120; Honigmann, *op. cit.*, index, s.v. Melitene; Canard, Histoire, 262–64; *EI*², s.v. Malaṭya. i. Pre-Ottoman History (E. Honigmann).

263. Balādhurī, *op. cit.*, 191–92; Yaʿqūbī, *Taʾrīkh*, II, 580–81; Ṭabarī, trans. Balʿamī, IV, 531–32; *Kitāb al-ʿuyūn*, 389; Ibn al-Athīr, *op. cit.*, VI, 479; J. B. Bury,

The Reason for the Byzantine Ruler's Behaving Thus with the Muslims

It has been mentioned that the reason for that was the position into which Bābak had fallen, because of his being driven into a tight corner by al-Afshīn, his reduction to the verge of destruction, and al-Afshīn's continuous pressure on him. When he was close to final perdition and became convinced that his own resources were now too weak to combat al-Afshīn, he wrote to the king (*malik*)[264] of the Byzantines, Theophilus, son of Michael, son of George, informing him that the king of the Arabs had sent his armies and warriors against him, even to the point of sending his tailor (he meant Jaʿfar b. Dīnār) and his cook (he meant Aytākh),[265] and that no one remained behind at his headquarters. [He accordingly told him], "If you want to march
[1235] out against him, know that there is no one in your way who will prevent you." Bābak sent that communication of his to the king of the Byzantines in the hope that, if he could induce the king to mount an attack, some of the difficulties that he himself was at that point enduring would be dispelled by al-Muʿtaṣim's having to transfer some of the armies then facing Bābak to combat the king of the Byzantines and by his attention's being thus deflected from Bābak.[266]

History, 259–62; Vasiliev, *Byzance*, 274–75, 293–94; Sadighi, *op. cit.*, 257; Rekaya, "Mise au point sur Théophobe," 55–56; Rosser, *op. cit.*, 268.

264. Thus used slightingly in reference to the Emperor.

265. Contemptuously referring to the *nisbah*s, or gentilics, of these two commanders, al-Khayyāṭ ("the tailor") and al-Ṭabbākh ("the cook"); see Ṭabarī, III, 1194–95 (p. 46 and nn. 151, 152, above).

266. According to Ṭabarī, trans. Balʿamī, IV, 531, Bābak, in his plea to Theophilus for help, pretended that he was a Christian and would, if victorious, endeavor to convert his followers to Christianity; cf. Bury, *History*, 259–62. However, Sadighi, *op. cit.*, 257, correctly noted that chronological difficulties are involved here. If Bābak really did send an appeal to Theophilus, it must have been a reasonable time before his final defeat at al-Badhdh in Ramaḍān 222 (August 836), and it seems improbable that Theophilus, after an appeal for immediate action, should have waited for several months, until 223 (which began in December 837), before launching his diversionary attack. Rosser, *op. cit.*, 267–68, accepts Ṭabarī's information at face value and speaks of Theophilus' being "obligated to help Bābak when the latter requested it in 837." But Rekaya discounts completely the laconic information of Ṭabarī, trans. Balʿamī, not repeated in any of the later Arabic sources, and denies that there could have been any alliance between Bābak and Theophilus, much less that Bābak would have

It has been mentioned that Theophilus set out with a force of 100,000 men—or, it has been said, more than that—including 70,000 odd regular army (*al-jund*) and the rest auxiliary troops (*atbāʿ*), until he reached Zibaṭrah.[267] He had with him a group of the Muḥammirah[268] who had been involved in the revolt in Jibāl and had subsequently joined up with the Byzantines at the time when Isḥāq b. Ibrāhīm b. Muṣʿab had fought with them; their leader was Barsīs (?).[269] The Byzantine king had assigned stipends to them, had provided them with wives, and had enrolled them as [regularly paid] warriors, utilizing their services in those affairs of the greatest importance to him. When the king of the Byzantines entered Zibaṭrah, killing the menfolk, enslaving the children and womenfolk, and burning it down, it was reported that the fleeing refugees came as far as Sāmarrā. The people of the frontier zones of Syria and al-Jazīrah, and the people of al-Jazīrah itself, sallied forth (i.e., for a counterstroke), with the exception of those lacking either a mount or weapons. al-Muʿtaṣim regarded this event as a great calamity, and it has been reported that when news of it finally reached him, he raised a call to arms in his palace. Then he mounted his horse and attached behind his

---

promised to become a Christian. Moreover, the chronological difficulties, already noted by Sadighi, make it very unlikely that Theophilus's Zibaṭrah campaign could have resulted from the direct prompting of Bābak, even though it is possible that the latter, increasingly desperate as al-Afshīn gradually and methodically tightened the noose around al-Badhdh, did send a general appeal to the Emperor. See Rekaya, "Mise au point sur Théophobe," 55–59.

267. Masʿūdī, *Murūj*, VII, 133–34 = par. 2816; cf. Vasiliev, *Byzance*, 330, who states that Theophilus had in his army contingents under the kings of the Burjān (?), Bulghars (B.r.gh.r), Slavs, and others.

268. Literally, "wearers of red," in Persian *surkh-jāmagān* (also Persian *surkh-ʿalamān* "those with red banners"), a term that Islamic authors applied also to the Mazdakite sect of pre-Islamic Persia. The color red thus seems generally to be associated with change, a break with tradition, and the forging of new ideas or ways of life. See Sadighi, *op. cit.*, 108, 188, 219–21; Scarcia Amoretti, *op. cit.*, 514.

269. The commander of this group of the Khurramiyyah of al-Jibāl who entered Byzantine service is named in other sources as Naṣīr/Nuṣayr or Theophobus, as noted (p. 3 n. 10, above). Vasiliev, *Byzance*, 138 n. 3, following Adontz, suggested that the man's original name may have been Narsī, Narseh (from ancient Iranian Nariyathaha; see Justi, *op. cit.*, 221–25), rendered in Arabic script as *Narsīs*. This seem quite possible. The assertion of Rekaya, "Mise au pont sur Théophobe," 45 n. 4, tht wc should follow the varant of ms. C in n. *e* for the preceding word, *raʾīsuhum*, and read instead *yusammīhim Barsīs*, "they were called Persians," seems less likely.

saddle shackles, an iron plowshare, and a provision bag, but he did not deem it advisable actually to set out until all arrangements had been completed.[270]

According to what has been mentioned, he held a meeting in the Public Audience Chamber, having summoned thither a group of persons from the City of Peace, including the judge of the city, ʿAbd al-Raḥmān b. Isḥāq,[271] and Shuʿayb b. Sahl,[272] accompanied by 328 men whose testimony was regarded as legally admissible;[273] and he made them bear formal witness to the arrangements for the disposal of his estates. He set aside one-third
[1236] for his children, one-third for God, and one-third for his mawlās, and then he camped on the western bank of the Tigris. That was on Monday, the second of Jumādā I (April 1, 838). He sent ʿUjayf b. ʿAnbasah, ʿAmr al-Farghānī,[274] Muḥammad Kūtah,[275] and a group of other commanders to Zibaṭrah as succor for its people, but [on arrival] they found that the king of the Byzantines had gone back to his land after perpetrating what we have previously recorded. They waited for a short while until the people gradually returned by degrees to their villages and became calm.[276]

---

270. Some later sources, including *Kitāb al-ʿuyūn*, 390; Ibn al-Athīr, *op. cit.*, VI, 480; and Ibn al-Ṭiqṭaqā, *al-Kitāb al-fakhrī*, 209–10, trans., 229, include a folkloric story that a captive Hāshimite woman in ʿAmmūriyyah cried out to al-Muʿtaṣim for help when he was in his palace at Sāmarrā; he heard her appeal and answered it by preparing for battle. It is, of course, quite likely that appeals for help from Muslim survivors or refugees from Zibaṭrah reached the Caliph, as is implied by v. 46 of Abū Tammām's celebrated ode on the capture of ʿAmmūriyyah (see. p. 121 n. 339, below), which speaks of a "cry from Zibaṭrah," *ṣawt*[an] *Zibaṭriyy*[an], to which al-Muʿtaṣim responded. More soberly, Yaʿqūbī, *Taʾrīkh, II*, 580–81, cf. Vasiliev, *Byzance*, 275, relates that al-Muʿtaṣim was deeply disturbed, sat down on the ground, distributed pay to the troops, and encamped with them immediately at the base of al-ʿUyūn, to the west of the Tigris, departing on campaign of the sixth of Jumādā I 223 (April 5, 838). According to Masʿūdī, *Murūj*, VII, 135 = par. 2817, he arrived at this camp four days previously.

271. Ḥanafī scholar, involved in the enforcement of the *Miḥnah* in al-Maʾmūn's reign. See Ṭabarī, III, 1120, 1121; al-Khaṭīb, *op. cit.*, X, 260–61 no. 5376; Watt, *The Formative Period of Islamic Thought*, 285.

272. Judge of al-Ruṣāfah in East Baghdad; see al-Khaṭīb, *op. cit.*, IX, 243–44 no. 4816.

273. *Ahl al-ʿadālah*, i.e., *ʿudūl*, those qualified by their probity to act in various legal capacities of attesting and verifying; see EI^2, s.v. ʿAdl (E. Tyan).

274. On the Farghānan element in the ʿAbbāsid armies, see p. 49 n. 158, above.

275. Literally, "the short" (Persian *kūtah*).

276. In Ṭabarī, trans. Balʿamī, IV, 532, al-Muʿtaṣim personally marches to Zibaṭrah. It seems that Theophilus marched from there farther eastward into

When al-Muʿtaṣim had [finally] got the upper hand over Bābak, he said, "Which place in the Byzantine lands is the most impregnable and securely fortified?" He was told, "ʿAmmūriyyah.[277] No Muslim has ever made an attempt upon it since the coming of Islam; it is the very heart (literally, "eye") and core of Christendom. In the view of the Christians, it is even more exalted in estimation than Constantinople."[278]

Al-Muʿtaṣim's Campaign against ʿAmmūriyyah

In this year al-Muʿtaṣim set out with a military expedition into the Byzantine lands. It has been said that he departed thither from Sāmarrā in 224 (838/839)—or, alternatively, in 222 (836/837)[279]—after he had killed Bābak.[280]

It has been mentioned that he equipped himself in a manner

Little Armenia and subdued various local Armenian princes; see Bury, *History*, 260–61.

277. I.e., the central Anatolian city, in the Anatolikon theme, the classical Phrygia, with a strong fortress and the seat of an archbishopric. It was of particular concern to Theophilus as the seat of his dynasty, the Amorian emperors, and had been attacked four times by the Arabs—despite what is said here by the Caliph's responders—in the previous two centuries, beginning with the raid of the governor of Syria Muʿāwiyah b. Abī Sufyān in 25 (646). See Yāqūt, *Muʿjam*, IV, 158; Le Strange, *Lands*, 137–38; 153; Bury, *History*, 262–63; Vasiliev, *Byzance*, 160–61; *EI*[2], s.v. ʿAmmūriyya (M. Canard).

278. *Kitāb al-ʿuyūn*, 390; Ibn al-Athir, *op. cit.*, VI, 480; Vasiliev, *Byzance*, 145, 293–95.

279. The date given by Yaʿqūbī and Masʿūdī, Jumādā I 223 (see p. 96 n. 270, above), seems more accurate.

280. The main additional primary sources for the ʿAmmūriyyah campaign are Yaʿqūbī, *Taʾrīkh*, II, 580–81 (brief); Khalīfah, *op. cit.*, II, 787–88 (brief); Balādhurī, *op. cit.*, 192 (brief); Masʿūdī, *Tanbīh*, 169–70, 354, 355–56, trans. 230–32, 454, 456, idem, *Murūj*, VII, 134–37 = pars. 2817–18; *Kitāb al-ʿuyūn*, 389–95; Azdī, *op. cit.*, 426–27; Ibn al-Athīr, *op. cit.*, VI, 480–88; Ibn al-Ṭiqṭaqā, *op. cit.*, 209–11, trans., 229–30. Many of the relevant excerpts from these sources and from others are translated into French by Canard in Vasiliev, *Byzance*, 271–394; he notes that Ṭabarī's account is by far the most detailed and important. Supplementary information from Christian Syriac and Armenian chronicles is noted in Vasiliev, *Byzance*, 145 n. 2.

Secondary sources include accounts based on the above sources and in varying detail; Edward Gibbon, *Decline and Fall*, VI, 44–46; Bury, *History*, 262–72; Vasiliev, *Byzance*, 144–75; idem, *History*, I, 276–77; Canard, "Byzantium," 710–11. Bury, in "Mutasim's March," endeavors to solve some of the problems connected with the itineraries of the Caliph and his commanders Ashnās and al-Afshīn.

that no previous caliph had ever done in regard to weapons, military supplies, implements, leather water troughs for the animals, mules, beasts of burden for carrying water (or: leather waterskins, *rawāyā*), goatskins for water, iron tools, and naphtha. He placed Ashnās[281] in charge of his vanguard, with Muḥammed b. Ibrāhīm[282] following him, Aytākh on his right wing, Jaʿfar b. Dīnār b. ʿAbdallāh al-Khayyāṭ on his left wing, and ʿUjayf b.
[1237] ʿAnbasah in charge of the center.[283] When he entered the Byzantine lands he encamped on the Lamas River,[284] by Salūqiyah,[285] near the sea, a day's journey from Ṭarsūs.[286] It is here that the ransoming takes place when there is an exchange of prisoners between the Muslims and the Byzantines.[287]

Al-Muʿtaṣim sent al-Afshīn Khaydhar b. Kāwūs to Sarūj[288] and instructed him to start out from there and enter [the Byzantine territory] via the pass (*darb*) of al-Ḥadath,[289] specifying for him a

---

281. Abū Jaʿfar Ashnās was a Turkish general and governor of al-Jazīrah, Syria, and Egypt in 25–30 (840–45). The name looks more Persian than Turkish, and Ṭabarī, III, 1017, gives a fanciful story explaining how it originated. It is found elsewhere in Iranian onomastic, and Justi, *op. cit.*, 44, conjectured an origin from *-shinās* "knowing, knower," with an omitted previous element; but the name remains basically unexplained.

282. Member of the Muṣʿabī line, parallel to that of the Ṭāhirids, brother of Isḥāq b. Ibrāhīm al-Musʿabī (see Ṭabarī, III, 1165 [p. 3 and n. 8, above]), governor of Fārs. He was regarded by al-Muʿtaṣim as one of the great men of state from his brother al-Maʾmūn's time; see Ṭabarī, III, 1328 (p. 214, below). He did, however, become involved in disputes with his nephew Muḥammad b. Isḥāq b. Ibrāhīm during al-Mutawakkil's caliphate, and these brought about his execution. See Nafīsī, *Taʾrīkh-i khāndān-i Ṭāhirī*, 30; Kaabi, *op. cit.*, I, 327.

283. For the various estimates of the numbers of the Muslim troops and their beasts, see Vasiliev, *Byzance*, 146 n. 1.

284. Classical Lamos, the modern Turkish Lamas Su, which runs from the Taurus Mountains down through the plain of Cilicia. See Le Strange, *Lands*, 133; *EI²*, s.v. Lamas-Ṣū (X. de Planhol).

285. The classical Seleucia, modern Turkish Selefke. See Yāqūt, *Muʿjam*, III, 242; Le Strange, *Lands*, 133; idem, *Palestine*, 530.

286. The most important and the most disputed of the frontier fortresses; it lay on the Cilician plain and commanded the southern approaches to the Cilician Gates. See Yāqūt, *Muʿjam*, IV, 28–29; Le Strange, *Lands*, 133; *EI¹*, s.v. Ṭarsūs (F. Buhl).

287. On these exchanges, see *EI²*, s.v. Lamas-Ṣū (X. de Planhol).

288. A town of al-Jazīrah, in Ḍiyār Muḍar, to be associated with the classical names Anthemusia and Batnae. See Yāqūt, *Muʿjam*, III, 216–17; Le Strange, *Lands*, 108; Canard, *Histoire*, 92–93; *EI¹*, s.v. Sarūdj (M. Plessner).

289. Al-Ḥadath, Greek Adata, was a town of the frontier *ʿawāṣim* between Marʿash and Malaṭyah, used by the ʿAbbāsids as a base for incursions into Byzantine territory; the famed pass lay northwest of the town, traversing the

day when he was to enter it.[290] He also assigned a day [of departure] for his own army and that of Ashnās, allowing between this day and the one of al-Afshīn's entry into Byzantine territory an amount of time corresponding to the difference of the two distances involved, the amount of time that he deemed adequate for the armies to come together in one place, i.e., Anqirah.[291] He organized the attack on Anqirah carefully, so that when God conquered it for him he could proceed against ʿAmmūriyyah, as there was nothing greater in the Byzantine lands upon which he had fixed his intentions than these two towns or any worthier goal for which he was aiming.

Al-Muʿtaṣim ordered Ashnās to enter via the pass of Ṭarsūs and to wait for him at al-Ṣafṣāf.[292] Ashnās set out on a Wednesday, the twenty-second of Rajab (June 19, 838), and al-Muʿtaṣim sent Waṣīf[293] forward after him and in command of al-Muʿtaṣim's own advance guard. He himself set off on Friday the twenty-fourth of Rajab (June 21, 838). When Ashnās reached Marj al-Usquf[294] a letter from al-Muʿtaṣim dispatched from al-Maṭāmīr[295] reached

---

eastern part of the Taurus range. See Yāqūt, *Muʿjam,* II, 227–29; Le Strange, *Lands,* 121–22; idem, *Palestine,* 443–44; Honigmann, *op. cit.,* see index s.v. Adata; Canard, *Histoire,* 272–73; *EI*², s.v. al-Ḥadath (S. Ory).

290. The Greek sources state that it was at this point that al-Afshīn's Turks were joined by an Armenian army commanded by the prince of Vaspurakan and the amīr of Malaṭyah; see Vasiliev, *Byzance,* 148.

291. Classical Ankyra of Galatia, in the Bucellarian theme, also known in Arabic sources as Qalʿat al-Salāsil "Fortress of the Chains." See Yāqūt, *Muʿjam,* I, 271–72; Le Strange, *Lands,* 149–50; Vasiliev, *Byzance,* 151 n. 2; *EI*², s.v. Anḳara (F. Taeschner).

292. This fortress, often in the plural al-Ṣafāṣif "the Willows," lay beyond the southern end of the Cilician Gate. See Yāqūt, *Muʿjam,* III, 413; Le Strange, *Lands,* 134–35, 139; Vasiliev, *Byzance,* 149; Honigmann, *op. cit.,* 42; Canard, *Histoire,* 284.

293. Turkish slave commander (*waṣīf* being a common term for "slave" in medieval Islam; Dozy, *Supplément,* II, 810), purchased by al-Muʿtaṣim in Baghdad and the owner of extensive land grants, or *qaṭāʾiʿ*, at Sāmarrā, eventually including those confiscated from al-Afshīn. He was finally killed in an insurrection of Turkish troops in 253 (867). See Yaʿqūbī, *Buldān,* 256, 258, 262, 264–65, trans., 45, 50, 54–55, 58; Ṭabarī, II, 1687–88; Herzfeld, *op. cit.,* III, 243.

294. "The Bishop's Meadow" lay to the west of the Podandos River; its possible location is discussed by Bury, "Mutasim's March," 121–22, 124, and by Canard, in Vasiliev, *Byzance,* 412. See also Le Strange, *Lands,* 138; Vasiliev, *Byzance,* 149; Honigmann, *op. cit.,* 45–46 n. 9.

295. Literally, "subterranean chambers, storehouses, strongholds"; these lay in the region of Malacopia, Arabic Malaqūbiyah. See Bury, "Mutasim's March," 121–22; Le Strange, *Lands,* 138; Honigmann, *op. cit.,* 46; *EI*², s.v. Maṭmūra (Ch. Pellat).

him, informing him that the [Byzantine] king was in front of him hoping that the [Muslim] forces would cross the Lamas (the Halys[296]) and that he (al-Muʿtaṣim) would take up a position by the fording place and thereby take them by surprise; Ashnās
[1238] therefore was to remain at Marj al-Usquf. Jaʿfar b. Dīnār was in charge of al-Muʿtaṣim's rear guard, and al-Muʿtaṣim informed Ashnās in his letter that he was awaiting the arrival of the rear guard because in it were the baggage, mangonels, provisions, etc.—the rear guard was in fact still in the narrow defile of the pass and had not yet emerged—so he was ordering Ashnās to stay put until the commander of the rear guard and the troops accompanying him were safely through and could go forth into the open country and reach Byzantine territory.[297]

Ashnās waited at Marj al-Usquf for three days until [another] letter from al-Muʿtaṣim arrived, ordering him to send one of his commanders on a nocturnal foray to seek out a man from the Byzantines whom they could question about the doings of the [Byzantine] ruler and those accompanying him. Hence Ashnās sent ʿAmr al-Farghānī with 200 cavalrymen, and they traveled all through the night until they came to the fortress of Qurrah.[298] They sallied forth in search of a man from the area outside the fortress but were unable to find anyone. The commander of

---

296. The classical Halys is the modern Turkish Kızıl Irmak, the longest river of Asia Minor; see *EI*², s.v. Ḳîzîl Irmāḳ (Cl. Huart). The apparent confusion of the Cilician Lamas Su with the Kızıl Irmak has attracted discussion, beginning with Bury, "Mutasim's March," 122–23. Vasiliev, *Byzance*, 146 and n. 4, suggested that it arose from corrupt readings of orthographically similar Arabic renderings of the names. In the same work Canard argues that it would have been pointless for the caliphal army to be within the great bend of the Halys if it was heading for Anqirah and suggests that the river intended is the Hylas; the orthographical confusion would thus be Hylas-Halys-Lamas.

297. It thus emerges, as Bury notes in "Mutasim's March," 120–21, that the Muslim attack on Anqirah was to be three-pronged. Al-Afshīn, commanding what might be called the Eastern Army, was to cross the Taurus range via al-Ḥadath, while the two divisions of the Western Army, under the Caliph himself and Ashnās, were to start from Cilicia and cross the mountains through the Cilician Gate, the aim being to converge simultaneously on their goal in Phrygia. To this end, the starting times of the armies and the distances to be covered had been carefully calculated beforehand, as Ṭabarī's narrative here shows.

298. Greek Koron, a fortress in Cappadocia and residence of the *kleisurarch* of that province. See Bury, "Mutasim's March" 123; Vasiliev, *Byzance*, 101–2, 150; Honigmann, *op. cit.*, 45.

Qurrah was aware of their presence, so went out with all the cavalry who were with him in al-Qurrah and concealed himself in ambush in the mountain that lay between Qurrah and Durrah,[299] a large mountain that flanks a rural district called "the *rustāq* of Qurrah."

ʿAmr al-Farghānī realized that the commander of Qurrah had become aware of their presence, so he proceeded onward toward Durrah and concealed himself there during that night. When the first gleams of dawn were visible he sent out his forces in three squadrons and ordered them to ride swiftly, so that they might bring back to him a captive who had intelligence regarding the [Byzantine] king. He arranged with them in advance to meet him, bringing the captive, at a certain place that the guides knew, and he sent two guides with each squadron. They rode forth at dawn and then split up in three directions. They took prisoner a number of Byzantines, including some from the king's army and some from the frontier regions (*al-ḍawāḥī*).[300] ʿAmr singled out one of the Byzantine captives, a man from the cavalry force of [1239] Qurrah, and questioned him about what was happening. The man told him that the king and his army were near to him, to the other side of the Lamas (of the Halys), four farsakhs away, and that the commander of Qurrah had become aware of their presence during that night and had ridden away and hidden himself in an ambush in that mountain above them. ʿAmr continued to remain in the place where he had arranged to meet his troops and ordered the guides who were with him to spread out among the mountain tops and thereby assume vantage points above the squadrons that he had sent out, fearing that the commander of Qurrah would fall upon one of the squadrons in their absence. The guides saw them and signaled to them [concerning the new orders], so they went forward; and they and ʿAmr met up in a place different from the one where they had originally been told to meet. They halted for a

299. Bury, "Mutasim's March," 123–24, and Canard, in Vasiliev, *Byzance*, 412, conjecture that it is to be identified with the modern Nora-halvadere (*pace* Vasiliev, *Byzance*, 150, who suggested Doara, which lay farther north, near the modern Hacı Bektaş).

300. Sing. *ḍāḥiyah*, literally, "outer, border region," in effect a no-man's-land between the Arabs and the Greeks. See Honigmann, *op. cit.*, 39–40; Bosworth, "Byzantine Defence System," 123–24.

short while and then traveled onward, seeking to regain the main army and having taken a number of prisoners from the [Byzantine] king's army.

They came to Ashnās on the Lamas (the Halys), and he asked them what had been happening, They informed him that for over thirty days the king had been fixed in one spot, awaiting the crossing of the Lamas (the Halys) by al-Muʿtaṣim and his vanguard, so that he might fall upon them from the other side of the river. [They also mentioned] that information had come to him (the king) recently that a powerful army had traveled from the direction of al-Arminiyāq[301] and had penetrated well into the country—meaning al-Afshīn's troops—and that these last had come up behind him. The king of the Byzantines had accordingly ordered one of his own kinsmen, the son of his maternal uncle, to act as deputy over his army and had himself gone forth with a detachment of his army seeking the whereabouts of al-Afshīn.

[On hearing all this] Ashnās sent the man who had given him this information to al-Muʿtaṣim, and he repeated the information to him. Al-Muʿtaṣim thereupon sent out a group of guides from his army, and he guaranteed to each one 10,000 dirhams if they should safely deliver his letter to al-Afshīn. In this letter he informed al-Afshīn that the Commander of the Faithful was remaining [where he was] and that he should likewise remain
[1240] [where he was], for fear of the possibility of the king of the Byzantines' attacking him. He also wrote a letter to Ashnās, ordering him to send, from his own resources, a messenger from among the guides who knew the mountains and tracks and could pass as Byzantines; and he guaranteed to each of them 10,000 dirhams if they could deliver the letter. He further wrote to him [in this same letter] that the king of the Byzantines had advanced toward him, so he could remain where he was until a letter should reach him from the Commander of the Faithful [with further instructions]. The messengers proceeded in the direction of al-Afshīn, but none of them was able to catch up with him

301. Arabization of the name of the Armeniakoi theme, which lay in the northeastern part of Asia Minor and bordered on independent Armenia; Qudāmah b. Jaʿfar, *Kitāb al-kharāj*, 258, renders it as *ʿamal al-Arminiyāq*. See Vasiliev, *History*, I, 228; Bosworth, "Byzantine Defence System," 122.

because he had penetrated into the Byzantine lands (i.e., more deeply than had been assumed).

Al-Muʿtaṣim's matériel and baggage finally reached the army camp with the commander of the rear guard. Al-Muʿtaṣim now wrote to Ashnās ordering him to advance, which he did, with al-Muʿtaṣim one stage[302] behind him, one group halting to camp while the other journeyed forward [and vice versa], but without any news from al-Afshīn reaching them until they were [only] three stages from Anqirah.

Al-Muʿtaṣim's army was reduced to extreme distress because of lack of water and fodder. In the course of his march[303] Ashnās had captured a number of prisoners, whose execution he had ordered until only one of them, an aged man, remained. The aged man said, "What good will killing me do you, when you are in this parlous condition and your troops also are suffering from lack of water and provisions? Now in this vicinity are a group of people who have fled from Anqirah for fear lest the king of the Arabs descend upon them. They are close to us here, and they have with them a considerable quantity of grain, food, and barley. Send a party of men with me so that I can hand over this group to them, and then set me free!"

So Ashnās's herald proclaimed, "Whoever feels lively and ready for action, let him ride forth!" And there rode with him around 500 cavalrymen. Ashnās went out until he had gone a mile from [1241]
the army, and those soldiers who were eager for action went forth with him. He rode forward, whipped his mount, and galloped furiously for about two miles. Then he stopped to look at his troops behind him, and those who could not keep up with the main body because of the inadequacy of their mounts he sent back to the army camp. He handed over the captured man to Mālik b. Kaydar (al-Ṣafadī)[304] and told him, "When this fellow

302. I.e., a day's march, *marḥalah*, on which see *EI*², s.v. Marḥala (Ed.).

303. According to Michael the Syrian, Ashnās, on his march between al-Ṣafṣāf and Anqirah, captured and razed the citadel of Nīshī'ā, i.e., the episcopal seat of Nyssa, south of the Halys; see Vasiliev, *Byzance*, 152.

304. Subsequently governor over the *ṣalāt* in Egypt, as deputy of Ashnās, during the years 224–26 (839–41). He died at Alexandria in 233 (848); see Kindī, *Kitāb al-wulāt*, 195.

shows you captives and extensive plunder, release him according to our undertaking!"

The aged man traveled with them until the time for the evening prayer, and he led them to a river valley with abundant herbage. The troops were able to pasture their mounts on the herbage until the mounts were satisfied; and they, the troops, were able to eat their evening meal and drink until they were refreshed. Then he took them along until he brought them out of the valley with its lush vegetation. Ashnās pressed on from where he was camped in the direction of Anqirah, and he ordered Mālik b. Kaydar and the guides accompanying him to meet him there. The aged man from the local inhabitants (*al-shaykh al-ʿilj*) led them onward for the remainder of the night, leading them around on a mountain but not conducting them from out of it, so that the guides complained to Mālik b. Kaydar, "This man is leading us around in circles." Mālik questioned him regarding the guards' accusations, and he replied, "They have spoken truly. The group of people whom you seek are outside the confines of the mountain, but I am afraid to leave the mountain at night, lest they hear the noise of the horses' hooves on the rocks and take flight. If we leave the mountain [now] and see no one there, you will kill me; however, I shall lead you round on this mountain until dawn, and then, when it is morning, we will go forth upon them, and I will show them to you, so that I shall be preserved from your killing me."

Mālik said to him, "Woe upon you! Bring us to a halt upon this
[1242] mountain, so that we may take a rest." The aged man replied, "Just as you think fit." So Mālik and the troops stopped on the rocks, holding fast in their hands the bridles of their mounts, until the dawn broke. When the dawn began to gleam the aged man said, "Send two men to climb up this mountain and see what is on it and to seize anyone they come upon there." So four of the troops climbed up and took prisoner a man and a women and brought them down. The local inhabitant questioned them as to where the group of people from Anqirah had spent the night, and they named for them the spot where the people from Anqirah had stayed. Then the aged man said to Mālik, "Release these two, for we promised them a safe-conduct so that they would guide us." So Mālik set them free. Then the local inhabitant went with

Mālik's troops to the place that he (i.e., acting on the information of the two captives) named to them. He brought them out above the camp, that is, the camp of the people of Anqirah, who were on the edges of some salt workings (*mallāḥah*). When the people of Anqirah saw the [Muslim] troops they shouted to the women and children, and these last went inside the works while they (the menfolk) waited for the Muslim troops on the edges of the works, fighting with spears, as there was no room to fight with stones or to use cavalry. The Muslim troops seized a number of captives from them. Among those who fell into their hands was a number of those who had long-standing wounds acquired some time previously. They questioned these captives about their wounds, and the captives said, "We were in the king's battle with al-Afshīn."[305] They instructed them, "Tell us about the affair!"

They accordingly told them that the king had been encamped four farsakhs away from the Lamas (the Halys) when a messenger had come to him with the news that a formidable army had entered from the vicinity of al-Arminiyāq. He had therefore appointed as deputy leader over his forces a member of his own family and had ordered him to stand fast in his position: If the vanguard of the king of the Arabs should come upon him, he (the deputy) was to attack him so that he himself (the Byzantine emperor) could go forth and attack the army that had entered al-Arminiyāq, that is, al-Afshīn's army.

Their leader (that of the Byzantine troops captured with the refugees from Anqirah) said, "Yes, [this is true]. I was one of those
who went with the king; we attacked them at the time of the [1243]
morning worship, and we put them to flight and killed all their infantrymen. Then our own troops split up into groups to pursue them (the fleeing Muslim troops), but at noon their cavalry

305. This battle had taken place on the plain of Dazimon, at Anzen near Tokat, Greek Dokeia, in northern Cappadocia, showing that al-Afshīn had penetrated deep into Byzantine territory from al-Ḥadath. According to the Greek sources, Theophilus's army included a contingent of Persians with the Persian commander Theophobus, and the Emperor also had with him the *domesticus* Manuel; these Persians were, of course, the Khurramī refugees from al-Jibāl who had fled west in 218 (833) under their leader Naṣīr/Nuṣayr, now the convert (Masʿūdī, *Murūj*, VII, 136 = par. 2818, *rajul min al-mutanaṣṣirah*) Theophobus; see p. 3 n. 10, above. See further, Bury, *History*, 264–66; Vasiliev, *Byzance*, 154–59; Rekaya, "Mise au point sur Théophobe," 61–63; Rosser, *op. cit.*, 68–69.

returned and engaged us in battle fiercely until they pierced our ranks and mingled with us and we with them. We did not know in which squadron was the king. We continued in this fashion until the time of the afternoon worship. After that we returned to the place where [previously] the king's army, of which we were a part, had been, but we did not come upon him. Hence we went back to the place of the camp that he had left behind on the Lamas (the Halys). There we found that the army had mutinied and the troops had abandoned the king's relative, the one whom he had appointed as his deputy leader over the army.[306] We remained there for the next night, and the following morning the king met us with a small contingent of troops. He found that his army had been broken up and thrown into confusion, so he arrested the man whom he had made his deputy and executed him. He also wrote to the towns and strongholds that, if they intercepted any deserter from the royal army, they were to flog him with whips, and then the fugitive was to return to a place that the king named, to which he himself repaired, so that all the troops might gather together and encamp in order to resist the king of the Arabs. He sent one of his servants, a eunuch, to Anqirah, with the instructions to remain there and guard the local populace in case the king of the Arabs should descend upon it."

The captive continued, "The eunuch proceeded to Anqirah, and we with him, but lo and behold, the people of Anqirah had left the city empty and had fled from it. The eunuch wrote to the king of the Byzantines telling him this news, and the king wrote back ordering him to travel onward to ʿAmmūriyyah."[307] He stated, "I

---

306. According to the Greek sources, either Manuel or Theophobus engaged in treacherous discussions with the Arabs during the battle, but Masʿūdī, *Murūj*, VII, 136 = par. 2812, reports that Theophilus lost the greater part of his patricians in the battle and himself escaped only through the aid of Naṣīr/Nuṣayr and his companions. He was able to reassemble the remnants of his forces on the plain of Khiliokōmon near Amasya. Theophilus's gratitude toward Theophobus later manifested itself in the Emperor's refusal to extradite him to the Caliph in order to stop the latter's march on Constantinople. See Ṭabarī, III, 1254 (p. 117 n. 327, below); Vasiliev, *Byzance*, 156–58; Rekaya, "Mise au point sur Théophobe," 62–63.

307. Theophilus now retreated westward to Dorylaeum in the Opsikion theme, or, according to the Greek sources, even as far as Nicaea, where he awaited news of what had happened at Amorion. It may have been from this refuge in

asked about the place for which its people"—meaning the people of Anqirah—"had made, and they told me that they were at the salt workings, so we joined up with them there."

[On hearing this], Mālik b. Kaydar said, "Leave behind all the people. Take just what you have, and leave the rest." The troops accordingly abandoned the captives (the women and children) and the [captured] soldiers and turned back, making for Ashnās's camp, and on their way they drove before them a great number of [1244]
sheep and goats and also cattle. Mālik set free that aged man who had been captured and went on to Ashnās's camp with the prisoners until he reached Anqirah. Ashnās remained encamped for one day, and then the following morning al-Muʿtaṣim joined him. He told al-Muʿtaṣim what the captive had told him, and al-Muʿtaṣim rejoiced at that. On the third day good news came from the direction of al-Afshīn, reporting that he was safe and sound and that he was on his way to the Commander of the Faithful at Anqirah.[308]

He related: Just one day after that al-Afshīn reached al-Muʿtaṣim at Anqirah. They remained there for some days. Then al-Muʿtaṣim proceeded to divide the troops into three armies: The first army was on the left wing, under the command of Ashnās; al-Muʿtaṣim was in the center; and al-Afshīn was on the right wing. Between each army was a distance of two farsakhs. He further ordered that each component army should have a right wing and a left wing and that they should burn down and destroy the villages and capture anyone they found in them. When it was time to encamp all the soldiers in the army were to come together with their particular commander and their chief. They were to do this all the way between Anqirah and ʿAmmūriyyah, a distance

---

northwestern Anatolia that the Emperor had to go to Constantinople in order to quell a plot to replace him on the throne, a rumor having spread that he had been killed in battle. This story is reported by Michael the Syrian, who may in fact have confused it with the information in Greek sources (the credibility of which may be suspect) that Persian troops in the imperial army rebelled at Sinope with the intention of proclaiming Theophobus emperor. See Vasiliev, *Byzance*, 158–59; Rekaya, "Mise au point sur Théophobe," 63; Rosser, *op. cit.*, 268–71.

308. It was after the Anzen defeat that the Emperor sent his first embassy to the Caliph, with the aim of securing peace and a Muslim withdrawal. It reached al-Muʿtaṣim when the siege of ʿAmmūriyyah was about to begin, and he kept the envoys in his camp until the city had fallen and a second Byzantine embassy arrived. See Ṭabarī, III, 1254 (p. 117, below) and the sources listed in n. 280, above.

of seven stages, until all the troops should have reached ʿAmmūriyyah.

He related: When the troops all converged on ʿAmmūriyyah, the first to arrive there was Ashnās, who reached ʿAmmūriyyah on Thursday in the early morning and then circled around the place. He encamped two miles away in a place that had water and herbage. When the sun rose next morning, al-Muʿtaṣim rode up; and he, too, circled around the city. Then on the third day al-Afshīn arrived. At this point the Commander of the Faithful divided the city between his commanders as they were circling around it. He allotted to each one of them a certain number of the city's defensive towers, according to the relative strength of that commander's forces, whether greater or lesser, so that each
[1245] commander had between two and twenty towers. Meanwhile, the inhabitants of ʿAmmūriyyah had entrenched themselves behind their fortifications and had prepared for a siege.

The people of ʿAmmūriyyah had [previously] captured a man of the Muslims, who had then become a Christian and married among them.[309] He had hidden himself away when the Byzantines had entered the fortress, but when he saw the Commander of the Faithful he came into the open and went over to the Muslims. He came to al-Muʿtaṣim and told him that there was a place in the city where the stream had borne down on it, owing to heavy rainstorms, so that the water had been carried down against it, with the result that the wall had collapsed at that place. The king of the Byzantines had written to the governor of ʿAmmūriyyah, ordering him to rebuild that place, but the governor had been dilatory over rebuilding it until the time when the king had set out from Constantinople, heading for some destination or other. The governor feared lest the king, passing through that district, should pass by the wall and see that it had not been rebuilt. At that point he had sent for skilled artisans, and

309. This is the first of two acts of treachery that, according to Ṭabarī, brought about the fall of ʿAmmūriyyah. The Christian sources are somewhat confused as to whether there was a single or a double betrayal; see p. 114 n. 318, below. The first traitor, originally a Muslim but converted to Christianity, may be the Manikophagos of one Byantine Greek source; as Vasiliev remarks, this name, "he who gnaws his manacles," would fit a former captive very well; see *Byzance*, 162–63, 169 n.

the facade of the wall had been repaired with stones laid one upon the other; but the rear surface of the wall, facing the city, he merely filled up with rubble (*ḥashw*). Then he had constructed on top of it battlements just as it had been there before. That man (the renegade) gave information to al-Muʿtaṣim about that particular place that he had described, and al-Muʿtaṣim gave orders for his own tent to be pitched in that place. He also set up mangonels[310] against the reconstructed part of the wall, and the wall was breached in that spot. When the people of ʿAmmūriyyah saw the breach in the wall, they hung down over it great balks of timber, each lapped over another, but when the rocks hurled by the mangonels fell on those timbers they shattered. So they hung down further pieces of timber with packsaddles over them to furnish a shield over the wall, but when the [fire of the] mangonels bore down hard on that place, the wall was split open. [1246]

Yāṭis (Aetius)[311] and the eunuch wrote a letter to the king of the Byzantines, informing him about the state of the wall, and they sent the letter with a man who spoke Arabic fluently and a Greek youth. They let them out through the outer protecting wall (*al-fāṣil*), and they crossed the defensive trench and emerged in the neighborhood of the force of royal princes and nobles (*abnāʾ al-mulūk*) attached to ʿAmr al-Farghānī. When the two men came up out of the trench, they (the attackers) did not recognize them; hence asked them where they came from. They replied, "We're from your comrades." They asked further, "Whose command are you under?" But the two men did not know any of the commanders of the army to name them to their questioners. As the latter could not identify the two men, they brought them to ʿAmr al-Farghānī Ibn ʾr. b. khā (?), who sent them to Ashnās, who in turn sent them to al-Muʿtaṣim.

Al-Muʿtaṣim questioned and searched them, and he found on them a letter from Yāṭis to the king of the Byzantines, in which Yāṭis told him that a very large army (that of the Muslims) had surrounded the city, that the place had become barely tolerable

310. *Majānīq*; see *EI*², s.v. Mandjanīḳ (D. R. Hill).

311. Described as Theophilus's maternal uncle in Yaʿqūbī, *Taʾrīkh*, II, 581. Aetius was the *strategos* of the Anatolikon theme; see Bury, "Mutasim's March,"267, and Vasiliev, *Byzance*, 147 and n. 1, on the commanders of the opposing Byzantine forces.

for them, and that his entry into that place had been a mistake. [Yāṭis continued] that he had therefore determined upon riding forth, bringing with him the elite of his companions on whatever mounts were within the fortress. He would open the gates by night without any warning (*ghaflatan*) and would go forth and attack the [Muslim] forces, whatever the outcome might be; some would manage to escape, and the rest would fall in battle, but he would then get free of the fortress and come and join the king. When al-Muʿtaṣim had read the letter, he ordered a purse of money (*badrah*)[312] for the man who could speak Arabic and the
[1247] Greek youth accompanying him, who both thereupon became Muslims. He presented them with robes of honor and gave orders so that, when the sun rose, the two men were paraded around [the walls of] ʿAmmūriyyah. The two men stated that Yāṭis would be in such-and-such a tower, so al-Muʿtaṣim ordered them to halt for a long while opposite the tower where Yāṭis was. In front of them two men bore the dirhams that they had been given, and they themselves wore the robes of honor and had with them the letter, until Yāṭis and all the Byzantines comprehended what they had done and hurled insults at them from the walls. Then al-Muʿtaṣim ordered that the two men be removed.

Al-Muʿtaṣim commanded that the soldiers take turns on guard duty all through each night [and that] the cavalry be on hand, spending the nights mounted and with their weapons at the ready, stationed there, lest the gate be opened at night and any man [of the people of ʿAmmūriyyah] slip out of the city. The troops continued to spend their nights that way, taking turns, on the backs of their mounts with their weapons ready, the mounts being saddled, until the stretch of wall between two towers in the place that had been described to al-Muʿtaṣim as poorly reconstructed collapsed. The troops of the army heard the crash, and they looked up, thinking that the enemy had broken out in an attack on one of the squadrons, until al-Muʿtaṣim sent someone to go round the troops in the encampment, informing them that that noise was the sound of the wall that had fallen down; as a result, the troops were jubilant.

When al-Muʿtaṣim had [originally] halted before ʿAmmūriyyah,

312. On this term see p. 65 n. 184, above.

he had observed the width of its defensive trench and the length of its walls, and he had driven along the road with him a great quantity of sheep. His plan in doing that was that he would utilize powerful mangonels proportionate to the height of the [1248]
wall, each mangonel manned by four persons and constructed as firmly and skillfully as possible. He mounted them on platforms on wheeled carts, and in regard to this he further planned to hand over the sheep to the troops, a single sheep for each man. The man was to eat its flesh, stuff its skin with earth, and then to bring these skins, stuffed with earth, for throwing into the defensive trench; this last was done. He further constructed large movable siege towers (*dabbābāt*),[313] each one capacious enough to hold ten men, and he had them carefully built so that he could roll them forward over the earth-filled skins when the trench became filled; this, too, was done. The skins were hurled down [into the trench] but did not fall in a regular, even-surfaced pattern, because the men were afraid of the rocks being thrown down by the Byzantines. They fell in an uneven layer, and it was not possible to level them. So al-Muʿtaṣim ordered earth to be thrown on them until the surface of the trench became level, and then a siege tower was pushed forward. He had it rolled, but halfway across the trench it became stuck on those skins; the crew were still inside and able to get free of it only with great effort. The wheeled cart remained fixed and immobilized there, and no stratagem could free it until ʿAmmūriyyah had been conquered. Thus the siege towers, mangonels, scaling ladders, and such remained ineffective and in the end were [broken up and] burned.

The next morning (after the collapse of the section of the wall) he attacked them at the breach. Ashnās and his men led the first assault, but the place was narrow, and they were unable to fight [properly] there. Al-Muʿtaṣim thereupon gave orders, and the big mangonels that were scattered around the perimeter of the wall were brought together in one spot and deployed around the

313. For this siege instrument, see Dozy, *Supplément*, I, 421; Levy, *op. cit.*, 440. Already in 149 (766) al-Manṣūr's generals had used mangonels and such movable towers as these for the conquest of Kamakh (Greek Kamakha) to the south of modern Turkish Erzincan; see Balādhurī, *op. cit.*, 184–85.

breach. Then he ordered that place to be bombarded. On the second day it was the turn of al-Afshīn and his troops to give battle; they fought well and were able to advance. Al-Muʿtaṣim
[1249] was waiting, on horseback, opposite the breach, accompanied by Ashnās, [al-]Afshīn, and the leading commanders, while the subordinate commanders were waiting on foot.

Al-Muʿtaṣim commented, "How well the battle is going today!" And ʿAmr al-Farghānī added, "The battle is going better today than yesterday!" Ashnās heard these words but controlled himself. However, when al-Muʿtaṣim went back to his tent for the midday meal and the commanders also went back to their tents for their meals and Ashnās drew near to the entrance of his own tent, the commanders dismounted from their horses in his honor, as was their custom, with ʿAmr al-Farghānī and Aḥmad b. al-Khalīl b. Hishām among them. They stepped before him, as usual, at his tent, but Ashnās said to them, "O you misbegotten sons [*awlād al-zinā*]! How can you walk before me? It would have been better if you had fought yesterday, rather than waiting there with the Commander of the Faithful. You now say that the conduct of the fighting today is better than yesterday, as if others than you were fighting then! Get back to your tents!"[314]

When ʿAmr al-Farghānī and Aḥmad b. al-Khalīl b. Hishām went back, one of them said to the other, "Don't you see what this slave, the son of a whore"—he meant Ashnās—"has done with us today? Wouldn't it be easier to go over to Byzantine territory than to endure what we have heard today?" ʿAmr al-Farghani, who had special information, said to Aḥmad b. Khalīl, "O Abū al-ʿAbbās, God will relieve you in the near future of his attitude, so rejoice!" And he led Aḥmad to suspect that he had [private] information. Aḥmad kept on pressing him with questions, and ʿAmr revealed to him what they were up to, saying, "The preparations regarding al-ʿAbbās b. al-Maʾmūn have been completed, and very soon we shall openly declare our allegiance to him and kill al-Muʿtaṣim,
[1250] Ashnās, and others." Then he told Aḥmad, "I would advise you to

314. This altercation seems to reflect the jealousies and hostilities of the Abnāʾ and Iranian elements (Khurāsānian and Transoxanian) toward the Turkish slaves, feelings that soon afterward assumed concrete form in the conspiracy to murder al-Muʿtaṣim and replace him with his nephew al-ʿAbbās b. al-Maʾmūn; see Ṭabarī, III, 1256–68 [pp. 121–23], below).

go to al-ʿAbbās, to step forward and become numbered among those sympathetic to his cause."

Aḥmad replied, "I don't believe this project will come to fruition." but ʿAmr told him, "It's already accomplished and finished!" And he directed him to al-Ḥārith al-Samarqandī, the kinsman of Salamah b.ʿUbaydallāh b. al-Waḍḍāḥ,[315] who was in charge of recruiting men to al-ʿAbbās's side and administering to them the oath of allegiance. ʿAmr said to Aḥmad, "I will bring you and al-Ḥārith together, so that you become one of the circle of our supporters." Aḥmad told him, "I am with you if this matter can be completed within ten days, but if it drags on beyond that then I can have nothing to do with you." Al-Ḥārith went along to al-ʿAbbās and informed him that ʿAmr had mentioned him (al-ʿAbbās) to Aḥmad b. al-Khalīl, but al-ʿAbbās said to him, "I don't like al-Khalīlī becoming cognizant of any part of our business. Keep away from him, and don't include him in any aspect of your affairs. Leave it between just the two of them." So they kept away from him.[316]

On the third day the battle was fought by the Commander of the Faithful's own troops in particular, together with the Maghāribah[317] and Turks, the overall commander being Aytākh. They fought and did well, and under their attacks the breach in

---

315. Possibly a kinsman, a first cousin, of the Khurāsānian general Hārūn b. Nuʿaym b. Waḍḍāḥ, employed in the campaign against the Zuṭṭ in lower Iraq in 219 (834–35); see Ṭabarī, III, 1167 (p. 8, above). The common grandparent Waḍḍāḥ may have been the Khurāsānian commander Abū Budayl Waḍḍāḥ b. Ḥabīb, who was active in the last years of the Umayyads and under al-Mahdī; see Ṭabarī, II, 1888, III, 496; Crone, *op. cit.*, 167.

316. Cf. Vasiliev, *Byzance*, 165–66.

317. The sources give little exact information about the ethnic or local origins of these "Westerners," in contradistinction to the detailed and specific information on the Khurāsānians and Transoxanians and their land grants at Sāmarrā (see pp. 28 n. 105, 49 n. 159, above). But they seem to have included, first of all, Bedouins who had long been located in the two *ḥawfs*, or "districts," of the Egyptian desert, to the east and west respectively of the Nile delta (those of Qays and Yaman, according to Masʿūdī, *Murūj*, VII, 118 = par. 2801, recruited by al-Muʿtaṣim), then Berbers from North Africa and possibly blacks brought as slaves from East Africa. They had their own *qaṭāʾiʿ* in Sāmarrā (Yaʿqūbī, *Buldān*, 263, trans., 55) and achieved particular power in caliphal affairs in the troubled middle decades of the third (ninth) century. See Herzfeld, *op. cit.*, 99, 112; *EI*², s.v. Maghāriba (M. Talbi). As to their numbers, it is mentioned, on the authority of the *rāwī* Ḥamdūn b. Ismāʿīl (for whom see Ṭabarī, III, 1314 (p. 196 n. 570, below), that 4,000 Maghāribah were involved in a ceremonial parade on the

the wall was enlarged. The fighting continued thus until many of the Byzantines were wounded. At the time when al-Muʿtaṣim's army had sat down before them, the king of Byzantium's commanders had divided among themselves the defensive towers, each commander and his troops being allotted a number of towers. The commander responsible for the place where the
[1251] wall had been breached was a man of the Byzantine commanders called W.n.dū, whose interpretation in Arabic is "bull."[318] This man and his troops fought strenuously night and day, but the whole weight of the fighting was on the shoulders of him and his troops alone, and neither Yāṭis nor anyone else would reinforce him with a single Byzantine soldier. When night came, the commander who was in charge of the breach went to the [other] Byzantines and said, "The whole weight of the fighting is on me and my troops, and I have no one left who has not been wounded. So send some of your own troops to man the breach and fire back for a while, for if you don't you will be disgraced and the city lost." They nevertheless refused to help him with a single man and told him, "The wall is intact in our section, and we aren't asking you for any assistance; so manage as best you can in your section, for you can expect no reinforcements from us."

As a result, W.n.dū and his comrades resolved to go out to the Commander of the Faithful al-Muʿtaṣim, asking him for a guarantee of safe-conduct for their families and [having been assured of this] to yield up to him the fortress, with all its contents of fittings, goods, weapons, etc. So when morning came he appointed his troops to hold the two sides of the breach while he went forth, saying, "I intend to go to the Commander of the Faithful," and instructing his soldiers not to fight until he should

occasion of the ʿĪd; see Ibrāhīm al-Bayhaqī, *op. cit.*, ed. Schwally, 165 = ed. Ibrāhīm, I, 250.

318. This name is corruptly written in the sources, but, if, as Ṭabarī says, it is to be equated with *thawr* "bull," then the correct reading is probably B.y.dū, corresponding to the Boiditzes of the Greek chronicles, described as having derived his surname from the ox (*boidon*) and stigmatized as the traitor who delivered the city to the Arabs. Bury, *History*, 269–71, and Vasiliev, *Byzance*, 167–70, 188–90, discuss at length the rather confused accounts in the Christian sources of the treacherous delivery of the impregnable fortress of Amorion to the Muslims; some of them mention only a single act of treachery.

return. He went forth till he came to al-Muʿtaṣim and stood in his presence.

Meanwhile, the [Muslim] troops were advancing to the breach, the Byzantines having held back from fighting, until they reached the wall. The Byzantines were making signs with their hands and saying, "Don't be afraid!" while the troops were at that moment advancing. W.n.dū was sitting with al-Muʿtaṣim, and the latter called for a horse and set W.n.dū on it; and he set his face forward [1252] until the troops proceeded with them to the edge of the breach. ʿAbd al-Wahhāb b. ʿAlī was in front of al-Muʿtaṣim, and he gestured to the troops with his hand that they were to enter, and they duly entered the city. At that point, W.n.dū turned (toward the Caliph) and seized his own beard with his hand. Al-Muʿtaṣim asked him, "What's the matter with you?" He replied, "I came because I wanted to hear your words and to let you hear mine, but you have acted treacherously with me!" Al-Muʿtaṣim, however, said, "Anything you want to ask, I guarantee to fulfill for you; say what you wish, for I shall not gainsay you." W.n.dū protested, "How can you say that you won't gainsay me, when the troops have already entered the city?" Al-Muʿtaṣim said, "Place your hand on whatever you want, and it is yours, and say whatever you want, and I will truly grant it to you. So W.n.dū remained in al-Muʿtaṣim's tent.

Yāṭis was in his tower with a group of Byzantines gathered around him. A detachment of them went along to a big church situated in one corner of ʿAmmūriyyah and fought there fiercely, but the Muslim troops burned the church over them; they were burned to death to the last man. Yāṭis remained in his tower with his soldiers and the remainder of the Byzantines, but the swords [of the enemy] wrought havoc among them, and all were either slain or wounded. At that, al-Muʿtaṣim rode on until he arrived and halted opposite Yāṭis, this place being near Ashnās's troops, and these last cried out, "O Yāṭis, this is the Commander of the Faithful!" The Byzantines shouted down from the top of the tower, "Yāṭis isn't here!" They replied, "Yes he is; tell him that the Commander of the Faithful is waiting." But they responded, [1253] "Yāṭis isn't here!" So the Commander of the Faithful went onward in an angry state. But when he had passed beyond [them] the Byzantines cried out [mockingly], "Yāṭis is here, Yāṭis is here!" Al-Muʿtaṣim accordingly came back and halted just opposite the tower. Then he gave orders regarding the ladders that had already been got ready, and one of them was carried forward and placed against the tower where Yāṭis was. Al-Ḥasan al-Rūmī, a slave of Abū Saʿīd Muḥammad b. Yūsuf's, climbed up it, and Yāṭis spoke to him.[319] Al-Ḥasan said, "This is the Commander of the Faithful, so descend the submit to his judgment." Then he went back down and told al-Muʿtaṣim that he had seen Yāṭis and spoken with him. Al-Muʿtaṣim instructed him, "Tell him that he must come down!" Al-Ḥasan went up a second time, and Yāṭis, girded with a sword, came out of the tower and stood on it, with al-Muʿtaṣim watching him meanwhile. Yāṭis then took off his sword from around his neck[320] and handed it over to al-Ḥasan and finally came down and presented himself before al-Muʿtaṣim, who lashed him in the face with a whip. Al-Muʿtaṣim returned to his tent and said, "Bring him here." Yāṭis walked a little distance, and then a messenger from al-Muʿtaṣim came to him [and instructed the Caliph's attendants], "Set him on a mount," so they conveyed him to the Commander of the Faithful's tent.[321]

The troops drew near from every direction with male prisoners and women and children captives until the encampment was full. Al-Muʿtaṣim commanded Basīl al-Tarjumān[322] to sort out the male prisoners and to set the noble and high-born Byzantines[323] on one side and the rest on another; and Basīl did this. Then al-Muʿtaṣim gave orders that his commanders should be in charge of the lots to be sold. Thus he gave Ashnās charge of what had come from his sector and told him to proclaim its sale. He gave al-Afshīn charge of what had come from his sector and told him
[1254] to proclaim and sell it. Aytākh was to deal with what came from his sector likewise and Jaʿfar al-Khayyāṭ similarly with what was

319. Presumably in Greek, since al-Ḥasan was of Greek (*rūmī*) origin.

320. A sign of submission.

321. Aetius's surrender effectively marked the fall of the city, which very probably took place on Tuesday, the seventeenth of Ramaḍān (August 12, 838); Yaʿqūbī, *Taʾrīkh*, II, 581. The Christian sources are imprecise, but there seem to be some grounds for stating that the duration of the siege was quite short, only twelve or fifteen days. See Vasiliev, *Byzance*, 170–71, 275.

322. I.e., "the interpreter, translator."

323. These amounted a considerable number, according to the Greek chronicles, including, in addition to Aetius, the *patricius* and *strategos* Theophilus, the *drungarius* Constantine, etc.; see Vasiliev, *Byzance*, 171.

in his sector. At the side of each of these commanders he appointed a man from Aḥmad b. Abī Duwād's staff to keep an account of the gains that the commander made (*yuḥṣī ʿalayhi*).[324] The various lots were sold in five days. What proved salable of them was sold, and he ordered that the remainder should be thrown on the fire. Al-Muʿtaṣim then started back for the region of Ṭarsūs.

When it was Aytākh's day (i.e., to sell his share of the plunder)—this being before al-Muʿtaṣim was to set out on his return journey—the troops pounced upon the spoils that Aytākh was in the process of selling. This was also the day on which ʿUjayf had arranged with the troops to fall upon al-Muʿtaṣim. Al-Muʿtaṣim galloped out alone [against the looters] with drawn sword, so that the troops fell back on each side before him and desisted from plundering the spoils. Al-Muʿtaṣim then returned to his tent. However, the next morning he gave orders that bids for the women and children captives were to be invited only three times, to speed up the sale; if someone raised the price after the third call, [well and good]; but if not the whole lot[325] was to be sold anyhow. He was involved doing that on the fifth day [of the sale]. The slave captives were being proclaimed for sale in groups of five and ten and the extensive spoils of goods and equipment in one block.[326]

He related: The king of the Byzantines had sent an envoy (i.e., to negotiate peace) when al-Muʿtaṣim first besieged ʿAmmūriyyah, but al-Muʿtaṣim ordered the envoy to be made to stay at a watering place three miles from ʿAmmūriyyah, where the troops were providing themselves with good drinking water; he would not let the envoy come to him until he had conquered ʿAmmūriyyah. Only then did he allow the envoy to go back to the king of the Byzantines, which he did.[327]

---

324. I.e., a representative of the chief judge was deputed to see that the division was handled fairly—an obvious precaution in the light of the quarrels mentioned below—and to take the ruler's fifth of all the spoils of war.

325. Following *Glossarium*, CCCLXXIII, for *ʿilq* in this context.

326. According to Michael the Syrian, the Caliph ordered that captured children should not be separated from their parents; see Vasiliev, *Byzance*, 172.

327. This is the embassy mentioned at p. 107 n. 308, above, to which was added a second embassy from Theophilus after the fall of the city. The two

Al-Muʿtaṣim went back in the direction of the frontier region (*al-thughūr*), as he had heard that the king of the Byzantines intended to set out following his (al-Muʿtaṣim's) tracks or else aimed at harrying the Muslim forces.[328] He accordingly pro-
[1255] ceeded along the main highway for one stage but then returned to ʿAmmūriyyah and ordered the troops to turn back also. He now turned aside from the main highway onto the road leading to the Wādī al-Jawr.[329] He distributed the prisoners among the commanders; and to each one of these last he gave a group to guard. The commanders in turn divided them among their troops. They traveled along a road for about forty miles, a waterless stretch, and they executed every prisoner who, because of the intense thirst he was suffering, refused to keep up with them. The troops entered the desert on the road through the Wādī al-Jawr; they were struck by thirst, so that both men and beasts kept

embassies seem to be conflated by Yaʿqubī, *Taʾrīkh*, II, 581, trans. in Vasiliev, *Byzance*, 275, and the details given here and by Michael the Syrian may relate to both embassies, though the plea for the return of the captives from ʿAmmūriyyah must obviously have been made by the second embassy. In his letter(s) Theophilus expressed contrition for the destruction of Zibaṭrah, promising to rebuild it and return the captives from there plus all other Arabs in Greek hands. Michael the Syrian alone adds further material: that the leader of the second delegation, the *patricius* Basil, asked for the release of Aetius and the other captives of ʿAmmūriyyah, offering a ransom of 200,000 *centenaria*. Al-Muʿtaṣim, however, demanded the extradition of Naṣr Khurdanāyā (i.e., Theophobus; see pp. 3 n. 10, 105 n. 305, above), his son, and the *domesticus* Manuel, who had once been a refugee in Muslim territory but had subsequently returned to Byzantine service. Basil refused these demands and presented a further letter from Theophilus, couched in menacing terms, after which al-Muʿtaṣim angrily dimissed the embassy and sent back the Emperor's presents. See Bury, "Mutasim's March," 266; Vasiliev, *Byzance*, 172, 174–75; Rekaya, "Mise au point sur Théophobe," 64–65.

328. The general assumption would be that al-Muʿtaṣim razed the walls of ʿAmmūriyyah completely, though Michael the Syrian states that he was able to pull down only a small part of the walls. Nevertheless, though Idrīsī and Ḥamdallāh Mustawfī Qazwīnī describe it as still flourishing, the city fell into ruins after the eighth (fourteenth) century. Its ruined site was identified only in the nineteenth century by Western travelers like William Hamilton as being that called by the local Turks Hergān-Qalʿe. See W. M. Ramsay, *Historical Geography of Asia Minor*, 230; Vasiliev, *Byzance*, 173–74.

329. This, with varying orthographies of the second element, is located by the geographers twelve miles from ʿAmmūriyyah; though unattested, a form like Wādī al-Ghawr "watercourse of the hollow" might perhaps be correct. See Vasiliev, *Byzance*, 172 n. 3.

falling down [dead], and some of the prisoners killed some of the soldiers and escaped.[330]

Al-Muʿtaṣim had traveled on ahead of the army and now came to meet the troops with water that he had brought from the place where he had encamped; nevertheless, many of the troops died of thirst in that valley. The troops told al-Muʿtaṣim, "These prisoners have killed some of our soldiers." So he immediately ordered Basīl al-Rūmī to sort out those prisoners who were of high rank, and these were set on one side;[331] then he further ordered that the remainder were to be taken up the mountains and brought down into the valleys [beyond] and executed en masse. These amounted to 6,000 men, killed in two places, in the Wādī al-Jawr and in another place. Al-Muʿtaṣim pressed on from there in the direction of the frontier zone until he reached Ṭarsūs. Water troughs made from leather had been set down for him around his encampment and all the way to the encampment at ʿAmmūriyyah; these were now filled, and the troops drank from them, untiring in their demand for water.

The battle between al-Afshīn and the king of the Byzantines [1256]
took place, it has been recorded, on Thursday, the twenty-fourth of Shaʿbān (July 21, 838),[332] while al-Muʿtaṣim sat down before ʿAmmūriyyah on Friday, the sixth of Ramaḍān (August 1, 838)[333] and came back [from the expedition] after fifty-five days.[334]

---

330. This return march must have been through the deserts to the west and south of the Tuz Gölü.

331. The Christian sources state that forty-two distinguished Byzantine prisoners were carried off to Sāmarrā, imprisoned there for seven years, and finally killed by al-Wāthiq in 230 (845) after refusing to convert to Islam; subsequently they entered Greek hagiology as "the Forty-Two Martyrs of Amorion." See Bury, *History*, 271–72.

332. Actually a Sunday.

333. Actually a Thursday.

334. Both Arab and Byzantine military operations along the *thughūr* and Byzantine naval activities as far as the Syrian coast continued over the next four years. According to Masʿūdī, *Murūj*, VII, 136–37 = par. 2818, al-Muʿtaṣim had, after his ʿAmmūriyyah victory, planned an expedition by land and sea against Contantinople, but the conspiracy centered on al-ʿAbbās b. al-Maʾmūn forced his hurried return to Syria and al-Jazīrah. It seems, however, that naval operations were in fact undertaken in the last year or so of his life, probably in 227 (841–42), though the Arabic historical sources do not mention them. Canard has noted a lengthy eulogy by the poet Buḥturī of the Amīr Aḥmad b. Dīnār b. ʿAbdallāh, probably the son of Hārūn al-Rashīd's mawlā Dīnār b. ʿAbdallāh, who had been

Al-Ḥusayn b. al-Ḍaḥḥāk al-Bāhilī[335] recited these verses eulogizing al-Afshīn and mentioning the battle between him and the king of the Byzantines:

The one protected (*al-maʿṣūm*; by God, i.e., al-Muʿtaṣim) made firm the power of Abū
Ḥasan (al-Afshīn) more securely than the pillar of Iḍam.[336]
All glory falls below that which he established
for the house of Kāwūs,[337] the lords of the Persians.
Al-Afshīn is nothing but a sword drawn
by God's power (or: His divine decree, *qadar*) in the hand of al-Muʿtaṣim.
He left no inhabitant at al-Badhdh,
except for images like those of Iram.[338]

---

briefly governor of al-Jibāl under al-Ma'mūn (Yaʿqūbī, *Ta'rīkh*, II, 553) and had quelled a revolt in Yemen for that Caliph (Ṭabarī, III, 1062–63). He is described as having achieved a glorious naval victory against the Byzantines, and this may be the expedition aimed at Constantinople that the Greek historians mention as commanded by one Apodeinar (Ibn Dīnār?) and destroyed by a great storm; Vasiliev placed this event in 842. See Buḥturī, *Dīwān*, ed. Beirut, 398 ff. = ed. al-Ṣayrafī, II, 980–85 no. 387; Bury, "Mutasim's March," 273–74; Margoliouth, *op. cit.*, 270; Vasiliev, *Byzance*, 176–77, 406–7.

Military operations, not recorded by Ṭabarī or other Arab historians but detailed by Michael the Syrian, also continued in the fronter region through the last years of al-Muʿtaṣim's life. They were conducted by the Amīr Abū Saʿīd Muḥammad b. Yūsuf [Ṭabarī, III, 1171 [p. 15 and n. 58, above]; from such raids as these he derived his *nisbah* al-Thaghrī) and by the garrison commander of al-Maṣṣīṣah (Mopsuestia) in Cilicia, Bashīr. See Bury. "Mutasim's March," 275; Vasiliev, *Byzance*, 175–76. In the course of fighting near al-Maṣṣīṣah in 225 (839–40) Bashīr and Abū Saʿīd defeated and killed Naṣīr/Nuṣayr, or Theophobus, the leader of the Persian and Kurdish troops from the Khurramiyyah of al-Jibāl in the Byzantine army. The event was celebrated by the poets Abū Tammām and Buḥturī, the latter an eye witness to the events in question. See Margoliouth, *op. cit.*, 269–70; Canard, "Les allusions," 398, 400–1, 403–4; H. Grégoire, "Manuel et Théophobe," 416; Rekaya, "Mise au point sur Théophobe," 65–67.

335. ʿAbbāsid court poet, often dubbed al-Khalīʿ "the debauchee, the libertine" (i.e., one of several *mājin*, or "frivolous, scoffing" poets of this period; see *EI*², s.v. Mudjūn [Ch. Pellat]), who died *ca.* 250 (865); he was in particular favor with al-Muʿtaṣim and his successors. *GAS*, II, 518–19; *EI*², s.v. al-Ḥusayn b. al-Ḍaḥḥāk (Ch. Pellat).

336. Described by Yāqūt, *Muʿjam*, I, 215, as a mountain in eastern Arabia between al-Yamāmah and Ḍariyyah.

337. I.e., that of al-Afshīn; on the ancient Iranian name Kāwūs, Avestan Kawa Usa, see Justi, *op. cit.*, 334–36.

338. This verse is also cited by Yāqūt in his entry on Badhdh, *Muʿjam*, I, 361. Iram Dhāt al-ʿImād "Iram of the Pillars," in Qur'ān LXXXIX:6, was generally

Then he brought forward as a present its ruler Bābak, as a captive, and as one taken in pledge, in double fetters, humbly expressing contrition.
And he pierced Theophilus with a well-aimed lance thrust, which shattered both his armies together and routed him.
The greater part of them were slain, and those who did escape of them were as meat on a chopping block (i.e., pounded and cut to pieces).[339]

In the year, al-Muʿtaṣim imprisoned al-ʿAbbās b. al-Maʾmūn and ordered him to be publicly cursed.

The Reason for al-Muʿtaṣim's Imprisoning al-ʿAbbās b. al-Maʾmūn

It has been mentioned that the reason for this was that, when al-Muʿtaṣim sent ʿUjayf b. ʿAnbasah, together with ʿAmr b. ʾr.b.khā al-Farghānī and Muḥammad Kūtah, to the Byzantine lands at the time of the trouble with the king of the Byzantines at Zibaṭrah, he did not give ʿUjayf a free hand regarding expenditure on salaries and supplies as al-Afshīn had been given a free hand, al-Muʿtaṣim having found ʿUjayf's conduct and activities unsatisfactory. This became apparent to ʿUjayf, at which he reprehended al-ʿAbbās for his previous actions at the time of [1257]

---

taken by the commentators to refer to a mighty city in the Arabian Desert, which had been destroyed by God as part of His punishment of the tribe of ʿĀd; see *EI*², s.v. Iram (W. M. Watt).

339. Al-Ḥusayn b. al-Ḍaḥḥāk, *Dīwān*, 99–100. These verses and others by this poet are also cited in Masʿūdī, *Tanbīh*, 169–70, trans., 231–32. Canard, "Les allusions," on Arabic poetry alluding to Byzantine-Arab warfare, has been mentioned in n. 334, above; he notes that these allusions are fairly meager and vague but do on occasion add further details to the accounts of the Muslim and Christian historians. See his listing of and comments on the poetry of Buḥturī and, above all, Abū Tammām, 397–403; for a detailed assessment of Abū Tammām's verse, see Haq, *op. cit.*, 24–29. The most famous example is, of course, the *qaṣīdah* in praise of al-Muʿtaṣim's victory at ʿAmmūriyyah, which begins *al-sayfu aṣdaqu anbāʾan min al-kutubi* (Abū Tammām, *Dīwān*, I, 40–74 no. 3, analyzed by S. P. Stetkevych in "The ʿAbbāsid Poet Interprets History," 60–64, and discussed by M. M. Badawi, "The Function of Rhetoric in Medieval Arabic Poetry," 43–56. It is somewhat surprising that Ṭabarī, who has quoted from Abū Tammām's ode on the fall of al-Badhdh (III, 1233–34 [pp. 92–93, above]) does not cite this even more famous poem of his.

al-Maʾmūn's death, when he had given allegiance to Abū Isḥāq (al-Muʿtaṣim), and for his inadequate measures then,[340] and he encouraged al-ʿAbbās to repair the resultant damage. Al-ʿAbbās undertook to do that and he secretly plotted with a man called al-Ḥārith al-Samarqandī, a kinsman of ʿUbaydallāh b. al-Waḍḍāḥ[341] and a person with whom al-ʿAbbās was on intimate terms.

Al-Ḥārith was a well-educated, intelligent person, skilled in intrigue, so al-ʿAbbās sent him out as his emissary and liaison officer to the commanders [of al-Muʿtaṣim]. He used to circulate around the army camp until a number of commanders came to be on close terms with him and swore allegiance to him (as al-ʿAbbās's representative), including some from [the Caliph's] close entourage. For each one of al-Muʿtaṣim's great commanders he nominated one of his followers whom he trusted, chosen from those who had sworn allegiance to him, and gave him responsibility for that, saying, "When we give the appropriate order, each one of you is to fall upon the person whom we have assigned to you to kill." They each pledged that to him, whereupon he would say to the man who had sworn allegiance to him, "O so-and-so, you are to kill so-and-so," and the man would reply, "All right!" He appointed one of al-Muʿtaṣim's close intimates, who had sworn allegiance to him, to be responsible for [killing] al-Muʿtaṣim, one of al-Afshīn's entourage for al-Afshīn, and one of Ashnās's entourage for Ashnās, all these from the Turks who had sworn allegiance to him; and they gave him their agreement en bloc.

When they were about to enter the mountain pass en route for Anqirah and ʿAmmūriyyah, al-Afshīn having [already] entered [the Byzantine lands] from the region of Malaṭyah, ʿUjayf advised al-ʿAbbās to fall upon al-Muʿtaṣim in the pass while he had few troops with him and the main army had become separated from him and thereupon kill him and return to Baghdad, for the troops would rejoice at the prospect of returning home from the expedition. However, al-ʿAbbās refused to do this and said, "I won't spoil this campaign until they have entered the Byzantine

340. See Ṭabarī, III, 1164 (p. 1, above).
341. *Ibid.*, 1250 (p. 113 and n. 315, above).

lands and conquered ʿAmmūriyyah." At this, ʿUjayf said to al-ʿAbbās, "O sleeping one, how long will you remain asleep? ʿAmmūriyyah is as good as already captured,[342] and the man (i.e., al-Muʿtaṣim) can now be dealt with. Secretly incite some of the troops to plunder these small amounts of captured spoils, and, when al-Muʿtaṣim hears the news of this looting, he will immediately ride forth. You can then give orders for him to be killed here on the spot." Al-ʿAbbās nevertheless refused, saying, "I shall wait until he travels through the pass (i.e., on the way back), for he will be as isolated then as he was on the original way out, and he will be more vulnerable than he now is here." [1258]

But ʿUjayf had already actually ordered some troops to plunder the baggage and equipment, so some of the spoils in Aytākh's encampment were actually looted. [As foreseen], al-Muʿtaṣim rode out at the gallop [to the looting], but the troops quieted down, for al-ʿAbbās did not give permission to act freely to any of those men with whom he had a covenant, so that they did nothing, reluctant to undertake any action without his orders.

News of what had been happening on that day reached ʿAmr al-Farghānī. He had a relative, a beardless youth, among al-Muʿtaṣim's close entourage, and the youth came to drink with ʿAmr's sons that night. He informed them that the Commander of the Faithful had ridden in haste and that he himself had run before him, and he reported, "The Commander of the Faithful became angry today and ordered me to draw my sword, saying, 'Anyone who plants himself in front of you, strike him!'" ʿAmr heard that report from the youth and was fearful that something unpleasant might happen to him, so he said to the youth, "O my son, you are foolish! Don't spend too much time with the Commander of the Faithful tonight! Keep to your tent, and if you hear any shoutings like these shoutings (of the discontented troops and looters), or any uproar, or anything at all, don't leave your tent, for you are indeed just an inexperienced lad, and you don't yet know how troops can behave." The youth then comprehended ʿAmr's speech.

342. This makes better sense in the context than the translation in Ṭabarī, trans. Marin, 77: "ʿAmmūriyya is already conquered." On this usage of the perfective form of the verb, see W. Wright, *A Grammar of the Arabic Language*, II, 2 A, par. 1 (e); cf. H. Reckendorf, *Arabische Syntax*, 301, par. 155.2.b.

Al-Muʿtaṣim set out from ʿAmmūriyyah making for the frontier region. Al-Afshīn dispatched Ibn al-Aqṭaʿ[343] by a road
[1259] different from that of al-Muʿtaṣim and ordered him to press on rapidly[344] to a place he named and to meet him at a certain point along the road, so Ibn al-Aqṭaʿ proceeded onward. Al-Muʿtaṣim also traveled onward toward the frontier region and journeyed until he reached a place where he halted for rest and refreshment and so that the troops might make their way through the defile that lay ahead of them. Ibn al-Aqṭaʿ, with the plunder he had gained, met al-Afshīn's troops, the camps of al-Muʿtaṣim and al-Afshīn being separate from each other, with two miles or more between them.

Ashnās fell ill, so al-Muʿtaṣim rode out at the time of the morning prayer to visit the sick man. He came to his tent and visited him, at a time when al-Afshīn had not yet caught up with him. Al-Muʿtaṣim set off back, when al-Afshīn met him on the road. Al-Muʿtaṣim said to him, "Are you heading for Abū Jaʿfar (Ashnās)?" At the time of al-Muʿtaṣim's departure from his visit to the sick Ashnās, ʿAmr al-Farghānī and Aḥmad b. al-Khalīl both set out to the vicinity of al-Afshīn's encampment so that they might see what captives Ibn al-Aqṭaʿ had brought and purchase any of them that took their fancies. So they headed for the vicinity of al-Afshīn's camp, but al-Afshīn himself, on his way to visit Ashnās, met them. They dismounted and greeted him, while Ashnās's doorkeeper (*ḥājib*) observed the two of them from afar. Al-Afshīn went on to Ashnās and then returned. Meanwhile, ʿAmr and Aḥmad had proceeded to al-Afshīn's encampment, but the captives had not yet been brought out; hence they stood on one side waiting for the public bidding for captives to begin in order to purchase some of them.

Ashnās's doorkeeper went into his master's presence and said, "ʿAmr al-Farghānī and Aḥmad b. al-Khalīl met al-Afshīn as they

343. I.e., the Amīr of Malaṭyah ʿAmr b. ʿUbaydallāh b. al-Aqṭaʿ, whose father had, during al-Amīn's reign, yielded up the fortress of Kamakh to the Byzantines in order to secure the freedom of his son. See Balādhurī, *op cit.*, 185; Canard, "Les allusions," 446.

344. Vocalizing *yughīra*, form IV of *gh-w-r*, rather than *yaghīra*, form I of *gh-y-r* "provide provisions" ("and ordered him to bring provisions to a place"), as in Ṭabarī, trans. Marin, 78.

were going toward his encampment. They dismounted and greeted him and then continued onward to his encampment." At that, Ashnās summoned Muḥammad b. Saʿīd al-Saʿdī[345] and said to him, "Go to al-Afshīn's encampment and look if you can see [1260] ʿAmr al-Farghānī and Aḥmad b. al-Khalīl there; observe with whom they stop and what they are up to." Muḥammad b. Saʿīd did this and found the two stationary on the backs of their mounts. He asked them, "What has detained you here?" They replied, "We stopped to await Ibn al-Aqṭaʿ's captives' being brought out so that we might buy some of them." Muḥammad b. Saʿīd said to them, "Appoint an agent to purchase on your behalf." But they replied, "We don't want to buy anything we don't see personally."

Muḥammad went back and informed Ashnās about that. The latter told his doorkeeper, "Say to those two, 'It would be better for you if you stuck to your own encampment' "—meaning [by "those two"] ʿAmr and Ibn al-Khalīl—" 'and don't keep wandering hither and thither.' " The doorkeeper accordingly gave them this message. They were perturbed by it and put their heads together and decided to go to the camp intelligence officer (*ṣāḥib khabar al-ʿaskar*) and ask to be removed from responsibility to Ashnās as their military superior. They therefore went to him and said, "We are the Commander of the Faithful's slaves, and he can attach us to whomsoever he wishes. But this fellow (i.e., Ashnās) treats us with contempt; he has reviled and threatened us, and we are afraid that he is going to take measures against us. So let the Commander of the Faithful attach us to whomsoever [else] he wishes." The intelligence officer repeated that to al-Muʿtaṣim the very same day.

The striking of camp coincided with the time of the morning worship. When the troops set out the armies traveled separately. Ashnās, al-Afshīn, and all the commanders in the Commander of

---

345. Ms. C has the variant (n. *l*) of "al-Ṣughdī" for this *nisbah*, which would actually fit well with the Transoxanian Iranian origin of many of al-Muʿtaṣim's senior military commanders. The Banū Saʿd b. Zayd Manāt were a clan of Tamīm (cf. Ṭabarī, III, 1146; Ibn al-Kalbī, *op. cit.*, I, Tafel 75, II, Register, 497; *EI*[1], s.v. Tamīm [G. Levi della Vida]), but Muḥammad b. Saʿīd may well have been of non-Arab mawlā origin, with a forebear who had become affiliated to the genuinely Arab Banū Saʿd.

the Faithful's army went on [together]; they appointed their deputies over the armies, and these were to travel with the armies. Al-Afshīn was in command of the left wing and Ashnās was over the right wing. When Ashnās went to al-Muʿtaṣim, the latter told him, "Punish ʿAmr al-Farghānī and Aḥmad b. al-Khalīl in an exemplary fashion, for they have made fools of themselves."

With that, Ashnās galloped off to his encampment. He asked
[1261] for ʿAmr and Ibn al-Khalīl. He found ʿAmr all right, but Ibn al-Khalīl had already gone forward with the left wing of the army, hastening toward the Byzantines. They brought ʿAmr al-Farghānī to Ashnās, who said, "Bring whips!" ʿAmr remained stripped for a long time, but the whips were not brought. ʿAmr's paternal uncle, who was a Persian (*aʿjamī*), spoke to Ashnās on ʿAmr's behalf, with the latter meanwhile waiting there. Ashnās thereupon said, "Carry him away and dress him in a *qabāṭāq*,"[346] so they bore him away on a mule in a canopied litter (*qubbah*) and took him to the camp. Aḥmad b. al-Khalīl galloped up, and Ashnās said, "Imprison this fellow with him." So he was made to dismount from his steed and put [in the litter] as the counterbalance[347] to ʿAmr, and the two of them were delivered to Muḥammad b. Saʿīd al-Saʿdī, who was to keep them under guard. He pitched for them a twin-poled tent[348] with a room and a table [for food], and he spread out for them mattresses and bedding,[349] and provided a tank of water. Their baggage and their slave boys remained in the encampment, and Muḥammad did not take away any of these. The two of them remained thus until they reached the mountain of al-Ṣafṣāf, Ashnās being in command of the rear guard (of the whole forces) and Bughā [al-Kabīr] being in command of the rear guard of al-Muʿtaṣim's [section of the] army.

When the army came to al-Ṣafṣāf and the Farghānī youth, who was a relative of ʿAmr's, heard of ʿAmr's imprisonment, he mentioned to al-Muʿtaṣim the conversation that had gone on between him and ʿAmr that night, including ʿAmr's words to

---

346. Not identified exactly, but possibly a gown, either sleeveless or with short sleeves, to be equated with the *b.gh.l.tāq* mentioned in Dozy, *Vêtements*, 81–84.

347. Here *ʿadīl*; in Ṭabarī, III, 1325 (p. 211, below), the term *zamīl* is used. Such a litter had two seats, one on each side of the mount.

348. *Fāzah*; see p. 81 n. 211, above.

349. *Ṭayyah*, translated as "platform" in Ṭabarī, trans. Marin, 80.

him, "If you perceive an uproar, stay inside your tent." Al-Muʿtaṣim said to Bughā, "Do not set out tomorrow morning until you go first to Ashnās; then take over custody of ʿAmr from him and bring him to me." This took place at al-Ṣafṣāf. Bughā halted with his banners, awaiting Ashnās. Muḥammad b. Saʿīd appeared with ʿAmr and Aḥmad b. al-Khalīl, at which Bughā said to Ashnās, "The Commander of the Faithful has ordered me to bring ʿAmr to him immediately." ʿAmr was therefore made to descend [from the litter], and some other man was placed in the litter with Aḥmad b. al-Khalīl to counterbalance it, and Bughā brought ʿAmr [1262] to al-Muʿtaṣim. Aḥmad b. al-Khalīl sent one of his slave boys to ʿAmr, so that he might learn what had been done with him. The slave boy came back and informed him that ʿAmr had been taken to the Commander of the Faithful's presence, had stayed there for a while, and then had been handed over to Aytākh and that, when he came in, the Commander of the Faithful had questioned ʿAmr about the words he had said to the youth who was his relative but that ʿAmr had denied this and had stated, "This lad was drunk and did not understand; I didn't say anything of what he has mentioned." Al-Muʿtaṣim gave orders, however, and ʿAmr was handed over to Aytākh.

Al-Muʿtaṣim traveled onward till he came to the entrance of the defiles leading to al-Budandūn,[350] and Ashnās remained there for three days waiting for the Commander of the Faithful's troops to emerge safely from it, because he was in charge of the rear guard.

Aḥmad b. al-Khalīl now wrote a letter to Ashnās telling him that he had valuable information for the Commander of the Faithful, Ashnās being at that moment stationed at the defile of al-Budandūn. Ashnās dispatched to him Aḥmad b. al-Khaṣīb[351] and Abū Saʿīd Muḥammad b. Yūsuf to ask him about the nature

---

350. I.e., the Podandos River in Cilicia, north of Ṭarsūs; see Honigmann, *op. cit.*, 44–45, 82. It was here that the Caliph al-Maʾmūn suffered his fatal illness in 218 (833). See Ṭabarī, III, 1133; Vasiliev, *Byzance*, 122.

351. I.e., Aḥmad al-Jarjarāʾī, at this time secretary to Ashnās, later to the prince al-Muntaṣir and, after the latter became Caliph, vizier; he died in 265 (879). He had a residence at Samarrā when it was first laid out. See Herzfeld, *op. cit.*, 113, 212, 217–18, 230; Sourdel, *Vizirat*, I, 262–65, 287–89; *EI*², s.v. al-Djardjarāʾī (D. Sourdel).

of this information, but Aḥmad averred that he would communicate it to no one but the Commander of the Faithful personally. The two envoys returned and reported that to Ashnās, who said, "Go back, and swear to him that I myself have sworn by the life of the Commander of the Faithful that, unless he reveals this information to me, I will have him flogged to death."

They retraced their steps and repeated these words to Aḥmad b. al-Khalīl. He made all those present with him leave, and only Aḥmad b. al-Khaṣīb and Abū Saʿīd were left. He then communicated to them what ʿAmr al-Farghānī had proposed to him concerning al-ʿAbbās; he explained to them everything that
[1263] he knew and gave them information about the activities of al-Ḥārith al-Samarqandī. The two of them then went back to Ashnās and informed him about the whole affair. At this, Ashnās sent for blacksmiths, and they brought two blacksmiths from the army. He provided them with iron and told them, "Make for me shackles like those now on Aḥmad b. al-Khalīl, and get it done immediately," and they did that. Now at the time for the evening worship Ashnās's doorkeeper used to spend the night at Aḥmad b. al-Khalīl's in company with Muḥammad b. Saʿīd al-Saʿdī. But on this particular night, at the time for the evening worship, the doorkeeper went to al-Ḥārith al-Samarqandī's tent, made him come out, and took him along to Ashnās. The latter put him in shackles and ordered the doorkeeper to bear him to the Commander of the Faithful, and the doorkeeper did this. Ashnās's departure coincided with the time for the morning worship. When he reached the place of his encampment, al-Ḥārith met him, [now] wearing robes of honor and in the company of al-Muʿtaṣim's officials. Ashnās said to him, "What's all this?"[352] Al-Ḥārith replied, "The shackles that were on my leg have now been transferred to al-ʿAbbas's leg!"

When al-Ḥārith had come to him al-Muʿtaṣim had questioned him about his activities, and al-Ḥārith had confessed that he was al-ʿAbbās's secret agent (*ṣāḥib al-khabar*), revealing to the caliph everything he had done and providing information about all those commanders who had pledged allegiance to al-ʿAbbās. Al-Muʿtaṣim then freed al-Ḥārith and presented to him robes of

352. *Mah*, literally, "steady on there!"; see W. Wright, *op. cit.*, I, 295.

honor but did not move against those commanders because of their numbers and the many who were specifically named among them.

Al-Muʿtaṣim was much disquieted over al-ʿAbbās's plot. When he marched out to the mountain pass he sent for al-ʿAbbās, set him free,[353] treated him kindly, and led him to believe that he (the caliph) had forgiven him. He ate his midday meal with al-ʿAbbās and then sent him back to his tent. At night he summoned al-ʿAbbās, made him his partner in conviviality over *nabīdh*,[354] and plied him [with it] until he had rendered him intoxicated and then made him swear an oath not to conceal from him any aspect of his undertaking. Consequently al-ʿAbbās disclosed to him his plan and gave him the names of all those who [1264]
had clandestinely entered into his plot, and [he further disclosed to him] how each one of them had become involved in it. Al-Muʿtaṣim recorded this and kept it safe. After that, he summoned al-Ḥārith al-Samarqandī and questioned him about the occasion and reasons [of those involved in the plot]. Al-Ḥārith repeated to him and confirmed al-ʿAbbās's story, whereupon al-Muʿtaṣim ordered al-ʿAbbās to be shackled. He told al-Ḥārith, "I made it easy for you to have lied so that I might consequently have a just cause for shedding your blood, but you did not do so, hence have escaped." Al-Ḥārith replied, "O Commander of the Faithful, I am not a liar!" At that point al-Muʿtaṣim handed over al-ʿAbbās to al-Afshīn.[355]

From then onward al-Muʿtaṣim pursued those commanders relentlessly, and the whole lot of them was arrested. He ordered that Aḥmad b. al-Khalīl be transported on a mule with a packsaddle but no saddleblanket, left in the sun whenever he

---

353. The sequence of events in the unmasking of the plot against al-Muʿtaṣim is not entirely clear. It may be that al-ʿAbbās was put in irons on two occasions (see below), or perhaps, as Marin suggests (Ṭabarī, trans. Marin, 81 n. 383), al-ʿAbbās had been under some sort of surveillance as a suspect.

354. This was properly any intoxicating drink fermented from anything but grapes, e.g., dates; see *EI*[1], s.v. Khamr (A. J. Wensinck), and *EI*[2], s.v. Khamr. 1. Juridical Aspects (A. J. Wensinck).

355. According to Yaʿqūbī, *Taʾrīkh*, II, 581, the great sum of 116,000 dīnārs was found with al-ʿAbbās when he was arrested. This was divided out among the regularly salaried troops (*murtaziqah*), two dīnārs each; al-Muʿtaṣim made up from his own resources the difference between this and the larger sum required, so that all these troops could benefit.

halted, and fed with a single loaf of bread per day. ʿUjayf b. ʿAnbasah was arrested among those commanders who were seized, and he was handed over, together with the rest of the commanders, to Aytākh, [except that] Ibn al-Khalīl was handed over to Ashnās. ʿUjayf and his companions were transported along the road on mules with packsaddles but no blankets. Al-Shāh b. Sahl, the hereditary leader of the people of a region of Khurāsān called Sijistān,[356] was also arrested. Al-Muʿtaṣim sent for him when al-ʿAbbās was also there in his presence and said to him, "O son of a whore, I treated you with kindness, but you were ungrateful!" Al-Shāh b. Sahl replied to him, "If only this son of a whore who is with you now"—meaning al-ʿAbbās— "had left me alone, you yourself would not at this moment be able to sit in this session and call me a son of a whore!" With that, al-Muʿtaṣim ordered his decapitation. Al-Shāh was the first of the commanders, in company with his retainers (*ṣaḥb*), to be killed.

ʿUjayf was handed over to Aytākh, who loaded him with numerous iron fetters and had him transported on a mule in a
[1265] litter without any saddle blanket.

As for al-ʿAbbās, he was in the custody of al-Afshīn. When al-Muʿtaṣim halted at Manbij,[357] al-ʿAbbās was hungry and asked for food. Ample food[358] was brought to him, and he ate, but when he asked for water this was refused, and he was wrapped in a felt blanket (*misḥ*). As a result, he died at Manbij, and one of his brothers prayed over him.[359]

As for ʿAmr al-Farghānī, when al-Muʿtaṣim halted in a garden in Niṣībīn,[360] he sent for the owner of the garden and told him to

---

356. Perhaps the scion of a local dynasty of Sīstān, which fell within the governorate of Khurāsān, held at this time by ʿAbdallāh b. Ṭāhir, who appointed deputies over Sīstān to fight the local Khārijites, as related in the relevant section of the anonymous local history of the region, the *Taʾrīkh-i Sīstān*, 181 ff., trans., 144 ff., though there is no mention there of al-Shāh b. Sahl.

357. A town on the Euphrates, in al-Jazīrah, where there was a bridge of boats over the river. See Yāqūt, *Muʿjam*, V, 205–7; Le Strange, *Lands*, 107; idem, *Palestine*, 501–2; Canard, *Histoire*, 87–88; *EI*[2], s.v. Manbidj (N. Elisséeff).

358. Very salty food, according to Yaʿqūbī, *Taʾrīkh*, II, 581.

359. Ibn al-Athīr, *op. cit.*, VI, 489–92; Ibn al-ʿAdīm, *op. cit.*, I, 69.

360. A town on the Hirnās River in al-Jazīrah. See Yāqūt, *Muʿjam*, V, 288–89; Le Strange, *Lands*, 94–95; Canard, *Histoire*, 103; *EI*[1], s.v. Naṣībīn (E. Honigmann).

dig a pit, to the depth of a man's height, in a place that he indicated by making a sign with his head. The owner of the garden began to dig it out. Then he sent for ʿAmr, al-Muʿtaṣim being at that time seated in the garden, having drunk several cups of *nabīdh*. He did not utter a word to ʿAmr, nor did ʿAmr speak to him until, when ʿAmr was there before him, al-Muʿtaṣim ordered, "Strip him!" He was stripped and flogged with whips by the Turks. The pit was meanwhile in process of being excavated until, when the digging was completed, the owner of the garden reported, "I have dug it out." At that, al-Muʿtaṣim issued orders, and ʿAmr's face and body were beaten with wooden cudgels; he was beaten continuously until he fell to the ground. Then al-Muʿtaṣim said, "Drag him to the pit and throw him into it." ʿAmr meanwhile did not speak or utter a sound all through that day until he died. He was hurled into the pit, and it was filled up with earth on top of him.

As for ʿUjayf b. ʿAnbasah, when he reached Bāʿaynāthā,[361] a little distance above Balad,[362] he died in the litter.[363] [His corpse] was thrown down and left with the commander of the garrison, who ordered that he be buried there. Hence he took the corpse to the side of a ruined wall; he threw the corpse down by it, and the corpse was buried there. It has been recorded from ʿAlī b. Ḥasan al-Raydānī that he said: ʿUjayf was in the custody of Muḥammad b. Ibrāhīm b. Muṣʿab. Al-Muʿtaṣim inquired of Muḥammad about ʿUjayf and asked him, "O Muḥammad, is [1266]
ʿUjayf not dead yet?" He replied, "O my lord, he will die today." Muḥammad then went back to his tent and said to ʿUjayf, "O Abū Ṣāliḥ, what do you have a craving for?" He answered, "Some *isfīdbāj*[364] and *fālūdhaj* sweetmeats."[365] Muḥammad ordered a

361. A town in al-Jazīrah on the al-Mawṣil-Naṣībīn road, to the northwest of Balad. See Yāqūt, *Muʿjam*, I, 325; Le Strange, *Lands*, 99; Canard, *Histoire*, 106, 110.

362. A town on the Tigris to the north of al-Mawṣil, the modern Eski Mawṣil. See Yāqūt, *Muʿjam*, I, 481–82; Le Strange, *Lands*, 99; Canard, *Histoire*, 106, 117.

363. According to Yaʿqūbī, *Taʾrīkh*, II, 582, ʿUjayf was brought from Adana in Cilicia in heavy chains, with a felt gag sewn over his mouth and a large fetter round his neck.

364. A dish made with meat, onions, etc.; see Dozy, *Supplément*, I, 22.

365. See p. 89 n. 237, above.

meal of all these foodstuffs to be made for him, and ʿUjayf ate. He asked for water, but this was denied him, and he kept on asking and pleading for it until he died. He was then buried at Bāʿaynāthā.[366]

He continued to relate: As for the Turk who had undertaken to al-ʿAbbās to kill Ashnās whenever al-ʿAbbās should give the order—he being regarded with great favor by Ashnās, treated by him as a boon companion, and never denied access to him by day or night—al-Muʿtaṣim ordered him to be imprisoned. Ashnās imprisoned him next to himself in a house whose door he bricked up with clay, and he used to provide him with a loaf of bread and a pitcher of water each day. One day the Turk's son came to him, and he talked with him from behind the wall, saying, "O my dear son, if only you could get me a knife, I could free myself from this place." His son kept on using various subterfuges until he managed to get a knife to him; the Turk then killed himself with it.

As for al-Sindī b. Bukhtāshah,[367] al-Muʿtaṣim ordered that he should be given back to his father, Bukhtāshah, because Bukhtāshah had not been smeared in any way by al-ʿAbbās's conspiracy. Al-Muʿtaṣim said, "This venerable shaykh should not be afflicted through [the loss of] his son." And he ordered the son to be set free.

As for Aḥmad b. al-Khalīl, Ashnās handed him over to Muḥammad b. Saʿīd al-Saʿdī, who dug a pit for him in al-Jazīrah at Sāmarrā. One day, al-Muʿtaṣim asked about him and said to
[1267] Ashnās, "What is Aḥmad b. al-Khalīl doing?" Ashnās told him, "He is with Muḥammad b. Saʿīd al-Saʿdī, who had a pit dug for him and then covered it over, leaving, however, a hole so that bread and water could be lowered down to him." Al-Muʿtaṣim replied, "This fellow must, I think, have grown fat under these

---

366. Yaʿqūbī, *Taʾrīkh*, II, 582, states that ʿUjayf's son Ṣāliḥ asked the Caliph for permission to drop his father's name from his *nasab* and to be called Ṣāliḥ al-Muʿtaṣimī; he also cursed his father and cut off all connection with him.

367. The consonants and vocalization of this name are uncertain; conceivably his father was one of the local rulers of Transoxania or the east. Al-Sindī survived and regained favor, for he is heard of in 248 (862) commanding the right wing on the summer raid (*ṣāʾifah*) into Byzantine territory; see Ṭabarī, III, 1481.

conditions." Ashnās told Muḥammad b. Saʿīd about that, and the latter ordered that Aḥmad b. Khalīl should be given water and that it should be poured over him in the pit until he died and the pit was filled up. Accordingly, water was continuously poured over him, but the sand soaked it up, and he did not drown, nor did the pit fill. Ashnās therefore ordered him to be handed over to Ghiṭrīf al-Khujandī.[368] This was done; he lingered with him for a few days and then died and was buried.

As for Harthamah b. al-Naḍr al-Khuttalī,[369] he was governor of al-Marāghah and was one of those whom al-ʿAbbās named as among his fellow conspirators. Al-Muʿtaṣim gave written orders that he should be transported in irons, but al-Afshīn spoke up for him and asked al-Muʿtaṣim for Harthamah to be awarded to him as a gift. This al-Muʿtaṣim did. Al-Afshīn thereupon wrote a letter to Harthamah b. al-Naḍr informing him that the Commander of the Faithful had given his person over to himself and that he (al-Afshīn) had now appointed him governor over the region where he would receive the letter. Harthamah was brought to al-Dīnawar[370] at nightfall in shackles and flung down in the caravanserai, still fastened in irons. Then the letter reached him in the course of the night; morning came, and he was governor of al-Dīnawar.

The remainder of the commanders, comprising Turks, men of Farghānah, and others, none of whose names have been preserved, were killed in their entirety.[371]

---

368. I.e., from Khujandah in Farghānah; see Yāqūt, *Muʿjam*, II, 347–48; Le Strange, *Lands*, 479; Barthold, *Turkestan*, 164–66; *EI*², s.v. Khudjand(a) (C. E. Bosworth).

369. I.e., from Khuttal or Khuttalān, a principality to the north of the upper Oxus; see Yāqūt, *Muʿjam*, II, 346–47; Le Strange, *Lands*, 438–39; Barthold, *Turkestan*, 69; *EI*², s.v. Khuttalān (C. E. Bosworth).

370. An important town in al-Jibāl, known in earliest Islamic times as Māh al-Kūfah. See Yāqūt, *Muʿjam*, II, 545–46; Le Strange, *Lands*, 189, 227; Schwarz, *op. cit.*, 473 ff.; Barthold, *Historical Geography*, 207–8; *EI*², s.v. Dīnawar (L. Lockhart).

371. According to *Kitāb al-ʿuyūn*, 398, al-Muʿtaṣim killed some seventy commanders in all, the greater part of those participating in the ʿAmmūriyyah campaign, by various methods: beheading, strangling, gibbeting on a wooden beam, etc. The result of this mass slaughter must have been a considerable diminution in the Khurāsānian and Transoxanian element among the leading commanders of the army and a corresponding rise in the influence of the Turkish

Al-Muʿtaṣim reached Sāmarrā safely and in the best of circumstances. On that day al-ʿAbbās was publicly called "The Accursed One." and al-Maʾmūn's [other] sons by Sundus[372] were handed over to Aytākh. They were imprisoned in an underground cellar in his house, where they later died.[373]

[1268] In this year, in Shawwāl (August–September 838), Isḥaq b. Ibrāhīm [al-Muṣʿabī][374] was wounded by one of his servants (or: eunuchs, *khādim*).[375]

In this year Muḥammad b. Dāwūd led the Pilgrimage.[376]

---

slave element, a trend accentuated a year or so later by the arrest and condemnation of the Iranian al-Afshīn (Ṭabarī, III, 1303–13, 1314–18 [pp. 179–93, 195–200, below]). See also Ibn al-Athīr, *op. cit.*, VI, 492–93; Herzfeld, *op. cit.*, 144.

372. This name literally means "fine silk brocade," the sort of name one would expect a slave concubine to have. The sons are named by Azdī, *op. cit.*: Hārūn, Aḥmad, ʿĪsā, and Ismāʿīl.

373. According to Ṭabarī, III, 1383, Aytākh took charge of executions for al-Muʿtaṣim and al-Wāthiq, and many important prisoners were committed to his charge. For the other primary sources on the conspiracy around al-ʿAbbās and its aftermath, see Yaʿqūbī, *Taʾrīkh*, II, 581–82 (with several details not in Ṭabarī); Masʿūdī, *Murūj*, VII, 136–37 = par. 2818; Azdī, *op. cit.*, 427–28; *Kitāb al-ʿuyūn*, 395–98; Ibn al-Athīr, *op. cit.*, VI, 489–93. See also Vasiliev, *Byzance*, 166–67.

374. I.e., the governor of Baghdad; see p. 3 n. 8, above.

375. The general term *khādim* "servant" was extensively used in this period as a euphemism for such blunter terms as *khaṣī* and *majbūb*, as has been emphasized and documented in great detail by Ayalon, *Military Reforms*, 3–4, 42–43; idem, "On the Eunuchs in Islam," 74–89; and *EI*², s.v. Khaṣī. I. In the Central Islamic Lands (Ch. Pellat).

376. Khalīfah, *op. cit.*, II, 787; Ibn al-Athīr, *op. cit.*, VI, 494; but, according to Azdī, it was ʿAlī b. Dāwūd al-Hāshimī who led this rite.

The Events of the Year 224

(November 23, 838–November 11, 839)

These included the open rebellion of Māzyār b. Qārin b. Wandāhurmuz[377] in Ṭabaristān against al-Muʿtaṣim and his warfare against the people of the plain and the chief towns there.[378]

---

377. On the etymology of the name Māzyār, see Justi, *op. cit.*, 201–2; and Marquart, *Untersuchungen*, II, 56 and n. 4: "helper, friend of Māhīzad"; cf. the form Māyazdyār in Balādhurī, *op. cit.*, 134, 339–40.

378. The roots of this episode lay in the complex family rivalries in the petty Caspian principalities but became entangled with tensions within the caliphate from the time of al-Ma'mūn and his minister al-Faḍl b. Sahl, on one side, and the Ṭāhirids, on the other. Essentially, it involved the Qārinid family, local rulers in the mountainous inland parts of Ṭabaristān, and their rivals in the Elburz Mountains region, the Bāduspānids and Bāwandids of Jabal Sharwīn. The Qārinids first appear in history, as opposed to legend, with the revolt of Māzyār's grandfather Wandād-Hurmuzd against the Muslim tax collectors of al-Mahdī in 165 (781–82). Qārin succeeded his father at some point during al-Ma'mūn's reign and was then succeeded, after only a short reign, apparently toward the end of al-Ma'mūn's caliphate, by his own son Māzyār. The Qārinid domains were at this time shrinking under pressure from the neighboring Bāwandid prince Shahriyār. At one point Māzyār had to flee Ṭabaristān altogether and take refuge at al-Ma'mūn's court, where he became a Muslim, in effect a client of al-Faḍl b. Sahl, and the first of his line to embrace the Islamic faith. He assumed the name of Abū al-Ḥasan Muḥammad b. Qārin and the title "Mawlā of the Commander of the Faithful." Māzyār's fortunes now began to revive. He defeated the Bāwandids and

The Reason for Māzyār's Open Rebellion against al-Muʿtaṣim and His Severe Measures with the People of the Plain

It has been mentioned[379] that the reason for that was that Māzyār b. Qārin had an antipathy toward the house of Ṭāhir and would refuse to hand over the land tax (*kharāj*) to the Ṭāhirids (i.e., through their intermediacy). Al-Muʿtaṣim would write to him, ordering him to convey the taxation to ʿAbdallāh b. Ṭāhir, and Māzyār would say, "I won't convey it to him, but I *will* convey it [directly] to the Commander of the Faithful." So, when al-Māzyār brought the taxation to him, al-Muʿtaṣim would direct one of his

---

sought to extend his authority, by oppressive and brutal methods, into the coastal plain of Ṭabaristān, with its centers at Āmul and Sāriyah. First al-Ma'mūn and then al-Muʿtaṣim confirmed him in his position as *Ispahbadh*, or prince, of Ṭabaristān, and Māzyār was thus able to adopt grandiloquent titles (see Yaʿqūbī, *Ta'rīkh*, II, 582; Ṭabarī, III, 1298 [p. 172, below]). He became more and more tyrannical and independent, maltreating both the Muslim population of the coastal towns and the Zoroastrian *dihqān* class of landowners. He refused, as Ṭabarī here details, to send the land tax of Ṭabaristān to the Caliph via his family's ancient rivals the Ṭāhirids, who, as governors of Khurāsān, were at least nominally his suzerains; he insisted on sending it directly to Iraq. Finally, he revolted against the central government.

The primary sources for Māzyār's earlier career and his revolt are Balādhurī, *op. cit.*, 339–40; Yaʿqūbī, *Ta'rīkh*, II, 582–83; Ṭabarī's account here; Ibn al-Faqīh, *Mukhtaṣar Kitāb al-buldān*, 305–7, trans., 362–63; and Masʿūdī, *Murūj*, VII, 137–39 = pars. 2819–22 (followed by *Kitāb al-ʿuyūn*, 399–403, and Ibn al-Athīr, *op. cit.*, VI, 495–505 (but totally omitted in Ṭabarī, trans. Balʿamī). From a somewhat later date the local chronicles of the Caspian region include Ibn Isfandiyār, *op. cit.*, 145–57, and Ẓahīr al-Dīn Marʿashī, *Ta'rīkh-i Ṭabaristān*, 114–18, 231.

Secondary sources include Rabino di Borgomale, "Les dynasties du Māzandarān," 408–9; Sadighi, *op. cit.*, 290–303 (mainly on Māzyār's part in al-Afshīn's trial but pointing out, 301–2 n. 4, that Ṭabarī's account of Māzyār's revolt includes material from four sources of varying reliability plus two short fragments, unimportant but with some extra details); E. M. Wright, *op. cit.*, 125; Rekaya, "Māzyār"; idem, "La place des provinces" (stressing that Māzyār's uprising was not an anti-Islamic movement of Iranian socioreligious protest against the incoming Arabs but rather a familiar early Islamic type of rebellion by a provincial governor against the central government in distant Iraq, there being no doubt about Māzyār's continued adherence to the Islamic faith); Mottahedeh, *op. cit.*, 75–76; Bosworth, "Ṭāhirids and Ṣaffārids," 100; Madelung, "Minor Dynasties," 204–5; Scarcia Amoretti, *op. cit.*, 506; Frye, *Golden Age*, 116–117; Kabbi, *op. cit.*, 253–57; *EI*[1], s.v. Māzyār (V. Minorsky); *EI*[2], s.v. Ḳārinids (M. Rekaya).

379. This short section, from an unnamed authority, at III, 1267–68, is the first of the sources drawn upon by Ṭabarī for his account of the revolt.

own officials, as soon as the money should reach Hamadhān, to collect the whole of it together and hand it over to ʿAbdallāh b. Ṭāhir's representative, so that the latter might take it back to Khurāsān.[380] This was his procedure for a complete run of several years, with Māzyār showing his detestation of the house of Ṭāhir until the affair between them grew serious.

From time to time al-Afshīn used to hear talk from al-Muʿtaṣim, indicating that he would like to remove the Ṭāhirids from Khurāsān.[381] When al-Afshīn had overcome Bābak and had secured in al-Muʿtaṣim's counsels a position such that no one had [1269]
precedence before him, he came to covet the governorship of Khurāsān. He got news of Māzyār's antipathy toward the Ṭāhirids and hoped that it would become a reason for removing ʿAbdallāh b. Ṭāhir. He therefore began intriguing by means of letters to al-Māzyār,[382] endeavoring to win him over by an appeal to fellow feelings as a Persian of noble birth and status (*yastamīluhu*

380. This compromise perhaps indicates that the Caliph was somewhat unwilling to throw his weight entirely behind the authority of the Ṭāhirids in Khurāsān, as would follow from the anti-Ṭāhirid talk attributed below to al-Muʿtaṣim; see, further, n. 381, below.

381. That a deep distrust and hostility existed between al-Muʿtaṣim and ʿAbdallāh b. Ṭāhir became something of an *idée fixe* in subsequent *adab* works (see, e.g., the anecdote about an exchange of letters between the two in Ibrāhīm al-Bayhaqī, *op. cit.*, ed. Schwally, 477–78 = ed. Ibrāhīm, II, 196–97, and the episode in Shābushtī, *Kitāb al-diyārāt*, 139–40, related on the authority of al-Faḍl b. Marwān (cf. G. Rothstein, "Zu aš-Šābuštī's Bericht," 164) and in the work of later historians (e.g., the Ghaznavid historian Gardīzī's statement, *op. cit.*, ed. Ḥabībī, 136 = ed. Nāẓim, 7, that al-Muʿtaṣim plotted to poison ʿAbdallāh, who had slighted him during al-Maʾmūn's reign). Barthold, *Turkestan*, 208–9, accepted such stories as true and attributed to the Caliph a deep hatred for ʿAbdallāh. The whole question is considered at length by Kaabi, *op. cit.*, 247–53, who suggests that it was in the nature of things for the Caliph to be suspicious of the Ṭāhirids' immense power in both Iraq and Khurāsān and that, in the light of these suspicions, the stories in the sources must contain some truth. Certainly ʿAbdallāh never left his governorate to come to the caliphal court (a reluctance prominently mentioned in the stories about their mutual coolness). But Kaabi points out that in practice both sides acted with prudence and restraint. Al-Muʿtaṣim recognized the fundamental importance of a well-governed, prosperous Khurāsān for the stability of his caliphate, while ʿAbdallāh never displayed any sign of insubordination or desire for independence, fully acknowledging his dependence on the Caliph, for example, by forwarding the tribute, including Turkish military slaves, regularly to the capital in Iraq.

382. As is already apparent, the name Māzyār sometimes appears with and sometimes without the Arabic definite article.

bi-al-dahqanah), telling him of his (al-Afshīn's) affection for him and that he had been promised the governorship of Khurāsān. This induced al-Māzyār to stop delivering the taxation due from him to ʿAbdallāh b. Ṭāhir.[383]

ʿAbdallāh b. Ṭāhir, for his part, kept continually dispatching letters about al-Māzyār to al-Muʿtaṣim until he made the latter fearful and angry about him.[384] This impelled al-Māzyār to rise up in rebellion and withhold taxation.[385] He took up a firm position in the mountains of Ṭabaristān and its outlying fringes, which was making al-Afshīn rejoice and leading him to covet the province. Al-Muʿtaṣim thereupon wrote to ʿAbdallāh b. Ṭāhir, ordering him to make war upon Māzyār, while al-Afshīn wrote to al-Māzyār ordering him to make war on ʿAbdallāh b. Ṭāhir and telling him that he would favorably represent his best interests at al-Muʿtaṣim's court.[386] Al-Māzyār would stand up against ʿAbdallāh b. Ṭāhir and resist him, to the point that al-Muʿtaṣim

---

383. See Rekaya, "Māzyār," 159–61. Despite the doubts thrown by Rekaya on the translation of the phrase *yastamīluhu bi-al-dahqanah*, given here and earlier by Minorsky, it still seems preferable to his "pour attirer (par la promesse de lui consentir la qualité de) dihqān." Such a promise would hold nothing fresh for Māzyār, already virtually an independent ruler in Ṭabaristān.

384. For ʿAbdallāh b. Ṭāhir's role in the affair of Māzyār, see Kaabi, *op. cit.*, 253–55, who emphasizes that the dispute between Māzyār and ʿAbdallāh was purely political and secular in origin; Māzyār was attempting to establish for himself a position in the Caspian provinces analogous to that of ʿAbdallāh in Khurāsān. A further factor was the earlier hostility between the Ṭāhirids and Sahlids, Māzyār having a connection with the latter (see n. 378, above).

385. *Kafara wa-ghadara*, in the words of Balādhurī, *op. cit.*, 339, who places the event six years and a few months after al-Muʿtaṣim's accession, i.e., in 224; but the rebellion may well have begun earlier, and Māzyār seems to have made his preparation in 223 (837–38). The use of *kafara* does not imply Māzyār's apostasy from Islam, and no other early sources state this. The verb is used here in its earliest signification, "to show ingratitude" > "to rebel." Only the fifth (eleventh)-century historian Gardīzī, *op. cit.*, ed. Nāẓim, 8 = ed. Ḥabībī, 136–37, explicitly attributes to Māzyār the doctrines of Bābak and the adoption of red garments like those of the Khurramiyyah, and the seventh (thirteenth)-century source of Ibn Isfandiyār, *op. cit.*, 153, speaks of Māzyār's demolition of mosques in the coastal region of Ṭabaristān and his grant of public offices to Zoroastrians.

386. That al-Afshīn urged Māzyār on in his rebellion is repeated by Ṭabarī at III, 1305 (p. 182, below). As Rekaya points out, in the words exchanged at al-Afshīn's trial between him and Māzyār, reported by Yaʿqūbī, *Taʾrīkh*, II, 583, Māzyār categorically avers that al-Afshīn had never corresponded with him, though acknowledging that his steward or agent (*wakīl*) had on occasion been kindly received by al-Afshīn.

would of necessity have to send him and others to ʿAbdallāh b. Ṭāhir (i.e., to take the situation in hand and restore order).

It has been mentioned from Muḥammad b. Ḥafṣ al-Thaqafī al-Ṭabarī[387] that, when al-Māzyār resolved on rebellion, he summoned his people to pledge allegiance. This they pledged to him, but unwillingly, so he took hostages from them and imprisoned them in the Iṣbahbadh's fortress (*burj*). He also ordered the peasant cultivators on the estates to rise up against the owners of those estates and to plunder their wealth.[388] Al-Māzyār had [previously] been corresponding with Bābak, egging him on and offering him assistance. Hence, when al-Muʿtaṣim had completed his campaign against Bābak and was free, he let it become widespread among the people that the Commander of the Faithful planned to travel to Qarmāsīn[389] and was sending al-Afshīn to al-Rayy[390] to combat Māzyār.[391] [1270]

387. This account, at III, 1269–82, 1282–93, is the second and longest of the four given by Ṭabarī: highly detailed, circumstantial, and apparently worthy of credence; cf. Sadighi, *op. cit.*, 301 n. 4. Minorsky, in *EI*[1], s.v. Māzyār in the bibliography, questioned whether the *rāwī* Muḥammad b. Ḥafṣ might not be a kinsman of the Mūsā b. Ḥafṣ who became governor of Ṭabaristān, Rūyān, and Dunbāwand under al-Maʾmūn in 207 (822–23) but died in 211 (826–27); he was succeeded there by his son Muḥammad (Ṭabarī, III, 1066, 1098).

388. This item of information has been used by certain modern writers to support the assertion that Māzyār's revolt was rooted in the ancient Iranian customs and ways of thought, aiming at a restoration of past glories and involving a kind of primitive communism and a hatred of the landowning classes similar to that of the Mazdakites in Sāsānid times. Rekaya ("Māzyār," 157–68; "La place des provinces," 145–46) has refuted this thesis, pointing out that what we have here is simply a policy on the part of Māzyār to eliminate his political opponents, those opposed to the extension of his arbitrary power, in which he used whatever means came to hand. Minorsky noted that Māzyār's violence and tyranny against all opposition in Ṭabaristān remained proverbial in the time of Ẓahīr al-Dīn Marʿashī (ninth [fifteenth] century); *EI*[1], s.v. Māzyār, and cf. Ibn Isfandiyār, *op. cit.*, 152, and Marʿashī, *op. cit.*, 118.

389. The town of al-Jibāl more recently known as Kirmānshāh. See Yāqūt, *Muʿjam*, IV, 330–31; Le Strange, *Lands*, 186–88; Schwarz, *op. cit.*, 480–82; Barthold, *Historical Geography*, 195–198; *EI*[2], s.v. Kirmānshāh (A. K. S. Lambton).

390. A town in northern Persia on the highroad to Khurāsān, commanding the approaches to Ṭabaristān and Gurgān; it lay just south of modern Tehran. See Yāqūt, *Muʿjam*, III, 116–21; Le Strange, *Lands*, 214–17; Schwarz, *op. cit.*, 740–81; Barthold, *Historical Geography*, 122–26; *EI*[1], s.v. Raiy (V. Minorsky).

391. The question whether there had really been any collusion between Bābak in Ādharbayjān and Arrān, on one hand, and Māzyār in Ṭabaristān, on the other, has aroused the interest of modern historians. Some recent Persian scholars have

When al-Māzyār heard about the people being thrown into a state of alarm through hearing news of that, he ordered that a cadastral survey[392] be made of the land, except for [the lands of] those who came to an agreement for paying taxation on their estates at a rate three times a [normal] tithe; action would be taken against anyone who refused to come to such an agreement and an increased assessment, and never a diminished one, levied against him.[393] Then he composed a letter to the official of his responsible for collecting the land tax, this official being a man called Shādhān b. al-Faḍl, the text of which was as follows:

> In the name of God, the Merciful, the Compassionate.[394] Information has been continually reaching us, and we have given it full credence, on the subject of what foolish people in Khurāsān and Ṭabaristān are disquietingly spreading concerning us, the [false] reports that they are engendering against us, and the

---

assumed the existence of a vast, anti-Arab conspiracy, involving not only Bābak but also the Byzantine Emperor Theophilus (see Ṭabarī, III, 1234–35 [p. 94 and n. 266, above]) and al-Afshīn, echoing the words, put into Māzyār's mouth at the time of his capture by ʿAbdallāh b. Ṭāhir by the later historian Ibn Isfandiyār, *op. cit.*, 155, that for many years he and Bābak and Afshīn Ḥaydar b. Kāwūs (read thus for "Afshīn and Ḥaydar b. Kāwūs" in Ibn Isfandiyār's text) had been plotting the downfall of the Arabs and the restoration of the ancient Persian empire. This seems even more unlikely than the possibility of limited contact between Bābak and Māzyār, for which there is no solid evidence. Sadighi's conclusion, *op. cit.*, 297 ff., was that all such accusations are highly dubious (even if the idea of a revival of former Persian glories does seem to have been in circulation at the popular level in some regions), affirmed by Rekaya, "Māzyār."

What does seem true is what Ṭabarī states here: that al-Afshīn coveted the government of Khurāsān and, having acquired an access of prestige through the capture of Bābak and through his part in the campaign against ʿAmmūriyyah and the Greeks, thought that, if ʿAbdallāh b. Ṭāhir became embroiled in the revolt of Māzyār over a long period of time and proved unable to suppress it, al-Afshīn himself would then be able to put himself forward to the Caliph as the one person in the empire who could save the situation in the east (cf. Ṭabarī, III, 1305 [p. 182, below]).

392. I.e., a *misāḥah*, for which term see F. Løkkegaard, *Islamic Taxation*, 108 ff., and *EI*[2], s.v. Misāḥa. 3. As a Technical Financial Term (Ed.).

393. Māzyār was clearly boosting his financial resources in preparation for a long war against the Ṭāhirids.

394. One would not expect Māzyār to begin his letter with the *basmalah* if he had in fact apostatized from Islam.

violent feeling against our dynasty and the critical attacks on our system of government that they are inciting their local leaders to nurture, the correspondence with our enemies, the expectation of civil strife, and the awaiting of changes of fortune among us, thereby denying favors [received from us] and making little of the security, tranquility, ease of life and riches that God has bestowed on them in preference [to others].

No commander or intelligence officer[395] comes to al-Rayy, nor does any envoy, young or old, reach us without saying thus-and-thus, and these foolish people stretch out their necks (i.e., hasten) toward him and engage at length in their tales to which God has already given the lie and their fanciful desires (i.e., for a forthcoming upheaval), which He has already frustrated time after time. The first [disappointment] does not deter them from indulging in the second, nor does fear of God or ordinary apprehension scare them away from that. All this we have patiently overlooked and have swallowed its bitterness to spare the whole of them and in furtherance of their welfare and security. But our desire to spare them has only increased them in obstinacy, and our refraining from punishing them has only incited them more. If we delay the process of the perception of the land tax (*iftitāḥ al-kharāj*)[396] out of consideration and tenderness for them, they say, "[He—i.e., the tax collector—has been] dismissed," and, if we hasten to begin the process, they say "[He needs it urgently] for some emergency that has arisen." They are not restrained by violence if we act [1271]
roughly or by kindness if we act generously. But God is sufficient for us, and He is our patron; upon Him we repose our trust and to Him we return repeatedly.

We have already ordered a letter to be written to the

395. For *wa-lā mushrif*, ms. O and the Cairo edition, X, 80, offer *wa-lā musharriq wa-mugharrib* "no traveler making his way eastward or making his way westward."

396. I.e., the opening of the financial year, a tern of the financial *dīwān*s, see Bosworth, "Abū ʿAbdallāh al-Khwārazmī," 134–35.

tax collector (*bundār*)[397] of Āmul[398] and to that of al-Rūyān[399] concerning the completion of the process of collecting the land tax (*istighlāq al-kharāj*)[400] in their respective districts, and we have granted them a delay in this until the end of the month of Tīr-Māh.[401] Take cognizance of that, exact the amount of taxation due to you, and raise what has been imposed on the people of your district in its entirety; do not let the month of Tīr-Māh reach its close with a single dirham outstanding to you, for if you turn away from that to doing something else your recompense from us will inevitably be gibbeting. So watch out for yourself, protect your own life's blood, and exert yourself diligently in your work. Forward your letter to al-ʿAbbās,[402] and beware of making excuses.[403] Report on the celerity and diligence with which you are proceeding, for we have been hoping that this procedure will constitute something that will distract them from spreading false news and act as a deterrent from putting off [payment of the required tax].

In recent days they have bruited abroad the rumor that the Commander of the Faithful—may God grant him

---

397. This Persian term (literally, "one who possesses a firm basis") had come by Seljuq times to apply generally to the tax collector = Arabic *ʿāmil* but seems originally to have designated commercial agents or speculators who purchased items of the land tax collected in kind. See *Glossarium*, CXLI-CXLII; BGA IV, 194; Løkkegaard, *op. cit.*, 244 n. 110.

398. The main town of the coastal plain of Ṭabaristān. See Yāqūt, *Muʿjam*, I, 57–58; Le Strange, *Lands*, 370; Barthold, *Historical Geography*, 238–42; *EI*², s.v. Āmul (L. Lockhart).

399. The westernmost district of Ṭabaristān. See Le Strange, *Lands*, 373–74; Barthold, *Historical Geography*, 233–34.

400. Again a technical financial term, often in the form *ighlāq* (literally, "closing, completing") *al-kharāj*; see Bosworth, "Abū ʿAbdallāh al-Khwārazmī," 135.

401. I.e., the fourth month of the Persian solar calendar, corresponding to late June–early and middle July. The equivalent month in the Avestan calendar is named after Tishtrya; and cf. Armenian Trē (Marquart, *Untersuchungen*, 1, 64 and n. 55).

402. Note *i* by the editor suggests that this person may be the Abū Ṣāliḥ Sarkhāstān named later as Māzyār's deputy in Sāriyah.

403. For *al-taʿdhīr*, the editor's reading of an ambiguous ductus in the mss., the Cairo edition, IX, 82, has *al-taghrīr* "(beware of) rashly exposing yourself to destruction."

nobility!—is going to Qarmāsīn and is sending al-Afshīn to al-Rayy. By my life, if indeed he—may God grant him strength!—does that, it is one thing by means of which God will grant us joy, will provide us with pleasure through his company with us, will enlarge the hope for what we have in the past been accustomed to enjoy of his benefits and favor, and will humble both his enemies and our own enemies. For he—may God grant him nobility!—will certainly not neglect his affairs or abandon his frontier districts and his personal attention to the management of the outlying provinces of his empire simply on account of alarmist reports spread about his tax collectors and slanderous talk about his close associates. Nor will he—may God grant him nobility!—send out his army when he sends it out, nor will he dispatch his commanders, when he dispatches them, except against a [1272] rebel.

Accordingly, read out this letter of ours to the land-tax collectors who are with you, in order that those of them who are present may convey it to those who are absent. Speak to them in harsh terms about exacting fully the taxation, and as for he who intends to break off short the work of levying it (*kasrihi*),[404] let him openly reveal his shortcomings in order that God may bring down on his head what He has brought down [in the past] on his likes. They have an example in the various imposts liable from the people of Jurjān,[405] al-Rayy, and the adjoining districts. The caliphs lightened the land tax due from them, and the obligation to pay the taxes normally raised (*al-rafāʾiʿ*)[406] was removed from them only because of the need that they (the people of Jurjān, etc.) had to combat

404. Again a technical financial term, with the cognate form in *māl munkasir*, relating to tax arrears that, for one reason or another, could not be collected and had to be written off; see Bosworth, "Abū ʿAbdallāh al-Khwārazmī," 136.

405. Persian Gurgān, classical Hyrcania, the region and also its main town, at the southeastern corner of the Caspian Sea. See Yāqūt, *Muʿjam*, II, 119–22; Le Strange, *Lands*, 376–81; Barthold, *Historical Geography*, 115; *EI*[2], s.v. Gurgān (R. Hartmann-[J. A. Boyle]).

406. For this term, see *Glossarium*, CCLVII; in Ṭabarī, trans. Marin, 88, *rufiʿat ʿanhum* is misinterpreted as "raised revenue from them."

the mountain peoples and because of the incursions of the errant Daylamīs;[407] but now God has relieved the Commander of the Faithful—may God exalt him in might!—of all that and has constituted the mountain peoples and the Daylamīs into a force of troops and auxiliaries.[408] God is worthy of praise!

He related: When al-Māzyār's letter reached Shādhān b. al-Faḍl, his collector of the land tax, the latter demanded the tax from the people and collected the whole of it within a space of two months, whereas it used previously to be collected in twelve months, a third every four months.

Then a man called ʿAlī b. Yazdād al-ʿAṭṭār, who was one of the group of persons from whom a hostage had been taken, fled and abandoned al-Māzyār's territory. Abū Ṣāliḥ Sarkhāstān,[409] al-Māzyār's deputy over Sāriyah,[410] was informed of that. He assembled the leading citizens of the town of Sāriyah and began to upbraid them, saying, "How can the king repose any confidence in you, and how can he trust you when this ʿAlī b. Yazdād was one of those who had given his oath, pledged his allegiance, and handed over a hostage but has now broken his oath, departed, and left his hostage behind, while you yourselves are not being true to your pledges and not really condemning this breach of faith and violation of an oath? How can the king trust you, and how can he
[1273] treat you again as you will like?" One of them replied, "We'll kill

407. For the first three centuries or so of Islam, the Caspian coast and the lands to the south of the Elburz range suffered from the incursions of the Daylamīs, predatory mountain people of the western Elburz region who were still pagans; they were converted to Shīʿī Islam by Ḥasanid ʿAlid *duʿāt*, or missionaries, toward the end of the third (ninth) century. See *EI*², s.v. Daylam (V. Minorsky).

408. Ibn al-Faqīh, *op cit.*, 306, trans., 362–63, speaks of Māzyār's earlier desire to implant Islam in Daylam and of a successful expedition thither by his commander al-Surrī (see Ṭabarī, III, 1274 [p. 147 and n. 417, below]). This success can only have been temporary, as the real Islamization of Daylam came later; see n. 407, above.

409. Somewhat dubiously interpreted by Justi, *op. cit.*, 277, 289, and Marquart, *Untersuchungen*, II, 56 n. 5, as meaning "he whose desire is set upon the ruler"; but the element *khʷāst* seems to mean here "seek (out)."

410. Beside Āmul the other main town of the Ṭabaristān coastal plain, at times alternating with Āmul as the administrative center of the province. See Yāqūt, *Muʿjam*, III, 170–71; Le Strange, *Lands*, 370, 375; Barthold, *Historical Geography*, 238–39; *EI*¹, s.v. Sārī (Cl. Huart).

the hostage so that no one else will flee again." Sarkhāstān asked them, "Will you really do that?" They replied, "Yes!" whereupon he wrote to the custodian of the hostages and ordered him to send al-Ḥasan b. ʿAlī b. Yazdād, who was hostage for his father['s good behavior]. But, when they brought him to Sāriyah, the people repented of what they had said to Abū Ṣāliḥ and began to turn violently against the person who had advised killing him. Sarkhāstān then gathered them all together, having previously had the hostage brought in, and addressed them, "Verily, you guaranteed to perform a certain thing; here is the hostage [in question], so put him to death now!" However, ʿAbd al-Karīm b. ʿAbd al-Raḥmān al-Kātib said, "May God guide you in an upright way! [In the past] you granted a delay of two months to those who abandoned this land. Regarding this hostage who is now before you, we ask you to grant him a respite of two months [before killing him]. Then if his father comes back [well and good]; if not you can put into effect your will regarding him."

He related: Sarkhāstān became angry with the people. He summoned the commander of his personal guard, a man called Rustam b. Bārūyah, and ordered him to gibbet the youth. This last asked him to grant him leave to perform two *rakʿahs*.[411] He gave him permission, but the youth took a long time over his act of worship, for he was trembling with fear, and a palm trunk had already been erected for his execution. They therefore dragged the youth from his worship and stretched him on the gibbet, tying his throat round it until he was strangled and expired on it.

[After this] Sarkhāstān ordered the people of the town of Sāriyah to go forth to Āmul, and he ordered the commanders of the garrisons to summon the people of the trenches (*ahl al-khanādiq*) (?),[412] both Abnāʾ and Arabs, to be present. They were duly brought in, and he proceeded with the people of Sāriyah to Āmul, saying to them, "I wish to call you to bear witness for the people of Āmul, and the people of Āmul as witnesses for you,

---

411. I.e., the middle part of the *ṣalāt*, or worship, from the recitation of the *Fātiḥah* to the second *sujūd* or prostration, a certain number of *rakʿahs* making up the whole *ṣalāt*; see *EI*[1], s.v. Ṣalāt (A. J. Wensinck).

412. The reference here is obscure, unless it refers to the defensive works that the inhabitants of the lowland settlements had been constructing to protect themselves.

and I will restore your estates and wealth; if then you stick to obedience and to providing good counsel, we shall from our own resources increase to you twofold what we [previously] took from
[1274] you." When they reached Āmul he gathered them together at the palace of al-Khalīl b. Wandāsfajān,[413] and made the people of Sāriyah go to one side apart from the rest, and he placed al-Lawzajān (?)[414] in charge of them. He wrote down the names of all the people of Āmul until not a single one of their names was hidden from him, and after that he passed them in review, according to their names, until they were all gathered together and not one of them had been left behind. Armed men surrounded them, and they were all paraded in ranks, he having appointed over each one two armed guards. He ordered the man in charge of them to cut off the head of anyone who held back in walking,[415] and the man drove them along with their hands pinioned behind their backs until he brought them to a mountain called Hurmuzdābādh,[416] eight farsakhs from Āmul and eight farsakhs from the town of Sāriyah. There he put them in irons and imprisoned them. They amounted to a total of 20,000. This happened in the year 225 (839/840), according to what has been mentioned from Muḥammad b. Ḥafṣ, but other relaters of historical traditions and a number of persons who were alive at that time state that it happened in 224 (838/839), and I believe that the latter is more likely to be correct, since the killing of Māzyār took place in 225 and the measures that he took against the people of Ṭabaristān were one year previous to that.

The narrative returns to the story of Māzyār and what he did to the people of Āmul, according to what has been mentioned from

---

413. Following *Addenda et emendanda*, DCCLXXIV, and Ibn al-Faqīh, *op. cit.*, 305 and n. *1*, trans., 362. The original Middle Persian form of this name is *Windād-ispān*, literally, "having attained peace, tranquility"; see Justi, *op. cit.*, 370.

414. Reading of this name dubious.

415. *Kāʿa ʿan al-mashy*, literally, "walked on one side of the foot." The verb *kāʿa* means basically "to walk on its knuckles (of a dog)"; see *WbKAS*, I, 437–38.

416. This was the site of Māzyār's main stronghold; see Ṭabarī, III, 1291–92 (p. 165, below). From Ṭabarī's account of subsequent operations in the area, III, 1289–92, Minorsky concluded that it must have lain in the valley of the Tālār river, or river of ʿAlīābād; see *EI*², s.v. Māzandarān (V. Minorsky-[C. E. Bosworth]).

Muḥammad b. Ḥafṣ. He related: Māzyār wrote to al-Durrī[417] to do the same thing with the leading men of the Arabs and the Abnā' who were with him at Muzn,[418] and he placed them in irons, imprisoned them, and appointed guards over them in their prison.

When Māzyār became assured of his position and his power and his domination of the people became firmly established, he [1275] gathered together his followers and ordered Sarkhāstān to demolish the walls of the town of Āmul. Sarkhāstān accordingly did this, to the accompaniment of music from drums and flutes, and then proceeded to the town of Sāriyah and did the same there. Then Māzyār sent his brother Qūhyār to the town of Ṭamīs,[419] which is situated in the province of Ṭabaristān on the frontier of Jurjān, and he demolished its walls and its inner *madīnah*[420] and allowed its people to be taken as lawful spoil. Those who were able fled, but others suffered in the general calamity. After that Sarkhāstān set out for Ṭamīs, and Qūhyār came back from it and then joined his brother al-Māzyār. Sarkhāstān built a wall from Ṭamīs to the [Caspian] Sea and made it stretch out into the sea for a distance of three miles (or: its extension into the sea amounted to a distance of three miles). The Persian emperors had originally constructed this wall between themselves and the Turks because in their time the Turks used to raid the people of Ṭabaristān. Sarkhāstān encamped with his forces at Ṭamīs; he surrounded it with a secure trench and guard towers, provided it with a strong gate, and posted trustworthy men there as custodians.[421]

---

417. This name appears in Ibn al-Faqīh, *op. cit.*, 306, trans., 363, as al-Surrī, previously sent by Māzyār against the Daylamīs; see p. 144 n. 408, above.

418. Amending the text's *Marw* in accordance with *Addenda et emendanda*, DCCLXXIV, and Ibn al-Faqīh, *op cit.*, 305, 306; this is also the reading of the Cairo edition, IX, 100. According to Ibn al-Faqīh, *op cit.*, 305–7, trans., 362–63, and Yāqūt, *Muʿjam*, V, 122, it was a place from which raids were launched into pagan Daylam by the Muslim governors.

419. On this place, see n. 421, below.

420. I.e., the core area of a town, that part of it around the citadel (*qalʿah, arg*) containing the markets, Friday mosque, government offices, etc. (Persian *shahrastān*), as opposed to the surrounding suburbs (*rabaḍ, bīrūn*); on the frequent tripartite structure of eastern Islamic towns, see Barthold, *Turkestan*, 78.

421. Ṭamīs(ah), modern Tammīshah, lies on the eastern border of Ṭabaristān adjoining Jurjān; according to Yāqūt, *Muʿjam*, IV, 41, the Emperor Khusraw Anūshirwān built a causeway there to carry the highway to Jurjān and Khurāsān

The people of Jurjān grew apprehensive and feared for their property and their town, and small group of them fled to Naysābūr.[422] The news reached ʿAbdallāh b. Ṭāhir and al-Muʿtaṣim, so the former dispatched against Māzyār his paternal uncle al-Ḥasan b. al-Ḥusayn b. Muṣʿab,[423] together with a powerful army with which to secure Jurjān. He ordered him to make his camp at the trench; hence al-Ḥasan b. al-Ḥusayn encamped at those defenses that Sarkhāstān had constructed, just the width of the trench separating the two armies. ʿAbdallāh b. Ṭāhir further dispatched Ḥayyān b. Jabalah[424] with 4,000 men to Qūmis,[425] where he made his camp on the edge of the mountains
[1276] of Sharwīn. For his part, al-Muʿtaṣim sent from his headquarters

---

over the marshes facing the Caspian; see also Le Strange, *Lands*, 375, and Barthold, *Historical Geography*, 232, 238 n. 49. There were certainly walls here in Sāsānid times, part of a system of man-made defenses intended to protect or to block points of entrance into Persia against invading armies, nomadic hordes, etc.; other such defenses were to be found along the Iraqi desert fringes, in the Caucasus, and in Jurjān. The Tammīshah walls, extending into the Caspian, were probably a second line of defense behind those in Jurjān farther east. Anūshirwān is popularly associated with the construction of various walls but may have simply repaired or reconstructed them. The ancient Tammīshah walls were demolished by Māzyār but then rebuilt by his commander Sarkhāstān. Recent excavations at the site have yielded finds of Kushan and Kushano-Sāsānid provenance, clearly indicating early settlement in the area. See Marquart, *Untersuchungen*, II, 56; A. D. H. Bivar and G. Fehérvári, "The Walls of Tammīsha," 35–50; Frye, "Sasanian System of Walls," 13–14.

422. Ibn Isfandiyār, *op cit.*, trans. 153–54 (also Kaabi, *op cit.*, I, 254, and II, 81–83), gives the text of an Arabic *qaṣīdah* by a certain Abū al-Qāsim Hārūn b. Muḥammad, which was addressed to the Caliph al-Muʿtaṣim on behalf of the people of Āmul, complaining of Māzyār's tyranny and seeking deliverance from the hands of ʿAbdallāh b. Ṭāhir.

423. I.e., the brother of the first Ṭāhirid governor of Khurāsān, Ṭāhir Dhū al-Yamīnayn and uncle of Isḥāq b. Ibrāhīm al-Muṣʿabī, governor of Baghdad (on whom see p. 3 n. 8, above). In the past there had been ill feeling over the succession in Khurāsān after Ṭāhir's death, with a brief rebellion by al-Ḥasan in Kirmān in 208 (823–24), for which, however, he was pardoned; see Ṭabarī, III, 1066. After Māzyār was defeated, al-Ḥasan remained in that office till his death in 231 (846); see Ṭabarī, III, 1357. On al-Ḥasan, see Nafīsī, *Taʾrīkh-i khāndān-i Ṭāhirī*, 29–30 (giving the date of his death as 231 [845–46]; the present writer has not been able to find this event exactly dated thus in the text of Marʿashī as edited by Shāyān); Kaabi, *op. cit.*, I, 189, 254–55, 293, 296.

424. Described in Ṭabarī, III, 1282 (p. 156, below), as a mawlā of ʿAbdallāh b. Ṭāhir's.

425. The small province (classical Komisēnē) the center of which was Dāmghān, lying to the southeast of the Elburz range along the Khurāsān highway.

Muḥammad b. Ibrāhīm b. Muṣʿab, Isḥāq b. Ibrāhīm's brother, with a large army, attaching to him the commander al-Ḥasan b. Qārin al-Ṭabarī[426] and the force of Ṭabarī troops who were at court. He also sent Manṣūr b. al-Ḥasan Hār, the lord of Dunbāwand,[427] to the city of al-Rayy that he might enter Ṭabaristān from the direction of al-Rayy, and he despatched Abū al-Sāj [Dīwdād] to al-Lāriz[428] and Dunbāwand.

When the cavalry surrounded al-Māzyār from every side he sent at that point Ibrāhīm b. Mihrān,[429] the commander of his police, and ʿAlī b. Rabban al-Kātib al-Naṣrānī,[430] together with the deputy of the commander of the guard,[431] to the people of the towns (of Āmul and Sāriyah) who had been imprisoned by him, [saying], "The [Arab] cavalry have crept up round me on every side. I imprisoned you only so that this fellow"—he meant al-Muʿtaṣim—"might make overtures to me on your behalf; but

---

See Yāqūt, *Muʿjam*, IV, 414–15; Le Strange, *Lands*, 364–68; Schwarz, *op. cit.*, 809–28; Barthold, *Historical Geography*, 87, 121; *EI*², s.v. Ḳūmis (C. E. Bosworth).

426. Probably a member of the Bāwandid family, a son of Qārin, himself son of Sharwīn b. Surkhāb, who had died in al-Ma'mūn's reign. See Justi, *op. cit.*, 431; Rabino di Borgomale, "Les dynasties du Māzandarān," 412.

427. The region of Ṭabaristān around the highest point of the Elburz chain, Mount Demavend. See Le Strange, *Lands*, 371; Schwarz, *op. cit.*, 785–92; *EI*²; s.v. Damāwand (M. Streck).

428. Variously described as a town of al-Rūyān (Ibn al-Faqīh, *op.cit.*, 303, trans., 359) and as a village with a citadel near Āmul (Yāqūt, *Muʿjam*, V, 7), See also *EI*², s.v. Lār and Lāridjān (J. Calmard).

429. Later described (in Ṭabarī, III, 1540, year 251 [865]) as the owner of a house in Sāmarrā and called al-Naṣrānī al-ʿAskarī—the latter presumably because, although Christians were commonly secretaries and financial officials, it was less common that they should be military men. After the collapse of Māzyār's cause Ibrāhīm must have entered the caliphal service.

430. ʿAlī b. Sahl Rabban, a Nestorian Christian from Khurāsān, subsequently passed into the caliphal service and, under al-Mutawakkil, converted to Islam. It was after this, in *ca.* 240 (854–55), that he wrote his celebrated defense of his new faith, *Kitāb al-dīn wa-al-dawlah*; see *GAL*, S I, 415; *GCAL*, II, 120; *GAS*, III, 236–40.

431. The repetition of the whole phrase *khalīfat ṣāḥib al-ḥaras* shortly afterward (III, 1277 l. 3) inclines one to think that *khalīfah* here means "deputy," rather than a personal name, as Marin takes it, Ṭabarī, trans. Marin, 91. This seems also to be the opinion of the editor of the text here, who, at III, 1277 n. *a*, suggests, on the basis of ms. C, that the personal name Muḥammad might perhaps be inserted here before the word *khalīfah*; it is also the opinion of the compiler(s) of the indexes, who do not include this person under the name Khalīfah.

he has not made a move. I have heard that al-Ḥajjāj b. Yūsuf[432] once became angry at the ruler of al-Sind because of a woman of the Muslims who had been captured and taken to al-Sind, to the point that he sent an expedition against that land and expended whole treasuries until he had rescued the woman and returned her to her own city. But this fellow does not care about 20,000 people and is not sending to me anyone to inquire about you! I will certainly not move forward and engage him in warfare while you are in my rear, so hand over to me the land tax for two years, and I will then release you. Those among you who are strong young men I will send forth to battle, and to those who fulfill their promise to me I will return their wealth and possessions, but, for those who fail to keep their promise, I shall have already assessed their blood money. Further, those who are aged men or
[1277] feeble I will appoint as guards or doorkeepers."

A man called Mūsā b. Hurmuz al-Zāhid[433]—of whom it was said that he had not drunk water for the previous twenty years—said, "I will hand over to you two years' land tax and assume responsibility for this matter. But the deputy of the commander of the guard said to Aḥmad b. al-Ṣuqayr, "Why don't you speak out, for you used to be the most highly favored of the people in the Ispahbadh's eyes? I used to see you eating with him and lolling back on his cushion, and this was something that the prince did with no one else. Thus you are more suitable for taking charge of this affair than Mūsā." Aḥmad replied, "Mūsā will certainly not be able to assume responsibility for collecting a single dirham. He answered you in this foolish manner only because of the stress that he and all the people are under.[434] If your master had known that we had a single dirham, he would not have imprisoned us; in fact, he imprisoned us only after cleaning us out of all the possessions and treasuries we had. If he seeks to acquire landed estates by means of this wealth, we will

432. The celebrated Umayyad governor of the East (75–95 [694–714]), known for his firm rule over the turbulent Arab tribes of Iraq but also, as here, for his meticulous oversight and care for the welfare of the Muslims. See *EI*², s.v. al-Ḥadjdjādj b. Yūsuf (A. Dietrich).

433. I.e., "the ascetic."

434. Following Ṭabarī, trans. Marin, 92, rather than the reading of the editor in n. *g*, which seems to make less sense in the context.

give it to him." ʿAlī b. Rabban al-Kātib said to him, "The estates belong to the ruler [anyway] and not to you," and Ibrāhīm b. Mihrān added, "I implore you by God, O Abū Muḥammad, not to say this sort of thing!"[435] Aḥmad said to him, "I wasn't saying anything until this fellow spoke to me the words you just heard."

At that point the envoys, accepting the guarantee of Mūsā al-Zāhid, went back and informed al-Māzyār of his undertaking. A group of fiscal agents [*suʿāt*][436] attached themselves to Mūsā al-Zāhid and said, "So-and-so is capable of paying 10,000, and so-and-so 20,000, more or less"; and they began to appropriate the wealth of those subject to the land tax and of others as well. When this process had gone on for some days Māzyār sent envoys again, demanding the money and seeking fulfillment of what Mūsā al-Zāhid had guaranteed, but he was unable to collect the merest [1278] trace of that or any reliable information about it. The truth of Aḥmad's words was established, and the offense became firmly fixed to him (i.e., to Mūsā al-Zāhid). Al-Māzyār had [actually] realized that the people did not have the wherewithal to pay; he wanted only to make trouble between those liable to the land tax and the merchants and artisans who were not liable to it.[437]

He related: Sarkhāstān had with him a group of vigorous and brave youths whom he had chosen from the sons of commanders[438] and others of the people of Āmul. He gathered together in his own house 260 of those youths whose presence in his vicinity he feared, ostensibly for interrogation purposes. Then

435. *Lammā sakatta ʿan hādhā al-kalām*; for this sense of *lammā* after an oath, see W. Wright, *op. cit.*, II, 340A, par. 186 Rem *c*, and Reckendorf, *op. cit.*, 512, par 262. 12.

436. Sing. *sāʿī*, literally, "someone who busies himself with an affair," whence in later usage "courier, agent of the *barīd* or postal service"; see Dozy, *Supplément*, I, 656. Here it must refer to the agents of the *Dīwān* who went out into the field personally to collect taxes in money or kind.

437. Again, the implication is that Māzyār was following a policy of encouraging divisiveness and disunity among the various social classes of Ṭabaristān, in order to strengthen his own authoritarian rule.

438. This is the literal translation of *abnāʾ al-quwwād*, yet it seems clear, from the mention of the Abnāʾ (in the technical sense) just below that what is intended is a reference to the Abnāʾ resident in the towns of Ṭabaristān and regarded, despite their Khurāsānian origin, as hostile to Māzyār, perceived as the representative of purely Iranian feeling; the rendering in Ṭabarī, trans. Marin, 93, "some officers of the *Abnāʾ*," thus seems more accurate.

he sent a message to selected cultivators (*al-akarah al-mukhtārīn*) of the *dihqāns* (i.e., to the local Persian agrarian population) and told them, "The sympathies of the Abnā' are [inevitably] with the Arabs and with the partisans of the ʿAbbāsid régime (*al-musawwidah*; literally, "the wearers of black"),[439] and I do not feel safe from their treachery and scheming. I have assembled together the suspect persons from among those whose presence I fear, so kill them, in order that you, too, may feel secure and that there may not be in your military forces anyone whose sympathies are in conflict with your own aspirations." At that, he ordered their hands to be pinioned behind them and their handing over to the *dihqān* cultivators by night, and this was done. They took them to a *qanāt*[440] thereabouts, then killed them and threw their corpses into the inspection shafts of that *qanāt* and returned home. But, when they recovered their senses, they regretted what they had done and were filled with fright at it.

When al-Māzyār realized that the people had nothing with which they could pay him, he sent a message to the select group of cultivators—the ones who had killed the 260 youths—and said to them, "I herewith grant to you as lawful spoil the dwellings of the owners of the estates and their womenfolk also, except for any of their daughters who are beautiful maidens,[441] for they are to become the ruler's (i.e., his own) property." He went on to tell
[1279] them, "Go to the prison and kill all the owners of the estates first; then after that take possession of the houses and womenfolk that I have bestowed upon you." But the men were too faint hearted to do that. They were stricken with fear and behaved cautiously and did not do what he had ordered them to do.

He related: The men appointed by Sarkhāstān to guard the walls of Āmul) used to talk by night with al-Ḥasan b. al-Ḥusayn b. Muṣʿab's guard, there being just the width of the trench between

---

439. See p. 31 n. 120, above.

440. I.e., a subterranean irrigation tunnel, which would have vertical shafts at intervals for inspection and cleaning; see EI^2, s.v. Ḳanāt. I. In Iran (A. K. S. Lambton).

441. *Jāriyah* seems here to have the general sense of "girl, maiden," rather than the more specific sense of "slave girl"; the Arabic lexicographers take it as the female equivalent of *ghulām* and explain unconvincingly that it is derived from the woman's activity and running about (verb *jarā* "to run, flow").

them, to the point that they grew to be on familiar terms with each other. Al-Ḥasan's guard and Sarkhāstān's guardians of the wall conspired together for the latter to hand over the walls to the besiegers. They accordingly did that, and al-Ḥasan b. al-Ḥusayn's guard entered via that spot to Sarkhāstān's camp, unknown to either al-Ḥasan b. al-Ḥusayn or to Sarkhāstān. Al-Ḥasan's troops observed a band of persons entering from the wall, so they joined them in entering [the town]. The inhabitants looked at each other (i.e., in astonishment) and were thrown into perturbation. Al-Ḥasan b. al-Ḥusayn b. Muṣʿab arrived and began shouting to the populace to keep them back, saying, "O people, I fear for your safety lest you become like the people of Dāwandān!"[442] But the troops of Qays b. Zanjūyah, who was one of al-Ḥasan b. al-Ḥusayn's men, continued going on until they set their banner on top of the wall in Sarkhāstān's camp. The news finally reached Sarkhāstān that the Arabs had broken through the wall and entered the town unexpectedly. Accordingly, his only thought was of flight, he being at that moment in the bathhouse (*ḥammām*). He heard the shouting, so came forth and fled, clad only in a thin shift (*ghilālah*).[443]

When al-Ḥasan b. al-Ḥusayn found himself impotent to get his followers to come back, he said, "O God, they have indeed disobeyed me but have obeyed you, O God, so watch over them and succor them." Al-Ḥasan's forces continued to follow the [first [1280]
wave of] troops until they reached the gate in the wall; they broke it down and poured in, without anyone hindering them, until they had gained control over all who were in the camp, with one group [of the troops] continuing the search (i.e., for fugitives).

It has been mentioned from Zurārah b. Yūsuf al-Sijzī[444] that he

442. Said by Yāqūt, , *Muʿjam*, II, 434–35, to have been a place near the site of the later Islamic town of Wāsiṭ in lower Iraq; the inhibitants in ancient times fled in order to avoid the plague, were nevertheless killed by divine action, but were brought to life again by the prophet Ezekiel (Arabic Hizqīl; see T. P. Hughes, *Dictionary of Islam*, 114). In traditional exegesis, Qur'ān II: 244/243, was taken to refer to the inhabitants of Dāwandān. In early Islamic times a Christian monastery, the Dayr Hizqīl, was located there. See Yaʿqūbī, *Buldān*, 321, trans., 164; Yāqūt, *Muʿjam*, II, 540–41.

443. A garment worn by both sexes, more recently the equivalent of an undershirt. See Dozy, *Vêtements*, 319–23; *EI*², s.v. Libās, i, ii (Y. K. Stillman).

444. I.e., the man from Sijistān, or Sīstān, on the border between modern Persia and Afghanistan.

said: I passed onward in the search, and while I was thus engaged I came to a spot on the left side of the road. I was afraid to penetrate farther into it, but then I rushed headlong into it with my spear without, however, seeing anyone. I shouted out, "Who are you? Woe upon you!" when behold, a well-built, elderly man cried out "*Zīnhār*!" meaning "Quarter!"[445] He related: I rushed upon him and seized him and pinioned him securely with cords, and, lo, it was Shahriyār, the brother of Abū Ṣāliḥ Sarkhāstān, the chief of the army. He related: I handed him over to my commander, Yaʿqūb b. Manṣūr. Night descended, preventing us from continuing the search, whereupon the troops returned to their camp. Shahriyār was brought to al-Ḥasan b. al-Ḥusayn, who had his head cut off.

As for Abū Ṣāliḥ, he went onward until he was some five farsakhs from his camp, being ill at this time. He was also tormented by thirst and fear. He halted in a thicket on the right-hand side of the road at the foot of a mountain, tethered his mount, and threw himself down on his back. One of his own slave boys and also one of his retainers called Jaʿfar b. Wandāmīd[446] recognized him and saw him reposing there. Sarkhāstān cried out, "O Jaʿfar, a drink of water, for I have become afflicted by thirst!" He (Jaʿfar) related: I replied, "I have no vessel with me with which I can get water from this place." Sarkhāstān said, "Take the top of my quiver and get me water in that." Jaʿfar related: At that, I went along to a number of my comrades and
[1281] told them, "This devil has brought about our destruction, so why should we not ingratiate ourselves by means of him with the ruling power (i.e., the ʿAbbāsid central government) and secure for ourselves a guarantee of safe-conduct?" They asked him, "How shall we achieve this through him?" He related: He made them stand round him and told them, "Help me for brief moment, and I will spring upon him." So Jaʿfar took a large beam of wood, Sarkhāstān being meanwhile laid out on his back, and hurled himself on Sarkhāstān; they overpowered him and made him fast by pinioning him to the beam. Abū Ṣāliḥ cried out to them, "Take

445. Persian *zinhār* "protection, refuge, security."

446. The latter element probably a compressed form of the name Windād-umīd, literally, "bringing about the attainment of hope," see Justi, *op. cit.*, 370.

from me 100,000 dirhams and leave me alone, for the Arabs will not give you anything." They said to him, "Produce it forthwith!" But he replied, "Bring some scales!" They protested, "Where are there any scales here?" But he replied, "And where is there anything for me to give you? But go with me to my house, and I will furnish you with bonds and guarantees of payment; truly, I will fulfill my promises to you and lavish wealth upon you."

Nevertheless, they took him along to al-Ḥasan b. al-Ḥusayn, one of whose cavalry detachments came out to meet them, and these cavalrymen cut off their heads. They seized Sarkhāstān from them, intending themselves to profit by him, and then al-Ḥasan's men conveyed Sarkhāstān to al-Ḥasan himself. When they brought him before al-Ḥasan, the latter summoned the military leaders of Ṭabaristān, such as Muḥammad b. al-Mughīrah b. Shuʿbah al-Azdī, ʿAbdallāh b. Muḥammad al-Quṭquṭī al-Ḍabbī, al-Fatḥ b. Q.rāṭ, and others,[447] and asked them, "Is this Sarkhāstān?" They replied "Yes!" Then he said to Muḥammad b. al-Mughīrah, "Arise and kill him in revenge for your son and brother!" Muḥammad went up to him and struck him with sword; the blows found their mark, and he was killed.

The Story of the Poet Abū Shās [1282]

The poet Abū Shās, whose full name was al-Ghiṭrīf b. Ḥusayn b. Ḥanash, was a youth of Iraqi origin but raised in Khurāsān, well educated and knowledgeable.[448] Sarkhāstān had attached Abū Shās to himself to learn from him the characteristics and ways of thought of the Arabs. When Sarkhāstān suffered his fate Abū Shās was in his military camp, together with riding beasts and baggage. A group of the Bukhāriyyah[449] from al-Ḥasan's troops suddenly fell upon him, seizing as plunder everything that he had with him, and several wounds were inflicted on him. Hence he rapidly snatched up a water jar he had by him, placed it on his shoulder,

447. From their names and the context, apparently members of the Arab or Abnāʾ military class settled in the towns of Ṭabaristān.

448. Obviously a poet of purely local fame; he is not mentioned in Abū al-Faraj al-Iṣfahānī, *Aghānī*.

449. I.e., troops drawn from the Iranian population of Bukhārā; cf. p. 49 n. 159, above.

took a drinking cup in his hand, and shouted, "Water freely available!" (*al-mā' li-al-sabīl*)[450] until he took advantage of a moment of inattentiveness on the part of the soldiers and fled from his tent, despite his wounds. When he passed by the tent of ʿAbdallāh b. Muḥammad b. Ḥumayd al-Quṭquṭī al-Ṭabarī, al-Ḥasan b. al-Ḥusayn's secretary, a slave boy spotted him, and they, that is, his slaves, recognized him also, he at that moment having the water jar on his shoulder, giving out water. They took him into their tent and told their master what Abū Shās was doing. He was accordingly brought into the presence of their master (ʿAbdallāh b. Muḥammad), who gave him a mount, provided him with [rich] clothing, and showed him the highest honor. He mentioned him to al-Ḥasan b. al-Ḥusayn and told Abū Shās, "Compose an ode on the Amīr!" Abū Shās, however, replied, "By God, fear and dread have blotted out what there was of the Qur'ān in my breast, so how can I compose a satisfactory ode?"

Al-Ḥasan sent Abū Ṣāliḥ Sarkhāstān's head to ʿAbdallāh b. Ṭāhir, but he did not leave his camp.

The Continuation of the Operations against Māzyār and His Capture and Execution

It has been mentioned from Muḥammad b. Ḥafṣ that Ḥayyān b. Jabalah, the mawlā of ʿAbdallāh b. Ṭāhir, had drawn near, in the
[1283] company of al-Ḥasan b. al-Ḥusayn, to the vicinity of Ṭamīs. He entered into correspondence with Qārin b. Shahriyār and encouraged him to give obedience, promising him that he would guarantee him possession of the mountain territories that his father and grandfather had held. Qārin was actually one of Māzyār's commanders and the son of his brother.[451] Māzyār had

450. *Sabīl*, in full *fī sabīl Allāh*, denotes anything made available by pious charity but is used especially in connection with the provision of drinking water. From this arises the later usage, certainly from Mamlūk times onward, of *sabīl* alone = "drinking fountain, source of fresh water provided by charity" and of the verbal noun *tasbīl* = "the charitable distribution of drinking water." See Dozy, *Supplément*, I, 630; Lane, *Manners and Customs*, Chapter 14, 332–33; *EI*[1], s.v. Sabīl (T. W. Haig).

451. This nephew of Māzyār was his governor in the Jabal Sharwīn and the eastern part of the Elburz range adjoining Jurjān. For his services in abandoning Māzyār's cause, he was rewarded after his uncle's fall by the grant of Jabal

sent him out with his [further] brother ʿAbdallāh b. Qārin, attaching to them a number of his trusty commanders and faithful relatives of his. When Ḥayyān endeavored to win over Qārin, the latter guaranteed to Ḥayyān that he would hand over to him the mountains and the town of Sāriyah as far as the frontier with Jurjān, on condition that Ḥayyān would make him ruler over the mountain territories held by his father and grandfather once he (Qārin) had fulfilled his pledge to Ḥayyān. Ḥayyān wrote to ʿAbdallāh b. Ṭāhir about this, and ʿAbdallāh set down formally, in writing and duly sealed, everything he asked, but he wrote back also to Ḥayyān that he should halt for a while and not enter the mountains or penetrate deeply into them until something should come from Qārin that would indicate his good faith, lest there be some trickery on his part.

Ḥayyān wrote to Qārin in these terms, and Qārin forthwith summoned ʿAbdallāh b. Qārin, Māzyār's brother, together with all his commanders, to a feast. When they had all eaten, laid down their weapons, and felt completely at ease, his own troops, who were armed to the teeth, surrounded them, pinioned them in bonds, and sent them to Ḥayyān b. Jabalah. When they reached Ḥāyyān he made sure of them and then rode forth with his forces until they entered the mountains of Qārin (*jibāl Qārin*).

News of this event reached Māzyār and disturbed him deeply. His brother al-Qūhyār said to him, "You have 20,000 Muslims in your custody, ranging from shoemakers to tailors, and you have given your attention to them; but now you are faced with the question of your own security and that of your family and kindred, so what are you going to do now with these prisoners in your custody?" He related: At that, Māzyār ordered the release of all who were in his custody. Then he summoned Ibrāhīm b. Mihrān, the commander of his police guard; ʿAlī b. Rabban al-Naṣrānī, his secretary; Shādhān b. al-Faḍl, the chief fiscal [1284]
officer (*ṣāḥib kharājihi*); and Yaḥyā b. al-Rūzbahār, his assayer and banker (*jahbadhahu*[452]), who were all members of the

Sharwīn, and in 227 (842) he became a Muslim; see Madelung, "Minor Dynasties," 205–6.

452. On this term, which may be of Persian origin and derive from Sāsānid administrative practice, see *EI*², s.v. D̲j̲ahbad̲h̲ (W. J. Fischel).

element of plains dwellers in his entourage, and said to them, "Your womenfolk, your residences, and your estates are all in the [coastal] plain, which the Arabs have now entered. I do not wish to bring down on you ill fortune, so go back to your dwellings and obtain guarantees of safety for yourselves." He then gave them gifts and accorded them permission to return, and they went away to their dwellings and obtained guarantees of safety for themselves.

When the people of the town of Sāriyah heard the news of Sarkhāstān's capture, the plundering of his camp, and Ḥayyān b. Jabalah's invasion of Sharwīn's mountain territories, they rose up and attacked Māzyār's governor (*ʿāmil*) in Sāriyah, who was called Mahrīstānī b. Shahrīz, but he fled from them and saved his skin. The populace threw open the gate of the prison and released those jailed there. After that Ḥayyān arrived at the town of Sāriyah; news of his arrival in Sāriyah reached Qūhyār, Māzyār's brother, whereupon he set free from his imprisonment Muḥammad b. Mūsā b. Ḥafṣ, the governor of Ṭabaristān, set him on a mule with a saddle, and dispatched him to Ḥayyān in order that Ḥayyān might accord him a guarantee of safety and so that Ḥayyān might grant him the mountain territories that his father and grandfather had held, [this] on condition that he would hand over Māzyār to Ḥayyān. To make that firm, he would offer him the guarantees of Muḥammad b. Mūsā b. Ḥafṣ and Aḥmad b. al-Ṣuqayr. When Muḥammad b. Mūsā came to Ḥayyān and told him about Qūhyār's message to him, Ḥayyān said to him, "Who is this?" meaning Aḥmad. Muḥammad b. Mūsā replied, "The leading figure of the region; the representatives (*al-khulafāʾ*) [of the central government] know him,[453] as does the Amīr ʿAbdallāh b.
[1285] Ṭāhir." Ḥayyān then sent for Aḥmad, and he came to him. He ordered Aḥmad to set out for the garrison at Khurramābādh[454] in

453. The Cairo edition, IX, 91, has *wa-baqiyyat al-khulafāʾ* "and the best of the representatives (of the central government)."

454. A village in the province of al-Rayy, according to Yāqūt, *Muʿjam*, II, 361. It is to be distinguished from the better-known Khurramābādh in Lur-i Kūchik; see Le Strange, *Lands*, 200–1. One should, however, note the existence, in modern times, of at least one other Khurramābād in Māzandarān itself, the chief place of the district of Tunakābun; also Rabino di Borgomale, *Mázandarán and Astarábád*, 23. A location on the coastal plain of Ṭabaristān seems better to fit the

the company of Muḥammad b. Mūsā. Now Aḥmad had a son called Isḥāq who had previously fled from Māzyār, spending the daylight hiding in the dense undergrowth and traveling by night to an estate called Sāwāsh.r.yān on the main highway from Qidḥ[455] al-Iṣbahbadh, where lay Māzyār's fortress.

It has been mentioned from Isḥāq that he said: I was at this estate when a number of Māzyār's troops passed me by, having with them riding beasts that were being led and other [? animals or things]. He related: I leaped onto one of the horses, a stout animal of mixed breed (*ḥajīn*); I rode it bareback and brought it to the town of Sāriyah, and there I handed it over to my father. When Aḥmad decided to set off for Khurramābādh he was riding that horse. Ḥayyān observed him [on it] and was filled with admiration for the horse. He turned to al-Lawzajān, who was one of Qārin's retainers, and said, "I see this shaykh on a noble horse, whose like I have rarely seen!" Al-Lawzajān told him, "This horse was Māzyār's." Ḥayyān thereupon dispatched a message to Aḥmad, asking him to send the horse to him so that he might look it over, and Aḥmad sent it on to him. When Ḥayyān had examined it at length and had inspected it closely he found that it had scarred forelegs, so he lost interest in it and gave it back to al-Lawzajān. He further told Aḥmad's envoy, "This belonged to Māzyār, and Māzyār's property belongs to the Commander of the Faithful."

The envoy returned and informed Aḥmad [about that]. Aḥmad grew angry against al-Lawzajān because of it, and Aḥmad sent him an insulting message. Al-Lawzajān protested, "I've commit- [1286]
ted no fault over this," returning the horse to Aḥmad, together with a horse of inferior breed (*birdhawn*) and a sprightly one of mixed breed (*shihrī fāriḥ*);[456] and he ordered his envoy to deliver

events described in Ṭabarī, III, 1291 (p. 165, below), when the captive Māzyār was sent to Sāriyah from Khurramābādh.

455. *Qidḥ* is presumably used here in the sense of "share, portion," hence "The Ispahbadh's allotment of land"; cf. Qidḥ al-S.l.tān in Ṭabarī, III, 1288 (p. 162, below). It appears to be an alternative designation for Burj al-Iṣpahbadh, mentioned at III, 1269 (see p. 139, above).

456. The word *fāriḥ* is supplied from one of the mss. utilized in the Cairo edition, IX, 91.

them both to him.[457] Aḥmad became angry at how Ḥayyān had treated him and said, "Can this weaver[458] send to a shaykh like myself and treat him as he has done?" At that he wrote to Qūhyār, "Woe upon you! Why do you act so mistakenly in your undertaking? You spurn a man like al-Ḥasan b. al-Ḥusayn, the paternal uncle of ʿAbdallāh b. Ṭāhir, and accept a guarantee of security from this servile wretch of a weaver! You are handing over your brother and diminishing your own prestige (or: power, *qadr/qadar*). Al-Ḥasan b. al-Ḥusayn will bear a secret hatred for you for leaving him and cleaving to one of his vilest slaves!"

Qūhyār wrote back to him, "I have indeed acted mistakenly in the first part of this affair, but I have promised the man that I would come to him the day after tomorrow, and I would not feel safe, if I were to break my word to him, that he would not rise up against me, launch an attack on me, and treat as lawful plunder my properties and possessions. Moreover, if I were to fight with him and as a result were to kill some of his retainers and blood were to flow between us, deeply felt hatred would result. Consequently, this matter that I am working toward would be brought to nothing." Aḥmad wrote to him, "When the day appointed for the meeting comes round, send to him a man from your own household, and write a letter to him that you have been afflicted with an illness that prevents you from moving and that you require medical treatment for three days. Then if you are restored to health [well and good]; if not you will come to him in a litter. We ourselves will prevail upon him to accept that story from you and [the promise of your] coming to him in due course."

Aḥmad b. al-Ṣuqayr and Muḥammad b. Mūsā b. Ḥafṣ wrote to al-Ḥasan b. al-Ḥusayn, who was at that moment in his army camp at Ṭamīs awaiting orders from ʿAbdallāh b. Ṭāhir and a
[1287] reply to his letter announcing the killing of Sarkhāstān and the conquest of Ṭamīs. They wrote to him, "Ride to us so that we can hand over to you Māzyār and the mountain territory; otherwise, he will escape from you, and you will lose the chance of

457. There is some ambiguity here as to whether al-Lawzajān sent the latter two horses or all three of them; cf. Ṭabarī, trans. Marin, 98 n. 463. For these terms denoting various breeds of horse, see EI^2, s.v. Faras (F. Viré).

458. The trade of weaver (*ḥāʾik*) was generally regarded with contempt as mean and debased; see R. Brunschvig, "Métiers vils en Islam," 50–54.

vengeance."[459] They sent the letter with Shādhān b. al-Faḍl al-Kātib and ordered him to journey as speedily as possible. When al-Ḥasan got the letter, he rode off immediately and covered three days' [normal] distance in a single night until he reached Sāriyah; then when the day broke he pressed on to Khurramābādh on what was the day of the appointed meeting with Qūhyār. Ḥayyān heard the sound of the drums accompanying al-Ḥasan; hence he rode out and met him a farsakh's distance away.

Al-Ḥasan said to him, "What are you doing here? Why are you making your way to this place? You have conquered the mountain territories of Sharwīn, yet you have abandoned them and come here! What guarantee do you have that an opportunity may not present itself to the people there and that they will not act treacherously with you, so that all you have achieved will crumble to pieces around you? Get back to the mountains, send out garrisons to the outlying parts and districts, and keep such a close eye on the people there that they will have no opportunity to act treacherously, even if they intend it." Ḥayyān replied, "I am just about to go back, and I want only to transport my baggage and give orders for departure to my men." Al-Ḥasan, however, told him, "Your yourself get moving, and I'll send on your baggage and your troops after you. Spend tonight in the town of Sāriyah, so that they may catch up with you, and then set off in the morning." Ḥayyān accordingly left immediately, just as al-Ḥasan had ordered him, for Sāriyah.

There then reached Ḥayyān a letter from ʿAbdallāh b. Ṭāhir, instructing him to camp at Labūrah[460] in the mountains of Wandāhurmuz,[461] this being the most strongly fortified place in

---

459. Vocalizing the text here as *fa-lā naqm*[a]; the Cairo edition, IX, 92, has less plausibly *fa-lā taqum* "so don't arise!"

460. This is the Lafūr frequently mentioned by Ibn Isfandiyār (*op. cit.*, index), on the eastern source of the Bābul river, which runs down to Bārfurūsh. Subsequently it was ruled by local Ispahbadhs; see Rabino di Borgomale, *Mázandarán and Astarábád*, 118, 147); Ibn Isfandiyār *op. cit.*, 95, states that in his time (early seventh [thirteenth] century) the noble families of Lafūr traced their descent back to the Qārinids, early rulers of the district. See also p. 180 n. 511, below.

461. At III, 1295 (pp. 168–69, below), Ṭabarī describes the mountain of Māzyār's grandfather Wandād-Hurmuz as in the center of the mountains of Ṭabaristān between that of his brother Wandās.b./f.jān and the Jabal Sharwīn of the Bāwandid prince; see Rabino di Borgomale, *Mázandarán and Astarábád*, 2.

his mountains and the spot where the greater part of Māzyār's wealth was stored. ʿAbdallāh gave further orders to Ḥayyān that
[1288] he should not prevent Qārin from doing what he wished in regard to those mountains and treasures. Qārin accordingly carried off that wealth of Māzyār's deposited there and Māzyār's treasuries at Asbāndarah,[462] together with what Sarkhāstān had at Qidḥ al-S.l.tān,[463] and took possession of the whole of it. Thus because of that horse everything that had presented itself to Ḥayyān as a favorable opportunity crumbled about him. Ḥayyān b. Jabalah died after that, and ʿAbdallāh sent in his place and over his troops Muḥammad b. al-Ḥusayn b. Muṣʿab, with orders that he should not prevent Qārin from doing anything he wished.

Al-Ḥasan b. al-Ḥusayn arrived at Khurramābādh. Muḥammad b. Mūsā b. Ḥafṣ and Aḥmad b. al-Ṣuqayr came to him; they engaged in private discussions with him, and he said to them, "May God reward you handsomely [for that]!" He himself wrote to Qūhyār, who came to Khurramābādh and went to al-Ḥasan, who rewarded him and showed him honor and agreed to everything he asked. The two of them fixed on a certain day [for the betrayal of Māzyār]. Then al-Ḥasan dismissed Qūhyār, who now went to Māzyār and informed him that he had secured for him a guarantee of safe-conduct and made it firm for him. Al-Ḥasan b. Qārin had written to Qūhyār from where Muḥammad b. Ibrāhīm b. Musʿab was, pledging to him desirable rewards from the part of the Commander of the Faithful, and in response Qūhyār had pledged to him what he had pledged to others, all this being aimed at deterring them from making war, and had gone over to al-Ḥasan's side. Muḥammad b. Ibrāhīm rode off from the town of Āmul, and the information [about all this] reached al-Ḥasan b. al-Ḥusayn.

It has been mentioned from Ibrāhim b. Mihrān that he was engaged in conversation at Abū al-Saʿdī's, and when the meridian approached he went back in the direction of his residence. His
[1289] way went past the door of al-Ḥasan's tent. He related: When I drew opposite his tent, lo, al-Ḥasan appeared, riding alone with merely three Turkish slave retainers of his following him. He

462. The reading of this name in the manuscripts is very doubtful.

463. The vocalization of the second element of this name is uncertain.

related: I threw myself off my mount and greeted him, at which he said, "Mount!" When I had remounted he said, "Where is the road to Ārum?"[464] I replied, "It goes through this valley." He said to me, "Proceed in front of me." He related: So I proceeded until I reached a pass two miles from Ārum. He related: I became very afraid and expostulated, "May God guide the Amīr uprightly! This is a fearful place; not less than a thousand cavalrymen ought to venture along this path! I would advise you to turn back and not enter it!" He related: But he roared at me, "Go on!" So I went on, almost bereft of my reason, although we did not see anyone along the road until we reached Ārum. Then he said to me, "Where is the road to Hurmuzdābādh?" I replied, "Over the mountain, by this track." He related: He told me, "Travel along it!" I protested, "May God make the Amīr mighty! [I seek the help of] God in preserving you and ourselves and all this body of troops with you!"[465] He related: But he shouted back at me, "Get going, O son of a stinking, uncircumcised whore!" He related: I said to him, "May God make the Amīr mighty! Cut my head off yourself, for this would be preferable to me than Māzyār's killing me and than the Amīr ʿAbdallāh b. Ṭāhir's fastening the blame on me!" He related: He thereupon upbraided me so roughly that I thought he was going to lay violent hands on me, and I went along, having completely lost heart. I said to myself, "At any moment now we shall all be seized, and I shall be brought before Māzyār; he will upbraid and threaten me and will say, 'You have acted as a guide against me!'" This was our situation when we reached Hurmuzdābādh as the sun began to gleam. Al-Ḥasan said to me, "Whereabouts around here was the prison where the Muslims were kept?" I replied, "On this very spot." He related: He dismounted and sat down, while we were at this time silent and holding back, with the cavalry catching us up in separate groups, because he had ridden forth without the troops' knowing; [1290]
they knew about it only after he had gone.

---

464. Thus vocalized by the editor of the text; perhaps it is to be identified with the village Arim, in the mountainous district of Sawādkūh to the south of Sārī, listed by Rabino di Borgomale, *Māzandarān and Astarābād*, 115.

465. *Allāh*^{a} *Allāh*^{a} *fī nafsika*, with a verb like *astaʿīnu* or *astaghīthu* understood; the expression is badly mistranslated in Ṭabarī, trans. Marin, 101.

Al-Ḥasan summoned Yaʿqūb b. Manṣūr and said to him, "O Abū Ṭalḥah, I want you to go to al-Ṭālaqāniyyah[466] and then, employing your subtle stratagems, take care of Abū ʿAbdallāh Muḥammad b. Ibrāhīm b. Muṣʿab's army there for two or three hours or more, whatever you can manage." There was a distance of two or three farsakhs between him and al-Ṭālaqāniyyah. Ibrāhīn continued to relate: While we were standing waiting in al-Ḥasan's presence, behold, he summoned Qays b. Zanjūyah and told him, "Proceed to the defile (*darb*) of Labūrah. It is less then a farsakh away, so go forth with your troops to the defile." He related: When we had performed the sunset worship and the night had come on, behold, a group of horsemen appeared before me, bearing lighted wax candles and coming from the Labūrah road. Al-Ḥasan said to me, "O Ibrāhīm, what is there on the Labūrah road?" I replied, "I can see lights and horsemen who have approached from that road." He related: I was filled with bewilderment and did not know what our situation was until the lights drew near to us. I was looking, and behold there was al-Māzyār, together with al-Qūhyār. I was not fully aware [of the position] until they both dismounted. Al-Māzyār advanced and greeted al-Ḥasan as Amīr, but the latter did not return to him the salutation and instead told Ṭāhir b. Ibrāhīm and Aws al-Balkhī, "Take him into your custody!"

It has been mentioned from the brother of Ummīdwār b. Khwāst Jīlān[467] that on that same night he went with a group of men to Qūhyār and told him, "Fear God! You have now taken the
1291] place of our leading men, so permit me to round up all these Arabs, for the troops are in a confused state and starving, and there is no road open to them for fleeing. You will thereby do away with their power and authority forever. Do not repose any trust in anything that the Arabs may give you, for they never keep

---

Grammatically the construction is analogous to those of *taḥdhīr* and *ighrā'*; see W. Wright, *op. cit.*, II, 74–75.

466. Not identified but unconnected with the Ṭālaqāns of Khurāsān and Daylam. Rabino di Borgomale, *Mázandarán and Astarábád*, 22, notes however the existence of a Ṭalaqānī clan today, in the district of Tunakābun in western Māzandarān.

467. For the first element of this name the text has *W.m.y.d.wār*; a more correct orthography (Persian *umīdwār* "hopeful") appears in the editor's n. *l*, as given by Ẓahīr al-Dīn Marʿashī.

their trust." Qūhyār, however, said, "Don't do that!" [Ummīdwār's brother continued to relate:] By that time Qūhyār had already ranged the Arabs against us and had handed over Māzyār and the members of his family to al-Ḥasan that he himself might enjoy the sole possession of royal power and that no one might contend with or oppose him.

When dawn had come al-Ḥasan sent Māzyār in the custody of Ṭāhir b. Ibrāhīm and Aws al-Balkhī to Khurramābādh and ordered them to take him to the town of Sāriyah. Al-Ḥasan rode on and took possession of the Wādī Bābak as far as al-Kāniyyah,[468] coming up with and encountering Muḥammad b. Ibrāhīm b. Muṣʿab, who was traveling toward Hurmuzdābādh to seize al-Māzyār. Al-Ḥasan said to him, "O Abū ʿAbdallāh, where are you heading?" He replied, "I am seeking al-Māzyār." Al-Ḥasan said, "He is at Sāriyah; he came to me, and I sent him on to there." Muḥammad b. Ibrāhīm was left in a state of great perturbation, for al-Qūhyār had planned to act treacherously with al-Ḥasan and to hand over al-Māzyār to Muḥammad b. Ibrāhīm. But al-Ḥasan had forestalled him over that, and al-Qūhyār was afraid that al-Ḥasan would attack him when he observed him in the middle of crossing the mountains, for Aḥmad b. al-Ṣuqayr had previously written to al-Qūhyār, "I do not see you either cultivating friendly relations or showing hostility to ʿAbdallāh b. Ṭāhir. Information about your position and the assurances given by you has been written down and sent to him, so don't act in a two-faced manner (literally, "two-hearted," *dhā qalbayn*)." At that he paid heed to what had been said (*ḥadhirahu*),[469] and handed al-Māzyār over to al-Ḥasan.

Muḥammad b. Ibrāhīm and al-Ḥasan al-Ḥusayn went to Hurmuzdābādh, burned down al-Māzyār's palace there, and plundered his possessions. They then proceeded to al-Ḥasan's [1292]
army camp at Khurramābādh. They sent [men] to al-Māzyār's brothers, and these last were imprisoned in his residence with guards appointed over them. Then al-Ḥasan rode on to the town of Sāriyah and remained there, al-Māzyār being imprisoned near

468. The pointing of the consonants and the vocalization of these two place names are uncertain.

469. Or "he (sc. al-Ḥasan) gave him a warning," vocalizing *ḥadharahu*, as in the Cairo edition, IX, 95.

al-Ḥasan's tent. Al-Ḥasan also sent to Muḥammad b. Mūsā b. Ḥafṣ asking him about the shackles with which al-Māzyār had loaded him (i.e., had loaded Muḥammad b. Mūsā); Muḥammad sent them to al-Ḥasan, and al-Ḥasan fettered al-Māzyār in these same shackles.

Muḥammad b. Ibrāhīm came to al-Ḥasan at the town of Sāriyah to ask about and discuss with him the wealth and possessions of al-Māzyār and his family. The two of them wrote to ʿAbdallāh b. Ṭāhir concerning this matter and awaited his orders. A letter from ʿAbdallāh reached al-Ḥasan, commanding him to hand over al-Māzyār, his brothers, and the members of his family to Muḥammad b. Ibrāhīm, so that the latter might convey them to the Commander of the Faithful, al-Muʿtaṣim. ʿAbdallāh did not make any move regarding their wealth and possessions but ordered Muḥammad b. Ibrāhīm to take the whole of al-Māzyār's wealth and possessions and to guard them. Al-Ḥasan then sent for al-Māzyār and had him brought in and questioned him about his wealth and possessions. Al-Māzyār stated that these last were deposited with a group of the leading citizens and persons noted for their probity, whom he named, of Sāriyah, ten individuals in all. At this al-Ḥasan also summoned al-Qūhyār and in a written document imposed on him an obligation, making him responsible for extracting the whole[470] of the wealth and possessions that al-Māzyār had said were in the custodianship of his treasurers and the keepers of his accumulated wealth. Al-Qūhyār assented to this duty laid upon him and formally bound himself to it before witnesses; then al-Ḥasan ordered the witnesses whom he had assembled to go to al-Māzyār and bear witness for him.

It has been mentioned by one of them that he said: When we went in to al-Māzyār's presence I was afraid lest Aḥmad b. al-Ṣuqayr might frighten him with [harsh] speech, so I told him, "I would like you to restrain yourself with him and not to mention what you have been advised about him." Aḥmad accordingly remained silent during the entire proceedings. Al-Māzyār now
[1293] affirmed, "I bear witness that the whole of what I brought along and what accompanied me, of my personal wealth, amounts to

470. *Tawfīr*, in its sense of "exacting the whole of something due"; see Ibn Manẓūr, *Lisān al-ʿArab*, VII, 150.

96,000 dīnārs, seventeen emeralds, sixteen rubies, eight loads of baskets bound with leather and containing various items of clothing, a crown and a sword decorated with gold and jewels, a golden dagger studded with jewels, and a large chest filled with jewels," he having placed it (the document) before us, which I had then handed over to Muḥammad b. al-Ṣabbāḥ, ʿAbdallāh b. Ṭāhir's treasurer and intelligence officer over the troops, and to al-Qūhyār. He related: We then went back to al-Ḥasan b. al-Ḥusayn, and he said, "Did you bear witness for that fellow?" He related: We replied, "Yes." He said, "This is something that I would have preferred to do myself, but I wanted his unimportance and contemptible status in my eyes to be made manifest."

It has been mentioned from ʿAlī b. Rabban al-Naṣrānī al-Kātib that that chest containing jewels belonging to al-Māzyār, his grandfather, Sharwīn, and Shahriyār, was sold for 18 million dirhams, and al-Māzyār brought the whole of this sum to al-Ḥasan b. al-Ḥusayn on condition that he would proclaim publicly that al-Māzyār had come to him under a guarantee of safe-conduct; that he (al-Ḥasan) had given him a guarantee of safety for his person, his wealth and possessions, and his children; and that he had made over to him [the government of] the mountain held by his father. However, al-Ḥasan b. al-Ḥusayn refused to accept this and held back from taking it (i.e., the wealth of al-Māzyār and his family); he was the most incorruptible of men with regard to taking dirhams and dīnārs.

When it was morning he sent off al-Māzyār with Ṭāhir b. Ibrāhīm and ʿAlī b. Ibrāhīm al-Ḥarbī, but a letter arrived from ʿAbdallāh b. Ṭāhir with instructions to send him with Yaʿqūb b. [1294]
Manṣūr. They had meanwhile already traveled three stages with al-Māzyār; so al-Ḥasan despatched an envoy, brought al-Māzyār back, and then sent him with Yaʿqūb b. Manṣūr.

After this al-Ḥasan b. al-Ḥusayn ordered al-Qūhyār, al-Māzyār's brother, to convey the wealth that he had pledged and provided him with mules from the army, at the same time ordering a force of soldiers to accompany him. Al-Qūhyār, however, refused, saying, "I don't need them," and he and his personal slave retainers (*ghilmān*) set out with the mules. When he entered the mountain zone he opened the treasuries, removed the wealth, and got it ready for transporting himself. But al-Māzyār's Daylamī slave retainers (*mamālīk*), amounting to 1,200 in number, rose up against him and said to him, "You betrayed our master and handed him over to the Arabs, and now you have come to carry off his wealth." They thereupon seized him and made him fast in irons. Then, under cover of night, they killed him and carried off as plunder that wealth and the mules. News of this reached al-Ḥasan, and he sent an army against those who had killed al-Qūhyār, and Qārin also sent a force of his own troops to capture them. Qārin's commander captured a number of the plunderers, including one of al-Māzyār's paternal cousins called Shahriyār b. al-Maṣmughān,[471] who was the leader of the slave troops and the one who had egged them on. Qārin sent him on to ʿAbdallāh b. Ṭāhir, but when he reached Qūmis he died. A group of those Daylamīs had set out along the way through the foothills and jungle, heading for al-Daylam. Muḥammad b. Ibrāhīm b. Muṣʿab became aware of them, hence sent out, from the forces at his disposal, the troops of Ṭabaristān and others until these troops came up against and confronted the Daylamīs and blocked their road, and they were thus captured. He then sent them to the town of Sāriyah with ʿAlī b. Ibrāhīm. Muḥammad b. Ibrāhīm's route of access when he entered from Shalanbah[472] was (or: was from Shalanbah) on the road from al-Rūdhbār[473] to al-Rūyān.

It has been said[474] that the deterioration of Māzyār's position and his final ruin were at the hands of one of his paternal cousins
[1295] called . . . ,[475] who ruled over all the mountain regions of Ṭabaristān, while al-Māzyār controlled the plain, this being the division between them as they had inherited it. It has been mentioned from Muḥammad b. Ḥafṣ al-Ṭabarī that the mountain regions of Ṭabaristān consisted of three mountains: that of

---

471. Maṣmughān was an ancient title of Ṭabaristān, held by a local dynasty of the Damāwand region, the Zarmihrid elder branch of the Qārinids, but by this time it seems to have become a proper name and to have been adopted in the younger branch of the Qārinids, that of Māzyār. See the discussion of this complex topic in *EI*², s.v. al-Maṣmughān (V. Minorsky).

472. Described by Yāqūt, *Muʿjam*, III, 360, s.v. Shalambah, as a place in the region of Damāwand; see also Ibn Isfandiyār, *op. cit.*, 28.

473. The Rūdhbār situated in Daylam, one of the many places with this name. See Yāqūt, *Muʿjam*, III, 77; Le Strange, *Lands*, 173.

475. There is a lacuna here in the texts of both manuscripts.

Wandāhurmuz in the middle of the Ṭabaristān mountains; second, the mountain of his brother Wandās.b/f. jān b. al-Andād b. Qārin; and, third, the mountain of Sharwīn b. Surkhāb b. Bāb.[476] When al-Māzyār's authority grew strong, he sent to that paternal cousin of his—or, as has been said, to his brother al-Qūhyār—and compelled him to stay with him at his court, meanwhile entrusting the governorship of the mountains to one of his own men, called Durrī. When al-Māzyār had a need for troops to combat ʿAbdallāh b. Ṭāhir he summoned his cousin—or his brother al-Qūhyār—and told him, "You are more familiar with your mountain than anyone else." He revealed to him the matter of al-Afshīn and the latter's [secret] correspondence with him and told him, "Go to that region of the mountain and guard the mountain for me." Al-Māzyār also wrote to al-Durrī, ordering him to come to him, which al-Durrī did, and he gave him military forces and sent him against ʿAbdallāh b. Ṭāhir. He thought that he had made firm for himself the mountain through his cousin—or his brother al-Qūhyār—because he did not imagine that anyone could come upon him via the mountain, because there was no way for [the access of] armies or the possibility of fighting there on account of the numerous defiles and [dense] trees. He further made sure of the places where he feared [possible access] by [1296]
means of al-Durrī and his forces, and he reinforced him with warriors and troops from his own army.

ʿAbdallāh b. Ṭāhir sent his paternal uncle al-Ḥasan b. al-Ḥusayn b. Muṣʿab with a large army from Khurāsān against al-Māzyār, and al-Muʿtaṣim sent Muḥammad b. Ibrāhīm b. Muṣʿab, together with an intelligence officer called Yaʿqūb b. Ibrāhīm al-Būshanjī, the mawlā of al-Hādī, known as Qawṣarah,[477] who was to write intelligence reports about the army. Muḥammad b. Ibrāhīm met al-Ḥasan b. al-Ḥusayn, and the

476. I.e., for Bāw/Bāv, sc. the Bāwandid Ispahbadhs. On this threefold division of the mountains, see EI^2, s.v. Māzandarān (V. Minorsky-[C. E. Bosworth]); the second would adjoin Daylam, as it was the starting point for expeditions against the Daylamīs (see p. 147 n. 418, above), and third would lie in the southeastern part of Ṭabaristān.

477. Literally, "a basket of dates woven from palm fibers," perhaps indicative of an originally servile status for this Khurāsānian. Būshanj was a town in what is now western Afghanistan. In connection with the attachments of this al-Būshanjī to Muḥammad b. Ibrāhīm b. Muṣʿab, it may not be without significance that the

armies advanced together toward al-Māzyār until they were close to him. Al-Māzyār, meanwhile, was not in any doubt that he had made secure for himself the place where the mountains faced him (faced al-Ḥasan b. al-Ḥusayn, his enemy?)[478] and was at this moment in his capital with only a small group of men. But the secret rancor that al-Māzyār's cousin nursed in his heart against al-Māzyār, the latter's treatment of him, and al-Māzyār's removal of him from his mountain impelled the cousin to write to al-Ḥasan b. al-Ḥusayn and tell him about everything that was happening in his camp, including the fact that al-Afshīn had been in correspondence with al-Māzyār. Al-Ḥasan forwarded al-Māzyār's cousin's letter to ʿAbdallāh b. Ṭāhir, and ʿAbdallāh in turn sent it with an envoy to al-Muʿtaṣim. ʿAbdallāh and al-Ḥasan b. al-Ḥusayn then wrote back to al-Māzyār's cousin—or, it has been said, al-Qūhyār—and they both promised him whatever he might wish. Al-Māzyār's cousin had informed ʿAbdallāh b. Ṭāhir that the mountain where he then was had belonged to him and his father and his forefathers before al-Māzyār[479] and that the latter, at the time when al-Faḍl b. Sahl had appointed him ruler over Ṭabaristān, had snatched the mountain from his possession and compelled him to remain at his court, treating him with
1297] contempt. Accordingly, ʿAbdallāh b. Ṭāhir made the stipulation to him that, if the cousin should rise up against al-Māzyār and use stratagems so that the mountain should pass into his own possession, as it had always previously been, no impediment would be placed in his way regarding it, nor would he be pursued with military force. Al-Māzyār's cousin agreed to these terms, so ʿAbdallāh b. Ṭāhir wrote out for him a document with that stipulation and in it gave him the requisite assurances.

Al-Māzyār's cousin promised al-Ḥasan b. al-Ḥusayn and their troops that he would lead them into the mountain. When the

region around Būshanj was the original home of the Ṭāhirid family and the birthplace of Ṭāhir Dhū al-Yamīnayn himself. See Yāqūt, *Muʿjam*, I, 508–9; Le Strange, *Lands*, 431; Barthold, *Historical Geography*, 60; Kaabi, *op. cit.*, I, 65.

478. One might also follow here the variant in n. *g* and read "the place in front of (*tilqāʾ*) the mountain."

479. *Min qabli* "before" seems to be the best vocalization here, in the light of the unequivocal phrase just below, "as it had always previously been"; the Cairo edition, IX, 99, vocalizes *min qibali* "under the suzerainty of."

time of the appointed meeting came round ʿAbdallāh b. Ṭāhir ordered al-Ḥasan b. al-Ḥusayn to advance to engage al-Durrī in battle and in the middle of the night sent out a powerful force under one of his commanders. They met up with al-Māzyār's cousin in the mountain; he delivered the mountains over to them and conducted them into the mountains. Al-Durrī drew up his own army in ranks against the opposing force; al-Māzyār in his palace was meanwhile quite unaware of what was happening until the [Arabs'] infantrymen and cavalry planted themselves at the very gate of his palace. Al-Durrī was at this time engaged in battle with the other army. The caliphal troops surrounded and besieged al-Māzyār and brought him forth in accordance with (or: "for," *ʿalā*) the Commander of the Faithful al-Muʿtaṣim's judgment.

ʿAmr b. Saʿīd al-Ṭabarī[480] has mentioned that al-Māzyār was out hunting and the [Arab] cavalry came upon him during the hunt. He was taken prisoner, and his palace was entered forcibly and the whole of what was in it captured. Al-Ḥasan b. al-Ḥusayn brought along al-Māzyār, with al-Durrī still at this time fighting the enemy facing him and unaware of al-Māzyār's capture; he remained oblivious of the situation until ʿAbdallāh b. Ṭāhir's troops came up behind him. His own troops were cut up and scattered and he himself put to flight, fleeing and seeking to enter the land of al-Daylam. His companions were slain, and the caliphal troops pursued and overtook him when he had with him only a small group of his retainers. He turned round and fought with them but was slain and his head taken and then sent to ʿAbdallāh b. Ṭāhir, into whose hands al-Māzyār had already [1298]
passed.

ʿAbdallāh b. Ṭāhir promised al-Māzyār that, if he would show him al-Afshīn's letters, he would ask the Commander of the Faithful to pardon him, and he warned al-Māzyār that he had learned that al-Māzyār had the letters in his possession. Al-Māzyār acknowledged the truth of that; the letters were sought for and found, and there turned out to be a considerable number of

480. This is the fourth of Ṭabarī's authorities for Māzyār's revolt (III, 1297–98), noted by Sadighi, *op. cit.*, 302 n. 4, as differing on some points from the principal account of Muḥammad b. Ḥafṣ and containing some errors.

letters. ʿAbdallāh b. Ṭāhir took them and sent them, together with al-Māzyār, to Isḥāq b. Ibrāhīm, commanding him not to allow the letters out of his hands, or al-Māzyār either, unless directly into the hands of the Commander of the Faithful, lest some stratagem be employed regarding the letters and al-Māzyār. Isḥāq followed his instructions and delivered them out of his own hands into those of al-Muʿtaṣim. Al-Muʿtaṣim then questioned al-Māzyār about the letters, but he refused to acknowledge them, whereupon al-Muʿtaṣim ordered al-Māzyār to be beaten until he died. His corpse was then gibbeted at the side of Bābak's.[481]

Al-Maʾmūn used to write to al-Māzyār, "From ʿAbdallāh al-Maʾmūn to the Jīl-i Jīlān,[482] Iṣbahbadh-i Iṣbahbadhān, Bishwār Khurshād,[483] Muḥammad b. Qārin, mawlā of the Commander of the Faithful."[484]

It has been mentioned that al-Durrī's position began to deteriorate when, after al-Māzyār's reinforcing him with an army, the news reached him of Muḥammad b. Ibrāhīm's descent of Dunbāwand. He thereupon sent his brother Buzurj-Jushnas,[485] reinforcing him with Muḥammad and Jaʿfar, the two sons of Rustam al-Kalārī,[486] and with troops from the frontier region and
[1299] from al-Rūyān, and he ordered them to proceed to the boundary of

---

481. I.e., in Sāmarrā, at the *ʿaqabat Bābak*; see Ṭabarī, III, 1231 (p. 88, above). For ʿAbdallāh b. Ṭāhir's relations with Māzyār and ʿAbdallāh's part in Māzyār's fate, see Kaabi, *op. cit.*, I, 255–57.

482. I.e., Māzyār claimed authority over Gīlān, the province to the west, as well as over Ṭabaristān.

483. Minorsky amended this phrase, in *EI*[1], s.v. Māzyār, to Patishwārjarshāh, without, however, giving his interpretation; perhaps he was following Marquart's Patashwārgar-shāh, listed by Ibn Khurradādhbih, *op. cit.*, 17, as an early Sāsānid provincial ruler's title. See Justi, *op. cit.*, 99; Marquart, *Untersuchungen*, II, 71–72; Herzfeld, *op. cit.*, 145.

484. Yaʿqūbī, *Taʾrīkh*, II, 582, gives these titles and says that, when Māzyār started getting pretensions, he no longer called himself by the humble title of "client of the Commander of the Faithful," but adopted *muwālī* ("partner, associate") *Amīr al-Muʾminīn*. See also Herzfeld, *op. cit.*, 145; Rekaya, "Māzyār," 150–52.

485. Text, *b.z.r.j.sh.n.s.* The element *j.sh.n.s* is the usual Arabized rendering of the Persian name Gushnasp (literally, "stallion"), the whole name thus meaning "great stallion." see Justi, *op. cit.*, 354–55; Ṭabarī, trans. Nöldeke, 110 n. 3.

486. Kalār is the district of western Ṭabaristān lying between Tunakābun and Kujūr, at this time adjoining the frontier of pagan Daylam and ruled by the Bāduspānids; see Rabino di Borgomale, *Māzandarān and Astarábád*, 27, 154–55.

al-Rūyān and al-Rayy to ward off the army. Al-Ḥasan b. Qārin had been corresponding with Rustam's sons Muḥammad and Jaʿfar, who were among the leaders of al-Durrī's troops, inciting the two of them [to betray their commander]. When the armies of al-Durrī and Muḥammad b. Ibrāhīm met, Rustam's two sons plus the troops from the two frontier regions and from al-Rūyān turned against al-Durrī's brother Buzurj-Jushnas, took him captive, and joined up with Muḥammad b. Ibrāhīm as his vanguard. Al-Durrī, together with his family and all his troops, was in his fortress at a place called Muzn.[487] When the news reached him of the treachery of Rustam's two sons, Muḥammad and Jaʿfar, and the rallying to their side of the troops from the two frontier regions and from al-Rūyān and of his brother Buzurj-Jushnas's capture, he became deeply grieved on account of that. He submitted [to the will of] his followers, whose only thought was for themselves, and the whole body of them split up, seeking guarantees of safe-conduct for themselves and contriving to save their skins as best they could. Al-Durrī then sent to the Daylamites (i.e., for reinforcements), and 4,000 of them rallied to his side. He held out inducements to them, gave them hope of largesse, and offered them gifts. Then he rode on, bearing his wealth and possessions with him, and proceeded as if his intention were to rescue his brother and attack Muḥammad b. Ibrāhīm, but in reality he intended to enter al-Daylam and seek the Daylamites' military assiatance against Muḥammad b. Ibrāhīm. At that point Muḥammad b. Ibrāhīm and his army met him, and a bitter battle ensued.

After al-Durrī had gone the prison guards fled, and the prisoners broke their fetters and escaped, and every one of them reached his own land. It happened that the men from Sāriyah who had been in al-Māzyār's jail and those persons who had been in al-Durrī's one got free on the very same day, this being the thirteenth of Shaʿbān in the year 225 (June 18, 840) according to Muḥammad b. Ḥafṣ; others, however, say that this took place in the year 224 (i.e., on June 30, 839).

It has been mentioned from Dāwūd b. Qaḥdham that Muḥam- [1300]

487. With the same emendation of this name as in Ṭabarī, III, 1274 l. 16 (p. 147 n. 418, above).

mad b. Rustam said:[488] Al-Durrī and Muḥammad b. Ibrāhīm met in combat on the coast of the [Caspian] Sea between the mountain chain, the jungle, and the sea, the jungle being contiguous with the border of al-Daylam. Al-Durrī was a courageous and valiant warrior. He hurled himself single-handed against Muḥammad's troops until he put them to flight. Then he went off to one side, not however fleeing precipitately and intending to go into the jungle. But one of Muḥammad b. Ibrāhīm's followers, called Find[489] b. Ḥājibah, attacked him and took him prisoner, and he was brought back.[490] The troops pursued al-Durrī's men, and everything that al-Durrī had with him—personal equipment, money, riding beasts, and weapons—was seized. Muḥammad b. Ibrāhīm ordered al-Durrī's brother Buzurj-Jushnas to be killed, and then al-Durrī himself was summoned. He stretched out his forearm, and it was cut off from the elbow; his leg was stretched out, and that was cut off from the knee. The same thing was done with the other forearm and leg. He squatted down on his backside, but did not utter a word or tremble at all. Muḥammad b. Ibrāhīm then ordered his head to be chopped off. He furthermore seized al-Durrī's men and had them transported in fetters.

In this year Jaʿfar b. Dīnār became governor of Yemen.[491]

In this year, al-Ḥasan b. al-Afshin married Utrunjah, the daughter of Ashnās, and consummated the marriage at al-Umarī,[492] the palace of al-Muʿtaṣim, in Jumādā II (April–May 839). He invited to the marriage celebrations the general populace

488. Dāwūd b. Quḥdham is otherwise unknown as an authority for this information, but his informant, Muḥammad b. Rustam, is presumably the Muḥammad son of Rustam al-Kalārī mentioned earlier.

489. This name seems to have perplexed the copyists, and also Marin, but is in fact not unknown in early Arabic onomastic (literally, "peak, mountain," hence a name for a powerfully built man); cf. the Jāhilī poet al-Find al-Zimmānī represented in Abū Tammām, *Ḥamāsah*, 9–12, trans. in C. J. Lyall, *Translations*, 5–7 no. III.

490. Reading *wa-sturjiʿa*, since *istarjaʿa*, which is transitive except in the denominative sense of "to exclaim 'Indeed we belong to God!'," requires an object in the active voice.

491. Ibn al-Athīr, *op. cit.*, VI, 508.

492. The palace built by and thus named after the commander ʿUmar b. Faraj al-Rukhkhajī (cf. p. 12 n. 42, above). See Yaʿqūbī, *Buldān*, 258, trans., 48–49; Herzfeld, *op. cit.*, 95.

of Sāmarrā. I was informed that they sprinkled the populace there with costly perfume (*ghāliyah*)[493] in silver vases and that [1301] al-Muʿtaṣim personally charged himself with the task of looking after those attending.[494]

In this year ʿAbdallāh al-Warthānī assumed a rebellious attitude at Warthān.[495]

In this year Minkajūr al-Ushrūsanī, a kinsman of al-Afshīn, rebelled in Ādharbayjān.[496]

The Reasons behind Minkajūr's Rebellion in Ādharbayjān

It has been mentioned that, when al-Afshīn had concluded the affair of Bābak and had returned from al-Jibāl, he appointed as governor of Ādharbayjān—which was one of the regions in his own charge and for which he was responsible—this Minkajūr. In Bābak's capital, in one of Bābak's dwellings, Minkajūr came

---

493. This was a mixture of musk, ambergris, and olibanum, used only on the most festive occasions; see Herzfeld, *op. cit.*, 144 n. 2. An anecdote given by Hilāl al-Ṣābiʾ emphasizes, however, al-Muʿtaṣim's extreme detestation of the smell of *ghāliyah*; *op. cit.*, 32–33, trans., 30–31.

494. Masʿūdī, *Murūj*, VII, 133 = par. 2815; Ibn al-Athīr, *op. cit.*, VI, 508; Herzfeld, *op. cit.*, 144. For the use of *tafaqqada* in the sense of "to look after, care for," see Dozy, *Supplément*, II, 271.

495. A town on the south bank of the Araxes, hence on the border between Mūqān and Arrān. See Yāqūt, *Muʿjam*, V, 370–71; Le Strange, *Lands*, 176–77, Schwarz, *op. cit.*, 1047–53. The rebel Warthānī is described in Balādhurī, *op. cit.*, 329, as one of the mawlās of al-Rashīd's wife Zubaydah. Yaʿqūbī, *Taʾrīkh*, II, 580, records the revolt of Muḥammad b. ʿUbaydallāh al-Warthānī, against whom al-Afshīn dispatched Minkajūr; but the rebel secured *amān* and came to al-Muʿtaṣim's court. He must have been reinstated in Mūqān, for Yaʿqūbī, *Taʾrīkh*, II, 583, goes on to record that Minkajūr, in the course of his own revolt (see below), killed Warthānī and other officials of the ʿAbbāsids. The form of the name in Azdī, *op. cit.*, 429, and Ibn al-Athīr, *op. cit.*, VI, 508, sc. Muḥammad b. ʿAbdallah, is doubtless less correct. See also Schwarz, *op. cit.*, 1051.

496. See Herzfeld, *op. cit.*, 144. The rebel is described by Yaʿqūbī, *Taʾrīkh*, II, 579, as Minkajūr al-Farghānī and as the maternal uncle of one of al-Afshīn's sons. Minorsky, in *Studies in Caucasian History*, 111 n. 1, suggested that the ford, now a dam, of Mingechaur over the Kur River in Arrān is named after him. The first element of what looks much more like a Turkish than an Iranian name may be *ming/bing* "1,000" or *mengü* "eternal, everlasting" (see Clauson, *Etymological Dictionary*, 345–47, 350–51), both of them common components in early Turkish onomastic. We may have here a Turkish slave soldier sold at or imported into Farghānah, rather than one of the indigenous population of that province.

across a large sum of money, which he then appropriated for himself without either al-Afshīn's or al-Muʿtaṣim's knowing about it (or: "being informed about it"). The head of the postal and intelligence service in Ādharbayjān was an adherent of the Shīʿah called ʿAbdallāh b. ʿAbd al-Raḥmān. He wrote to al-Muʿtaṣim with the information about that hoard of wealth and Minkajūr in turn wrote branding the accusation a lie. Arguments and disputes broke out between Minkajūr and ʿAbdallāh b. ʿAbd al-Raḥmān until Minkajūr finally determined to kill the latter. ʿAbdallāh sought the aid of the people of Ardabīl, and they shielded him from Minkajūr's intentions, so that as a result Minkajūr attacked them.

News of this reached al-Muʿtaṣim, who thereupon ordered al-Afshīn to send a man to remove Minkajūr from office; so al-Afshīn dispatched one of his commanders with a powerful army. When Minkajūr heard about this, he threw off allegiance, gathered around himself the vagabonds and desperadoes (*al-ṣaʿālīk*), and left Ardabīl. Al-Afshīn's commander spotted him and attacked him, and Minkajūr was put to flight. He went to one of the fortresses of Ādharbayjān that Bābak had destroyed, a
[1302] well-defended site on an inaccessible mountain. There he rebuilt and repaired it and fortified himself within it. However, before less than one month had elapsed, Minkajūr's followers who were with him in the fortress rose up against him; they betrayed him and handed him over to that commander who had previously fought with him. The latter brought him to Sāmarrā, where al-Muʿtaṣim ordered him to be imprisoned; al-Afshīn also came under suspicion regarding Minkajūr's affair.[497] It has been said that the commander sent to wage war on this Minkajūr was Bughā al-Kabīr, and it has further been said that when Bughā encountered Minkajūr the latter went out to him with a guarantee of safe-conduct.[498]

497. I.e., for allegedly inciting Minkajūr to rebellion; Yaʿqūbī, *Taʾrīkh*, II, 579, explicity adduces this incitement, plus the fact that the army originally sent against Minkajūr under Abū al-Sāj Dīwdād was really intended as reinforcement for him, forcing the Caliph to send an army under Bughā al-Kabīr actually to quell the outbreak.

498. Yaʿqūbī, *Taʾrīkh*, II, 579–80, also has information on events in northwestern Persia and Armenia at this time that is not in Ṭabarī and records Minkajūr's

In this year Yāṭis al-Rūmī died, and [his corpse] was gibbeted at the side of Bābak.[499]

In this year, in the month of Ramaḍān (July–August 839), Ibrāhīm b. al-Mahdī died, and al-Muʿtaṣim led the worship at his funeral.[500]

In this year Muḥammad b. Dāwūd led the Pilgrimage.[501]

---

appointment as governor there; the relevant passage is translated by Marquart, *Osteuropäische und ostasiatische Streifzüge*, 460–61.

499. Masʿūdī, *Murūj*, VII, 138–39 = par. 2821, states that the corpses of Bābak, Māzyār, and then Yāṭis all bent toward each other on their respective gibbets and quotes some verses of Abū Tammām on this.

500. Ibn al-Athīr, *op. cit.*, VI, 508.

501. Khalīfah, *Taʾrīkh*, II, 789; Ibn al-Athīr, *op. cit.*, VI, 508.

The Events of the Year 225

(November 12, 839–October 30, 840)

These included al-Warthānī's coming to al-Muʿtaṣim in al-Muḥarram (Novermber–December 839) with a guarantee of safe-conduct.[502]

In this year, Bughā al-Kabīr brought Minkajūr to Sāmarrā.[503]

In this year al-Muʿtaṣim went to al-Sinn, appointing Ashnās as his deputy. Also in this year, in Rabīʿ I (January–February 840), he installed Ashnās on a throne, awarding him a crown and a ceremonial girdle.[504]

In this year Ghannām the apostate (*al-murtadd*) was burned.[505]

---

502. This would refer to Warthānī's reinstatement after his submission; see p. 175 n. 495, above.

503. See Ṭabarī, III, 1301–2 (pp. 175–76, above).

504. *Kitāb al-ʿuyūn*, 404; Herzfeld, *op. cit*, 145–46. Ashnās was now high in the Caliph's favor, and in this year also al-Muʿtaṣim appointed him overall governor of the vast region of al-Jazīrah, Syria, and Egypt (in practice, gubernatorial powers in these provinces were exercised by deputies while Ashnās himself remained in Iraq). See Kindī, *op. cit.*, 194–95; Ibn al-ʿAdīm, *op. cit.*, I, 69, according to whom al-Muʿtaṣim gave to Ashnās, in total, 40 million dirhams during the last years of his life; P. von Sivers, "Military, Merchants and Nomads," 222–23.

505. This character and episode remain enigmatic; all we have is a laconic mention by Jāḥiẓ in *Kitāb al-ḥayawān*, I, 9, implying that Jāḥiẓ had previously written against him.

In this year al-Muʿtaṣim grew angry with Jaʿfar b. Dīnār on account of his attack on those of the Shākiriyyah[506] who were [1303]
with him and imprisoned him in the custody of Ashnās for fifteen days. He dismissed him from the governorship of Yemen and gave it to Aytākh, but then he relented toward Jaʿfar.

In this year al-Afshīn was dismissed from the caliphal guard (*al-ḥaras*), and Isḥāq b. Yaḥyā b. Muʿādh took over the office.[507]

In this year ʿAbdallāh b. Ṭāhir sent Māzyār (i.e., to the caliphal court).[508] Isḥāq b. Ibrāhīm [b. Muṣʿab] went out to al-Daskarah[509] and conducted Māzyār to Sāmarrā in Shawwāl (August 840), and he ordered Māzyār to be transported on an elephant. Muḥammad b. ʿAbd al-Malik al-Zayyāt said,

The elephant has been painted and adorned with dyestuff, as is
the custom with such a beast,
[for] it is bearing the Jīlān of Khurāsān.

---

506. This group (*shākir*, Persian *chākir* "servant," according to the lexicographers; Herzfeld suggested, *op. cit.*, 99, that the word was derived from Middle Persian *shkar*, cf. New Persian *shikār* "hunt, hunting," but this does not have any very obvious connection with his adducing of instances in the *Kitāb al-aghānī*, where *shākirī* clearly means "personal attendant, bodyguard." These last instances accord however with the usage in Central Asia of *chākir/chākar* to denote the personal guard of rulers there, both Iranian and Turkish; see Minorsky, *Sharaf al-Zamān Ṭāhir Marvazī*, 94) formed a body of mercenaries in the caliphal serivce. In the Arabic historical sources the *Dīwān al-Jund wa-al-Shākiriyyah* is clearly distinguished from the *Dīwān al-Mawālī wa-al-Ghilmān*, that of the clients and military slaves (Yaʿqūbī, *Buldān*, 267, trans., 61; idem, *Taʾrīkh*, II, 596, reign of al-Mutawakkil). By the middle years of the third (ninth) century, the old *jund* of free Arab warriors (cf. *EI*², s.v. Djund [D. Sourdel]) had virtually disappeared, and both the new *jund* and the *shākiriyyah* must have been paid, presumably non-Arab soldiers. See Hoernerbach, *op. cit.*, 264–66; Bosworth, "Recruitment, Muster and Review," 69. Shaban, *op. cit.*, 64–65, suggests that the *shākir*s of this period were the personal guards of Iranian and Turkish princes and local rulers of Central Asia, brought into the caliphal army, like al-Afshīn himself; this seems quite feasible.

507. Isḥāq was the grandson of a Khurāsānian commander, from Khuttal or al-Rayy, who served the first ʿAbbāsids; he was the son of al-Maʾmūn's governor of Armenia and al-Jazīrah, who unsuccessfully fought Bābak (see Ṭabarī, III, 1233 [p. 91, above]). Isḥāq governed Damascus for both al-Muʿtaṣim and al-Wāthiq. See Yaʿqūbī, *Taʾrīkh*, II, 584; Ibn al-Athīr, *op. cit.*, VI, 516; Herzfeld, *op. cit.*, 107, 145; Crone, *op. cit.*, 183–84; p. xv, above.

508. Ibn Isfandiyār, *op. cit.*, 154; cf. Marʿashī, *op. cit.*, 117, who says that Māzyār was confined in a box with only eyeholes and transported thus on a mule back to Iraq.

509. In full, Daskarat al-Malik, one stage from al-Nahrawān on the high road to Khurāsān. See Yāqūt, *Muʿjam*, II, 455; Le Strange, *Lands*, 62; *EI*², s.v. Daskara (A. A. Duri).

The elephant does not have its limbs painted and adorned except for a very momentous person (or: for a very momentous occasion).[510]

Māzyār refused to ride on the elephant, so he was brought in mounted on a mule with a packsaddle. [On this day], the fifth of Dhū al-Qaʿdah (September 6, 840), al-Muʿtaṣim sat in the Public Audience Chamber. He gave orders and brought Māzyār into confrontation with al-Afshīn, who had been imprisoned the previous day. Al-Māzyār acknowledged that al-Afshīn had been in correspondence with him and had persuaded him that it was right to show disobedience and rebelliousness. Al-Muʿtaṣim ordered al-Afshīn to be returned to his prison and Māzyār to be beaten with 450 lashes; he begged for water, was given some, and then expired immediately.[511]

In this year al-Muʿtaṣim became angry with al-Afshīn and imprisoned him.

The Reason for al-Muʿtaṣim's Anger against al-Afshīn and His Imprisoning Him

It has been mentioned that, during the time when al-Afshīn was engaged in his war with Bābak and was stationed in the land of the Khurramiyyah, all the presents that he received from the people of Armenia he invariably sent on to Ushrūsanah.[512] These
[1304] presents used to pass through [the territory of] ʿAbdallāh b. Ṭāhir,

510. These two verses are a repetition of those given in Ṭabarī, III, 1230 (p. 000, above), with the substitution of Jīlān, alluding to Māzyār's title Jīl-i Jīlān (Ṭabarī, III, 1298 [p. 172, above]), for Shayṭān in the first verse.

511. Balādhurī, *op. cit.*, 340; Masʿūdī, *Murūj*, VII, 138–39 = pars. 2820–21; *Kitāb al-ʿuyūn*, 403, placing this event in the previous year, 224; Ibn al-Athīr, *op. cit.*, VI, 510; E. M. Wright, *op. cit.*, 125; Herzfeld, *op. cit.*, 145; Rekaya, "Māzyār," 188–89. The Persian local historical sources, e.g., Marʿashī, *op. cit.*, 231, state that the line of Qārin, the Qārinwands, expired with Māzyār's execution. However, Madelung, "Minor Dynasties," 205, has pointed out that petty rulers in Lafūr (see Ṭabarī, III, 1287 [p. 161 n. 460, above]) are mentioned in the fourth (tenth) and fifth (eleventh) centuries and described as Qārinids; one branch at least of the family thus survived.

512. The province to the south of the great bend of the Jaxartes River, lying between it and the river of Soghdia; al-Afshīn's family were hereditary rulers of Ushrūsanah, continuing there after Khaydhar's death until 280 (893). See Yāqūt, *Muʿjam*, I, 197; Le Strange, 474–76; Barthold, *Turkestan*, 165–69, 211; Bosworth and Clauson, *op. cit.*, 7–8; *EI*[1], s.v. Osrūshana (J. H. Kramers).

who therefore wrote to al-Muʿtaṣim about this affair. Hence al-Muʿtaṣim wrote back to ʿAbdallāh b. Ṭāhir, ordering him to set down a detailed description of all the presents that al-Afshīn was sending to Ushrūsanah, and ʿAbdallāh did that. Whenever any of the money in question was ready and at hand with al-Afshīn, he would load it round the waists of his retainers in the form of dīnārs and waist purses (*al-hamāyīn*), as much as they could carry. A man used to carry 1,000 dīnārs and more round his waist. ʿAbdallāh was informed about this, so that one day, when al-Afshīn's envoys had halted at Naysābūr, having the presents with them, ʿAbdallāh b. Ṭāhir sent after them and apprehended them. He searched them and found the purses around their waists, which he took away from them, saying to them, "Where did you get all this money?" The replied, "There are presents given to al-Afshīn, and they're his property." ʿAbdallāh said, "You're lying; if my colleague al-Afshīn had wished to send such wealth as this, he would have written to me informing me about it so that I might order measures for guarding it and provide an escort for it, for that is an enormous sum! You are nothing but thieves!"

At that, ʿAbdallāh b. Ṭāhir confiscated the money and distributed it to the troops under his command. He wrote back to al-Afshīn, recounting to him what the men had said and himself saying [in his letter], "I am unable to believe that you can have sent such a sum of money as this to Ushrūsanah without writing to me informing me of it, so that I might provide an escort for it. So, if this wealth is not in fact yours, well, I have distributed it to the troops in place of the money that the Commander of the Faithful forwards to me each year (i.e., for the payment of their salaries). If, however, the money really is yours, as the men assert, then, when the money arrives from the Commander of the Faithful, I will return it to you. Again, if the position should be [1305]
otherwise, then the Commander of the Faithful has the best entitlement to this money. I simply gave it to the troops because I intend sending them out to the land of the Turks (i.e., on a campaign into the Central Asian steppelands)." Al-Afshīn thereupon wrote back to ʿAbdallāh, telling him that his own money and the Commander of the Faithful's money were one and the same and requesting that ʿAbdallāh set the men free, so that

they might proceed to Ushrūsanah. ʿAbdallāh b. Ṭāhir accordingly released them, and they went on their way. However, this was the reason for the hostility that arose between ʿAbdallāh b. Ṭāhir and al-Afshīn; thereafter, ʿAbdallāh began to keep a close watch on him.[513]

From time to time, al-Afshīn used to hear words from al-Muʿtaṣim that indicated that he wanted to remove the Ṭāhirids from Khurāsān. Al-Afshīn coveted the governorship of Khurāsān for himself, so he began to send letters to Māzyār, inciting him to rebel and undertaking to assume the task of defending him with regard to the ruling power (*al-sulṭān*), thinking that, if Māzyār should rebel, al-Muʿtaṣim would, will-nilly, have to send him to combat Māzyār, would remove ʿAbdallāh b. Ṭāhir from office, and would appoint him governor of Khurāsān instead. What subsequently transpired regarding Māzyār we have already recounted, and what happened regarding Minkajūr in Ādharbayjān we have already described.

What al-Muʿtaṣim had suspected regarding Minkajūr's affair and the fact that al-Afshīn's planning and express instructions to Minkajūr must have lain behind it became confirmed in the caliph's mind by al-Afshīn's correspondence with Māzyār in the terms that al-Afshīn had actually been carrying it on. Because of that, al-Muʿtaṣim's attitude toward al-Afshīn changed, and the latter sensed it and realized al-Muʿtaṣim's altered opinion of him but did not know what to do. He therefore resolved, according to what has been mentioned, to prepare rafts of inflated waterskins (*aṭwāf*)[514] in his palace and to employ the stratagem, on some day when al-Muʿtaṣim and his commanders were
[1306] otherwise occupied, of taking the road to al-Mawṣil and crossing the Zāb[515] on those waterskin rafts until he should reach the land of Armenia and then the land of the Khazars.[516] This plan proved, however, difficult to execute, so he prepared [instead] a great

513. Herzfeld, *op. cit.*, 145–46.

514. On these (sing. *ṭawf*), which were used for constructing rafts on the rivers of Iraq (known by the term *kelek*, for which see *EI*², s.v. Kelek [H. Kindermann]), see Bosworth, "Some Remarks on the Terminology," 84–85.

515. This river would be the Lesser Zāb, the left-bank affluent of the Tigris, which joints it at al-Sinn; see Le Strange, *Lands*, 90–91.

516. I.e., the land of the Turkish people of that name, north of the Caucasus and along the lower course of the Volga River. See D. M. Dunlop, *The History of the Jewish Khazars*; *EI*², s.v. Khazar (W. Barthold-[P. B. Golden]).

quantity of poison and decided on arranging a banquet, to which he would summon al-Muʿtaṣim and his commanders and then give them to drink [the poison]. If al-Muʿtaṣim were to refuse the invitation, he would seek the caliph's permission to invite his Turkish commanders, such as Ashnās, Aytākh, etc., on some day when the Commander of the Faithful was otherwise occupied. Then, when they came to him, he would ply them with food and drink and poison them, and then, when they had left his residence, he would go forth in the early part of the night, carrying on the backs of pack animals those waterskin rafts and other equipment for making a crossing, until he should come to the Zāb. He and his baggage would then cross on the rafts while the pack animals would swim across as best they could. He would then send on the rafts so that he might cross the Tigris and enter Armenia, the governorship of which he himself held. From there he would proceed to the land of the Khazars, seeking a guarantee of safe-conduct through them, thence go round from the land of the Khazars to that of the Turks, and return from the latter territory to the province of Ushrūsanah. Having achieved this, he planned to win over the Khazars into hostility against the Muslims. His preparations for this course of action got under way, but the whole affair took up an inordinate amount of time, and he was unable to achieve it.[517]

Al-Afshīn's commanders used to take turns (i.e., at guard duty) in the Commander of the Faithful's palace, as is the custom with commanders. A conversation had taken place between Wājan[518] al-Ushrūsanī and some person who had become aware of al-Afshīn's plans, and Wājan had told this person that, in his opinion, the scheme was not possible and could not be brought to a conclusion. The man who heard Wājan's words went away and [1307] related them to al-Afshīn. One of al-Afshīn's slaves (or: eunuchs, *khadam*[519]) and intimates, whose sympathies inclined toward Wājan, overheard what al-Afshīn said concerning Wājan; so, when Wājan came back from his turn of guard duty one night, this man went to him and told him that this matter (i.e., of

517. Herzfeld, *op. cit.*, 146.

518. On this Iranian name (the Bīzhan son of Gīw of the *Shāh-nāma*), see Justi, *op. cit.*, 367, and Herzfeld, *op. cit.*, 146 n. 1. Marquart, *Untersuchungen*, I, 68, cites Parthian *wējan, wēzhan, bēzhan* "of good stock."

519. See p. 134 n. 375, above.

Wājan's doubts about the feasibility of al-Afshīn's plans) had been related to al-Afshīn.

Wājan was accordingly put on his guard and immediately rode off in the dead of the night till he came to the Commander of the Faithful's palace at a time when al-Muʿtaṣim himself was asleep. So Wājan went to Aytākh and told him, "I have some important counsel for the Commander of the Faithful." Aytākh replied, "You're here at the wrong time; the Commander of the Faithful has gone to sleep!" Wājan told him, however, "I can't wait until morning!" Aytākh therefore knocked on the door of someone who would inform al-Muʿtaṣim about what Wājan said. Al-Muʿtaṣim sent back word, "Tell him to return to his house tonight and come back to me first thing in the morning." But Wājan replied, "If I return tonight, I shall die." At that, al-Muʿtaṣim sent the message back to Aytākh, "Have him spend the night with you." Aytākh had Wājan spend the night with him, and then, when it was morning, he went with him at the time of the dawn worship and introduced him into al-Muʿtaṣim's presence. Wājan told al-Muʿtaṣim everything he knew, at which al-Muʿtaṣim sent for Muḥammad b. Ḥammād b. D.n.q.sh al-Kātib[520] and dispatched him to summon al-Afshīn. The latter arrived, dressed in black robes, but al-Muʿtaṣim ordered these to be taken away from him and consigned him to prison. He was incarcerated in al-Jawsaq,[521] but then the caliph had a lofty prison built for him within al-Jawsaq, which he named al-Luʾluʾah ("the Pearl")[522] and which is known until today[523] as [the prison of] al-Afshīn.[524]

---

520. *Ḥājib* or door keeper to al-Muʿtaṣim, according to Masʿūdī, *Tanbīh*, 356, trans., 457. As Sourdel notes, *Vizirat*, I, 242, the office of *ḥijābah* was very much in the background during this period, and its holders are shadowy persons. Yaʿqūbī, *Taʾrīkh*, II, 584, included Muḥammad b. Ḥammād among a group of Turks who served as *ḥājib*s for al-Muʿtaṣim. From an anecdote in Tanūkhī, *op. cit.*, VI, 162–63, it emerges that Ḥammād b. D.n.q.sh had been a mawlā of al-Manṣūr's; the son Muḥammad was subsequently to become al-Muhtadī's *ṣāḥib al-shurṭah*, according to this same source.

521. On this palace, see pp. 26 n. 97, 87 n. 232, above.

522. Not to be confused with the Luʾluʾah Palace constructed later by al-Mutawakkil, at vast expense, in the Jaʿfariyyah district of Sāmarrā; see Herzfeld, *op. cit.*, 128, 132.

523. The words *ilā al-ān* are added in the Cairo edition, IX, 106.

524. Herzfeld, *op. cit.*, 146–47. Masʿūdī, *Murūj*, VII, 138 = par. 2820, uniquely has the detail that al-Afshīn was denounced by a secretary of his called Sābūr.

Al-Muʿtaṣim wrote to ʿAbdallāh b. Ṭāhir, telling him to employ a stratagem against al-Ḥasan b. al-Afshīn. Now al-Ḥasan had bombarded ʿAbdallāh b. Ṭāhir with letters [complaining] about Nūḥ b. Asad, informing him about Nūḥ's unjust and oppressive treatment of him regarding his (al-Ḥasan's) estates and his region.[525] So ʿAbdallāh b. Ṭāhir wrote to Nūḥ b. Asad informing [1308] him about what the Commander of the Faithful had written to him concerning al-Ḥasan, and he ordered him to gather together his forces and make preparations for al-Ḥasan b. al-Afshīn, so that, when the latter should come to him with a letter announcing his appointment to the governorship, Nūḥ was to secure his person and bring him to ʿAbdallāh. [At the same time], ʿAbdallāh b. Ṭāhir wrote to al-Ḥasan b. al-Afshīn, informing him that he had dismissed Nūḥ b. Asad from office and had appointed him (al-Ḥasan) governor of the region instead, and he sent to him the official letter of Nūḥ b. Asad's dismissal. At that, al-Ḥasan b. al-Afshīn set off with only a small force of his troops and few weapons until he reached Nūḥ. b. Asad, all this time under the delusion that he himself was the new governor of the region. But Nūḥ b. Asad seized him, placed him in secure bonds, and sent him to ʿAbdallāh b. Ṭāhir, who in turn sent him to al-Muʿtaṣim.[526]

The prison that was built for al-Afshīn was in the form of a minaret, and inside it was left just sufficient space for al-Afshīn to sit down.[527] The guards used to walk round the minaret's perimeter below it during their spells of duty.

It has been mentioned from Hārūn b. ʿĪsā b. al-Manṣūr[528] that he said: I was present in al-Muʿtaṣim's palace, where there were

525. Nūḥ b. Asad was one of the four Sāmānid brothers given governorships in Transoxania and eastern Khurāsān by al-Maʾmūn as a reward for their support. As governor in Samarqand, Nūḥ would endeavor at this time to extend his authority over the neighboring principality of Ushrūsanah, thus clashing with al-Ḥasan b. al-Afshīn. See Barthold, *Turkestan*, 209–11; Frye, "Sāmānids," 136.

526. Herzfeld, *op. cit.*, 147. Michael the Syrian, *Chronicle*, III, 103, says that ʿAbdallāh b. Ṭāhir, on the Caliph's orders, forced al-Ḥasan to divorce Utrunjah bt. Ashnās, whom he had married with such pomp the previous year; see Ṭabarī, III, 1300–1 (pp. 174–75, above).

527. Following Herzfeld's translation, *op. cit.*, 147 and n. 2, *pace* Ṭabarī, trans. Marin, 114.

528. A great-nephew of his, Isḥāq b. Muḥammad, is mentioned in the *Kitāb al-aghānī*; see Herzfeld, *op. cit.*, 147 n. 3.

also assembled Aḥmad b. Abī Duwād,[529] Isḥāq b. Ibrāhīm b. Muṣʿab, and Muḥammad b. ʿAbd al-Malik al-Zayyāt. Al-Afshīn was brought in, he not yet being in the strong prison. A group of prominent figures had been assembled to heap reproaches on al-Afshīn for what he had done, and not a single person of high social or official rank (*aḥad min aṣḥāb al-marātib*)[530] was left in the palace apart from the sons (i.e., the lineal descendants) of al-Manṣūr, the rest of the [generality of] people having been dismissed. The prosecutor (*al-munāẓir*)[531] chose for al-Afshīn was Muḥammad b. ʿAbd al-Malik al-Zayyāt, and those who had been

529. The prominent part played by the chief judge in the interrogation and condemnation of al-Afshīn is noteworthy. Sadighi, *op. cit.*, 291 ff., sees in the whole affair a reflection of Arab hatred of the Iranian element in the caliphate and its prominence (hence a continuation of the tension between the eastern part of the caliphate and the Arabs of the Iraqi and Syrian heartlands, discernible in the previous caliphates of al-Amīn and al-Maʾmūn). Later sources—but not Ṭabarī here—give another explanation for this personal hostility between the chief judge and al-Afshīn. In the Arabic sources of the fourth (tenth) century (sc. Abū al-Faraj al-Iṣfahānī, *Kitāb al-aghānī*, and Tanūkhī, *op. cit.*, VII, 246–47) we find a story that Aḥmad b. Abī Duwād had saved the life of the Arab general Abū Dulaf al-Qāsim al-ʿIjlī, who had commanded the volunteers during al-Afshīn's last campaign against Bābak (see Ṭabarī, III, 1206 ff. [pp. 59 ff. and n. 176, above]) and who is depicted in Arabic *adab* literature as an all-round Arab hero, after he had somehow fallen into al-Afshīn's power. Aḥmad had interceded for him, explaining to the Caliph about al-Afshīn's hatred for the Arabs and Arabic culture in all its aspects (see Sadighi, *op. cit.*, 291–92; Herzfeld, *op. cit.*, 140). The story is given at great length and with much circumstantial detail by the Persian historian of he Ghaznavid period Abū al-Faḍl Bayhaqī in his *Taʾrīkh-i Masʿūdī*, trans. of this section in A. de Biberstein-Kazimirski, *Menoutchehri*, 149–54. Whether or not full credence should be attached to Bayhaqī's highly ornamented narrative is uncertain; his authority for the story is one Ismāʿīl b. Shihāb, not recorded as a *rāwī* in Ṭabarī. But the authority for the briefer version in Abū al-Faraj al-Iṣfahānī, *Kitāb al-aghānī*, Būlāq ed., VII, 154–55 = ed. Ibrāhīm, VIII, 250–51) is Aḥmad b. Abī Ṭāhir Ṭayfūr (presumably from the lost later part of his history), and one must conclude that there is some substance to it.

530. In ʿAbbāsid court and ceremonial procedure these persons of rank (*martabah*) included other members of the ʿAbbāsid family, descendants of the Rightly Guided Caliphs, the Umayyad Caliphs, the ʿAlids, etc. The term *martabah* also denotes the physical embodiment of this status, in the form of a cushion or seat of a height appropriate to its user's rank. See Herzfeld, *op. cit.*, 140; Sourdel, "Questions de cérémonial," 139 ff.; *EI*², s.v. Marāsim. 1. Under the Caliphate and Fāṭimids (P. Sanders).

531. A term also used for the official charged with extracting the ill-gotten gains of fallen officials, if necessary by violence, the process being called *muṣādarah* or *munāẓarah*; see *EI*², s.vv. Muṣādara. 2. In the Mediaeval Caliphate; Mustakhridj (C. E. Bosworth).

assembled there included al-Māzyār, the ruler of Ṭabaristān; the Mūbadh;[532] al-Marzubān b. T.r.k.sh, who was one of the princes of al-Sughd;[533] and two men from among the people of al-Sughd. [1309]

Muḥammad b. ʿAbd al-Malik summoned first the two men, who were dressed in threadbare garments. Muḥammad ʿAbd al-Malik said to them, "What happened to you?" They uncovered their backs, which were stripped of flesh, and Muḥammad said to al-Afshīn, "Do you know these two men?" He replied, "Yes, this one is a muezzin and the other an imām. They built a mosque in Ushrūsanah, so I gave each of them 1,000 lashes because there exists between me and the princes of al-Sughd a covenant and stipulation that I should leave each people to their own religion and beliefs. These two men fell upon a house that contained their idols"—he meant [those] of the people of Ushrūsanah—"and then threw out the idols and turned it into a mosque. I accordingly gave them 1,000 lashes each because of their transgression and their keeping the people from their place of worship."[534]

Muḥammad now asked him, "What is a certain book that you have and that you have ornamented with gold, jewels, and satin brocade and that contains blasphemies against God?"[535] Al-Afshīn replied, "This is a book that I inherited from my father and that contains some of the wise counsels (*ādāb*) of the Persians. As for what you mention concerning blasphemies, I used to enjoy the wise counsels in it and ignore the rest. I found it already adorned, and there was nothing to impel me to remove

532. I.e., the chief priest of the Zoroastrian community, the Mōbadh-Mōbadhān; see *EI*², s.v. Mōbadh (M. Guidi-[M. G. Morony]).

533. Al-Marzubān (literally, "warden of the marches") b. T.r.k.sh (perhaps to be vocalized Türgesh, after the Western Turks, or Türgesh, who had been active in military intervention in Soghdia a century or so previously) was the *dihqān*, or local ruler, of a district near Samarqand, which was named Marzbān after him. See Barthold, *Turkestan*, 95; Le Strange, *Lands*, 466.

534. The two Muslim zealots were thus punished for their ill-considered and fanatical iconoclasm, which affronted the beliefs of the majority of the population of Ushrūsanah, not yet converted to Islam; al-Afshīn, though personally a Muslim, regarded it as conducive to social and religious harmony in his principality to curb the Muslims' excesses. Thus one does not have to assume, as does E. M. Wright, *op. cit.*, 57, that al-Afshīn was himself still a secret devotee of the old religion of his subjects.

535. There has been speculation that this may be an allusion to the illuminated, finely written books of the Manichaeans; see p. 200, below.

the decoration from it. Thus I left it as it was, like the *Book of Kalīlah and Dimnah*[536] and the *Book of Mazdak*[537] in your own house. I did not think that this was in any way going outside Islam."

Hārūn b. ʿĪsā b. al-Manṣūr continued: Then the Mūbadh came forward and said, "This man used to eat the flesh of strangled beasts, and he used to urge me to eat it also, alleging that it was more tender than meat that had been [ritually] slaughtered.[538] He used to kill a black ewe each Wednesday; he would sever it through the middle with a sword, walk between
[1310] the two halves, and then eat its flesh. One day he said to me, "I have fallen in with these people (i.e., the Muslims) regarding everything that I in fact detest, to the point that, for them, I have gone as far as eating oil, riding camels, and wearing sandals; however, no hair has so far ever fallen from me," meaning that he had never smeared himself (i.e., had never used depilatories on his pubic hair) or been circumcised. Al-Afshīn replied, "Tell me about this man who utters these words—is he trustworthy in his own religion?" Now the Mūbadh was a Magian who subsequently converted to Islam at the hand of al-Mutawakkil and became one of the latter's boon companions. They replied, "No." Al-Afshīn said, "Then what is the meaning of your accepting testimony from a man whom you don't trust or account competent to act as a valid legal witness?"[539] Then he went up to

---

536. I.e., the Arabic version of the *Fables of Bidpai*, based on the Sanskrit Panchatantra and translated into Arabic from the Pahlavi version by Ibn al-Muqaffaʿ (d. *ca.* 139 [756]); see *EI*², s.v. Kalīla wa-Dimna (C. Brockelmann).

537. This work, also translated into Arabic by Ibn al-Muqaffaʿ, apparently belonged, like *Kalīlah wa-Dimnah*, to the genre of *adab*, intended to divert, and was not a work of theology or polemic; see Ṭabarī, trans. Nöldeke, 461 n. 2. However, Sadighi, *op. cit.*, 295 n. 2, cites the Persian scholar ʿAbbās lqbāl to the effect that it is not a *Kitāb Mazdak* but a *Kitāb Marwak* (cf. the reading in Ṭabarī's text, n. *o*: *M.r.w.t.k*). Marwak was a legendary person to whom aphorisms and wise sayings were attributed; the book would thus still be a work of *adab*.

538. I.e., in the manner conforming to Islamic law, with the animal's throat cut and the blood drained. See Hughes, *op. cit.*, 697, s.v. Z̲abh; *EI*², s.v. D̲h̲abīḥa (G.-H. Bousquet).

539. Because he was a Zoroastrian, the Mūbadh's legal testimony (*ʿadālah*) could not be accepted as the equal of a Muslim's or, indeed, be regarded as admissible at all in a legal suit with a Muslim. See A. Fattal, *Le statut légal*, 361 ff.; on the role of the *ʿadl* in general, see J. Schacht, *Introduction to Islamic Law*, 193–94; *EI*², s.v. ʿAdl (E. Tyan).

the Mūbadh and said, "Was there any door running between my house and yours or any garret window by means of which you could look down upon me and know what I was doing?" He replied, "No." Al-Afshīn continued, "Didn't I let you come in to me, and didn't I communicate to you my inner secrets and tell you about the concept of Persian national consciousness (*al-aʿjamiyyah*) and my sympathies for it and for its exponents?" He replied, "Yes." Al-Afshīn went on, "Then in that case you were neither trustworthy in your own religion nor upright in keeping to your word, as you divulged openly, to my detriment, a secret that I had confided to you."[540]

Then the Mūbadh went aside, and al-Marzubān b. T.r.k.sh came forward. They said to al-Afshīn, "Do you know this man?" He replied, "No." Then al-Marzubān was asked, "Do you know this man?" He replied, "Yes, he is al-Afshīn." They told al-Afshīn, "This is al-Marzubān." The latter said to al-Afshīn, "O liar and trickster (*mumakhriq*), how long will you fend off [the truth] and confuse the issues?" But al-Afshīn replied, "O long-beard,[541] what are you talking about?" Al-Marzubān asked, "How do the people of your province address you in correspondence?" Al-Afshīn replied, "Just as they used to address my father and grandfather." Al-Marzubān said, "Explain that," but al-Afshīn retorted, "I won't." Al-Marzubān said, "Don't they write to you in such-and-such terms in the language of Ushrūsanah?"[542] Al-Afshīn admitted, "Yes, indeed." Al-Marzubān continued,
"Doesn't that mean in Arabic, 'To the God of Gods, from his [1311]
servant So-and-so, son of So-and-so'?" He said, "Yes, indeed." Muḥammad b. ʿAbd al-Malik now asked, "Do Muslims allow themselves to be addressed in this way? What have you left for Pharaoh when he said to his people, 'I am your supreme Lord'?"[543]

---

540. Herzfeld, *op. cit.*, 148.

541. This being taken as a sign of stupidity; see *Glossarium*, CCCXLIV.

542. In *Addenda et emendanda*, DCCLXXIV. Von Kremer plausibly suggested reading the Persian title *khudā-yi khudā* instead of the Arabic of the text *kadhā wa-kadhā*, presumably with the same meaning in Persian "lord of lords" (though this would actually require *khudā-yi khudāyān*).

543. Qur'ān, LXXXIX:24, taken as revealing Pharaoh's pretentions to divinity, an idea borrowed from the Jewish Aggada. In the Midrashim we also find the idea that Pharaoh falsely claimed divinity in order to delude the stupid Egyptians; see A. Geiger, *Was hat Mohammed aus dem Judenthume aufgenommen?* 157–58; L.

Al-Afshīn answered, "This was the custom of the people when addressing my father and grandfather and when speaking to myself before I became a Muslim, and I was reluctant to lower my status to a level inferior to them and thus adversely affect their obedience to me." Isḥāq b. Ibrāhīm b. Muṣʿab reproached him, "Woe to you, O Khaydhar,[544] how can you swear by God to us in such a way that we can consider you veracious, hold your oath reliable, and treat you like other Muslims when you claim for yourself what Pharaoh claimed?" Al-Afshīn replied, "O Abū al-Ḥusayn, this is a sūrah that ʿUjayf cited against ʿAlī b. Hishām,[545] and now you cite it against me! Consider carefully who may cite it against you tomorrow!"[546]

Hārūn b. ʿĪsā b. al-Manṣūr continued: Then Māzyār, the ruler of Ṭabaristān, was brought forward, and they said to al-Afshīn, "Do you know this man?" He replied, "No." Then they said to al-Māzyār, "Do you know this man?" He replied, "Yes, he's al-Afshīn." They said to al-Afshīn, "This is al-Māzyār," and he replied, "Yes, I recognize him now." They asked, "Did you enter into correspondence with him?" He replied, "No." They asked al-Māzyār, "Did he write to you?" And he replied, "Yes. his brother Khāsh wrote to my brother Qūhyār in these terms, 'Indeed, there has been no one to uphold this pure religion (literally, "white religion," *al-dīn al-abyaḍ*)[547] but myself, you,

---

Ginzberg, *The Legends of the Jews*, II, 347–48, V, 201 n. 87, 427 n. 175, VI, 354 n. 16, 423 n. 100.

544. The use of the *ism*, or given name, for someone of al-Afshīn's status would be regarded as contemptuous; al-Afshīn himself uses Isḥāq's *kunyah*, or patronymic, implying respectful intimacy, when replying to him.

545. Al-Maʾmūn's governor of Ādharbayjān, Jibāl, and Armenia but executed, with his brother Ḥusayn, after ʿUjayf b. ʿAnbasah had been sent against him, in 217 (832–32); see Ṭabarī, III, 1107–9.

546. As Sadighi, *op. cit.*, 297 n. 1, points out, the Arab accusers of al-Afshīn are unable to comprehend the purely protocolar nature of the titulature in a letter addressed to an Iranian prince.

547. Browne, *op. cit.*, I, 334, translates "this Most Luminous Religion." Herzfeld, *op. cit.*, 149 n. 2, takes *abyaḍ* here in the sense of "decisive, categorically true" and states that he is unable to discern any connection with the use of colors to denote various sectarian religious groups. White had, of course, been associated with the movement of al-Muqannaʿ in Transoxania, that of the "wearers of white," *Mubayyiḍah, Ispīdh-Jāmagān*. Certainly Islam is characterized in more than one source as the "black religion," in contrast to the "white religion" of the Persians; see Scarcia Amoretti, *op. cit.*, 500, 513.

and Bābak. But as for Bābak, he brought about his own death through his foolishness. I exerted myself to avert death from him, but his folly inevitably led him into falling into what he eventually fell into (i.e., his death). But if you rebel, these people [1312]
(the Arabs) will have no one except myself to launch against you. I have with me cavalry and valiant, fearless troops, and if I am sent against you there will be no one left to combat us apart from three groups—the Arabs, the Maghāribah, and the Turks. As for the Arab, he is like a dog; I will throw him a scrap of food and then beat his brains out with a mace. As for these flies"[548]—meaning the Maghāribah—"they are only a handful. As for those sons of devils"—meaning the Turks—"it is only a short period of time before they will have loosed off their arrows, and then the cavalry will swoop down on them in a concerted charge and destroy them to the last man.[549] [After that] the [true] religion will return to what it always was in the days of the Persians."

Al-Afshīn commented, "This fellow is marking an allegation against his own brother and my brother[550] that should not be imputed to me. Even if I had written such a letter as this to him in order that I might win him over to my side and that he might feel confident of my support and favor (literally, "my flank," *nāḥiyatī*),[551] it would not have been anything to be deprecated. For if I can aid the caliph with my hands, it is all the more fitting for me to aid him with cunning stratagems in order to seize him (Māzyār) unawares and bring him to the caliph, that I might thereby enjoy his favor as does ʿAbdallāh b. Ṭāhir with the caliph." Then al-Māzyār was sent away on one side.[552]

548. Presumably a contemptuous reference to the swarthy and dark skins of the Maghāribah.

549. Herzfeld, *op. cit.*, 149 n. 3, cites as a parallel to this judgment of the relative merits and demerits of these different groups of warriors similar words of al-Ma'mūn and al-Muʿtaṣim, used in a discussion, from Ibn Abī Ṭāhir Ṭayfūr's *Kitāb Baghdād.*

550. The variant reading of ms. O, "against me and against my brother." makes equally good sense.

551. For these transferred meanings of *nāḥiyah*, see *Glossarium*, DV.

552. E. M. Wright, *op. cit.*, 126, notes that al-Afshīn's evasiveness here—his defense that the letter was really his brother's and that, even if he himself had written it, it was for use as a stratagem to gain Māzyār's confidence and then capture him—leaves the impression that al-Afshīn had no strong desire to deny the genuineness of at least the letter's contents.

When al-Afshīn replied to al-Marzubān al-T.r.k.shī as recorded above and to Isḥāq b. Ibrāhīm in those above-mentioned terms, Ibn Abī Duwād chided him; but al-Afshīn said to him, "O Abū ʿAbdallāh, you lift your *ṭaylasān* with your hand and won't place it back on your shoulder until you have killed a great number by means of it."[553] Ibn Abī Duwād asked him, "Are you circumcised?" He replied, "No." Ibn Abī Duwād said, "So what kept you back from that, seeing that it signifies completion of one's Muslim faith and purification from uncleanliness?" Al-Afshīn replied, "Is there not a place in the Islamic faith for prudent dissimulation (*al-taqiyyah*)?"[554] He said, "Yes, certainly." Al-
[1313] Afshīn continued, "I was afraid to cut that member of my body, lest I die." Ibn Abī Duwād observed, "You may be pierced with spears and struck with swords, but still that does not prevent you from engaging in battle; yet you are anxious about cutting a foreskin!" Al-Afshīn replied, "That first eventuality is a necessary affliction that may befall me, and I shall have to bear it when it occurs. But this last is something that I would draw upon myself voluntarily, and I am not sure that it might not involve my death. Moreover, I was not aware that the omission of being circumcised means the renunciation of Islam."[555]

At that Ibn Abī Duwād exclaimed, "His case has now become clear to all of you. O Bughā"—he was adressing Bughā al-Kabīr Abū Mūsā al-Turkī—"seize him!" He related: Bughā clapped his hand on al-Afshīn's girdle and pulled him toward himself, saying, "I had been expecting this [condemnation] from you (from the assembled inquisitors) before now!" He drew the fullness of al-

---

553. I.e., by condemning men to death through the exercise of his judicial authority, symbolized by his wearing of the *ṭaylasān*, a loose hood or gown worn by the *faqīh*, or religious lawyer. See Dozy, *Vêtements*, 278–80; Herzfeld, *op. cit.*, 150 n. 2; p. 31 n. 120, above.

554. *Taqiyyah* or *kitmān*, the justifiable concealment of one's true religious views when under duress or threat of injury, recognized by Sunnīs but of special significance to the Shīʿah, who often suffered persecution or discrimination; see *EI*[1], s.v. Taḳīya (R. Strothmann).

555. Male circumcision is not, of course, prescribed in the Qurʾān, but in continuation of pre-Islamic practices and in accordance with much of ancient Near Eastern religion, above all that of the Hebrews, it came to be regarded very early in Islam as a touchstone of the faith; most of the law schools regard it as *mandūb*, recommended. See Rekaya, "Māzyār," 163; *EI*[2], s.v. Khitān (A. J. Wensinck).

Afshīn's *qabā'* over his head, and then he grasped the parts of the *qabā'* itself firmly at his neck and brought al-Afshīn out via the Bāb al-Wazīrī[556] to his prison.[557]

In this year ʿAbdallāh b. Ṭāhir caused al-Ḥasan b. al-Afshīn and Utrunjah bt. Ashnās to be conveyed to Sāmarrā.

In this year Muḥammad b. Dāwūd led the Pilgrimage.[558]

---

556. See Herzfeld, *op. cit.*, 96, 150, regarding the problems of locating this; it may have been a gate out of the Jawsaq Palace leading to Qaṣr al-Wazīrī or a doorway within the palace where the vizier usually worked. Whether the al-Wazīriyyah also mentioned in the sources for this period as being in Sāmarrā is to be identified with this Bāb al-Wazīrī or whether it was a separate locality is unclear; see also p. 200 n. 583, below.

557. Yaʿqūbī, *Taʾrikh*, II, 583; Masʿūdī, *Murūj*, VII, 137–39 = pars. 2819–21; *Kitāb al-ʿuyūn*, 405–6; Ibn al-Athīr, *op. cit.*, VI, 513–16; The trial of al-Afshīn has been translated almost entirely by Browne, *op. cit.*, I, 331–36; Sadighi, *op. cit.*, 294–304; and Herzfeld, *op. cit.*, 147–50, with comments and paraphrases, and analyzed by E. Wright, *op. cit.*, 56–59, 124–27; cf. also Kaabi, *op. cit.*, I, 255–57; Rekaya, "Māzyār," 163 ff., 189–90.

558. Khalīfah, *op. cit.*, II, 790; Ibn al-Athīr, *op. cit.*, VI, 516.

The Events of the Year 226

(October 31, 840–October 20, 841)

The Rebellion of ʿAlī b. Isḥāq in Damascus

These events included the rebellion of ʿAlī b. Isḥāq b. Yaḥyā b. Muʿādh,[559] who was in charge of police duties (*al-maʿūnah*)[560] at Damascus on the authority of Ṣūl Er-Tigīn,[561] involving an attack on Rajāʾ b. ʿAlī al-Ḍaḥḥāk, who was in charge of the department of tax collecting. He killed Rajāʾ and then feigned madness

559. The son of al-Muʿtaṣim's recently appointed commander of the guard; see Ṭabarī, III, 1303 (p. 179, above).

560. Von Sivers, *op. cit.*, 223, takes *maʿūnah*, however, as meaning here "auxiliary troops," and this would fit the context equally well; we are obviously dealing with locally raised or long-resident troops of the Syrian *jund*, who, as von Sivers points out, must have resented the appointment, a year previously, of a slave commander of the new caliphal guard from the east, Ashnās, as overall governor of Syria and al-Jazīrah, in place of the ʿAbbāsid ʿUbaydallāh b. ʿAbd al-ʿAzīz b. al-Faḍl b. Ṣāliḥ b. ʿAlī (see p. 178 n. 504, above). Finally, in regard to this ambiguous term *maʿūnah*, pl. *maʿāwīn*, one should note that it is also used in the sense of extraordinary taxes and levies for the support of officials. See Løkkegaard, *op. cit.*, 186–7; *EI*², s.v. Maʿūna (P. Crone).

561. For the origins of Ṣūl Er-Tigīn in the caliphal service, see Ṭabarī, III, 1194 (p. 44 and n. 148, above).

(*aẓhara al-waswās*).[562] [However,] Aḥmad b. Abī Duwād subsequently spoke up for him, and he was released from his prison.[563] Al-Ḥasan b. Rajā' used to encounter him on the street in Sāmarrā. Al-Buḥturi al-Ṭā'ī[564] said: [1314]

Through his impetuousness ʿAlī b. Isḥāq erased the traces of the strange haughtiness that was once in al-Ḥasan.
A certain serious happening made him forget his loud, futile talk and left in him nothing but surrender to fate.
He was not like Ibn Ḥujr[565] when he was angry or like the brother of Kulayb[566] or Sayf b. Dhī Yazan.[567]
It was never said to you regarding an act of blood vengeance that you sought,
"[The blood of] those noble souls is not [like] two bowls of milk curds."[568]

In this year Muḥammad b. ʿAbdallāh b. Ṭāhir b. al-Ḥusayn died, and al-Muʿtaṣim led the worship over him in Muḥammad's own house.[569]

In this year al-Afshīn died.

---

562. The verb *waswasa* is frequently used of the "whisperings" of Satan, but the interpretation followed here is that of von Sivers, *op. cit.*, 223, that he feigned madness or diabolical possession in order to provide an excuse for his rebellious actions.

563. Ibn al-Athīr, *op. cit.*, VI, 517.

564. Al-Walīd b. ʿUbayd(allāh), of the Buḥtur clan of the Banū Ṭayyi', (died 284 (897)), was a poet and author of an anthology called, like that of Abū Tammām, the *Ḥamāsah*. He was at this time a protégé of his fellow-Ṭā'ī the commander Abū Saʿīd Muḥammad b. Yūsuf (see p. 15 n. 58, above). See also *GAS*, II, 560–64, IX, 300–1; *EI*², s.v. al-Buḥturī (Ch. Pellat).

565. I.e., the famous pre-Islamic poet-king Imru' al-Qays b. Ḥujr al-Kindī.

566. I.e., Muhalhil b. Rabīʿah, avenger of Kulayb on the enemy tribe of Bakr in the pre-Islamic War of Basūs. See R. A. Nicholson, *Literary History*, 55–59; *EI*², s.v. Kulayb b. Rabīʿa (G. Levi della Vida).

567. The Ḥimyarite prince famed for his role in the expulsion of the alien Abyssinians from South Arabia in the sixth century. See Nicholson, *op. cit.*, 28–29; *EI*¹, s.v. Saif b. Dhī Yazan (R. Paret).

568. Al-Buḥturī, *Dīwān*, ed. al-Ṣayrafī, IV, 2246 no, 883.

569. This item of information cannot be correct, as Muḥammad b. ʿAbdallāh b. Ṭahir lived on until 253 (867), in al-Muʿtazz's caliphate, having played a leading role in affairs of the time. See Bosworth, "The Ṭāhirids and Arabic Culture," 68–69; Kaabi, *op. cit.*, I, 299–312.

Al-Afshīn's Death, the Treatment of Him at That Time, and What Was Done with His Corpse after His Death

It has been mentioned from Ḥamdūn b. Ismāʿīl[570] that he related: When the new fruits came into season al-Muʿtaṣim gathered some of them on a platter and told his son Hārūn al-Wāthiq, "Go personally with these fruits to al-Afshīn and convey them to him." So they were brought along with Hārūn al-Wāthiq until he
[1315] went up with them to al-Afshīn in the building that had been constructed for the latter's imprisonment and that was called Lu'lu'ah. Al-Afshīn looked at the platter but missed certain fruits (or: "looked for certain fruits," *iftaqada*), either ordinary plums (*ijjāṣ*) or plums of the *shāhlūj* variety,[571] and exclaimed to al-Wāthiq, "There is no god but God! What an excellent platter, except that there are no *ijjāṣ* or *shāhlūj* plums there for me!" Al-Wāthiq replied, "That's true! I'll go back and send the missing fruit to you," al-Afshīn not having at that point touched any of the fruit. When al-Wāthiq got ready to go back, al-Afshīn said to him, "Give my lord greetings, and tell him, 'I beseech you to send me a trustworthy person from your entourage, who will convey what I shall say.' "[572]

Al-Muʿtaṣim at this point gave orders to Ḥamdūn b. Ismāʿīl—it was this Ḥamdūn who was, during al-Mutawakkil's reign, imprisoned by Sulaymān b. Wahb[573] in the very same prison where al-Afshīn was incarcerated, and he related this story when he was actually in it. Ḥamdūn said: Al-Muʿtaṣim sent me to

---

570. Ibrāhīm, called Ḥamdūn, b. Ismāʿīl b. Dāwūd b. Ḥamdūn, was a courtier and boon companion of al-Ma'mūn, al-Muʿtaṣim, and their successors. With his son Abū ʿAbdallāh he figures frequently in anecdotes in Abū al-Faraj al-Iṣfahānī, *Aghānī*, passim, and in Ibrāhīm al-Bayhaqī, *op. cit.*, ed. Schwally, 164–68, 574–75 = ed. Ibrāhīm, I, 249–53, II, 328–30; see also Herzfeld, *op. cit.*, 151 n. 1. The Ḥamdūn family of boon companions ran to four generations; see A. G. Chejne, "The Boon-Companion," 335; Masʿūdī, *Murūj*, ed. Pellat, VI, 285–86.

571. This type of plum is also found in Persian, spelled *shāh-lūk*; see Vullers, *op. cit.*, II, 396. On *ijjāṣ*, see Dozy, *Supplément*, I, 10.

572. E. M. Wright, *op. cit.*, 127, takes al-Muʿtaṣim's offer of the fruit as a sign that he intended momentarily to relent toward al-Afshīn.

573. I.e., the man who was subsequently the vizier of al-Muhtadī and al-Muʿtamid and who had previously been secretary to Mūsā b. Bughā al-Kabīr and Aytākh; he died in 271 (884–85) or 272 (885–86). See Sourdel, *Vizirat*, I, 300–3, 310–13; *EI*[1], s.v. Sulaimān b. Wahb (K. V. Zettersteén).

al-Afshīn and told me, "He will spin out his tale for you, so don't dally there." He related: I accordingly went in to al-Afshīn, who had the platter of fruit still in front of him, not having touched a single piece or more from it. He said to me, "Sit down," so I sat down, and he tried to win me over by stressing his position as a noble figure among the Persians (*bi-al-dahqanah*). I told him, however, "Don't spin things out, for the Commander of the Faithful ordered me not to dally here with you, so make it short!" He said, "Tell the Commander of the Faithful, 'You were good to me and showed me honor, and people followed me submissively (literally, "walked at my heels"). But then you accepted statements about me that were not confirmed for you as being true, nor did you reflect on them with your own intelligence, just how this situation could occur and how it could be thought possible of me that I should do these things you had heard about. You are informed that I was in secret communication with Minkajūr, urging him to rebel, and you give it credence. You are also informed that I told the commander whom I sent against Minkajūr, "Don't actually fight him, but hold back and feign battle, and if you come into contact with one of our men, flee from him!" You are a [courageous] man; you have been familiar [1316]
with war, have fought against opponents, and have led armies. Is it possible that the head of an army would tell a body of troops that was about to encounter an enemy, "Behave in such-and-such a way!"? It would be inadmissible for anyone to behave in this fashion! And even if this were possible, it would not be fitting for you to accept its truth from an enemy whose ulterior motive you had already perceived. You are in a superior position over me (or: "you are always my first concern," *anta awlā bī*); I am merely one from among your slaves and a creature of yours.[574] But a fitting comparison between the two of us (i.e., in regard to the caliph's uncritical acceptance of calumnies against al-Afshīn), O Commander of the Faithful, is that of a man who tended and raised a calf of his until he had fattened it and it had grown big and was in a fine condition. He had friends who were longing to eat the calf's flesh, so they proposed to him that the calf should be

574. *Ṣanīʿuka*, in the sense of protégé, dependent; see Herzfeld, *op. cit.*, 151 n. 2.

slaughtered; but he refused their plea about that. At this, they all agreed to say to him one day, "Woe upon you! Why are you rearing this lion? This is a savage beast that has grown big, and, when a savage beast grows big, it reverts to its kind." The man answered them, "Woe upon you! This is a bovine's calf, not a savage beast!" But they replied, "This is a savage beast; ask whom you will about it! They had previously given instructions to all those who knew the man and had said to them, "If he asks you about the calf, tell him that it's a savage beast!" Hence whenever the man questioned another person about it and said to him, "Don't you see this calf, how fine it is!" the other person would reply, "It's a savage beast, a lion, woe upon you!" So [in the end] the man ordered the calf to be slaughtered. Now I am that calf, so how can I be a lion? [I ask the help of] God concerning my plight![575] You (al-Muʿtaṣim) have chosen me as one of your protégés and have raised me to a level of honor, and you are my lord and master. I implore God to incline your heart toward me!' "

Ḥamdūn related: I rose and went away, and I left the platter just
[1317] as it was, without al-Afshīn's having touched anything of it. Then it was only a short time afterward that it was reported that he was either dying or had already died. Al-Muʿtaṣim then said, "Show him to his son."[576] So they brought out al-Afshīn's corpse and flung it down in front of him, and he tore out his beard and his hair.[577] Then al-Muʿtaṣim gave orders, and al-Afshīn's corpse was borne away to Aytākh's house.[578]

Ḥamdūn related: Aḥmad b. Abī Duwād had summoned al-Afshīn from prison to the Public Audience Chamber and said to him, "O Khaydhar, it has reached the Commander of the Faithful that you are uncircumcised." He answered, "Yes." By asking that, Ibn Abī Duwād had only wanted him to bear witness against himself, for, if he exposed himself, weakness and lack of spirit would be imputed to him, and, if he did not expose himself, the accusation against him that he was uncircumcised would

575. *Allāh*[a] *Allāh*[a] *fī amrī*; see on this construction, p. 163 n. 465, above.

576. I.e., to al-Ḥasan, sent captive to Sāmarrā shortly before this by ʿAbdallāh b. Ṭāhir; see Ṭabarī, III, 1308 (p. 185, above).

577. I.e., as a sign of distress and mourning.

578. Al-Ḥasan himself was not released from prison until 250 (864), in al-Mustaʿīn's caliphate; see Ṭabarī, III, 1533.

be substantiated. But al-Afshīn answered, "Yes, I am uncircumcised."

All the commanders and other troops and courtiers (*al-nās*) were present at the palace on that day when Ibn Abī Duwād had brought al-Afshīn forth into the Public Audience Chamber. This had taken place before al-Wāthiq's visit to him with the fruit and before Ḥamdūn b. Ismāʿīl went to him.

Ḥamdūn related: I said to him (i.e., later, when al-Afshīn was back in his prison), "Are you [really] uncircumcised as you asserted [on that day]?" Al-Afshīn replied, "He (Ibn Abī Duwād) brought me forth to a place like that (i.e., to the Public Audience Chamber within the palace), with all the commanders and other people assembled, and then said to me what he said! He only wanted to dishonor me; if I had told him, 'Yes,' he would not have accepted my word but would have told me to expose myself so that he might dishonor me before all the people! Death would have been preferable for me, rather than exposing myself before all the people. But you, O Ḥamdūn, if you wish me to expose myself in your presence so that you can see me, I will do so." Ḥamdūn continued: I said to him, however, "In my opinion, you are a highly veracious person, and I don't want you to expose yourself."

When Ḥamdūn returned and conveyed al-Afshīn's message to al-Muʿtaṣim, the latter ordered that all but a little food should be denied to al-Afshīn, so he used to be given only a loaf of bread each day until he died.

After his death his body was taken along to Aytākh's house,[579]
and they brought it forth and gibbeted it on the Bāb al-ʿĀmmah, [1318]
so that the populace might see it. Then it was flung down at the Bāb al-ʿĀmmah, together with the wooden beam on which it had been gibbeted, and burned and the ashes carried away and thrown into the Tigris.[580]

579. Yaʿqūbī, *Buldān*, 262, trans., 54, places this in the second of the main streets of Sāmarrā, adjacent to the *qaṭāʾiʿ* and houses of the two Bughās, Sīmā al-Dimashqī, Waṣīf, and other Turkish commanders; see Herzfeld, *op. cit.*, 108.

580. The story of al-Afshīn's appeal to the Caliph, his adducing the story of the calf-lion, and his final fate, is given in a briefer form, also on the authority of Ḥamdūn, by Ibrāhīm al-Bayhaqī, *op. cit.*, ed. Schwally, 574–75 = ed. Ibrāhīm, II, 328–30. Abū Tammām wrote an ode in praise of al-Muʿtaṣim on the occasion of the gibbeting and burning of al-Afshīn's corpse (*Dīwān*, II, 198–209 no. 72), a

At the time when al-Muʿtaṣim ordered al-Afshīn to be imprisoned, on a certain night, he sent Sulaymān b. Wahb al-Kātib to make an inventory of everything in al-Afshīn's residence and to record it. Al-Afshīn's palace was at al-Maṭīrah.[581] In his residence was found a tabernacle (*bayt*) containing an image of a man, carved out of wood and covered with many ornaments and jewels and having in its ears two white stones with intricate gold filigree work over them. One of the men who were there with Sulaymān took one of these two stones, thinking that it was a jewel of great value—this being nighttime. But, when morning came and he pulled the gold filigree work off it, he found that it was a stone resembling the seashell called *ḥabarūn*, the kind of shell called "trumpet shell."[582] There were brought out of his residence grotesque figures (or: "paintings," *ṣuwar*) and such, idols and things of that ilk, together with the rafts made of inflatable skins and timber frameworks that he had got ready; and there were further items of his at al-Wazīriyyah.[583] Among them was found another idol, and among his books they found a book of the Magians called *Z.rāwah*[584] and many other books pertaining to his faith by means of which he used to worship his lord.[585] Al-Afshīn's death was in Shaʿbān 226 (May–June 841).[586]

---

poem described by Stetkevych as strongly anti-Iranian and anti-Shuʿūbī in sentiment; see her analysis, *op. cit.*, 55–60.

581. Al-Afshīn's *qaṭīʿah*, where his palace was built, was adjacent to the lands of others of his Ushrūsanī troops; the ruins of his palace are now called Jubayriyyah. See Yaʿqūbī, *Buldān*, 259, 262, trans., 51, 55; Herzfeld, *op. cit.*, 101. According to Yaʿqūbī, *Buldān*, 264–65, trans., 58, al-Afshīn's palace was taken over after his death by Waṣīf, who abandoned his old dwelling for this new one.

582. See *Glossarium*, CLXXIX.

583. Either a part of the Maṭīrah Palace, accessible by the Bāb al-Wazīrī (see p. 193 n. 556, above), or the district where lay the *qaṣr al-wazīrī*, the house of Abū al-Wazīr Aḥmad b. Khālid, who is said to have had a pioneer role in the original laying out of Sāmarrā; see Ṭabarī, III, 1179–80 (pp. 25–26, above); cf. Herzfeld, *op. cit.*, 91, 95–96.

584. Herzfeld, *op. cit.*, 152 n. 4, interprets this as being correctly *zuwārah*, *uzwārah*, rendered in Ibn al-Nadīm's *Fihrist* as *ūzwārsh*, meaning "interpretation, exegesis."

585. According to Masʿūdī, *Murūj*, VII, 139 = par. 2822, the idols were thrown on to the fire when al-Afshīn's corpse was burned and consumed.

586. Hence al-Afshīn remained in prison for nearly nine months. See Masʿūdī, *Murūj*, VII, 139 = par. 2822; *Kitāb al-ʿuyūn*, 407; Ibn al-Athīr, *op. cit.*, VI, 517–18; Sadighi, *op. cit.*, 303–5; E. M. Wright, *op. cit.*, 127–30; Herzfeld, *op. cit.*, 151–52.

In this year Muḥammad b. Dāwūd led the Pilgrimage by order of Ashnās, who himself made the Pilgrimage this year. He (Ashnās) was given charge over every place that he was to enter, and his name was mentioned with blessings in the worship from all the pulpits through which he passed, from Sāmarrā to Mecca and Medina. The one who mentioned him from the pulpit at al-Kūfah was Muḥammad b. ʿAbd al-Raḥmān b. ʿĪsā b. Mūsā,[587] [1319]
from the pulpit at Fayd[588] it was Hārūn b. Muḥammad b. Abī Khālid al-Marwarrūdhī,[589] from the pulpit at Medina it was Muḥammad b. Ayyūb b. Jaʿfar b. Sulaymān,[590] and from the pulpit at Mecca it was Muḥammad b. Dāwūd b. ʿĪsā b. Mūsā.[591] In all these districts he was greeted as *amīr*, and he continued to hold this administrative charge over them until he returned to Sāmarrā.[592]

The last two authorities note, in connection with al-Afshīn's idols or pictures, what were originally believed to be painted stone columns (called by Herzfeld *Bildsäulen* "picture columns"), discovered by the German team of archaeologists who first excavated Sāmarrā under the floor of the throne room in the Jawsaq al-Khāqānī. In fact, D. S. Rice subsequently showed that these are fragments of tall wine vessels (technically called *dann*, pl. *dinān*), with scenes painted on them of a secular nature and appropriate to wine drinking and other convivial activities; see his "Deacon or Drink," 15–23. Thus these finds cannot be cited as having any connection with Manichaean idols or paintings. With regard to the nature of al-Afshīn's own religious beliefs, Sadighi rightly points out that his ancestral religion can hardly have been Zoroastrianism, in the light of the prominence of these idols, but could well have been Buddhism, which had certainly been one of the faiths of pre-Islamic Transoxania; this, too, is the conclusion arrived at by Rekaya, "Māzyār," 163.

587. Probably the great-grandson of the first ʿAbbāsid Caliph al-Saffāḥ's brother Mūsā, hence a first cousin of the Muḥammad b. Dāwūd b. ʿĪsā b. Mūsā, mentioned in n. 591, below.

588. A settlement in Najd, important as the halfway point on the Pilgrimage route from al-Kūfah to the Holy Places in the Ḥijāz; see *EI*[2] Suppl., s.v. Fayd (C. E. Bosworth).

589. A commander of Abnā' descent whom Ṭabarī mentions at various points at serving al-Ma'mūn; his father had been the leader of the Baghdad opposition to al-Ḥasan b. Sahl during the early years of al-Ma'mūn's caliphate.

590. This man is mentioned in Abū al-Faraj al-Iṣfahānī, *Aghānī*, Būlāq ed., XII, 129–30 = ed. Ibrāhīm, XIV, 17, 19, as governor of al-Baṣrah and as the grandson of the Jaʿfar b. Sulaymān who was an ʿAbbāsid of the line of ʿAlī al-Sajjād and governor of al-Baṣrah, Mecca, and Medina in the caliphates of al-Manṣūr and al-Mahdī.

591. The great-grandson of the brother of al-Saffāḥ and governor of Mecca 221–33 (836–48).

592. Khalīfah, *op. cit.*, II, 791; Ibn al-Athīr, *op. cit.*, VI, 521.

The Events of the Year

227

(October 21, 841–October 9, 842)

These included the rebellion in Palestine of Abū Ḥarb al-Mubarqaʿ[593] al-Yamānī[594] and his defiance of the central government.

593. Literally, "the Veiled One." As noted by H. Eisenstein, "Erhebung," 454, Abū Ḥarb was by no means the first rebel in Islam to call himself thus. Cf. the Yemeni rebel of the Prophet's time al-Aswad or Dhū al-Khimār; the Transoxanian rebel of early ʿAbbāsid times al-Muqannaʿ; and the leader of the Zanj, or black slaves, in lower Iraq toward the end of the third (ninth) century ʿAlī b. Muḥammad, al-Burquʿī or al-Mubarqaʿ. (Eisenstein, *op. cit.*, 454 n. 3, noted that it must be this last rebel who is to be identified with the "al-Burquʿī" who Thaʿālibī claims, *op. cit.*, 142 trans. 110, was among the monsters who killed more than a million people in Islam, rather than the Palestinian al-Mubarqaʿ.) This Palestinian outbreak is examined in detail by Eisenstein, *op. cit.*, and *EI*², s.v. al-Mubarḳaʿ. He notes that Ṭabarī's account is the most detailed, the one upon which later writers, like Miskawayh, *Tajārib al-umam*, VI, 526–27; *Kitāb al-ʿuyūn*, 408; Ibn ʿAsākir, *op. cit.*, V, 311–12; and Ibn al-Athīr, *op. cit.*, VI, 522–23, largely depend. The only account clearly originating from a different source is the brief one given by Yaʿqūbī, *Taʾrīkh*, II, 586, which is inserted among the events of al-Wāthiq's reign and involves the exploits of Rajāʾ b. Ayyūb al-Ḥiḍārī (see below), who suppressed a rebellion of the Berbers of Cyrenaica, supported by dissident Arab elements, in 228 (842–43), after he had dealt with Ibn Bayhas in Damascus and al-Mubarqaʿ in Palestine, to which should be added von Sivers, *op. cit.*, 223–24.

594. Yaʿqūbī, *Taʾrīkh*, II, 586, calls him "Tamīm al-Lakhmī, known as Abū Ḥarb and with the *laqab* al-Mubarqaʿ."

The Reason for Abū Ḥarb al-Mubarqaʿ's Rebellion and Its Eventual Outcome

One of my acquaintances, who stated that he was familiar with the story of al-Mubarqaʿ's outbreak, has mentioned to me that the reason behind his rebellion against the central government was that a certain one of the troops wanted to lodge in his house while he himself was away and [only] his wife or sister there. She refused to let him (the soldier seeking a billet) do that, so he struck her with a whip that he had with him, and she fended it off with her forearm, but the whip hit her forearm and left marks on it. When Abū Ḥarb returned to his house she wept and complained to him about what the soldier had done to her and showed him the marks on her forearm from his blow. At that Abū Ḥarb took up his sword and went along to the soldier, catching him unawares,[595] and struck him with the sword until he killed him. He then took to flight, covering his face with a veil (*burquʿ*), so that he would not be recognized, and went into one of the mountains of the Jordan region. The government authorities sought him, but there was no report of him. [1320]

Abū Ḥarb used to appear openly during the daytime and sit out, veiled (*mutabarqiʿan*), on the mountain in which he had taken refuge, and people would see him and come to him. He would then exhort them and enjoin upon them good behavior and the prohibition of bad actions (*al-amr bi-al-maʿrūf wa-al-nahy ʿan al-munkar*), and he would mention the central government (*al-sulṭān*) and how it oppressed the people and would speak scathingly of it. He persisted in doing this habitually until a group of the peasant cultivators from that region and also the villagers responded to his call. He used to assert that he was an Umayyad, with the result that those who responded to him said, "This man is the Sufyānī!"[596] When his adherents and followers from this

595. *Ghārr*, literally, "neglectful, unprepared."

596. I.e., an awaited deliverer from the Sufyānid line of the Umayyads, who would arise and release Syria from the tyranny of the ʿAbbāsids. Outbreaks headed by such figures are mentioned up to the beginning of the fourth (tenth) century. The bibliography here is extensive. Earlier studies are reviewed in Madelung, "The Sufyānī," who is himself skeptical that the popular legend of the Sufyānī as a Syrian national hero was the mainspring of messianic beliefs about the Sufyānī and the Mahdī.

class of people grew numerous, he summoned the members of leading families and notables of the region. Out of these a good number of the leaders of the Yemenis[597] responded to his call, including a man named Ibn Bayhas, who commanded the obedience of the Yemenis,[598] and also two other men from the people of Damascus.[599]

The news [of this rebellion] reached al-Muʿtaṣim at the time when he was ill with the sickness from which he [eventually] died. He therefore sent Rajāʾ b. Ayyūb al-Ḥiḍārī[600] against Abū Ḥarb with about a thousand men from the local troops (*al-jund*). But when Rajāʾ reached Abū Ḥarb he found the latter with a vast host (literally, "a world, universe") of followers. The person who related this story to me about Abū Ḥarb's revolt mentioned that Abū Ḥarb had approximately 100,000 men. Rajāʾ was unwilling to engage forces with him, encamped opposite him, and procrastinated with him until it was the beginning of the season for the peasants' cultivating their lands and for their plowing.[601] The peasant cultivators in Abū Ḥarb's following went back to their plowing, and the landowners to their own estates, and Abū Ḥarb was left with a force of around 1,000 or 2,000 men. Rajāʾ now came out against him in battle, and the two armies met: that of Rajāʾ and that of al-Mubarqaʿ. When they came together Rajāʾ
[1321] scrutinized al-Mubarqaʿ's army and said to his companions, "I don't discern within his forces any man who has the equestrian and martial skills (*furūsiyyah*)[602] except him. He will sally forth

597. Yaʿqūbī, *Taʾrīkh*, II, 586, mentions men of Lakhm (Abū Ḥarb's own tribe), Judhām, ʿĀmilah, and Balqayn as responding specifically to him.

598. This same historian, however, gives him the *nisbah* "al-Kilābī" (hence from what was actually a North Arab tribe of the Rabīʿah group; see *EI*², s.v. Kilāb b. Rabīʿa [W. M. Watt]; from the Kilāb Bedouins of Syria were to spring, in the next century, the Mirdāsids of Aleppo) and states that he rallied round him a great many of the clans of Qays.

599. This participation of the *ahl Dimashq* doubtless refers to members of the local *jund*, who had broken out in revolt against the central government in Iraq during the previous year, as recorded by Ṭabarī, III, 1313–14 (pp. 194–95, above); see von Sivers, *op. cit.*, 223.

600. See, on him, p. 44 and n. 149, above.

601. Eisenstein, *op. cit.*, 456, notes that at this juncture, according to Ibn Khaldūn and, by inference, Ibn al-Athīr, the already sick al-Muʿtaṣim died.

602. See, on the ensemble of skills that made up this concept, *EI*², s.v. Furūsiyya (G. Douillet and D. Ayalon).

in person to display to his companions his manliness (*rujlah*), so don't hasten against him."

He related: The matter turned out just as Rajāʾ had predicted. Very soon al-Mubarqaʿ attacked Rajāʾ's forces. Rajāʾ instructed his men, "Leave a way open for him," and they did this until al-Mubarqaʿ passed right through their lines. Then he turned back again, and Rajāʾ again ordered his troops to leave a way open for him, and they did this until he passed right through them and returned to his own camp. Again Rajāʾ delayed any action and told his troops, "He will attack you once more, so leave a way open for him, but when he tries to return [this time] intercept him, and take him prisoner." Al-Mubarqaʿ behaved exactly thus. He attacked Rajāʾ's troops, and they left a way open for him until he passed right through them. Then he turned back again, but [this time] they surrounded him, captured him, and brought him down from his steed.

He related: Previously, when Rajāʾ had abandoned the idea of making a sudden onslaught on al-Mubarqaʿ, an envoy had come to him, sent by al-Muʿtaṣim, with the task of urging him on to action. Rajāʾ had seized the envoy and put him in fetters until the outcome of the struggle between him and Abū Ḥarb was as we have just mentioned; then he set him free. The same authority went on to relate: On the day when Rajāʾ brought Abū Ḥarb to al-Muʿtaṣim the latter upbraided Rajāʾ for what he had done to his envoy. Rajāʾ told him, "O Commander of the Faithful, may God make me your ransom! You sent me with 1,000 men against a force of 100,000. I shrank from launching an immediate attack, lest I myself and the troops with me perish to no avail whatever. Hence I proceeded carefully until the forces that he had with him had grown sparse. I found an opportunity and discovered ways and means to combat him. Then I rose up and attacked him at the moment when his forces had grown sparse and he was in a weak position while we were in a strong one. And now I have brought you the man as a prisoner!"

Abū Jaʿfar (al-Ṭabarī) says: Another source, as well as the one that I have mentioned as relating to me the story of Abū Ḥarb as I [1322]
have just described it, has asserted that his rebellion was actually in the year 226 (840–841) and that he came out in arms in

Palestine or at al-Ramlah.[603] They (the people of that region) said that he was the Sufyānī. He then came with 50,000 Yemenis and others, and Ibn Bayhas and two other men with him from the people of Damascus raised the standard of rebellion (*iʿtaqada*).[604] Al-Muʿtaṣim sent Rajāʾ al-Ḥiḍārī with a powerful force, and Rajāʾ attacked them at Damascus. He killed about 5,000 of the followers of Ibn Bayhas and his two associates, and he took Ibn Bayhas prisoner and killed his two companions. He attacked Abū Ḥarb at al-Ramlah, killed about 20,000 of his followers, and took Abū Ḥarb himself prisoner. He was transported to Sāmarrā, and he and Ibn Bayhas were incarcerated in the Maṭbaq prison.[605]

In this year Jaʿfar b. Mihrj.sh al-Kurdī rebelled. In al-Muḥarram (October–November 841) al-Muʿtaṣim sent Aytākh to the mountains of al-Mawṣil to combat him, and one of his soldiers fell upon Jaʿfar and killed him.[606]

In this year, in the month of Rabīʿ I (December 841–January

603. The administrative capital of the *jund* of Filasṭīn, some twenty-five miles northeast of Jerusalem. See Yāqūt, *Muʿjam*, III, 69–70; Le Strange, *Palestine*, 28, 38, 303–8; *EI*[1], s.v. al-Ramla (E. Honigmann).

604. Understanding the omission of an implied object like *liwāʾan*, as is pointed out by Eisenstein, *op. cit.*, 457 n. 13, *pace* Ṭabarī, trans. Marin, 126.

605. Einstein notes, *op. cit.*, 457, that neither the role of Ibn Bayhas in al-Mubarqaʿs uprising nor the relationship between the Damascus and Palestine movements is clear, nor is the chronology certain. Given the fact, however, that Rajāʾ waited for some time while Abū Ḥarb's peasant followers returned to work their fields and that al-Muʿtaṣim died in Rabīʿ I 227 (January 842), it may well be that the outbreak of al-Mubarqaʿ began in 226, rather than in 227, as Ṭabarī's second authority for the events related states. Nothing is recorded about the presumed eventual deaths of al-Mubarqaʿ and Ibn Bayhas. The Maṭbaq or Muṭbaq was a well-known jail within the Round City of al-Manṣūr at Baghdad. See Yaʿqūbī, *Buldān*, 240, trans., 15–16; Le Strange, *Baghdad*, 27; Lassner, *op. cit.*, 55, 243.

606. The reading of the second element of Jaʿfar's name is uncertain. Azdī, *op. cit.*, 430–31, starts to tell the story of this revolt in detail (placing it under the events of the year 224), but his recital is broken off in the extant manuscripts midway through the story. It was doubtless Azdī's account that Ibn al-Athīr, *op. cit.*, VI, 506–7, used for his own narrative of the revolt, placing it under the year 226. The outbreak clearly turned into a large-scale uprising of the Kurds in the mountain regions north and east of al-Mawṣil; Masʿūdī, *Tanbīh*, 355, trans., 456, counts its suppression among the major victories of al-Muʿtaṣim's reign. The caliphal governor of al-Mawsil, ʿAbdallāh b. al-Sayyid b. Anas al-Azdī, was himself unable to quell it; it was not until Aytākh was sent into the mountains of Dāsin (see Yāqūt, *Muʿjam*, II, 432: apparently the mountains of the modern Amadiyah [ʿImādiyyah] region) to combat Jaʿfar that the latter was defeated and killed.

842), the death of Bishr b. al-Ḥārith al-Ḥāfī took place. He was originally from Marw.[607]

In this year, al-Muʿtaṣim's death took place. According to what has been mentioned, it was on a Thursday, and some people say it was on the eighteenth of the month of Rabīʿ I (January 5, 842),[608] two hours after daybreak.

Al-Muʿtaṣim's Fatal Illness, the Length of His Life, and His Physical Characteristics [1323]

It has been mentioned that the beginning of his illness was when he was cupped (or "asked to be cupped") on the first of al-Muḥarram (October 21, 841) and fell ill at that point.[609] It has been mentioned from Muḥammad b. Aḥmad b. Rashīd from Zunām al-Zamīr,[610] who said: Al-Muʿtaṣim felt a momentary easing of his pain during his final illness and said, "Get a *zulāl*[611] ready for me, so that I may travel in it tomorrow." He related: He

---

607. Bishr was a renowned Khurāsānian mystic whose nickname al-Ḥāfī meant "the barefooted one." See al-Khaṭīb, *op. cit.*, VII, 67–80 no. 3517; Ibn Khallikān, *Wafayāt al-aʿyān*, I, 274–77 no, 114, trans., I, 257–60; *EI*², s.v. Bis͟hr al-Ḥāfī (F. Meier).

608. This date was in fact a Thursday. Masʿūdī, *Tanbīh*, 354, trans., 454, gives Thursday, the nineteenth of Rabīʿ I (also the date in Yaʿqūbī, *Taʾrikh*, II, 584, and Dīnawarī, *op. cit.*, 406), but in his *Murūj*, VII, 144 = par. 2829, he gives Thursday, the eighteenth of Rabīʿ I. *Kitāb al-ʿuyūn*, 409, and Ibn al-Athīr, *op. cit.*, VI, 523–24, follow Ṭabarī in giving the day of the month as the eighteenth. The figures for al-Muʿtaṣim's age at his death vary between forty-six and forty-nine years; see pp. 208–9, below.

609. According to Ibn Abī Uṣaybiʿah, citing Ḥunayn b. Isḥāq, in his biography of Salmawayh b. Bunān (*ʿUyūn al-anbāʾ*, I, 164–65; cf. *GAS*, III, 227), al-Muʿtaṣim used to be cupped regularly and then purged twice a year by his Christian physician Salmawayh, whom he trusted so implicitly that he called him "my father" and personally prayed over his grave when he died in 225 (840). After this the noted physician Yūḥannā or Yaḥyā b. Māsawayh (died in 243 [847]; cf. *GAS*, III, 231–36) treated al-Muʿtaṣim but allegedly reversed the order of treatment, thereby overheating the Caliph's blood and bringing about his death. For an anecdote on Ibn Māsawayh's prescribing for the Caliph, see also Masʿūdī, *Murūj*, VII, 104–6 = par. 2789.

610. Literally, "the reed pipe or flute player." i.e., the player on the *zamr* or *mizmār*, pace Ṭabarī, trans. Marin, 127 n. 606: "the lute player." Sunām was a celebrated performer on the reed pipe, who was patronized by caliphs from Hārūn al-Rashīd to al-Wāthiq; see Farmer, *op. cit.*, 131; *EI*², s.v. Mizmār (H. G. Farmer).

611. This was a small, light, swift river craft used especially for pleasure. See Kindermann, *op. cit.*, 35; al-Nukhaylī, *op. cit.*, 59–62.

sailed off in it, with myself accompanying him, and on the Tigris he passed along opposite his palaces. He said, "O Zunām, play for me [the tune of the verses]:

O dwelling place whose traces have not yet become effaced,
God forbid that your traces should ever disappear completely!
I have not wept [merely] for your ruined traces, but
I have wept for my life there within you as it has ebbed away.
His [past] life is the most fitting thing that a noble youth can weep over,
[but ultimately] the sad one must find consolation."

He related: I continued playing this melody until he called for a jar containing a *raṭl* [of wine] (*raṭliyyah*) and then drank a beakerful. I began to play my flute and repeated the melody. He meanwhile had taken up a napkin (*mandīl*)[612] before him and continued weeping, wiping his eyes with the napkin and sobbing until he went back to his palace, not having finished drinking the contents of the *raṭliyyah*.[613]

It has been mentioned from ʿAlī b. al-Jaʿd[614] that he said: When al-Muʿtaṣim was on the point of death, he began to murmur, "All possible stratagems have come to an end; there is no way out now left," until he was reduced to silence.[615] Others, however, have mentioned that he began to murmur, "I am being snatched away from the midst of all these people." He is also reported to have said, "If only I had known that my life-span would be thus short, I would not have done what I did."

When he died he was buried at Sāmarrā.[616] His caliphate lasted
[1324] for eight years, eight months, and two days. It is said that he was born in Shaʿbān 180 (796–797), but others place it in the year 179 (795–796). If he was born in 180, his complete life-span was forty-six years, seven months, and eighteen days, but, if he was

---

612. Or handkerchief; see *EI*^{2}, s.v. Mandīl (F. Rosenthal).

613. Ibn al-Athīr, *op. cit.*, VI, 523–24; Ibn al-Ṭiqṭaqā, *op. cit.*, 212, trans., 231–32.

614. ʿAbī b. al-Jaʿd al-Jawharī al-Baghdādī was a *muḥaddith* from whom Bukhārī related traditions and who died in 230 (844–45). See al-Khaṭīb, *op. cit.*, XI, 360–66 no. 6215; *GAS*, I, 105.

615. Ibn al-Athīr, *op. cit.*, VI, 524; Ibn al-Ṭiqṭaqā, *op. cit.*, 212, trans., 232.

616. In the Jawsaq Palace, as Yaʿqūbī specifies, *Taʾrīkh*, II, 584.

born in 179, his life-span was forty-seven years, two months, and eighteen days. According to what has been mentioned, he was fair-complexioned, with a black beard the hair tips of which were red and the end of which was square and streaked with red, and with handsome eyes.[617] He was born in the Khuld Palace.[618] He related: Some authors say that he was born in the year 180 in the eighth month (Shaʿbān), was the eighth caliph (of the ʿAbbāsids), in the eighth generation from al-ʿAbbas,[619] his life-span was eight and forty years, that he died leaving eight sons[620] and eight daughters, and that he reigned for eight years and eight months.[621]

Muḥammad b. ʿAbd al-Malik al-Zayyāt said,

I commented, when they consigned you to oblivion and hands
hovered over you, [throwing] earth and clay,
"Go forth, for what a fine guardian you were for the world,
and what an excellent protector of religion!
May God not restore the fortunes of a community that has lost
one like you, except through someone like Hārūn (al-Wāthiq)!"[622]

Marwān b. Abī al-Janūb, that is, Ibn Abī Ḥafṣah, said,

Abū Isḥāq died when the sun was still extending its light, and we
died too;

---

617. Masʿūdī, *Tanbīh*, 354, trans., 454; *Kitāb al-ʿuyūn*, 409; and Ibn al-Ṭiqṭaqā, *op. cit.*, 209, trans., 229, stress al-Muʿtaṣim's physical strength, and the last source notes also his illiteracy (*kāna ummiyy*[an] *lā yaktubu*).

618. The "Palace of Eternity," i.e., Paradise (cf. Qur'ān, XXV:17/16), was al-Manṣūr's palace, situated on the right bank of the Tigris opposite the Khurāsān gate and to the east of the Round City. See Le Strange, *Baghdad*, 101–5; Lassner, *op. cit.*, 55, 76; al-ʿAlī, *op. cit.*, 240, 343–47.

619. I.e., from the Prophet's uncle al-ʿAbbās b. ʿAbd al-Muṭṭalib.

620. Numbered by Yaʿqūbī, *Ta'rīkh*, II, 584, however, at six: Hārūn al-Wāthiq, Jaʿfar al-Mutawakkil, Muḥammad, Aḥmad (al-Mustaʿīn), ʿAlī, and ʿAbdallāh.

621. In a typically Arab search for *nawādir*, strange happenings and coincidences, the sources stress al-Muʿtaṣim's role as *al-Muthamman* "the man whose affairs were characterized by the number eight." See Masʿūdī, *Tanbīh*, 354–55, trans. 454–55; Ṭabarī, trans. Balʿamī, IV, 545–56; Thaʿālibī, *op. cit.*, 135–36, trans., 107; *Kitāb al-ʿuyūn*, 409; Ibn al-Athīr, *op. cit.*, VI, 524–25; Ibn al-Ṭiqṭaqā, *op. cit.*, 209, trans., 229.

622. Ibn al-Athīr, *op. cit.*, VI, 525.

but in the evening we were given Hārūn and were brought back to life!
Indeed, if Thursday has brought us what we have regarded with loathing,
it has also brought us that which we have come to love passionately (i.e., the new caliph al-Wāthiq)![623]

Something about al-Muʿtaṣim's Character and Behavior

It has been mentioned from Ibn Abī Duwād that he [often] mentioned al-Muʿtaṣim bi'llāh; he mentioned him profusely, gave detailed descriptions of him, spoke at length about his
[1325] merits, and expatiated on the openness of his character, the nobility of his lineage, the agreeableness of his manner, the easiness of his presence, and the pleasantness of his company. He said: One day, al-Muʿtaṣim said to me when we were at ʿAmmūriyyah, "What would you say to some fresh dates (*busr*),[624] O Abū ʿAbdallāh?" I replied, "O Commander of the Faithful, we are in the Byzantine lands, and fresh dates are in Iraq." He said, "You have spoken truly, but I have sent to the City of Peace, and they have brought two clusters of dates, which I know you love passionately." Then he said, "O Aytākh, bring in one of the date clusters," so he brought a cluster of fresh dates. Al-Muʿtaṣim thereupon stretched out his forearm and gripped the cluster with his hand, saying, "Eat, by my life, set to and eat them from my hand." I protested, "May God make me your ransom, O Commander of the Faithful! On the contrary, put them down, and I will eat as much as I want." He nevertheless replied, "No, by

623. Ṭabarī has here confused Abū al-Simṭ Marwān al-Aṣghar b. Abī al-Janūb (died *ca.* 248 [862]) with his grandfather Abū al-Simṭ Marwān al-Akbar b. Sulaymān, called Abū Ḥafṣah, the most talented of this famous poetic family (died in 182 [798]). Marwān al-Aṣghar must have been a eulogist of al-Muʿtaṣim, but only these two verses and two other fragments have survived from this period of his poetic career. See M. Y. al-Rasheed, *The Abū Ḥafṣah Family*, 67 ff., 131 n. 94, 179 nos. 202–3, 218, 250; *EI*², s.vv. Marwān al-Akbar b. Abī Ḥafṣa; Marwān al-Asghar b. Abi'l-Djanūb (J. E. Bencheikh).

624. I.e., fresh and still moist but not fully ripe, or *ruṭb*; see Ibn Manẓūr, *op. cit.*, V, 123–24.

God, only from my own hand!" He related: And, by God, he kept on uncovering his forearm and stretching forth his hand while I was plucking dates from the cluster and eating until he threw it away, completely stripped and without a single date left.[625]

Ibn Abī Duwād further related: I used often to act as his counterweight (or: "used often to ride behind him on his mount," *uzāmiluhu*)[626] during that journey of his (i.e., during the ʿAmmūriyyah campaign) until one day I said to him, "O Commander of the Faithful, if only one of your mawlās or court intimates would ride with you as counterweight and if you had a refreshing change from me to them for a period and then from them back to me for another period, that would be more inspiriting to your heart and more pleasant to your mind, and you would find it more restful." He said, "Sīmā al-Dimashqī[627] is acting as my counterweight today, but who will accompany *you* thus?" I replied, "Al-Ḥasan b. Yūnus."[628] He said, "Just as you like." He related: So I sent for al-Ḥasan, and he acted as my counterweight, and preparations were made for al-Muʿtaṣim to ride a mule, for he chose to ride alone. He related: He began to travel along at the side of my camel, and when he wished to talk to me he would raise his head toward me, and when I wanted to talk to him I would lower my head. He related: We came to a wadi
the depth of which we did not know, having left the main body of [1326]
the army behind us. Al-Muʿtaṣim said to me, "Stay where you are while I go forward and thus ascertain the depth of water and look

---

625. Ibn al-Athīr, *op. cit.*, VI, 525.

626. Cf. Ṭabarī, III, 1261–62 (p. 127, above), where, on the return from the ʿAmmūriyyah campaign, two conspirators against al-Muʿtaṣim are made to ride side by side in a litter on a mule. The verb *zāmala* and the noun *zamīl* (basically "traveling companion") can refer to journeying side by side or one behind the other (the rear person being called the *radīf*); see Ibn Manẓūr, *op. cit.*, XIII, 329–30.

627. A Turkish commander (to be distinguished by the *nisbah* from another slave officer, Sīmā al-Sharābī) and doorkeeper (*ḥājib*) of al-Muʿtaṣim, originally purchased by the Caliph from al-Faḍl b. Sahl. Sīmā held *qaṭāʾiʿ* at Sāmarrā; see Yaʿqūbī, *Buldān*, 256, 262, trans., 45, 54. Subsequently, it was he who, with Waṣīf, placed al-Mutawakkil on the throne; see Yaʿqūbī, *Taʾrīkh*, II, 584, 591; Herzfeld, *op. cit.*, 243.

628. Unidentified, unless he is the Abū ʿAlī al-Ḥasan b. Yūnus b. Mihrān al-Zayyāt, a traditionist mentioned by al-Khaṭīb. *op. cit.*, VII, 455 no. 4027, without, however, any date of birth, death, or *floruit*.

for shallow patches, and you follow in my tracks." He related: He thereupon went forward, plunged into the wadi, and began to search for shallow patches; at one time he would swerve to his right, another time to his left, and on some occasions he would go straight on, with me behind him, following in his track until we had crossed the wadi.

Ibn Abī Duwād also related: I sought to obtain from al-Muʿtaṣim 2 million dirhams for the people of al-Shāsh[629] for digging out one of their irrigation canals (*nahr*), which had silted up in early Islamic times and had thereby brought them hardship. He said to me, "O Abū ʿAbdallāh, what concern is it of mine or yours that you should take my money for the people of al-Shāsh and Farghānah?" But I replied, "They are your subjects, O Commander of the Faithful, and the farthest and the nearest one are alike in the benevolent oversight of the Imām!"[630]

Someone else has related that when al-Muʿtaṣim was roused to anger he did not care whom he killed or what he did.[631]

It has been mentioned from al-Faḍl b. Marwān that he said: Al-Muʿtaṣim took no pleasure in making buildings decorative and attractive to see; his sole aim was to make them solid. He also said: There was no item of expenditure on which he was more lavish in providing money than military campaigns.[632]

Muḥammad b. Rāshid has mentioned that Abū al-Ḥusayn Isḥāq b. Ibrāhīm (b. Muṣʿab) once said to him: The Commander of the Faithful al-Muʿtaṣim summoned me one day. I went into his presence, and he was wearing a silk-embroidered waistcoat (*ṣudrah*),[633] a girdle of gold, and red boots. He said to me, "O

---

629. Shāsh (Persian form: Chāch) was a district adjacent to the district of Īlāq, on the right bank of the Jaxartes; the town of Shāsh was on the site of modern Tashkent. See Yāqūt, *Muʿjam*, III, 308–9; Le Strange, *Lands*, 480–83; Barthold, *Turkestan*, 169–75; *EI*¹, s.v. Ta<u>sh</u>kent (W. W. Barthold); *EIr*, s.v. Čāč (C. E. Bosworth).

630. Ibn al-Athīr, *op. cit.*, VI, 525–26. Al-Muʿtaṣim's grudging attitude here hardly conforms to Masʿūdī's information, in *Murūj*, VII, 104 = par. 2788, that he was devoted to the improvement of his territories and their prosperity (*ʿimārah, ʿumrān al-arḍ*).

631. Ibn al-Athīr, *op. cit.*, VI, 526.

632. *Ibid.*

633. This garment, though only vaguely explained in the sources, clearly denoted a waistcoat or short jacket covering the chest (*ṣadr*); see Dozy, *Vêtements*, 246.

Isḥāq, I would very much like to play polo (*al-ṣawālajah*)[634] with you, so by my life you must dress in the same fashion as I." I sought to be excused from that, but he refused. So I got dressed in the same dress as his. Then a horse caparisoned with gold [1327] trappings was brought forward for him, and we entered the polo field (*al-maydān*).[635] When he had played for a while he said to me, "I see you're lazy and half-hearted, but I realize that you dislike this outfit." I replied, "That's true, O Commander of the Faithful!" He then dismounted and took my hand and proceeded onward, walking in my company, until he came to the chamber of the bathhouse.[636] He said, "Take my clothes, O Isḥāq," so I took his clothes until he was left naked. Then he ordered me to remove my own clothes, which I did, and the two of us entered the bath. We were unaccompanied by any slave boy, so I stood over him and rubbed him, and the Commander of the Faithful al-Muʿtaṣim undertook the task of doing the same for me.[637] Meanwhile, during the course of all this I was requesting him not to concern himself with me, but he refused. Then he left the bath, and I gave him his clothes and donned my own ones. Then he took my hand,

---

634. This term possibly designated the curved polo stick (Persian *chawgān*), rather than the game itself (*chawgān-bāzī*); see *EI*², s.v. Čawgān (H. Massé). The more usual Arabic form is *ṣawlajān*; see Dozy, *Supplément*, I, 854. For this episode, see Herzfeld, *op. cit.*, 152–53, locating the polo ground to the east of the Jawsaq Palace. There may well have been one there, for as many as twelve putative polo grounds have been identified among the remains of Sāmarrā, though the bottle-shaped course located to the east of the Jawsaq al-Khāqānī or Dār al-Khilāfah (clearly visible at the time of Sarre and Herzfeld's first survey during World War I but now largely plowed up) is characterized by Northedge as one of the five walled tracks at Sāmarrā obviously intended for horse racing (his Course 2: see "Racecourses," 37–38). Northedge pertinently observes that recent writers on horse racing in medieval Islam have not always distinguished properly between courses for horse racing and polo grounds; "Racecourses," 52 n. 79.

635. For such fields, see *EI*², s.v. Maydān (F. Viré); Herzfeld, *op. cit.*, 153 n. 2, pointed out that *maydān* in this context was a synonym for Middle Persian *asprēs* "polo, race ground."

636. *Ḥujrat al-ḥammām*. Here the general term *ḥujrah* must denote the first room of the bath, that for undressing and resting, the *apodyterium* of classical baths; in the central Islamic lands it was called the *maslakh* after the sixth (twelfth) century; Herzfeld, *op. cit.*, 153, calls this room *vestibulum*. See H. Grotzfeld, *Das Bad im Arabisch-Islamischen Mittelalter*, 28 ff, *EI*², s.v. Ḥammām (J. Sourdel-Thomine).

637. Rubbing and massaging, *tadlīk*, would normally be done by a special attendant, the *dallāk*; see Grotzfeld, *op. cit.*, 69–70.

and we walked on, the two of us together, until he reached his council chamber.

[When we were there] he said to me, "O Isḥāq, bring me a prayer rug (*muṣallā*)[638] and two pillows." I brought these to him, and he put down the pillows and lay down on his face as if to sleep. Then he said, "Bring [another] prayer rug and two [more] pillows," so I brought them, and he said, "Throw them down, and lie down on them opposite me." I swore that I would not do that, but I sat down on the rug. Aytākh al-Turkī and Ashnās entered, and he told them, "Just withdraw to a spot where, if I cry out, you will both be able to hear me." Then he said, "O Isḥāq, there is something on my mind (literally, "heart") that I have been pondering over for a long time, and I have only put you at your ease at this juncture so that I might divulge my inner thoughts to you." I answered, "Speak on, O my master, O Commander of the Faithful, for I am merely your slave and the son of your slave." He said, "I have been considering my brother al-Ma'mūn. He nurtured for his own service four men who turned out excellently, while I have nurtured for my own service likewise four men, none of whom has proved successful." I asked, "Who are these men whom your brother nurtured?" He replied, "Ṭāhir b.
[1328] al-Ḥusayn, whom you saw and heard of [his fame]; ʿAbdallāh b. Ṭāhir, a man of unparalleled quality; you yourself, for by God you are a person for whose like the ruling authority could never hope to find a substitute; and your brother Muḥammad b. Ibrāhīm—where is there his like? Whereas I myself have nurtured al-Afshīn, and you have seen what finally became of him; Ashnās, and what a feeble heart and coward he is!;[639] Aytākh, who is totally insignificant; and Waṣīf, who is an unprofitable servant." I said, "O Commander of the Faithful, may God make me your

638. The Caliph normally had his own *muṣallā* for special ceremonial occasions, supervised by an official called *ṣāḥib al-musallā*. The family of one Ṣāliḥ seems customarily to have exercised this function from the time of al-Manṣūr onward, certainly until al-Muʿtaṣim's reign, according to an anecdote in Tanūkhī, *op. cit.*, VI, 187–89, and possibly until the time of al-Muntaṣir; see Sourdel, "Questions de cérémonial," 131–32, 146.

639. *Fa-fashl*[un] *ayyuhu*. For *ayyu* in exclamations and to express surprise, see W. Wright, *op. cit.*, II, 316, Rem. *a*; Reckendorf, *op. cit.*, 33–34 par. 18.2, 40 par. 21.2. Neither, however, notes this particular use of *ayyu* + pronoun suffix *after* its qualifying noun, as opposed to the more usual *ayyu fashl*[in].

ransom! I can provide an answer, on condition of a guarantee of security from your wrath!" He replied, "Speak on!" I said, O Commander of the Faithful, may God make you mighty, your brother considered the roots and made use of them, and their branches flourished exceedingly; whereas the Commander of the Faithful has utilized only branches, which have not flourished because they have lacked roots." He replied, "O Isḥāq, the hardships that I have endured during the passage of this long period of time are indeed easier for me to bear than this answer!"[640]

It is mentioned from Isḥāq b. Ibrāhīm al-Mawṣilī[641] that he said: I went into the Commander of the Faithful al-Muʿtaṣim bi-Allāh's presence one day when he had with him a slave singing girl (*qaynah*)[642] from whom he derived great pleasure, and she was singing to him. When I had greeted him and taken my seat he said to her, "Carry on with what you were singing," so she sang again. He said to me, "What do you think of her, O Isḥāq?" I answered, "O Commander of the Faithful, I see her subduing [her instrument] with skill and mastering it with delicacy; whatever she brings forth, she raises it to a level superior to what it was previously. In her melody are fragments of small pearls more beautiful than the settings of pearls that one sees on people's throats." He exclaimed, "O Isḥāq, your description of her is more beautiful than she herself or her singing," and he told his son Hārūn (al-Wāthiq), "Listen to these words!"

It has been further mentioned from Isḥāq b. Ibrāhīm al-Mawṣilī that he said: I spoke to al-Muʿtaṣim regarding some matter, and he said to me, "O Isḥāq, when passion becomes dominant, one's [1329]
judgment becomes impaired." I told him, "O Commander of the Faithful, I used to wish that my youth would stay with me always, so that I might remain at your service, as I would like to do." He said to me, "Haven't you achieved your aim in this respect, then?" I replied, "Yes, certainly." He observed, "Thus

640. Ibn al-Athīr, *op. cit.*, VI, 526–27; Herzfeld, *op. cit.*, 152–54.

641. The famous musician and singer (150–235 [767–850]) and son of the equally celebrated musician Ibrāhīm al-Mawṣilī. See Farmer, *op. cit.*, 124–26; *EI*², s.v. Isḥāḳ b. Ibrāhīm al-Mawṣilī (J. W. Fück).

642. Such singing girls formed a highly trained, often well-educated class in ʿAbbāsid times; see *EI*², s.v. Ḳayna (Ch. Pellat).

now at present you are achieving what you intended, so the two aims are equally realized!"

It has been mentioned from Abū Ḥassān[643] that he said: Abū Isḥāq al-Muʿtaṣim's mother was a non-Arab slave (*muwalladah*) from al-Kūfah called Māridah.[644] It has been mentioned from al-Faḍl b. Marwān that he said: Al-Muʿtaṣim's mother was Māridah, of Soghdian origin, whose father had, however, grown up in the Sawād.[645] He related: I think he was actually from al-Bandanījīn.[646] Al-Rashīd also had from Māridah, in addition to Abū Isḥāq, Abū Ismāʿīl, Umm Ḥabīb, and two others whose names are unknown.

It has been mentioned from Aḥmad b. Abī Duwād that he said: Al-Muʿtaṣim gave alms, and at my own hand and through my own agency he bestowed the amount of 100 million dirhams.[647]

---

643. I.e., al-Ḥasan b. ʿUthmān al-Ziyādī, judge and *rāwī*, who had been involved in al-Maʾmūn's *miḥnah*, or inquisition proceedings (Ṭabarī, III, 1121, 1122–23), and who was a source for Ibn Abī Ṭāhir Ṭayfūr, whence for Ṭabarī, for events in the first half of the third (ninth) century.

644. Called by Masʿūdī, *Murūj*, VII, 103 = par. 2786, Māridah bt. Shabīb. See also Muḥammad b. Ḥabīb al-Baghdādī, *Kitāb al-muḥabbar*, 42; Ibn Qutaybah, *Kitāb al-maʿārif*, 392; Thaʿālibī, *op. cit.*, 126 trans., 102.

645. I.e., the "dark," because green and cultivated, region of central Iraq around Baghdad; see *EI*[1], s.v. Sawād (H. H. Schaeder).

646. A town lying to the east of Baghdad and the Tigris, the center of the rural district to Bādurāyā in the foothills of the Pusht-i Kūh range. See Yāqūt, *Muʿjam*, I, 499, Le Strange, *Lands*, 63.

647. Ibn al-Athīr, *op. cit.*, VI, 527; Herzfeld, *op. cit.*, 156. Despite such largesse, al-Muʿtaṣim was nevertheless able to leave in the state treasury at his death, according to Ibn al-Zubayr, *op. cit.*, 213–14 par. 300, 8 million dīnārs and 8 million dirhams, beside 33,000 riding beasts in the royal stables.

Bibliography of Cited Works

Primary Sources: Texts and Translations

Abū Dulaf, Misʿar b. Muhalhil al-Khazrajī. *Second Risālah*, ed. and trans. V. Minorsky as *Abū-Dulaf Misʿar ibn Muhalhil's Travels in Iran (circa A. D.* 950).Cairo, 1955.

Abū Tammām, Ḥabīb b. Aws al-Ṭā'ī. *Ḥamāsa*, ed. G. Freytag as *Hamasae Carmina cum Tebrisii scholiis*. Bonn, 1828.

———. *Dīwān bi-sharḥ al-Khaṭīb al-Tibrīzī*, ed. M. ʿA. ʿAzzām. 4 vols. Cairo, 1951–69.

al-Azdī, Abū Zakariyyā' Yazīd b. Muḥammad. *Ta'rīkh al-Mawṣil*, ed. ʿA. Ḥabībah. Cairo, 1387/1967.

al-Baghdādī, Abū Jaʿfar Muḥammad b. Ḥabīb. *Kitāb al-muḥabbar*, ed. I. Lichtenstaedter. Hyderabad, 1361/1942.

al-Balādhurī, Abū al-Ḥasan Aḥmad b. Yaḥyā. *Futūḥ al-buldān*, ed. M. J. de Goeje as *Liber expugnationis regionum*. Leiden, 1866.

al-Bayhaqī, Abū al-Faḍl Muḥammad b. Ḥusayn, *Ta'rīkh-i Masʿūdī*, ed. Q. Ghanī and ʿA. A. Fayyāḍ. Tehran, 1324 A.S.H./1945.

al-Bayhaqī, lbrāhīm b. Muḥammad. *Kitāb al-maḥāsin wa-al-masāwī*, ed. F. Schwally. Giessen, 1902. O. Rescher, *Index und Stellennachweise zu Fr. Schwally's Baihaqî-Ausgabe*, Stuttgart, 1923. Ed. M. A. Ibrāhīm. 2 vols. Cairo, 1380/1961.

al-Buḥturī, Abu ʿUbāda al-Walīd b. ʿUbayd (allāh). *Dīwān*. 2 vols. Beirut, 1962. Ed. Ḥ. K. al-Ṣayrafī. 4 vols. Cairo, 1963–72.

al-Dhahabi, Shams al-Dīn Abū ʿAbdallāh Muḥammad b. ʿUthmān. *Kitāb duwal al-Islām*. 2 vols. Hyderabad, 1337/1918–19.

al-Dīnawarī, Abū Ḥanīfah Aḥmad b. Dāwūd. *Kitāb al-akhbār al-ṭiwāl*, ed. ʿA. ʿĀmir and J. al-Shayyāl. Cairo, 1960.

Gardīzī, Abū Saʿīd ʿAbd al-Ḥayy b. al-Ḍaḥḥāk. *Kitāb zayn al-akhbār*, ed. M. Nāẓim. Berlin, 1928. Ed. ʿA. Ḥabībī. Tehran, 1347 A.S.H./1968.

Hilāl al-Ṣābiʾ, *Rusūm dār al-khilāfah*, ed. M. ʿAwwād. Baghdad, 1964. Trans. E. A. Salem as *Rusūm dār al-khilāfah (The Rules and Regulations of the ʿAbbāsid Court)*. Beirut, 1977.

Ḥudūd al-ʿālam, trans. V. Minorsky as *The Regions of the World: A Persian Geography 372 A. H. –982 A. D.* GMS N.S. XI. London, 1937.

al-Ḥusayn b. al-Ḍaḥḥāk al-Bāhilī al-Khalīʿ, Abū ʿAlī. *Dīwān*, ed. ʿA. A. Farāj as *Ashʿār al-Khalīʿ al-Ḥusayn b. al-Ḍaḥḥāk*. Beirut, 1960.

Ibn Abī Uṣaybiʿah, Abū al-ʿAbbās Aḥmad b. al-Qāsim. *ʿUyūn al-anbāʾ fī ṭabaqāt al-aṭibbāʾ*, ed. A. Müller. Vols. I–II. Cairo, 1290/1882. Vol. III. Königsberg, 1884.

Ibn al-ʿAdīm, Kamāl al-Dīn ʿUmar b. Aḥmad. *Bughyat al-ṭalab fī taʾrīkh Ḥalab*, ed. S. al-Dahhān. 3 vols. Damascus, 1370–87/1951–68.

Ibn ʿAsākir, Thiqat al-Dīn Abū al-Qāsim ʿAlī b. al-Ḥasan. *Tahdhīb Taʾrīkh madīnat Dimashq*, ed. ʿA. Badrān and A. ʿUbayd. 7 vols. Damascus, 1329–51/1911–32.

Ibn al-Athīr, ʿIzz al-Dīn Abū al-Ḥasan ʿAlī b. Muḥammad. *al-Kāmil fī al-taʾrīkh*. 13 vols. Beirut, 1385–87/1965–67.

Ibn al-Faqīh, Abū Bakr Aḥmad b. Ibrāhīm al-Hamadhānī. *Mukhtaṣar Kitāb al-buldān*, ed. M. J. de Goeje. BGA V. Leiden, 1885. Trans. H. Massé as *Abrégé du Livre des pays*. Damascus, 1973.

Ibn Isfandiyār, Muḥammad b. al-Ḥasan. *Taʾrīkh-i Ṭabaristān*, abr. trans. E. G. Browne as *History of Ṭabaristán*. GMS II. Leiden and London, 1905.

Ibn al-Kalbī, Abū al-Mundhir Hishām b. Muḥammad. *Jamharat al-nasab*, interp. and arr. with indices W. Caskel and G. Strenziok as *Ǧamharat an-nasab: Das genealogische Werk des Hišām ibn Muḥammad al-Kalbī*. 2 vols. Leiden, 1966.

Ibn Khallikān, Abū al-ʿAbbās Aḥmad b. Muḥammad al-Irbilī. *Wafayāt al-aʿyān wa-anbāʾ al-zamān*, ed. I. ʿAbbās. 8 vols. Beirut, 1968–72. Trans. Baron McGuckin de Slane as *Ibn Khallikan's Biographical Dictionary*. 4 vols. Paris, 1842–71.

Ibn Khurradādhbih, Abū al-Qāsim ʿUbaydallāh b. ʿAbdallāh. *al-Masālik wa-al-mamālik*, ed. M. J. de Goeje. BGA VI. Leiden, 1889.

Ibn Manẓūr, Jamāl al-Dīn Abū al-Faḍl Muḥammad b. Mukarram al-Anṣārī. *Lisān al-ʿArab*. 20 vols. Būlāq, 1300–8/1883–91.

Ibn al-Nadīm, Abū al-Faraj Muḥammad b. Isḥāq al-Warrāq. *Kitāb al-Fihrist*, ed. R. Tajaddud. Tehran, n.d. [1391/1971]. Trans. B. Dodge as *The Fihrist of al-Nadīm: A Tenth Century Survey of Muslim Culture*. 2 vols. New York, 1970.

Ibn Qutaybah, Abū Muḥammad ʿAbdallāh b. Muslim. *Kitāb al-maʿārif*, ed. Th. ʿUkkāshah. Cairo, 1960.

Ibn Sayyār al-Warrāq, Abū Muḥammad al-Muẓaffar b. Naṣr. *Kitāb al-ṭabīkh*, ed. K. Öhrnberg and S. Mroueh. Studia Orientalia . . . Societas Orientalis Fennica LX. Helsinki, 1987.

Ibn al-Ṭiqṭaqā, Ṣafī al-Dīn Muḥammad b. ʿAlī b. Ṭabāṭabā. *Kitāb al-fakhrī fī al-ādāb al-sulṭāniyyah wa-al-duwal al-islāmiyyah*. Cairo, 1317/1899. Trans. C. E. J. Whitting as *Al Fakhri: On the Systems of Government and the Moslem Dynasties*. London, 1947.

Ibn al-Zubayr, Qāḍī Abū al-Ḥusayn Aḥmad b. al-Rashīd. *Kitāb al-dhakhā'ir wa-al-tuḥaf*, ed. M. Ḥamīd Allāh and Ṣ. al-Munajjid. Kuwait, 1959.

al-Iṣfahānī, Abū ʿAbdallāh Ḥamzah b. al-Ḥasan. *Ta'rīkh sinī mulūk al-arḍ wa-al-anbiyā'*. Beirut, n.d. [ca. 1961].

al-Iṣfahānī, Abū al-Faraj ʿAlī b. al-Ḥusayn. *Kitāb al-aghānī*. 20 vols. Būlāq, 1285–86/1868–70. Vol. XXI, ed. R. E. Brünnow. Leiden, 1305/1887. Ed. M. A. Ibrāhīm *et al.* 24 vols. Cairo and Beirut, 1927–74.

———. *Maqātil al-ṭālibiyyīn*, ed. K. al-Muẓaffar. Najaf, 1385/1965.

al-Jāḥiẓ, Abū ʿUthmān ʿAmr b. Baḥr. *al-Bayān wa-al-tabyīn*, ed. ʿA. M. Hārūn. 4 vols. Cairo, 1380–81/1960–61.

———. *Kitāb al-bukhalā'*, ed. Ṭ. al-Ḥājirī. Cairo, 1971. Trans. C. Pellat as *Le Livre des avares de Ǧāḥiẓ*. Paris, 1951.

———. *Kitāb al-ḥayawān*, ed. ʿA. M. Hārūn. 7 vols. Cairo, 1357–64/1938–45.

al-Jahshiyārī, Abū ʿAbdallāh Muḥammad b. ʿAbdūs. *Kitāb al-wuzarā' wa-al-kuttāb*, ed. ʿA. I. Ṣāwī. Baghdad, 1357/1938.

al-Khalīfah, Abū ʿAmr b. Khayyāṭ. *Ta'rīkh*, ed. S. Zakkār. 2 vols. Damascus, 1967–68.

al-Khaṭīb al-Baghdādī, Abū Bakr Aḥmad b. ʿAlī. *Ta'rīkh Baghdād aw Madīnat al-Salām*. 14 vols. Cairo, 1349/1931.

al-Kindī, Abū ʿUmar Muḥammad b. Yūsuf. *Kitāb al-wulāt wa-Kitāb al-quḍāt*, ed. R. Guest as *The Governors and Judges of Egypt*. GMS XIX. Leiden and London, 1912.

Kitāb al-ʿuyūn wa-al-ḥadā'iq fī akhbār al-ḥaqā'iq, ed. M. J. de Goeje. Fragmenta Historicorum Arabicorum I. Leiden, 1871.

al-Kutubī, Abū ʿAbdallāh Muḥammad b. Shākir. *Fawāt al-wafayāt*, ed. I. ʿAbbās. 5 vols. Beirut, 1973–74.

Marʿashī, Ẓahīr al-Dīn b. Naṣīr al-Dīn. *Taʾrīkh-i Ṭabaristān u Rūyān u Māzandarān*, ed. ʿA. Shāyān. Tehran, 1333 A.S.H./1955.

Marwān b. Abī Ḥafṣah, Abū al-Simṭ Marwān b. Abī al-Janūb. *Dīwān*, ed. M. M. al-Y. al-Rasheed, in *The Abū Ḥafṣah Family of Poets, Together with a Critical Edition of the Poetry of the Principal Members of the Family*. Unpublished doctoral dissertation, The University of Manchester, 1980.

al-Masʿūdī, Abū al-Ḥasan ʿAlī b. al-Ḥusayn. *Kitāb al-tanbīh wa-al-ishrāf*, ed. M. J. de Goeje. BGA VIII. Leiden, 1894. Trans. Baron Carra de Vaux as *Le livre de l'avertissement et de la revision*. Paris, 1897.

———. *Murūj al-dhahab wa-maʿādin al-jawhar*, ed. and trans. C. Barbier de Meynard and Pavet de Courteille as *Les prairies d'or*. 9 vols. Paris, 1861–77. Ed. and partial trans. C. Pellat as *Les prairies d'or*, 9 vols. plus 2 index vols. Paris and Beirut, 1962–89.

Michael the Syrian. *Chronicle*, ed. and trans. J.-B. Chabot as *Chronique de Michel le Syrien, Patriarche Jacob d'Antioche*. 3 vols. Paris, 1899–1924.

Miskawayh, Abū ʿAbdallāh Aḥmad b. Muḥammad. *Tajārib al-umam wa-taʿāqib al-himam*, ed. M. J. de Goeje as *Pars sexta operis Tadjáribo 'l-Omami, auctore Ibn Maskowaih*. Fragmenta Historicorum Arabicorum I. Leiden, 1871. Trans. H. F. Amedroz and D. S. Margoliouth as *The Experiences of the Nations*, The Eclipse of the ʿAbbasid Caliphate: Original Chronicles of the Fourth Islamic Century I, II, IV, V. Oxford, 1920–21.

Narshakhī, Abū Bakr Muḥammad b. Jaʿfar. *Taʾrīkh-i Bukhārā*, ed. M. Riḍawī. Tehran, n.d. [ca. 1939]. Trans. R. N. Frye as *The History of Bukhara*. Cambridge, Mass., 1954.

Niẓām al-Mulk, Abu ʿAlī al-Ḥasan b. ʿAlī al-Ṭūsī. *Siyāsat-nāmah or Siyar al-mulūk*, ed. H. Darke. Tehran, 1340 A.S.H./1962. Trans. H. Darke as *The Book of Government or Rules for Kings*. London, 1978.

Qudāmah b. Jaʿfar, Abū al-Faraj, *Kitāb al-kharāj wa ṣināʿat al-kuttāb*, ed. M. J. de Goeje. VI. Leiden, 1889. Pp. 184–266.

al-Shābushtī, Abū al-Ḥasan ʿAlī b. Muḥammad. *Kitāb al-diyārāt*, ed. G. ʿAwwād. Baghdad, 1370/1951.

al-Ṭabarī, Abū Jaʿfar Muḥammad b. Jarīr. *Taʾrīkh al-rusul wa-al-mulūk*, ed. M. J. de Goeje *et al.* as *Annales quos scripsit Abu Djafar... at-Tabari*. 13 vols. plus 1 vol. *Indices* and 1 vol. *Introductio, glossarium, addenda et emendanda*. Leiden, 1879–1901. Ed. M. A. Ibrāhīm. 10 vols. Cairo, 1960–69. Partial trans. T. Nöldeke as *Geschichte der Perser und Araber zur Zeit der Sassaniden*. Leiden,

1879. Partial trans. E. Marin as *The Reign of al-Mu'tasim* (833–842). New Haven, 1951. Partial trans. F. Rosenthal as *General Introduction and From the Creation to the Flood.* The History of al-Ṭabarī I. Albany, 1989. Partial trans. C. E. Bosworth as *The Reunification of the 'Abbāsid Caliphate.* The History of al-Ṭabarī XXXII. Albany, 1987. Trans. Abū 'Alī Muḥammad Bal'amī as *Tārīkh-i Ṭabarī,* trans. H. Zotenberg as *Chronique de... Tabarî, traduite sur la version persane d'Abou-'Alî Mo'hammed Bel'amî.* 4 vols. Paris, 1867–74.

al-Tanūkhī, Abū 'Alī al-Muḥassin b. 'Alī. *Nishwār al-muḥāḍarah wa-akhbār al-mudhākarah,* ed. 'A. al-Shāljī. 8 vols. Beirut, 1391–93/1971–73.

Tārīkh-i Sīstān, ed. M. Bahār. Tehran, 1314 A.S.H./1935. Trans. M. Gold as *The Tārikh-e Sistān.* Literary and Historical Texts from Iran II. Rome, 1976.

al-Tha'ālibī, Abū Manṣūr 'Abd al-Malik b. Muḥammad. *Laṭā'if al-ma'ārif,* ed. I. al-Abyārī and Ḥ. K. al-Ṣayrafī. Cairo, 1960. Trans. C. E. Bosworth as *The Book of Curious and Entertaining Information.* Edinburgh, 1968.

al-Ya'qūbī, Abū al-'Abbās Aḥmad b. Isḥāq, called Ibn Wāḍiḥ. *Kitāb al-buldān,* ed. M. J. de Goeje. BGA VII. Leiden, 1892. Trans. G. Wiet as *Les pays.* Cairo, 1937.

———. *Ta'rīkh,* ed. M. T. Houtsma as *Historiae.* 2 vols. Leiden, 1883.

Yāqūt, Abū 'Abdallāh Ya'qūb b. 'Abdallāh al-Ḥamawī al-Rūmī. *Irshād al-arīb ila ma'rifat al-adīb,* ed. D. S. Margoliouth as *Dictionary of Learned Men of Yáqút.* GMS VI. 7 vols. London, 1923–31.

———. *Mu'jam al-buldān.* 5 vols. Beirut, 1374–76/1955–57.

Secondary Sources and Reference Works

Agius, D. A. *Arabic Literary works as a Source of Documentation for Technical Terms of the Material Culture.* Islamkundliche Untersuchungen XCVIII. Berlin, 1984.

al-'Alī, Ṣ. A. *Baghdād, Madīnat al-Salām, inshā'uhā wa tanẓīm sukkānihā fī al-'uhūd al-'abbāsiyyah al-ūlā I. al-Jānib al-gharbī.* Baghdad, 1985.

Anastos, M. V. "Iconoclasm and Imperial Rule 717–842," in *The Cambridge Mediaeval History* IV. *The Byzantine Empire* 1. *Byzantium and Its Neighbours,* ed. J. M. Hussey. Cambridge, 1966. Pp. 61–104.

Arazi, A., and A. El'ad. "'L'épître à l'armée': Al-Ma'mūn et la seconde da'wa," *SI* 66 (1987): 27–70; 67 (1988): 29–73.

al-Asil, Nāŷī. "La ciudad de al-Muʿtaṣim en al-Qāṭūl (Exploración y resultados)," *al-Andalus* 12 (1947): 339–57.

Ayalon, D. "The Military Reforms of Caliph al-Muʿtaṣim: Their Background and Consequences." Unpublished paper, Jerusalem, 1963.

———. "Preliminary Remarks on the *Mamlūk* Military Institution in Islam," in *War, Technology and Society in the Middle East*, ed. V. J. Parry and M. E. Yapp. London, 1975. Pp. 44–58.

———. "On the Eunuchs in Islam," *JSAI* (1979): 67–124.

Badawi, M. M. "The Function of Rhetoric in Medieval Arabic Poetry: Abū Tammām's Ode on Amorium," *JAL* 19 (1978): 43–56.

Barthold, W. "A History of the Turkman People," in *Four Studies on the History of Central Asia*. Leiden, 1962. Pp. 75–170.

———. *Turkestan Down to the Mongol Invasion*. GMS N.S. V, 3rd ed. London, 1968.

———. *An Historical Geography of Iran*, trans. S. Soucek, ed. C. E. Bosworth. Princeton, 1984.

Biberstein Kazimirski, A. de. *Menoutchehri, poète persan du 11ème siècle de notre ère (du 5ème de l'hégire): Texte, traduction et introduction historique*. Paris, 1887.

Bivar, A. D. H., and G. Fehérvári. "The Walls of Tammīsha," *Iran JBIPS* 4 (1966): 35–50.

Bosworth, C. E. *The Ghaznavids: Their Empire in Afghanistan and Eastern Iran* 994–1040. Edinburgh, 1963.

———. *The Islamic Dynasties: A Chronological and Genealogical Handbook*. Edinburgh, 1967.

———. "The Political and Dynastic History of the Iranian World (A. D. 1000–1217)," in *The Cambridge History of Iran* V. *The Saljuq and Mongol Periods*, ed. J. A. Boyle. Cambridge, 1968. Pp. 1–202.

———. "Abū ʿAbdallāh al-Khwārazmī on the Technical Terms of the Secretary's Art: A Contribution to the Administrative History of Mediaeval Islam," *JESHO* 12 (1969): 113–64. Repr. in *Medieval Arabic Culture and Administration*. London, 1982.

———."The Ṭāhirids and Arabic Culture," *JSS* 14 (1969): 45–79. Repr. in *Medieval Arabic Culture and Administration*. London, 1982.

———. "Recruitment, Muster and Review in Medieval Islamic Armies," in *War, Technology and Society in the Middle East*, ed. V. J. Parry and M. E. Yapp. London, 1975. Pp. 59–77.

———. "The Ṭāhirids and Ṣaffārids," in *The Cambridge History of Iran* IV. *The Period from the Arab Invasion to the Saljuqs*, ed. R. N. Frye. Cambridge, 1975. Pp. 90–135.

———. "The Byzantine Defence System in Asia Minor and the First Arab Incursions, *Proceedings of the Second Symposium on the History of Bilād al-Shām during the Early Islamic Period up to 40 A. H./640 A. D. (English and French Papers)*. Vol. I. Amman, 1987. Pp. 116–24.

———. "Al-Khwārazmī on the Secular and Religious Titles of the Byzantines and Christians," in *Mélanges Charles Pellat, CT* XXXV/139–40 (1987): 28–36.

———. "Some Remarks on the Terminology of Irrigation Practices and Hydraulic Constructions in the Eastern Arab and Iranian World in the Period 3rd–5th Centuries A. H./9th–11th Centuries A. D.," in *Journal of Islamic Studies* 2 (1991): 78–85.

———and G. Clauson, "Al-Xwārazmī on the Peoples of Central Asia," *JRAS* (1965), pp. 2–12. Repr. in *The Medieval History of Iran, Afghanistan and Central Asia*. London, 1977.

Brockelmann, C. *Geschichte der arabischen Literatur*. 5 vols. Leiden, 1937–43.

Browne, E. G. *A Literary History of Persia*. 4 vols. London and Cambridge, 1902–24.

R. Brunschvig, "Métiers vils en Islam," *SI* 16 (1962): 41–60.

Bury, J. B. "Mutasim's March through Cappadocia in A. D. 838," *JHS* 29 (1909): 120–29.

———. *A History of the Eastern Roman Empire from the Fall of Irene to the Accession of Basil I: A.D. 802–867*. London, 1912.

Canard, M. "Les allusions à la guerre byzantine chez les poètes Abū-Tammām et Buḥturī," in A. A. Vasiliev, *Byzance et les Arabes* I. *La dynastie d'Amorium (820–867)*. Brussels, 1935. Pp. 397–408.

———. *Histoire de la dynastie des H'amdânides de Jazîra et de Syrie*. Vol. I. Algiers, 1951.

———. "Byzantium and the Muslim World to the Middle of the Eleventh Century," in *The Cambridge Medieval History* IV. *The Byzantine Empire*, part 1. *Byzantium and Its Neighbours*, ed. J. M. Hussey. Cambridge, 1966. Pp. 696–735.

Chejne, A. G. "The Boon-Companion in Early ʿAbbāsid Times," *JAOS* 85 (1965): 327–35.

Clauson, G. *An Etymological Dictionary of Pre-Thirteenth Century Turkish*. Oxford, 1972.

Crone, P. *Slaves on Horses: The Evolution of the Islamic Polity*. Cambridge, 1980.

Dozy, R. P. A. *Dictionnaire détaillé des noms de vêtements chez les arabes*. Amsterdam, 1845.

———. *Supplément aux dictionnaires arabes*. 2 vols. Leiden, 1881.

Dunlop, D. M. *The History of the Jewish Khazars*. Princeton, 1954.

Eisenstein, H. "Die Erhebung des Mubarqaʿ in Palästina," *Orientalia* 55 (1986): 454–58.

Encyclopaedia of Islam. 4 vols. plus Supplement. Leiden, 1913–42. 2nd ed. 6 vols. plus supplement. Leiden and London, 1960–.

Farmer, H. G. *A History of Arabian Music to the XIIIth Century*. London, 1929.

Fattal, A. *Le statut légal des non-musulmans en pays d'Islam*. Beirut, 1958.

Fraenkel, S. *Die aramäischen Fremdwörter im Arabischen*. Leiden, 1886.

Frye, R. N. "Ṭarxūn-Türxūn and Central Asian History," *HJAS* 14 (1951): 105–29. Repr. in *Islamic Iran and Central Asia (7th–13th Centuries)*. London, 1979.

———. *The Golden Age of Persia: The Arabs in the East*. London, 1975.

———. "The Sāmānids," in *The Cambridge History of Iran* IV. *The Period from the Arab Invasion to the Saljuqs*, ed. R. N. Frye. Cambridge, 1975. Pp. 136–61.

———. "The Sasanian System of Walls for Defense," in *Studies in Memory of Gaston Wiet*, ed. M. Rosen-Ayalon. Jerusalem, 1977. Pp. 7–15.

Gaudefroy-Demombynes, M. *Le pèlerinage à la Mekke: Etude d'histoire religieuse*. Paris, 1923.

Geiger, A. *Was hat Mohammed aus dem Judenthum aufgenommen*? 2nd ed. Leipzig, 1902.

Gibbon, E. *The Decline and Fall of the Roman Empire*, ed. J. B. Bury. 7 vols. London, 1896.

Ginzberg, L. *The Legends of the Jews*. 7 vols. Philadelphia, 1911–38.

Goitein, S. D. *A Mediterranean Society: The Jewish Communities of the Arab World as Portrayed in the Documents of the Cairo Geniza*. I. *Economic Foundations*. Berkeley and Los Angeles, 1967.

H. Grégoire. "Manuel et Théophobe et l'ambassade de Jean le Grammairien chez les Arabes," in A. A. Vasiliev, *Byzance et les Arabes* I. *La dynastie d'Amorium (820–867)*. Brussels, 1935. Pp. 413–17.

Grotzfeld, H. *Das Bad im arabisch-islamischen Mittelalter. Eine kulturgeschichtliche Studie*. Wiesbaden, 1970.

von Grunebaum, G. E. *Muhammadan Festivals*. New York, 1951.

Haq, A. "Historical Poems in the Diwan of Abu Tammam," *IC* 14 (1940): 17–29.

Herzfeld, E. *Die Ausgrabungen von Samarra* VI. *Geschichte der Stadt Samarra*. Forschungen zur Islamische Kunst II. Hamburg, 1948.

Hinz, W. *Islamische Masse und Gewichte umgerechnet ins metrische*

System. Handbuch der Orientalistik, Ergänzungsband I/1. Leiden, 1955.

Hoernerbach, W. "Zur Heeresverwaltung der ʿAbbāsiden: Studie über Abulfarağ Qudāma: Dīwān al-ğaiš," *Isl.* 24 (1949–50): 257–90.

Honigmann, E. *Die Ostgrenze des byzantinischen Reiches von 363 bis 1071 nach griechischen, arabischen, syrischen und armenischen Quellen*. Brussels, 1935.

Hughes, T. P. *A Dictionary of Islam. Being a Cyclopaedia of the Doctrines, Rites, Ceremonies, and Customs. Together with Technical and Theological Terms, of the Muhammadan Religion.* London, 1885.

Ismail, O. S. A. "Muʿtaṣim and the Turks," *BSOAS* 24 (1966): 12–24.

———. "The Founding of a New Capital: Sāmarrāʾ," *BSOAS* 31 (1968): 1–13.

Jones, A. H. M. "Were Ancient Heresies National or Social Movements in Disguise?" *JTS* N.S. 10 (1959): 280–98.

Justi, F. *Iranisches Namenbuch*. Marburg, 1895.

Kaabi, M. *Les Ṭāhirides: Etude historico-littéraire de la dynastie des Banū Ṭāhir b. al-Ḥusayn au Ḫurāsān et en Iraq au III*ème *s. de l'Hégire/IX*ème*s. J.-C.* 2 vols. Tunis, 1983.

Kennedy, H. *The Prophet and the Age of the Caliphates: The Islamic Near East from the Sixth to the Eleventh Century*. London and New York, 1986.

Kindermann, H. *"Schiff" im Arabischen: Untersuchung über Vorkommen und Bedeutung der Termini*. Zwickau, 1934.

Kraemer, J., *et al. Wörterbuch der klassischen arabischen Sprache, auf Grund der Sammlungen von August Fischer, Theodor Nöldeke, Herrmann Reckendorf und anderer Quellen*. Wiesbaden, 1957–.

Lane, E. W. *An Arabic-English Lexicon, Derived from the Best and Most Copious Eastern Sources*. 8 vols. London, 1863–93.

———. *An Account of the Manners and Customs of the Modern Egyptians Written in Egypt during the Years 1833–1835*. Paisley and London, 1895.

Lassner, J. *The Topography of Baghdad in the Early Middle Ages: Text and Studies*. Detroit, 1970.

Le Strange, G. *Palestine under the Moslems: A Description of Syria and the Holy Land from A.D. 650 to 1500*. London, 1890.

———. *Baghdad under the Abbasid Caliphate from Contemporary Arabic and Persian Sources*. Oxford, 1900.

———. *The Lands of the Eastern Caliphate: Mesopotamia, Persia, and Central Asia from the Moslem Conquest to the Time of Timur*. Cambridge, 1905.

Levy, R. *The Social Structure of Islam*. Cambridge, 1957.

Løkkegard, F. *Islamic Taxation in the Classic Period, with Special Reference to Circumstances in Iraq*. Copenhagen, 1950.

Lyall, C. J. *Translations of Ancient Arabian Poetry, Chiefly Pre-Islamic*. London, 1930.

Madelung, W. "The Minor Dynasties of Northern Iran," in *The Cambridge History of Iran* IV. *The Period from the Arab Invasion to the Saljuqs*, ed. R. N. Frye. Cambridge, 1975. Pp. 148–249.

———. "The Sufyānī between Tradition and History," *SI* 63 (1984): 5–48.

Margoliouth, D. S. "The Historical Content of the *Diwan* of Buhturi," *JIH* 2 (1922–23): 247–71.

Marquart, J. *Untersuchungen zur Geschichte von Eran*. 2 vols. Göttingen and Leipzig, 1896–1905.

———. *Ērānšahr nach der Geographie des Ps. Moses Xorenacʿi*. Abhandlungen der Königlichen Gesellschaft der Wissenschaften zu Göttingen N.S. III/2. Berlin, 1901.

———. *Osteuropäische und ostasiatische Streifzüge: Ethnologische und historisch-topographische Studien zur Geschichte des 9. und 10. Jahrhunderts (ca. 840–94)*. Leipzig, 1903.

Mez, A. *Die Renaissance des Islâms*. Heidelberg, 1922. Trans. S. Khuda Bakhsh and D. S. Margoliouth as *The Renaissance of Islam*. Patna, 1937.

Minorsky, V. *Sharaf al-Zamān Ṭāhir Marvazī on China, the Turks and India: Arabic Text (circa A.D. 1120) with an English Translation and Commentary*. London, 1942.

———. "Caucasica IV. 1. Sahl ibn Sunbāṭ of Shakkī and Arrān," *BSOAS* 14 (1952): 505–14. Repr. in *The Turks, Iran and the Caucasus in the Middle Ages*. London, 1978.

———. *Studies in Caucasian History*. 3 vols. London, 1953.

———. *A History of Sharvān and Darband in the 10th–11th Centuries*. Cambridge, 1958.

Mottahedeh, R. "The ʿAbbāsid Caliphate in Iran," in *The Cambridge History of Iran* IV. *The Period from the Arab Invasion to the Saljuqs*, ed. R. N. Frye. Cambridge, 1975. Pp. 57–89.

Muth, F.-C. *Die Annalen von aṭ-Ṭabarī im Spiegel der europäischen Bearbeitungen*. Heidelberger Orientalische Studien V. Frankfurt, 1983.

Nafīsī, S. *Tārīkh-i khāndān-i Ṭāhirī* I. *Ṭāhir b. Ḥusayn*. Tehran, 1335 A.S.H./1956.

———. *Bābak-i Khurram-dīn. Dilāwar-i Ādharbāyjān*. Tehran, 1342 A.S.H./1963.

Nicholson, R. A. *A Literary History of the Arabs*. London, 1907.

Northedge, A. "Planning Sāmarrā: A Report for 1983–4," *Iraq* 47 (1985): 109–28.

———. "The Racecourses at Sāmarrā'," *BSOAS* 53 (1990): 31–56.

——— and R. Faulkner. "The 1986 Survey Season at Sāmarrā," *Iraq* 49 (1987): 143–73.

al-Nukhaylī, D. *al-Sufun al-islāmiyyah ʿalā ḥurūf al-muʿjam*. N.p. [Alexandrial], 1974.

Öhrnberg, K. *The Offspring of Fatima: Dispersal and Ramification*. Studia Orientalia . . . Societas Orientalis Fennica LIV. Helsinki, 1983.

Omar, F. *ʿAbbāsiyyāt: Studies in the History of the Early ʿAbbāsids*. Baghdad, 1976.

Patton, W. M. *Aḥmed ibn Ḥanbal and the Miḥna: A Biography of the Imām Including an Account of the Moḥammedan Inquisition Called the Miḥna, 218–234 A.H.* Leiden, 1897.

Pellat, C. *Le milieu baṣrien et la formation de Ǧāḥiẓ*. Paris, 1953.

Pipes, D. *Slave Soldiers and Islam: The Genesis of a Military System*. New Haven, 1981.

Rabino di Borgomale, H. L. *Mázandarán and Astarábád*. GMS N.S. VII. London, 1928.

———. "Les dynasties du Māzandarān de l'an 50 avant l'hégire à l'an 1006 de l'hégire (572 à 1597–1598), d'après les chroniques locals," *JA* 228 (1936): 397–474.

Ramsay, W. M. *The Historical Geography of Asia Minor*. Royal Geographical Society's Supplementary Papers IV. London, 1890.

al-Rasheed, M. M. al-Y. *The Abū Ḥafṣah Family of Poets, Together with a Critical Edition of the Poetry of the Principal Members of the Family*. Unpublished doctoral dissertation, The University of Manchester, 1980.

Reckendorf, H. *Arabische Syntax*. Heidelberg, 1921.

Rekaya, M. "Māzyār: Résistance ou intégration d'un province iranienne au monde musulman au milieu du IXe siècle ap. J.C.," *St. Ir.* 2 (1973): 143–92.

———. "Mise au point sur Théophobe et l'alliance de Bâbek avec Théophile (233/34–839/840)," *Byzantion* 44 (1974): 43–67.

———. "La place des provinces sud-caspiennes dans l'histoire de l'Iran de la conquête arabe à l'avènement des Zaydites (16–250 H./637–864 J.C.): Particularisme régional ou rôle 'national'?" *RSO* 48 (1974): 117–52.

Rice, D. S. "Deacon or Drink: Some Paintings from Samarra Re-examined", *Arabica* 5 (1958): 15–33.

Ritter, H. "Autographs in Turkish Libraries," *Oriens* 6 (1953): 63–90.

Rodinson, M. "Recherches sur les documents arabes relatifs à la cuisine," *REI* (1949): 95–165.

Rogers, J. M. "Sāmarrā: A Study in Medieval Town-Planning," in *The Islamic City: A Colloquium.*, ed. A. H. Hourani and S. M. Stern. Papers on Islamic History I. Oxford, 1970. Pp. 119–55.

Rosser, J. "Theophilus' Khurramite Policy and Its Finale: The Revolt of Theophobus' Persian Troops in 838." *Byzantina* 6 (1974): 265–71.

Rothstein, G. "Zu aš-Šābuštī's Bericht über die Ṭāhiriden (Ms. Wetzstein II, 1100 fol. 44ᵃ–54ᵃ)," in *Orientalische Studien Theodor Nöldeke . . . gewidmet* I, ed. C. Bezold. Giessen, 1906. Pp. 155–70.

Sadan, J. *Le mobilier au Proche Orient médiéval.* Leiden, 1976.

Sadighi, G. H. *Les mouvements religieux iraniens au IIième et au IIIième siècles de l'hégire.* Paris, 1938.

Saleh, A. H. "Les Bédouins d'Égypte aux premier siècles de l'Hégire," *RSO* 55 (1981): 137–61.

Scarcia Amoretti, B. "Sects and Heresies," in *The Cambridge History of Iran* IV. *The Period from the Arab Invasion to the Saljuqs*, ed. R. N. Frye. Cambridge, 1975. Pp. 481–519.

Schacht, J. *An Introduction to Islamic Law.* Oxford, 1964.

Schwarz, P. *Iran im Mittelalter nach den arabischen Geographen* 9 vols. Leipzig, Stuttgart, and Berlin, 1896–1936.

Serjeant, R. B. *Islamic Textiles: Material for a History up to the Mongol Conquest.* Beirut, 1972.

Sezgin, F. *Geschichte des arabischen Schrifttums.* 9 vols–. Leiden, 1975–.

Shaban, M. A. *Islamic History: A New Interpretation* II. *A.D. 750–1055 (A.H. 132–448).* Cambridge, 1976.

Siddiqi, A. *Studien über die persischen Fremdwörter im klassischen Arabisch.* Göttingen, 1919.

Sivers, P. von. "Military, Merchants and Nomads: The Social Evolution of the Syrian Cities and Countryside during the Classical Period, 780–969/164–358," *Isl.* 56 (1979): 212–44.

Sourdel, D. *Le vizirat ʿabbāside de 749 à 936 (132 à 324 de l'Hégire).* 2 vols. Damascus, 1959–60.

———. "Questions de cérémonial ʿabbaside," *REI* 28 (1960): 121–48.

Spuler, B. *Iran in früh-islamischer Zeit: Politik, Kultur, Verwaltung und öffentliches Leben zwischen der arabischen und der seldschukischen Eroberung 633 bis 1055.* Akademie der Wissenschaften und der Literatur, Veröffentlichungen der Orientalischen Kommission II. Wiesbaden, 1952.

Steingass, F. *A Comprehensive Persian-English Dictionary. Including the Arabic Words and Phrases to Be Met with in Persian Literature.* London, 1892. Repr. Beirut, 1970.

Stetkevych, S. P. "The ʿAbbāsid Poet Interprets History: Three Qaṣīdahs by Abū Tammām," *JAL* 10 (1979): 49–64.

Van Arendonck, C. *Les débuts de l'Imāmat Zaidite au Yemen.* Leiden, 1960.

Vasiliev, A. A. *Byzance et les Arabes* I. *La dynastie d'Amorium (820–867).* Brussels, 1935.

———. *History of the Byzantine Empire 324–1453.* Madison, 1952.

Vullers, J. A. *Lexicon Persico-Latinum etymologicum.* 2 vols. plus supplement. Bonn, 1855–67.

Waines, D. "A Prince of Epicures: The Arabs' First Cookbook," *Ur* 3 (1984): 26–29.

Watt, W. M. *The Formative Period of Islamic Thought.* Edinburgh, 1973.

Wellhausen, J. *Reste arabischen Heidentums.* 2nd ed. Berlin, 1897.

———. *Das arabische Reich und sein Sturz.* Berlin, 1902. Trans. M. G. Weir as *The Arab Kingdom and Its Fall.* Calcutta, 1927.

Wright, E. M. "Bābak of Badhdh and al-Afshīn during the Years 816–41 A.D.: Symbols of Iranian Persistence against Islamic Penetration in North Iran," *MW* 38 (1948): 43–59, 124–31.

Wright, W. *A Grammar of the Arabic Language.* 3rd ed. rev. W. R. Smith and M. J. de Goeje. 2 vols. Cambridge 1896–98.

Yule, H., and A. C. Burnell. *Hobson-Jobson: A Glossary of Colloquial Anglo-Indian Words and Phrases, and of Kindred Terms, Etymological, Historical, Geographical and Discursive,* new ed. W. Crooke. London, 1903.

Index

The index contains all proper names of persons, places, and tribal and other groups, as well as topographical data, occurring in the introduction and the text (but not normally in the footnotes), together with technical terms; where the latter are explained in the footnotes, they are also noted.

The definite article, the abbreviations b. *(for* ibn *"son") and* bt. *(for* bint *"daughter"), and everything in parentheses have been disregarded for purposes of alphabetization.*

A

B

N

P

Q

R

S